Enjoy the r_____

WITNESS STATEMENTS

Making The Bill: 1988

OLIVER CROCKER

D

DEVONFIRE

WITNESS STATEMENTS Making The Bill: 1988

By Oliver Crocker

First edition published November 2022 by Devonfire Books

Cover and spine design by Oliver Crocker and Robert Hammond
Cover illustrations by Robert Hammond
Internal design by Oliver Crocker
Proofread by Tessa Crocker

ISBN 978-1-8382819-2-2

Printed and bound by Book Printing UK, Peterborough.

DEVONFIRE

This book is dedicated to:

Richard Bramall (1944-2020)

&

Michael Ferguson (1937-2021)

who between them produced all 48 episodes
of *The Bill* broadcast in 1988.

CONTENTS

Light Relief! Tony Tyrer drew this funny picture for fellow floor manager Aidan Boulter, in homage to the opening scene of *Light Duties*, the first half-hour episode of *The Bill* to be broadcast.

INTRODUCTION
By Executive Producer Peter Cregeen (1988-89)

Setting up the bi-weekly series was a huge operation, and there were a multitude of problems to be solved, both creatively and operationally. Ironically, some of the writers, who had worked so hard to make the hour-long series such a success, initially found it difficult to adapt to the new format. While the new slot was half an hour, in reality it was only twenty-five minutes, because of the commercial break. Geoff McQueen, the creator of the series, wasn't actually available to write many stories for us at all, as he was busy developing other series at the BBC. Barry Appleton and Christopher Russell, two of our most successful writers, were eager to continue being involved, but we were going to need to find a huge number of new writers to meet our target.

Having to set up a totally new operation was not only a colossal expense, but also a major operational challenge. To my knowledge, no other ongoing drama had ever been made in this way. We were into unknown territory. Ewart Needham, Head of Technical Resources, found the cameras we needed in Japan, and organised all that we would need from his area to achieve our objectives.

We now needed two producers, one for each unit, and I was delighted when Michael Ferguson and Richard Bramall agreed enthusiastically to fulfil those roles. Together we had to work out how we were going to achieve two units filming simultaneously, both using many of the same actors. The only way it could run like clockwork on an ongoing basis was for both teams to report to Derek Cotty, our production manager, and to communicate with one another continuously. It could only become even more complicated when a third unit was introduced, at which point Nigel Wilson became our valued production co-ordinator.

There was such enthusiasm and commitment from all concerned that the programme became one of the most exciting experiences of my career. So many people are owed my own personal thanks for what they achieved – making *The Bill* a very important part of television history. 60 of those talented people have shared their memories of the first 48 half-hour episodes of *The Bill* for Oliver Crocker's fascinating book. I hope you enjoy reading about how we made these episodes as much as we all enjoyed making them.

1988 PRODUCTION NOTES

By Producers Richard Bramall and Michael Ferguson

In July 1988, press officer Rosane Chapman released publicity packs to journalists, containing a fascinating one-page document written by the producers, Richard Bramall and Michael Ferguson, which brings to life how the new bi-weekly series of *The Bill* was being produced...

Production Notes

After three very successful series – totalling 35 programmes – *THE BILL* has now developed into one of the most ambitious programmes undertaken by a television company.

Set entirely on location, two half-hour programmes are completed each week, with two production teams working in parallel with one another – colour coded for efficiency as the RED unit and the BLUE unit. The base at Barlby Road, London W10 is not only a location where half of the building is the permanent police station, it is also a production centre.

A minimum of six directors work to two producers, who work to an executive producer. Each programme has four weeks production preparation, five days shooting, ten days of editing and four days of dubbing. It is shot using lightweight Ikigami cameras and recorded on half-inch tape, and the recorder can be clamped on to the camera. There is none of the heavy artillery previously used to make a drama series. All the equipment fits into one small van. This van carries no Thames identification, enabling the use of its hand-held camera to record almost unnoticed around London streets to achieve essential realism. There is no scanner and only the minimum amount of lighting is used.

THE BILL is a breakthrough in British television production – as the first drama series to be shot in this way. All of the editing is completed in two purpose-built editing suites at Barlby Road. The script unit, casting department, make-up, wardrobe, design, accountancy and all elements of production management are based on site. At any one time there are approximately 180 people working there, including the cast.

LIGHT DUTIES
Written by Geoff McQueen
Directed by Derek Lister

Series 4: Episode 1
Broadcast: Tuesday 19 July 1988

Case Narrative
Roach and Carver pull a body from the river – the unfortunate corpse
has been fixed to a door with the word "grass" painted on it.

Regular Cast
Sgt. Cryer (Eric Richard), D.S. Roach (Tony Scannell), D.C. Carver
(Mark Wingett), P.C. Hollis (Jeff Stewart), P.C. Frank (Ashley Gunstock),
W.P.C. Ackland (Trudie Goodwin), W.P.C. Martella (Nula Conwell), P.C. Melvin
(Mark Powley), P.C. Edwards (Colin Blumenau), P.C. Stamp (Graham Cole),
Sgt. Peters (Larry Dann), D.C. Dashwood (Jon Iles), P.C. Haynes
(Eamonn Walker), Insp. Frazer (Barbara Thorn), Sgt. Penny (Roger Leach).

Guest Cast
D.S. Dougan (Andrew Secombe), D.I. Corrington (Anthony Dutton),
Jack Card (Eric Francis), Shop Owner (Richard Jamieson), Woman
Outside Shop (Jean Marlow), Marion (Susan Majolier), Ward Sister
(Judy Elrington), Hospital Registrar (Margaret Lawley).

Uncredited Personnel
W.P.C. Ford (Vikki Gee-Dare), P.C. (Oscar Peck), Stuntman (Tip Tipping),
2nd Unit Camera (Chas Watts), Chief Engineer (Dave Chislett), Press
Officer (Rosane Chapman), Librarian (Bridget Moore), Accountants
(Anne Shields, David Saggs).

Production Team
Stunt Arranger (Sean McCabe), Title Music (Andy Pask, Charlie Morgan),
Casting Director (Julia Lisney), Costume Designer (Jennie Tate), Make Up
Designer (Gilly Wakeford), Graphics (Jenni Phillips), Videotape Editor
(Tom Kavanagh), Lighting (Allen Harradine), Camera (Jamie Acton-Bond),
Sound (Stan Lee, Alan Lester), Production Buyer (Mike Ashby), Location
Manager (Eddie Mares), Floor Manager (Aidan Boulter), Stage Manager
(Marilyn Edwards), Production Manager (Derek Cotty), Production
Assistant (Susan Lewis), Technical Adviser (Wilf Knight), Programme

Associate (Valerie Farron), Series Script Editor (Kenneth Ware), Designers (Robin Parker, Deborah Ashforth, Pamela Blackwell, Peter Elliott, David Richens), Executive Producer (Peter Cregeen), Producer (Richard Bramall).

Observation Notes

Light Duties was shot between Monday 23rd and Friday 27th May 1988. The Production number was D4017 and the Videotape number was VTR/THS/45252. The scenes where Roach and Carver recover Terry Card's body were filmed along a section of river behind the Metropolitan Police Marine Policing Unit HQ, 98-102 Wapping High Street, E1W.

The shopping precinct scenes featuring P.C. Edwards, P.C. Stamp and Insp. Frazer were filmed at the Concorde Centre, Shepherd's Bush, W12. The centre was built in 1967 and was significantly redeveloped in the 1990s, becoming the West12 centre, which is still open today.

The final pub scene was filmed at The Latimer Arms, 198 Latimer Road, W10. The pub had also previously been used as the exterior of the Skinners Arms in a 1972 episode of *Steptoe & Son*. The pub closed in 1998 and the building has since been converted into flats.

Light Duties saw Susan Majolier make her debut as Marion, Chief Supt. Brownlow's loyal secretary. As well as appearing in over 60 episodes of *The Bill* over the next decade, Majolier's other TV credits include *Peak Practice*, *Men of Affairs* and a memorable role as a nurse in *Dad's Army*.

On Friday 13th May 1988, prior to filming on *Light Duties*, producers Richard Bramall and Michael Ferguson issued a two-page document named *"THE BILL* – A Shooting Day". Both men explained that they "would like there to be as few rules as possible" and published guidelines for the production teams. The overall shooting hours at base were advised to be 08:30-18:00, with teams heading out to location told that "travel time has to be sensibly worked out by the production unit, so that all concerned are able to leave the site by 18:30, having completed all their work." When considering each shooting day's wrap, the producers explain it was essential for production to allow the Wardrobe teams a "minimum of 30 mins to sort and make safe costumes."

Bramall and Ferguson also advised on times for meal breaks, with breakfast available in the canteen from 07:30, though in order to aid Wardrobe and Make-up staff in meeting the 08:30 deadline, a buffet breakfast will be "provided in the Green Room for principal artistes,

Wardrobe and Make-up only." Lunch was to be scheduled at any time between 12:00 and 14:00, to finish no later than 15:00. This flexibility was "to aid the sensible use of shooting time." There would also be an afternoon tea break "of about 15 mins for refreshments."

Light Duties was the first episode of *The Bill* directed by Derek Lister, who would go onto become one of the series' longest-serving directors, helming 57 episodes over the next 12 years, as well as being the lead director on the spin-off series *Beech is Back*. Lister began his directing career in the theatre, with productions at the Royal Shakespeare Company, Traverse, Soho, King's Head and the Royal Court. His many television credits include *Play for Today, Juliet Bravo, Coronation Street, Taggart, Rockliffe's Babies, Casualty* and Geoff McQueen's *Big Deal*.

As part of the publicity pack to promote the return of the series, Rosane Chapman issued a press release to promote *Light Duties*, which read:

"*THE BILL* - Thames Television's hit drama series for the past five years - returns to ITV screens tonight in an earlier evening slot as a half-hour programme twice a week, with an 'omnibus' repeat edition.

For the next 52 consecutive weeks, *THE BILL* will be shown every Tuesday and Thursday at 8.00pm, with a Friday afternoon repeat in the London area at 2.00pm.

There are 22 regular characters based at London's Sun Hill Police Station in this £10 million series – devised by Geoff McQueen – with Peter Cregeen as Executive Producer, and Richard Bramall and Michael Ferguson as the Producers.

The new regular characters will be introduced over the next few weeks. Tonight, viewers will meet two of them - Inspector Christine Frazer (Barbara Thorn) and PC Haynes (Eamonn Walker).

In *Light Duties* – written by Geoff McQueen and directed by Derek Lister - PC Hollis (Jeff Stewart) is running a book on who will get DI Galloway's job... DS Roach (Tony Scannell) desperately wants this promotion... Sgt Penny (Roger Leach) has returned to Sun Hill, but he has not fully recovered from the effects of his gunshot wound... And Sun Hill's first woman Inspector arrives..."

On Wednesday 25th May 1988, Barbara Thorn attended a photocall to promote *Light Duties*, posing for a series of promotional photos in her uniform, including one with a rose in her mouth and another with two real-life Met police officers, Graham Neale and Barry Leach.

All the writers on *The Bill* were given a document called "Character Notes and Background Information". Dated 5.2.88, the document was written and collated by script editor Tim Vaughan and described each of the 22 regular characters. The "soft spoken" Inspector Christine Frazer was listed as being 34 years old and "described – with a mix of admiration and awe – by other upper-echelon policemen as the most likely candidate for first Female Commissioner of the Met. This is an assessment with which Christine Frazer would not disagree. In short, the lady's on the make... and making it." The Backgound Information also describes the role of the Uniformed Inspector, explaining it is their job to "run the relief, allocate jobs and responsibilities..." The guide was written before Barbara Thorn's casting, and describes the role as a male: "He usually decides the allocation of work a week in advance. He has a small office on the ground floor, close to the Front Office."

Witness Statements

Barbara Thorn (Insp. Christine Frazer)

'In 1988, things weren't working out with my agent and I was getting frustrated that I wasn't working more in television, so I joined a co-operative agency, of which there were quite a few popping up at the time. The idea was that actors would get together and take turns in running the office and could put each other and their members up for acting work. I just happened to be in the office when a casting came through from *The Bill*, looking for an actress in her early 30s, to play the new police Inspector. I said to my colleagues in the office, "Has anyone put me up for this?" They hadn't, so I asked if anyone had any objection to me putting myself up for the part, which I did. I was very truthful and didn't big myself up. The next thing I know, I was asked to go in for a meeting the next day, where I met the casting director, Julian Oldfield.'

'I was then invited back to meet the two producers, Richard Bramall and Michael Ferguson. I then had a third meeting with the executive producer, Peter Cregeen, who asked me if I had a showreel, which I didn't... I went away and got someone to put some bits and pieces of my work together on VHS. That did the job and I was in. Having given them my videotape, they then gave me a load of videotapes of the first three series, because I hadn't seen *The Bill* at all! I then spent my evenings watching all these hour-long episodes, which was fantastic, because I got to know the characters that I'd be working with and the kind of stories they told. I was then asked to go and have some photographs taken and be the face of *The Bill* as part of Thames' autumn season publicity, which was very exciting!'

'I was told that Frazer had "set her sights high", but the character breakdown was quite vague, so I was given more or less free rein on how to play her. I also got to meet a real policewoman, Chief Inspector Judith Davidson, who was based at Notting Hill. I think they based Frazer on Judith, because there were a few similarities between us physically and I could also be very brusque when I needed to be! Prior to me joining *The Bill*, there had obviously been a female Inspector in *Juliet Bravo*, but that wasn't set in London - she was policing the countryside. I think I was the first female senior police officer, dealing with inner city crime. That gave the writers an opportunity to explore something new and I was given some magnificent stories.'

Derek Lister (Director)

'The producers of these half-hour episodes were Michael Ferguson and Richard Bramall. They had created a document detailing the ethos of observation, and how the series would only be seen through the eyes of the police. That ethos was a big determining factor for all our parameters as a director, but this rigid rule made me unhappy at the beginning, because I didn't go there to be told how to shoot. Richard Bramall was a nice bloke and he was only doing his job, but there were tensions between us. I felt that this amorphous ethos, that the police shouldn't see anything that was more than six feet away in shooting terms, was a bit doctrinaire. For myself and Bill Brayne, the director of the next episode, this felt like a really old-fashioned concept, because most cutting-edge documentaries at the time used a range of lenses; to exclusively use the on-the-shoulder look would have been terribly constricting. I'm not knocking the concept of the documentary style at all, but my argument was that if you hire me as a director, you've got to allow me to put some of myself into the programme. I'm of the generation of filmmakers where the idea was to be given an envelope and tear it up, we wanted to make something new and different and that's still my attitude, I'm not a 'box ticker'. As a director, when I got a script it was an empty glass and it was up to me what I put in it.'

'I went to see Peter Cregeen and questioned if he really wanted me to shoot the series on the same lens on every shot, with the camera stuck up an actor's nose or over their shoulder? Peter's a nice guy and he listened to me as a fellow drama director. That's why *Light Duties* opens with that long lens shot, where the camera was 100 yards away and I could wash things through the foreground. That to me was something we could do and still stay true to the idea of police observation, though they did make me cut other shots that a police officer couldn't have seen. I used to have a laugh with the cameramen, because I used so many lenses, they would end up with all these pieces of tape up their arms ready to mark up the different focus pulls! But they loved being asked to shoot properly and develop shots.'

'1988 was a pretty tumultuous time for Thames TV. They were under a lot of pressure from the Thatcher government, because of the fallout from the *Death on the Rock* documentary, which had aired just a month before we started shooting *Light Duties*. There was a real chance that they could lose their licence, so *The Bill* became the show that couldn't afford to fail and this first episode needed to hold its audience. The pressure on the production was really intense and there was near hysteria from the executives at Thames, who were around me like seagulls at the time, worried that if the cameras stopped moving for a millisecond, the audience would change channels and they'd all lose their jobs. *Light Duties* is one of the most pressured jobs I've ever had in that respect and it felt like a constant battle between the creative, the producers and the institution, though I do understand the pressure they were all under and why they were so nervous. Then luckily, a chap called W. Stephen Gilbert, who had been a producer at the BBC before becoming a critic, gave *Light Duties* a great review saying it had modern 1980s direction, which quietened things down for a bit.'

Jamie Acton-Bond (Camera)

'There was a friction between the two camera departments of Hanworth, who had worked on the first hour-long episodes of *The Bill*, and us at Teddington, who had agreed to do the new twice-weekly series after several Union meetings. They were upset when they found out how cheaply we were shooting the series, for "an apple and biscuit" as they called it... The two departments had different skill-sets of camera work: The Outside Broadcast team from Hanworth concentrated on live events i.e. horse racing, football matches, concerts and royal events. Our skill-set was that of drama and light entertainment. The directors found it an easier task shooting with us, due to our drama skills.'

'Myself, Rolie Luker and Roy Easton were the first three camera operators assigned to the half-hours. Prior to us going up to Barlby Road, we received our training down in Teddington from Chris Hodson, who taught us the art of *The Bill* and showed us the way it was done. We knew we were writing off our family lives for a while, because we would have to start at 6:00 in the morning every day and wouldn't be getting home until 9:00 at night. When we got to Barlby Road, the first thing the three of us did was establish what we called "the office", which was the Admiral Blake pub on the corner, where we often discussed methods and equipment. We were scheduled to work on two episodes at a time, within a three-week schedule. The first week was spent finding the locations and then each episode would be shot in a week. There were quite a few reshoots at weekends in the early days because of equipment failure.'

'We were all learning how to use the videotape machines out in the field, away from the studio and without an O.B. truck. Thames and Anglia Television had gone with the innovation of using the Panasonic M2 machines, which was the difference between VHS and Betamax. We went down the VHS route, though we discovered the ones that actually worked were the Betamax ones being used by most of the other television companies. There were days while we were setting up where we had to do retakes, because the VTRs didn't work! We would go back to base in the evening to review the footage and realise it hadn't come out... That's when the fridge in the corner became important, because that's when the beers came out! We then had Panasonic come down to sort out these early faults. We also had Vinten camera equipment, which were traditionally used in studio rather than location. Vinten, like Panasonic, were often with us to modify and improve. It was a big learning curve and a totally different way of working.'

Aidan Boulter (Floor Manager)

'There were 13 floor managers, six floor assistants and 12 stage managers at Thames Television, who all reported into the same Head of Department, John Wayne (no relation), who would be sent through the schedules of what programmes were coming up about six weeks in advance. We were lucky enough in those days, because we were staff, to be allocated programmes. I was first allocated *The Bill* in 1987, where I was floor manager on two of the hour-long episodes, directed by Mary McMurray. Many people assumed that, when the series was going to be shown twice weekly in an earlier time slot, the drama would be watered down. It wasn't a soap opera; these were individual standalone episodes, which each had their own merits and the stories that we were telling were often based on reality. *Light Duties* opens with a dead body strapped to a door floating in the Thames... I wouldn't call that family viewing! We were showing the audience what the police actually have to deal with and unfortunately life isn't all sweetness and light.'

'Sean McCabe was the stunt arranger on *Light Duties*, though as the gaffer he didn't do the stunt in the Thames himself. It is very rare to only have one stunt person involved, because sometimes they go wrong and you want somebody who knows their stuff to come to the rescue if necessary. The stuntman on the door was Tip Tipping, a former Royal Marine Commando who I worked with a few times. Tip was a really lovely guy, who unfortunately had a very sad ending and didn't survive a parachute stunt that went wrong a few years later. It was a terrible shame, because he left a wife and young kids behind.'

'We were very lucky on *The Bill* in those days, because we had complete cooperation from the Metropolitan Police. In that opening sequence of *Light Duties*, the boat Tony Scannell is standing on is a real police boat from Wapping police station, driven by the real crew, who were absolutely brilliant. They weren't out on the river for very long, the scene was done quite quickly. Nowadays, the actors would have to wear life jackets, with a safety boat on standby. Tony Scannell was fearless and more than happy to walk along the side of the boat for real without a harness; he was a mad Irishman and very funny. We also had Harry Secombe's son Andrew playing D.S. Dougan, who had the lovely line "Don't play the Wilf", which was a reference to our police advisor, the late Wilf Knight, who was a nice guy and tremendous help to me.'

Wilf Knight (Technical Adviser)
Archive Witness Statement, written in February 1988.
'The protocol of uniform is quite simple. Below 70°F, you will wear the uniform, which means helmet, jacket, trousers and boots, outside the police station. Inside the police station you may take your uniform off to walk around. People working inside the station, i.e. clerical staff of the police, as opposed to the civilian clerical staff, may

wear short-sleeve order with their epaulets on, but unless the temperature is 70°F, you will wear your jackets inside. When it becomes 70°F, you wear short-sleeve order. If you assume that it is going to be 70°F when you wake up, as in our long hot summer, then you put your short-sleeved shirt on with your open collar and you go to work, with your epaulets on. If it starts off at 61° and rises to 70° in the space of eight hours, you may well have started off with a long-sleeved shirt and tie and collar, in which case you roll up your sleeves to short-sleeve order.'

'If you're on the beat, you bring your jacket in. You come into the station, take your jacket off, hang it up in your locker room, and go out in short-sleeve order. To be honest with you, the temperature of 70° isn't adhered to unless you have a really sticky Station Commander; when it gets 65° then people often wear short-sleeve order. But the cardinal rule is if one wears short-sleeve order, they all wear short-sleeve order. An order goes out "short-sleeve order for today" and you put your short-sleeve order on. It came out rather badly in the episode *Skipper,* where Dinesh Patel and Bob Cryer were walking around the streets and Cryer was in short-sleeve and Dinesh was in full uniform. It stood out like a sore thumb. You do not go out in half-and-half, there must be uniformity.'

'In the station, Chief Supt. Brownlow may be wearing his uniform, but outside where there is a public image, it's uniformity even for him. If a short-sleeve order was declared, he would wear short-sleeve order. It's almost unthinkable, in actual fact, for him to do so – it's very rare. But certainly Chief Inspector and Uniformed Inspector would wear short-sleeve order. If the Chief Inspector of Operations is working in the police station, sometimes he may wear uniform and sometimes he may wear plain clothes. That is a choice for him. If, for instance, he's meeting civil dignitaries from the local authorities, he may want to wear his uniform to signify its body language. If he's just having a day around the station, or he's going out at lunchtime to meet someone for a particular event, a swan if you like, a drink in the pub, he would wear his plain clothes. And so he has an optional choice. But usually at official functions he would want to wear his uniform. An Operations Chief Inspector doesn't get a plain clothes allowance, whereas the CID officer does. You pay what you like for suits, Marks & Spencer through to Christian Dior, you wear what you like.'

THE THREE WISE MONKEYS

Written by Geoff McQueen
Directed by William Brayne

Series 4: Episode 2
Broadcast: Thursday 21 July 1988

Case Narrative

An armed robbery has been thwarted, but one of the villains has hijacked a car and its female driver.

Regular Cast

Sgt. Cryer (Eric Richard), P.C. Smith (Robert Hudson), W.P.C. Ackland (Trudie Goodwin), Sgt. Penny (Roger Leach), Ch. Supt. Brownlow (Peter Ellis), D.S. Roach (Tony Scannell), D.C. Dashwood (Jon Iles), Ch. Insp. Conway (Ben Roberts), Insp. Frazer (Barbara Thorn), Sgt. Peters (Larry Dann), D.C. Carver (Mark Wingett), W.P.C. Martella (Nula Conwell), P.C. Hollis (Jeff Stewart), P.C. Melvin (Mark Powley), P.C. Edwards (Colin Blumenau), P.C. Haynes (Eamonn Walker).

Guest Cast

Alfie (Chris Jenkinson), Lenny (Barry O'Rorke), D.C. Willis (Mark Carey), D.C. Hawtrey (Nick Brimble), Blakelynn (Tom Owen), Blue Sierra Driver (Colin Skeaping), Blue Sierra Passenger (Steve Wilsher).

Uncredited Personnel

W.P.C. Ford (Vikki Gee-Dare), W.P.C. (Karen England), P.C. (Oscar Peck), Chief Engineer (Dave Chislett), Press Officer (Rosane Chapman), Librarian (Bridget Moore), Accountants (Anne Shields, David Saggs).

Production Team

Stunt Arranger (Roy Alon), Casting Director (Julian Oldfield), Title Music (Andy Pask, Charlie Morgan), Costume Designer (Allard Tobin), Make Up Designer (Gilly Wakeford), Graphics (Jenni Phillips), Videotape Editor (Dave Lewinton), Lighting (John O'Brien), Camera (Roy Easton), Sound (John Osborne, Alan Lester), Production Buyer (Terry Allen), Location Manager (Eamonn Duffy), Floor Manager (Tony Tyrer), Stage Manager (Nigel J. Wilson), Production Manager (Derek Cotty), Production Assistant (Isobel Neil), Technical Adviser (Wilf Knight), Programme Associate (Valerie Farron), Series Script Editor (Kenneth Ware), Designers

(Robin Parker, David Richens), Executive Producer (Peter Cregeen), Producer (Michael Ferguson).

Observation Notes

The Three Wise Monkeys (Production No: D4015, VTR No: THS/45250) was the first half-hour episode to be filmed, between Monday 16th and Friday 20th May 1988.

Filming for the opening driving sequence with Dashwood and Roach began on Golborne Road W10. Jon Iles then drives over the bridge and turns left onto Southam Street, W10. They then drive onto the adjoining road for the scene of the crash, meeting Eamonn Walker outside 48 Southern Row, W10. The pub on the corner was then the Prince of Wales, but now operates as The Chilled Eskimo. The next driving sequence with Dashwood and Roach begins on East Row, W10. Ted then spots the blue Sierra down the adjoining Conlan Street, W10.

The scene where P.C. Smith, W.P.C. Ackland and the titular Three Wise Monkeys first spot the blue Sierra begins on St Mark's Road, W10, with Robert Hudson driving past Camelford Court on the left. He then reverses into Cornwall Crescent, which is where the suspect vehicle overtakes them. The following scene where Smith is ordered to get closer was filmed along the Harrow Road, under the Westway.

The chase continues with the cars turning in from Clarendon Road, W11, into Portland Road W11, passing Nottingwood House on the left. The finale of the chase takes place on what was a derelict site, with Princess Alice House on the Dalgarno Estate in the background. The area has since been redeveloped and is now Sunbeam Crescent, W10.

The Three Wise Monkeys also sees Sgt. Penny break down in the Sergeant's locker room, which is described in the Background Information document as having "Approximately 12 lockers, one armchair and mirror. Some football pictures etc stuck inside lockers. Supposed to be tidier than the PC's locker room".

The Three Wise Monkeys was the first episode directed by William Brayne, a Canadian who had started his career in the 1960s as a documentary cameraman. He moved into directing drama in 1973 on the series *Special Branch*, which he later claimed was due to the producers calling his number by mistake, instead of director Bill Bain. He soon gained a reputation as a reliable director with an eye for

13

action, earning him work on *The Sweeney, The Professionals, Dempsey and Makepeace* and *C.A.T.S. Eyes*. Brayne directed ten episodes of *The Bill*, culminating with the famous 1993 episode *The Short Straw*. Bill Brayne passed away in 2014, aged 76.

As part of the publicity pack promoting the series, press officer Rosane Chapman issued a press release for *The Three Wise Monkeys*: "Following an attempted armed robbery, PC Smith (Robert Hudson) and WPC Ackland (Trudie Goodwin) come close to death in a shoot-out between one of the robbers and three armed members of the Met's Tactical Support Group (including Chris Jenkinson and Barry O'Rorke) – in Thames Television's *THE BILL* tonight. Sgt Penny (Roger Leach) is clearly unwell. DS Roach (Tony Scannell) loses out to two DCs from Somerset (Nick Brimble and Mark Carey)... And for the first time, viewers will meet Chief Inspector Conway (Ben Roberts). Written by the series' creator Geoff McQueen, *The Three Wise Monkeys* is directed by William Brayne and produced by Michael Ferguson."

Also in the press on Thursday 19th May 1988, just prior to filming commenced on *The Three Wise Monkeys*, the Daily Star ran an article about the filming of the new end credits sequence being filmed for the half-hour episodes, performed by Robert Hudson (Yorkie) and Karen England, a supporting artist who worked on *The Bill* for over 15 years. England later worked as a pet behaviourist counsellor for 20 years and is now an energy healer and teacher of spiritual esoteric principles.

The second page of Michael Ferguson and Richard Bramall's "*THE BILL - A Shooting Day*" document laid out the guidelines for "Alteration of Overall Hours". The producers explained that a unit may start and finish shooting, "half an hour later than normal, with no penalty." They point out however, that all departments, especially Wardrobe, "should be consulted before such a day is scheduled." The section concluded that "In all matters concerning abnormal hours, over-runs or emergency re-scheduling" the unit should contact production manager Derek Cotty.

The second page also features guidelines for "Sharing Members of Cast Between Units", where the producers felt it would be "sensible that Floor Managers agree together the time at which a member of cast should leave one unit and join the other." If a floor manager anticipated failing to meet the agreed deadline, then their "first course of action should be to contact the Floor Manager of the other crew to see if some solution can be found locally." If no agreement could be found, this would also be a problem for production manager Derek Cotty to step in and resolve.

Witness Statements

Derek Cotty (Production Manager)

'By 1987, *The Bill* was an established ratings winner across the network, with its one-hour, one a week format, drawing a youthful and growing audience. Thames TV already enjoyed an enviable reputation for its light entertainment output, but now we were "top of the pops" for drama too. Then a bombshell. Our Director of Programmes, David Elstein, declared at an ITV chief's meeting that the format of *The Bill* was to change from its current hour-long self-contained episode a week slot, to two half-hour episodes a week, both with independent nightly concluding storylines, therefore retaining the programme's self-contained established style and format. To my knowledge, nobody on the production team was privy to this decision, so it came as a huge surprise to us all when the details were shared with us; not least myself, who was charged (in the nicest possible way) to come up with a scheduling solution that could accomodate the desired results. I accepted the challenge and within a week or so, had worked out a format by which, within very tight constraints, a shooting schedule could be achieved. However it was dependant on everyone in every department understanding what was required of them, and all pulling together and accepting a new way of doing things.'

'What it meant, practically, was that instead of shooting a one-hour episode every two weeks, we would in fact need to shoot two half-hours *every* week, so twice the amount of television we had been making before. Using a couple of the hour-long scripts, I worked out that the only way we could do it was if production were able to determine which actor was where at what time. We had a small band of artists, so as well as expanding that cast, it would also mean that the scripts could not be driven by a specific set of characters, i.e. they couldn't all be Ackland or Cryer stories, other characters would now have to take the lead at some point. I had a great big board and I worked out how it was possible, but it would have to be done my way in order to do it within the time period.'

'Discipline at all levels was essential, which proved difficult for some of our directors; who could no longer take a day to do whatever they could, because at 11:30 I would be taking some of the actors off one episode to start on another and it would then be down to the director to explain at the end of the day why they hadn't finished their shoot, which could not be allowed to happen. It seems tough now, but to succeed I knew the production had to be run like a military operation, every single day. *The Bill* worked because it was made by the best team of programme-makers in the business.'

'The producers of the bi-weekly were Michael Ferguson and Richard Bramall, who worked very much as a duo and were a good match. They intentionally chose experienced directors to work on the early half-hours, as younger directors would not have had the experience to be able to adapt to the format we were now working in. Directing *The Three Wise Monkeys* was Bill Brayne, who was an ageing, but very capable director, who had worked in both documentaries and drama.'

'It also took some time for the cast to adjust to this new and quite rigid way of life, having previously only been working on one script at a time. It became a different process for them learning lines overnight from two episodes that they'd be shooting scenes for the next day. They also had to do quite a bit of work themselves from a characterisation point of view, though that wasn't a problem once they got used to it. The actors from these early episodes are all very close to my heart. We also tried to ease the engineering side for the technicians when we got in new lightweight Ikigami cameras, which nobody had ever heard of. We had teething problems of course, but they did make a colossal difference, particularly from the numbers of people we had to have on the street, which was always an imposition when shooting on London streets. The parking was always a nightmare, even back then.'

John Osborne (Sound)

'Thames TV was a fantastic place to work and the shows they made were exceptional. Light entertainment, drama, children's, education and local news; Thames TV did it all and I was doing it all for them. On my first day at Thames, I walked in to Studio One and Tommy Steele was sitting on a Chroma key box twenty feet off the ground against a blue cyclorama recording *Quincy*. It was technically brilliant, with early camera syncing to his action on a keyed-in set and a miniature model tracking his every move. I'm sure it might not stand up much against modern techniques, but it was very clever at the time.'

'I left the studio and headed off to Studio 2 and to my surprise it was *The Kenny Everett Show*. I simply could not believe my luck, as he was a hero of mine. I can't say I was concentrating too much on the technical side, as I was staring longingly at the Hot Gossip dancers, dancing to Supernature, and very good they were too. I worked on that show on the floor as a sound technician and Fisher boom operator for years, until Kenny was eventually lured to the BBC. Walking past all his enormous props in the scene dock was for me as exciting as it gets. Over time I progressed up the ranks in the sound department mixing, dubbing and tape operating for music recordings.'

'In 1988, work had slowed down at Teddington and the working week became days of standbys and off days, with the occasional situation comedy at the weekend. Most of us became very listless and bored, fearing for our jobs if things didn't improve. But there was about to be the start of something big and that something was the new bi-weekly series of *The Bill*... In 1983, I worked on the *Woodentop* pilot, which was filmed at Teddington on five studio cameras, that were all individually recorded; a technique always used now, but then it was unusual. A very expensive process, but as this was a pilot they threw money at it.'

'When Thames commissioned a series, it was made by the OB department from Hanworth, using a small, conventional two-studio camera truck, with all the facilities of an OB shoot, and a decent amount of kit and crew. They made 35 episodes using this technique, which would have been expensive as an ongoing concern. Thames management eventually wanted to change lots of working practices across the board and saw a remodelling of these by using *The Bill* as a good place to start...'

'The OB department naturally disagreed with the new practices and they weren't prepared to compromise, so the management offered it to Teddington. As we hadn't worked much for several months, most of us jumped at the chance, which I'm sure created a rift between Teddington and OBs, but that's what happened. The management gave us a new recorder and some minimal kit and asked us to go and make it work. Mike Pontin, my head of Sound, called me in to his office and asked me to be involved, which was all very exciting! I asked him who I was going to work with and he said, "Whoever you choose." He was actually putting me in charge! Not surprisingly, I was extremely proud to be asked, so off I went to set about making the means to do this, as we had no kit and little experience. I designed the first equipment trolleys to put the sound and video equipment on, which were then made by the engineering department. They were brilliant if I say so myself and I still have one. The engineering department were incredible and helped out at every stage of the way.'

'And so, the new style *Bill* was born and recording began at Barlby Road. I worked on the first two shows of the new set-up, *The Three Wise Monkeys* and *Good Will Visit*, which I can remember like it was yesterday. Bill Brayne was the director, a somewhat brash Canadian who had previously worked on *The Sweeney* and *Minder*, so he knew his stuff. Sadly, we were all not quite ready technically for a number of reasons, so when he walked onto set at 1 second past 8am and shouted, "where the hell is the goddamn camera?" it was all a bit of a shock. He was surprisingly complimentary to me at the end of the shoot as we watched the rushes, but it would have been nice for us all if he'd been a little more understanding.'

'Over the years I've worked on hundreds of episodes, some very challenging ones technically, but always with great fun and collaboration, particularly from the cast who seemed to love it too. Everyone from the cast and crew were just lovely to work with and it was a truly collaborative experience, but most importantly it was just a fun place to work, with one enormous happy family.'

Robert Hudson (P.C. "Yorkie" Smith)

'When we started doing the half-hours, for some reason Yorkie was always either getting shot at, knocked out or blown up... danger must have been in my contract! I nearly didn't do the half-hours, because I didn't know how it was going to work at 8pm. They kept reassuring me that it wasn't going to be a soap and they were still going to be individual stories. The 9pm episodes had some quite meaty storylines that I didn't think they could get away with at 8pm. I thought I'd do it for a year and see how it went... Of course I'm so glad that I stayed and I realise now how revolutionary it was, with the handheld cameras and shooting with two units, it was way ahead of its time. It also worked so well because luckily they got a great bunch of actors who all got on so well together. And as a cast, we all loved working with new directors and looked forward to seeing what different camera angles they were going to try.'

'*The Three Wise Monkeys* was the one where the armed police shot the guy in the back and only just missed me. When we were planning the car chase, they wanted me to do all my own driving and the production team said they'd found us a quiet road to shoot on... Well of course, they wanted me driving down the lower tier of the Westway! I said, "What are you talking about, this isn't quiet?" and they said it had been quiet on the recce, at 3pm, but we were filming it during rush hour! We had £30,000 of camera equipment stuck out the side and I said I would not be driving unless they put a car behind me to stop anybody going past, who wouldn't see the camera until they'd knocked it off! They sorted that, but as I was responsible for Trudie Goodwin, three guest actors in the back and 30 grand's worth of camera on the side, all I was thinking during that scene was, "Should I be doing this?" Then they said on the radio "Can you drive a bit quicker Rob?"'

'Just as we got started on the half-hours, I was in the canteen having a coffee when Peter Cregeen, who was now the executive producer, walked over and explained that they were going to redo the feet on the credits and he asked me if I wanted to do it with Karen England, who was in a lot of *The Bill* episodes. They sprayed the street down, because the cobbles looked better when they were wet. Then we had to practice it, because you have to walk really close together, so we actually had our arms around each other, otherwise we wouldn't have been walking closely enough. The Daily Star came down to take photos of us doing it, so after we'd got it in the can, for a laugh we did the same thing, but from the waist up we were wearing Hawaiian shirts, sunglasses and sombreros!'

Karen England (W.P.C. & End Credits Legend)
'I was born and raised in Hong Kong and travelled around the world a lot with my parents in the 60s. We moved to the UK when I was 13 and I joined Rambert Ballet School when I was 16. After three years training, I went off and danced on cruise ships, which I enjoyed. Although, classical dancing was never really my thing, I found it quite

harsh and I did it because I was good at it, rather than having any yearning from within me to do it. I had a good time as a dancer, but there were long periods in between my contracts. So I signed up to a few agencies who supplied supporting artists for background work.'

'In those days the industry was very different; supporting artists were Equity members who did background work in between other entertainment jobs. That was how I met my husband, Oscar Peck, who had been a child actor and gone to stage school and like me was doing extra work in between contracts. Neither of us was aspiring to be a famous actor and never thought we were something that we weren't. After a while, we realised how much fun we were having and both just carried on doing it. For a time we made a really good living out of it, because we got known for being professional, never complaining, not looking at the camera and getting on with the job as part of a team.'

'Over the years, I have been working away in the background of many programmes, including *Doctor Who*, *Tenko* and some of the very first episodes of *EastEnders*. It was funny when *The Bill* came along, because my father had been a policeman, so maybe there was a look and a steadiness that ran in the blood? *The Bill* was a very friendly programme; we weren't treated like outsiders, everybody knew each other well and it was like a big family. There was obviously a lot of hanging around when you weren't working on set, so I would chat with my friends in the dressing room, or Oscar and I would play Scrabble, it was great fun. Then there would be a knock on the door and someone would ask you to come on set. In *The Three Wise Monkeys* you can see me in the custody area. Or sometimes they might ask me to do a line, which I was happy to do, though it was a bit nerve-wracking at first!'

'There's been quite a lot of incorrect information about the end credits reported over the years. I don't know who did them originally in 1984, but I first did them at Barlby Road with Robert Hudson in 1988. I don't really know why they asked me; maybe they had seen my dancer's calves? Robert and I had to be hip-to-hip with our arms around each other, so that we could walk in sync. The press took some photos of us wearing Hawaiian tops, which was fun. When the series moved to Merton, I did the credits again with Paul Page-Hanson. I used to keep quiet about it, because I was never trying to be famous, but it has brought people a lot of pleasure over the years finding out they were my legs. I'm very grateful that I have my own slice of TV history.'

GOOD WILL VISIT

Written by Barry Appleton
Directed by William Brayne

Series 4: Episode 3
Broadcast: Tuesday 26 July 1988

Case Narrative

It's P.C. Ramsey's first day at Sun Hill, but he doesn't get off to a very good start...

Regular Cast

Sgt. Cryer (Eric Richard), Sgt. Peters (Larry Dann), P.C. Ramsey (Nick Reding), P.C. Haynes (Eamonn Walker), Ch. Insp. Conway (Ben Roberts), D.S. Roach (Tony Scannell), D.C. Dashwood (Jon Iles), D.C. Carver (Mark Wingett), Sgt. Penny (Roger Leach), W.P.C. Ackland (Trudie Goodwin), P.C. Edwards (Colin Blumenau), P.C. Smith (Robert Hudson), P.C. Melvin (Mark Powley), P.C. Frank (Ashley Gunstock).

Guest Cast

Patrick Clancy (Malcolm Kaye), Harry Parker (Osaze Ehibor), Oriental (Philip Tan), Coxswain Bower (Terry Gurry), Leslie Fisk (Tony Portacio).

Production Team

Stunt Arranger (Terry Walsh), Casting Director (Julian Oldfield), Title Music (Andy Pask, Charlie Morgan), Costume Designer (Jennie Tate), Make Up Designer (Gilly Wakeford), Graphics (Jenni Phillips), Videotape Editor (Dave Lewinton), Lighting (John O'Brien), Camera (Roy Easton), Sound (John Osborne, Alan Lester), Production Buyer (Terry Allen), Location Manager (Eamonn Duffy), Floor Manager (Tony Tyrer), Stage Manager (Nigel J. Wilson), Production Manager (Derek Cotty), Production Assistant (Isobel Neil), Technical Adviser (Wilf Knight), Programme Associate (Valerie Farron), Series Script Editor (Kenneth Ware), Designers (Robin Parker, David Richens), Executive Producer (Peter Cregeen), Producer (Michael Ferguson).

Observation Notes

Good Will Visit (Production No: D4016, VTR No: THS/45251) was filmed between Monday 23rd and Friday 27th May 1988.

The scenes where Peters and Haynes investigate the damage caused by the Navy were filmed on Harlesden High Street, NW10.

The market scene where Ramsey intimidates Leslie Fisk was filmed on the corner of Alba Place and Portobello Road, Notting Hill, W11. Ramsey then picks up his Porsche on an intersection that no longer exists, between Latimer Road, W10 and the now truncated Treadgold Street, W11. The spot where Ramsey's Porsche was parked is now the site of the Saint Francis of Assisi Catholic primary school, which opened in 2005.

Good Will Visit saw veteran actress Jean Channon make her debut as Eileen, Conway's secretary, although she went uncredited on this episode. Channon's acting career began in the 1960s and her many television credits included *Emergency-Ward 10, Dixon of Dock Green, Bless This House, Z Cars, Public Eye, Doctor Who, Blake's 7, The Young Ones, Tales of the Unexpected* and *Big Deal.* Jean Channon passed away in 2007, aged 74. Also seen during the briefing scene are regular supporting artists Karen England and Oscar Peck.

Good Will Visit saw Nick Reding make his debut as P.C. Pete Ramsey. The character notes for Ramsey feature a lot of details introduced in Barry Appleton's script, where he is described as a 24-year old "tough, flash East End boy. His uniform is pressed, spotless, and seems to fit better than other people's; his car is a 1970s Porsche 911 in immaculate condition. Formerly a plain-clothes officer, he was moved to Sun Hill and put back in uniform after allegations that he cheated other police officers in a card game. The official story is that he needs to be near his sick mother who lives in the Sun Hill area. In one way, Ramsey is not a good policeman – he certainly breaks the rules. He'll take a backhander from an unlicensed trader or do a deal over a minor offence; he doesn't expect to pay for a new shirt or a packet of cigarettes. In another way, he's a very good policeman – bright, self-reliant and at ease in the inner city. He's not on the side of the villains... He's on the side of Peter Ramsey."

Witness Statements

Barry Appleton (Writer)
'A lot of good things happened for me because of *The Bill.* Michael Chapman was so pleased with my input on the first series that

he commissioned me to write an episode of his next drama for Thames, *Mr. Palfrey of Westminster.* In between the third series and the start of the half-hours, Thames was also commissioning me to write pilots for them. I had so much work coming in that it became too much for my agent to manage. Peter Cregeen kindly introduced me to the William Morris Agency, who took me under their wing and asked me to go to the States for pilot season. I was suddenly flavour of the month and I couldn't believe it, especially when I was still honing my craft. I learnt a lot from William Goldman's book *Adventures in the Screen Trade,* which is the best education that you could ever have for writing screenplays, it's an absolutely brilliant book.'

'I felt I could tell better stories in the half-hour format, because you didn't have time for padding, you could just go for it and I really enjoyed writing them. Before I started writing *Good Will Visit,* I took my grandchildren on board HMS Belfast, which is moored on the Thames by Tower Bridge; only a stone's throw from where the original studio was on Artichoke Hill. I was walking around on deck and thought "I've got to use this..." In fact there were two scenes that I wrote for the episode that saw Peters and Haynes actually on board HMS Belfast, talking to the Captain. But I don't think the Ministry of Defence liked the idea, so I had to cut down the whole storyline and those scenes were never filmed, sadly. I thought what they *were* able to do, with the sailors arriving at the station, was fabulous and done really well.'

'The other important thing about this series was that I created the character of Ramsey. I think there's a little bit of me in the character, because I was a Porsche lover as well, although I was never bent or anything like that. When I first wrote him, I had him joining the Met not because he wanted a career in the police, but saw it as a business opportunity. I toned that down, but we see traces of it in *Good Will Visit* at the market. I wanted a character that was going to go right on the edge and when I saw Nick Reding's brilliant performance, I thought perhaps we could go further and that Ramsey should really cross the line, but I wasn't sure how long they'd be able to keep him in the show for, because he was such a good actor. Many years later I saw Nick Reding being interviewed and he said Ramsey was his favourite character he'd played, which was wonderful. I loved Ramsey, I could have written a whole series about him.'

'The storyline with the bags of saffron is based on a case that actually happened when I worked on the Flying Squad. We were following these guys in a van that we suspected of selling drugs and when we stopped them, there were all these sacks of stuff. When we opened it, I knew what it was straight away, because my wife was a brilliant cook and she used a lot of it in her recipes. The other two detectives didn't know what it was, and I remember being a smart ass and telling them it was made from the dried stigmas of a crocus. They asked me if it was worth anything and I explained that if they bought a little pack of it from the supermarket, it would cost an arm and a leg. The amount we had caught was worth a lot of money. I slotted that in *Good Will Visit* and of course I made Ramsey the smart ass like me, I loved writing for him.'

Nick Reding (P.C. Pete Ramsey)

'It wasn't a huge leap for me to become an actor, because I grew up in an arty household. My mum had been a dancer and choreographer, as well as doing a bit of acting. After the Second World War, she started doing big theatre shows with variety artists, which toured all over the UK. She later became a personal assistant to stars like Ginger Rogers and Olivia de Havilland at Pinewood Studios, before training as a make-up artist and joining the BBC, which was where she met my dad, who worked there as a music producer. My parents weren't keen for me to become an actor, but I just wanted to do it and I left school at 15 with four O-levels. It's not until later in life you realise there are massive holes when you don't have a proper education, though I don't regret leaving school early, because I went straight into work as a stagehand in the West End and by the time I was 17 I'd earned my Equity card.'

'When *The Bill* came along, I'd just come back from travelling in the Far East for four months. My agent rang and told me that the series was going twice-weekly. I was aware that the show had been hugely popular on Friday nights, but I'd not seen much of it. I managed to catch some of the hour-long episodes and thought they were really good. My agent gave me the brief for Ramsey, but explained they were looking for an East Ender... I said, "That's fine, I'm a Londoner..." But she said, "No they want the real thing, because there's no rehearsal time and they don't want someone who is going to be putting on a performance." So when I went in for the audition, I just behaved like

Ramsey, chewing gum and saying, "All right" to all these terribly nice, middle-class television producers. When you're in an audition, if they ask a stupid question, you're supposed to come up with an exciting answer, whereas I did what I thought Ramsey would do, which was roll my eyes and look out the window. I think by the end they were thinking, "This guy *is* Ramsey!"'

'That day I was filming a Status Quo video, dancing with a girl on a bandstand in Hyde Park, when I got the call from my agent saying that they'd like me to go back to the Barlby Road studios. I went back in and they say that they'd like to offer me the part. Of course, I was still behaving like Ramsey, so I said, "Oh right... can I think about it?" I went away, phoned my agent and said, "They think I'm Cockney!" She said, "Well you'll have to keep it up then..." Which is what I did, although I shifted it down a bit. Barry Appleton set Ramsey up as a crooked officer in *Good Will Visit*, where you see him taking a bribe off a stallholder on the Portobello market. Being corrupt was the only way a young PC could have afforded to drive around London in a Porsche. That was a horrible car to drive; the clutch was really stiff and when you are driving a racing car around London, it feels like you are only doing 8 miles an hour, because you can't properly let it go. We actually used four different Porsches for filming, all sprayed gold to look like the same one.'

Wilf Knight (Technical Adviser)
Archive Witness Statement, recorded in February 1988.

'When an officer joins a station, they're given a number and become P.C. SO 123 or Sgt. SO 64. The two numbers are for Sergeants, three and upwards are for PCs. The very big stations might even run into four numbers, but you'll rarely see it. Always in our case, the numbers are preceeded by SO. It used to be that you just had the letter of your Division... then it ws decided that we all ought to know which Stations we came from. And so now if you are well equipped with that kind of knowledge you'll be able to walk round the West End and say "Good Lord, that person's from the Diplomatic Protection Group", because they've got DP on their shoulder and she's talking to a person from Tottenham Court Road, because she's got EO on her shoulder. The new boy who comes in could have the number of an officer who's left. The numbers are allocated from the Station, and recorded at District Headquarters. When you arrive, you're called in by your Chief

Inspector, who welcomes you to the station and says, "I want you to keep it clean, smell nice, turn up for work, do eight hours a day, don't get into trouble and don't make any of the WPCs pregnant... and by the way, your number's 579. Welcome to Sun Hill, please drive carefully."'

Larry Dann (Sgt. Alec Peters)

'I loved doing the comedy side of *The Bill* and it was when we moved onto the half-hours that they started to give me little stories where Alec did something silly. In *Good Will Visit*, he made a right old mess when he arrested a whole platoon of navy personnel! This was whilst he was asked to "puppy walk" Haynes, a process where new recruits are shown the ropes and taken around "the patch", which was usually done by a Sergeant. I rememeber we were filming along a busy row of shops in Harlesden and I got the feeling that Eamonn Walker didn't seem to be very happy filming this scene – one of his first on location. He took me aside and confided that he was getting "that look" from the Black community. I asked him if it was because he was playing a police officer, which of course it was. I wish I'd had more scenes with Eamonn and I am so pleased for his success in America.'

'I used to organise sporting events for charity and in the summer of 1988, we held a cricket match at Sutton. I had played there many times with my club and, knowing that I was in *The Bill*, I was asked if I could get some of the cast to come and play... Because of Eamonn's imposing height, I got him to open the bowling. As a joke, I had all the fielders standing in the slips (behind the stumps) with no one in front. In cricket terms, that made everyone think that Eamonn was a very, *very* fast bowler! Only Eamonn and I were in on the gag – which was that he didn't really play cricket at all! Eamonn took an enormous long run up... and then delivered one of the slowest balls you've ever seen! It was great fun!'

'The other highlight of *Good Will Visit* was that it featured my first scene with Ben Roberts, who was such a funny man. We used to get in trouble when we did scenes together, because I couldn't keep a straight face and he'd make me corpse. The directors would get furious with us, because they were under such pressure to get an episode out in a week and there are these two actors pissing themselves laughing. I had some great times with Ben, he was outrageous!'

HOME SWEET HOME
Written by Nicholas McInerny
Directed by Gareth Davies

Series 4: Episode 4
Broadcast: Thursday 28 July 1988

Case Narrative
Cryer assists the bailiff in carrying out an eviction order on squatters in a council flat.

Regular Cast
Sgt. Cryer (Eric Richard), Insp. Frazer (Barbara Thorn), P.C. Haynes (Eamonn Walker), P.C. Smith (Robert Hudson), W.P.C. Ackland (Trudie Goodwin), P.C. Ramsey (Nick Reding), P.C. Melvin (Mark Powley), P.C. Frank (Ashley Gunstock), Sgt. Peters (Larry Dann), Sgt. Penny (Roger Leach), W.P.C. Martella (Nula Conwell), D.C. Dashwood (Jon Iles), P.C. Hollis (Jeff Stewart), P.C. Edwards (Colin Blumenau).

Guest Cast
Hunt (Christian Rodska), Councillor Thomas (John Bowe), Marie Tucker (Sasha Mitchell), Wayne Tucker (Dean Packman), Sonja Bloomfield (Janet Dale), Mrs. Aldershot (Pauline Munro), Squatter (Nicholas Barnes), Librarian (Sarah Sherborne), Nosey Neighbour (Efua Taylor).

Uncredited Personnel
W.P.C. Ford (Vikki Gee-Dare), P.C. (Russell Brook), P.C. (Oscar Peck), D.C. (Kevin O'Brien), Press Officer (Rosane Chapman), Librarian (Bridget Moore), Accountants (Anne Shields, David Saggs).

Production Team
Casting Director (Julian Oldfield), Title Music (Andy Pask, Charlie Morgan), Costume Designer (Mandy Harper), Make Up Designer (Gilly Wakeford), Graphics (Jenni Phillips), Videotape Editor (Dave Lewinton), Lighting (Peter Bower), Camera (Rolie Luker), Sound (James Noble, Alan Lester), Production Buyer (Terry Allen), Location Manager (Sheila Loughrey), Floor Manager (Julian Meers), Stage Manager (Diana Paskin), Production Manager (Derek Cotty), Production Assistant (Carol Snook), Technical Adviser (Wilf Knight), Programme Associate (Valerie Farron), Series Script Editor (Kenneth Ware), Designers

(Robin Parker, Pam Blackwell), Executive Producer (Peter Cregeen), Producer (Michael Ferguson).

Observation Notes

Home Sweet Home (Production No: D4019, VTR No: THS/45254) was shot between Monday 30th May and Friday 3rd June 1988. The opening eviction scenes were shot at Wolfe House on the White City Estate, W12. The scenes set in Councillor Thomas' home were filmed in the St Stephen's area of Ealing, W13.

In the first of a number of billing errors, Roger Leach was incorrectly credited as playing Haynes rather than Eamonn Walker. This was also the first episode of *The Bill* not to feature Mark Wingett as Jim Carver.

Home Sweet Home and the following episode *All in Good Faith* were helmed by Gareth Davies, who, after a successful acting career, became a prolific television director. His many directing credits include *Z Cars*, *Play for Today*, *Oliver Twist*, *Follyfoot*, *The Diary of Anne Frank*, *The Darling Buds of May*, *Tales of the Unexpected* and *Dalziel and Pascoe*.

Witness Statements

Nicholas McInerny (Writer)

'I was both startled and pleasantly surprised to be asked to revisit my very first episode of *The Bill* that I wrote back in 1988. At the time I had just written for a series called *Gems*, which was an afternoon soap opera. I went to meet the script editor Kenneth Ware, who had a very sardonic sense of humour. He commissioned me to write *Home Sweet Home*, which was one of the first six half-hour episodes to be made. As I later learned, the process of writing for *The Bill* could be very tortuous and it certainly got more difficult later when it returned to the hour-long episodes. I was very lucky with *Home Sweet Home*, because from the first draft to the production script, only three lines were changed. It was probably the easiest script I ever wrote for the series.'

'Watching *Home Sweet Home* back, part of me wonders whether it is too slow? I question whether the public's attention span has changed with regards to how programmes are cut nowadays... If this episode had been made under the Paul Marquess regime, I expect some of the scenes that I wrote would have been shortened to give it more of a sense of pace. I personally like the slowness, because it suited the natural realism that the series was aiming for. To match that, the actors downplayed their dialogue, rather than elevating it, like in the opening scene between Cryer and the bailiff. That's quite a long scene with some really nice stuff about a range of social issues, from squatter's rights to middle class revolutionaries, that the slower pace gave us time to explore.'

'I noticed the word "bloody" was used three times in this episode. Every time we had a swear word in the script, it really had to be argued for. When the squatters open the door and are shown the warrant, in real life they're going to say something much worse than "Go to hell". That's an example of where you had to find an imaginative way to convey somebody's opinion of someone without resorting to swearing. In this case I put an angry dog in there and called them Dennis and Gnasher! It also amused me to see John Bowe's character smoking a cigarette, something we'd not be allowed to show on screen now.'

'I teach creative writing in lots of different arenas, where I talk about my experience writing for *The Bill*. I explain how you were only allowed a certain number of characters and locations in each episode and that you had to see everything purely from the police's point of view. Of course, many new writers think this is some terrible restriction, but in point of fact it's a way of making you work harder to create something that is more powerful. An example of that is the scene in *Home Sweet Home*, where Marie has locked herself in the bathroom with the kids and Insp. Frazer has to try and rationalise with Marie from behind a door. Then gradually there's an awareness that she's popping pills, and only then do they break the door down.'

'That's a five minute scene on the landing and I think that even towards the end of *The Bill*, there would have been much more of a fight creatively to somehow see behind the door. I think it was much more powerful just to show their faces and their reactions whilst they were working out what was happening, plus they were dealing with the drunken councillor and the social worker. I think if I wrote that script today, where things are much more political in television, I would have to make much more of a case for the character dying at the end. A story where a homeless woman would rather die than look after her children has quite a bleak outcome, which I'm not sure would get made today.'

Julian Meers (Floor Manager)
'When the half-hour format was first mentioned, I wondered if we

were going to be making a very different programme from what had started out as a little boutique programme, made in the East End by a breakaway production team from Teddington studios. Setting up at Barlby Road was a mega deal as we required a larger number of production staff to service two episodes a week, which required more leading characters. I remember having a conversation with Peter Cregeen about where to set up the water cooler on the production floor. Why? Because we wanted to maximise the time that people from different departments and units would spend having conversations and problem solving. It might seem crazy, but the placement of this water cooler actually created a better communication network because, while staff were queuing for their water, they weren't locked away in their offices. Such a straightforward solution to a water cooler location was typical of Peter Cregeen's influence, a wonderful executive producer who was creatively brilliant, practically understanding and sensitive to ideas from his team. I loved working for Peter.'

'We had to logistically work out how to make two episodes a week with the same cast, because up until that time we had never had to share the cast, they had previously worked exclusively on one hour-long episode at a time. So when we as the Red unit were shooting scenes like the opening raid in *Home Sweet Home*, we had five of our principal artists on location: Eric Richard, Trudie Goodwin, Ashley Gunstock, Mark Powley and Nick Reding. We had to think very carefully when scheduling this scene, because all five artists would have also been required by the Blue unit for scenes in another episode being shot in tandem that week. We were definitely flying by the seat of our pants logistically on these early twice-weekly episodes, until we found a system of delivery that worked. I think that sort of energy is actually creative and exciting, because no-one was able to sit back on their haunches. We could never be complacent at Barlby Road, the challenge of making the half-hour episodes created a great buzz and excitement on the set, which I believe showed in the completed episodes because we all genuinely cared and enjoyed making the series.'

'*Home Sweet Home* illustrates this well. Gareth Davies directed it with great aplomb and it's amazing how much we packed into 25 minutes. There's the great opener of a flour fight with some squatters. Given time restraints and no resetting time, it had to be one take or bust as we didn't have spare cleaned uniforms and all camera and audio equipment had to be protected from the flour. I also loved watching the actors work and the small little details they added to make it all real. For example, in that opening scene before the raid, Christian Rodska as Hunt does this lovely little bit of business with his Thermos, to help sell the idea they've had to be there early morning. Though in hindsight perhaps there were too many shots of John Bowe's character drinking.'

'*Home Sweet Home* was beautifully written by Nick McInerny, featuring themes that are still relevant today. I was captivated by the long scene set around the bathroom, which because of the 'police point of view' rules of *The Bill*, we never see inside of until the end of the episode. Gareth therefore created the drama though a series of reaction shots *outside* the bathroom and the drama being heightened considerably by the acting talent outside on the landing. But there were also other practical considerations for not seeing inside the bathroom as we only had five spread out location days to shoot 25 minutes and were up against the clock. *Home Sweet Home* was more challenging than other episodes as we had two children in the story, both under five years old, which had limitations on the amount of time we were allowed to have them on set. In other words, by not seeing the children inside the bathroom, we saved valuable time by not having to shoot complex set-ups with children in a confined shooting space. Putting aside practical considerations however, I do think Nick created a more powerful drama for the audience as their imaginations were forced to work as if it was a radio drama: "What is going on in there? How are they going to cope with this particular situation? How are the kids reacting etc." If this episode were made today, we might have seen inside the bathroom, which would be dramatically weaker.'

'I didn't meet Nick McInerny until 2020, when we recorded a commentary for this episode together on Zoom. Writers weren't encouraged to visit us while we were shooting, which was actually always a bit of a downside, because the artists would have welcomed the writers being on set. From my perspective too, it would have helped inform the writers about the production process. When a writer pens a driving scene for example, it is straightforward as a script, but practically we were losing valuable shooting time as we had to build and mount a substantial technical rig to the car before shooting the scene. As there wasn't space for the director to able to be in the car during recording, every take had to be checked on completion, often by the side of the road, before setting up for another take. When the scene finally wrapped, the car would have to be derigged of all the technical kit. In 1988 we had many more practical considerations to take account of that impacted our shooting time. However, in my book, the writer was always king, ideas are the driving force of the series and without them we didn't have a show. If there was another driving scene in the script it was essential we had to find a way to make it happen.'

Gareth Davies (Director)

'I was a bit nervous going into *The Bill*, because it was very complicated for the actors, who were divided up into colour-coded groups. I was given a chart and told which actors I could have and when. The actors had to prepare for scenes from completely different time periods, that they were going to do on the same day. In the morning they could be playing an emotional scene for one episode, then in the afternoon play a totally different sequence. I thought the way the actors dealt with the schedule was remarkable, because I thought it was going to be so complicated that it would fall over itself. The organisation by the production team was extraordinary and incredibly efficient and the main thing I remember about *The Bill* was it was a very, very happy show.'

'I cast my good friend Christian Rodska to play Hunt the bailiff in *Home Sweet Home*, a wonderful actor who I directed on lots of programmes, including an episode of *Z Cars*. The episode was called *Guns* and Christian's character was the leader of a gang of thugs planning an armed robbery at a racecourse, which was supposed to be Aintree, but in actual fact was Brighton. Obviously we always informed the local police that we were going to be filming and that there might be actors rushing about. I was shooting a scene where three police cars had to arrive and our characters would then rush into the stadium and have a big punch up with Christian's thugs. We rehearsed this highly organised sequence with experienced stuntmen, so that punches could be thrown and nobody would get hurt. I was directing from the mobile control room and counted our three police cars into the scene... "Car 1, go! Car 2, go! Car 3, go! Car 4... what the hell?!" A fourth police car arrived and the punch up started to get quite nasty, which was very confusing for everybody! It turned out that some real policemen from across the country borderline had picked up our signal on their radios and decided they would join in! They were amazed to find these thugs were actually actors, one of whom I overheard on the microphone saying, "No need to be so rough, luvvy!"

Sheila Loughrey (Location Manager)

'I joined the BBC as a secretary when I was 18, having seen the job advertised in a newspaper whilst working for a company on the Slough Trading Estate. I became a production assistant when I was 21. I found doing the continuity very hard work. I remember filming a Shirley Bassey performance from Pembroke Castle and thinking, "how do you write continuity for this?" Then when I was 24, I left the BBC and joined Thames Television as a P.A. and when I was about 30, a job came up as a trainee location manager, which I got. Not only was I the first trainee, but I was also the first female to work as a location manager at Thames Television. I had worked with Sandra Brown, the recently appointed Head of Department, before when she was a production manager. So the chaps felt my appointment was a "nudge-nudge, wink-wink" equal opportunities job, but I was soon accepted.'

'One of my first jobs as a trainee location manager was filming at night in a quarry, where the location manager had put storm lanterns all the way along this quarry. Then he told me that my job at the end of the night would be to go along and pick up all the lanterns in the pitch black, while he went home! There was no health and safety in those days; it was every woman for herself. That was my training really, it was non-existent with no structure as such, but I can't complain because I got the job and just got on with whatever I was asked to do. Another show I trained on was *The Benny Hill Show*, which we filmed at Thorpe Park every year when it closed for the season and we'd have Benny running around being chased by the girls.'

'I loved being a location manager because it gave me freedom and got me away from the vast amount of paperwork involved when working as a P.A. I also found that I could contribute a lot more to how each programme looked by finding the right location. I started working on *The Bill* in 1985. I'll always remember that when we were filming around the Isle of Dogs, they were halfway through pulling down the old Tate & Lyle sugar factory. I thought, "I've got to get this into an episode" and eventually I did. Wapping was such a fantastic location for the series and was really what *The Bill* was about to begin with. We still found some good architecture when we moved to West London. The opening of *Home Sweet Home* was filmed on the White City estate, while the house was in Ealing, which I picked because it had quite a large landing.'

ALL IN GOOD FAITH
Written by Barry Appleton
Directed by Gareth Davies

Series 4: Episode 5
Broadcast: Tuesday 2 August 1988

Case Narrative
Sun Hill is running an amnesty bin, in which the public are encouraged to hand in offensive weapons.

Regular Cast
Sgt. Cryer (Eric Richard), D.S. Roach (Tony Scannell), D.C. Dashwood (Jon Iles), D.C. Carver (Mark Wingett), Ch. Insp. Conway (Ben Roberts), Insp. Frazer (Barbara Thorn), W.P.C. Ackland (Trudie Goodwin), P.C. Ramsey (Nick Reding), Sgt. Peters (Larry Dann), P.C. Frank (Ashley Gunstock), P.C. Smith (Robert Hudson), Sgt. Penny (Roger Leach), W.P.C. Martella (Nula Conwell), P.C. Melvin (Mark Powley), P.C. Haynes (Eamonn Walker).

Guest Cast
Miss Lewis (Mary Maxted), Mrs. Duffy (Phyllis McMahon), Mrs. Tully (Betty Romaine), Pat Duffy (Leslie Schofield), Lock (Terry Russell), Woman in Foyer (Tricia Downs).

Production Team
Casting Director (Julian Oldfield), Title Music (Andy Pask, Charlie Morgan), Costume Designer (Jennie Tate), Make Up Designer (Gilly Wakeford), Graphics (Jenni Phillips), Videotape Editor (Dave Lewinton), Lighting (Peter Bower), Camera (Rolie Luker), Sound (Richard Bradford, Alan Lester), Production Buyer (Terry Allen), Location Manager (Sheila Loughrey), Floor Manager (Julian Meers), Stage Manager (Diana Paskin), Production Manager (Derek Cotty), Production Assistant (Carol Snook), Technical Adviser (Wilf Knight), Programme Associate (Valerie Farron), Series Script Editor (Kenneth Ware), Designers (Robin Parker, Pam Blackwell), Executive Producer (Peter Cregeen), Producer (Michael Ferguson).

Observation Notes

All in Good Faith (Production No: D4020, VTR No: THS/45255) was shot between Monday 6th and Friday 10th June 1988. The driving scenes with Dashwood and Ackland were filmed on Dalgarno Gardens, W10. The following scene where they talk to Miss Lewis on her doorstep was shot outside 72 Sidar Road, W11.

The scene where Roach and Carver meet Dashwood was filmed at the end of Freston Road, Ladbroke Grove, W10, with Dashwood's car parked outside No 191, which is now the home to the special education school Pupil Parent Partnership. The skateboard park and wasteground opposite where Dashwood's car is parked has been replaced by modern outdoor sports facilities. Different sections of Freston Road are used for filming locations in several of the 1988 episodes of *The Bill*.

The scenes in Mrs. Duffy's flat were filmed in Frinstead House, W10, a 21-storey tower residential block built in 1966 that is still in use today.

The scenes featuring Duffy being pursued were filmed around Carlton Vale, North Maida Vale, NW6. Duffy is first seen exiting Strome House, before being pursued out of Stratford Close and eventually apprehended down Malvern Mews, Kilburn NW6. For the scene where CID are driving Duffy back to Sun Hill, Mark Wingett drives the car down Carlton Vale before turning into Randolph Gardens, NW6.

Eamonn Walker was again erroneously billed as Roger Leach on the closing credits of *All in Good Faith,* which was also the first episode since the *Woodentop* pilot not to feature Colin Blumenau as Taffy.

Witness Statements

Barry Appleton (Writer)

'I was asked to set *All in Good Faith* mainly around the station, because they had spent a lot of money on *Good Will Visit.* I thought it would be nice to open with the amnesty box and seeing weapons being handed in. It was also an early storyline for Chief Inspector Conway, who was a bit naïve in some ways; he'd been at the Yard most of his career and was more of an administrator. There was nothing exciting about this storyline, but I thought it showed an interesting procedure, as they needed to check these weapons even if they were old souvenirs, because they could still do a lot of damage. It was Jon Iles himself who added that lovely moment of Dashwood not being able to get the knuckleduster off, which worked very well.'

'I also felt that Tony Scannell was a very good actor and that he needed something to get stuck into. I drew on my own experience of when I was a Sergeant in the Flying Squad and was made up to Acting D.I. There is pressure on you at that stage of your career, because you don't want to make a balls-up of an opportunity like that and you've got to think of your future. I enjoyed writing this storyline for Roach and I thought Scannell played it well. I based the story of the old lady who trapped the dodgy gasman on an old case where that actually happened - she didn't tell anybody until much later that he was still in the cellar!'

Gareth Davies (Director)

'I was brought up in the Valleys, in a place called Tredegar. As a boy, I joined an amateur dramatics society, which was wonderful. I traveled all over South Wales doing competitions and we toured various plays, which is when I got the bug and from that moment on it was all I wanted to do. My father was a Presbyterian minister, which people tend to think of as being very severe, but he wasn't at all; he was a very liberal man and had been a very good preacher in his time. He also loved the theatre and used to put on concerts, so the enthusiasm was in the household and he was quite happy and encouraged me to be an actor. I was lucky to get a scholarship to go to drama school, otherwise we wouldn't have been able to afford it.'

'I was then offered various jobs around the country with good repertory theatres, as well as the Old Vic, but first I had to go and do my national service, which put a shocking stop in my career. At the time I thought it was such a waste of time, and in military terms it was because I was never a very good soldier. I've never really regretted it, in a funny sort of way, even though I hated it then. It did at least make me realise that there was another world outside the theatre. I went to Italy, Austria, Germany and all sorts of places that I wouldn't have done otherwise. I also spent part of my service with the Forces broadcasting.'

'I then spent eight years working as an actor, starting in repertory theatre, before moving into television. My wife, Christine Pollon, and I were both in a soap opera together called *Compact* for a couple of years, where we had a wonderful time. Christine played Janet Ellis and I played Mark Viccars. Every Monday's episode went out live, then on Tuesday we recorded Wednesday's episode, so that we could stay in the studio for two days and not to have to change our set-ups, which was obviously more efficient. But even the recorded episode was done "as live" where you couldn't really break, or the poor old director would end up on the naughty step and get their wrist slapped. I wouldn't recommend it as the ideal way to make programmes, though it was exciting and gave us very good experience. You had to get it right and you learned how to ad-lib and get your way out of situations. Nothing makes you more wide awake than knowing you've got 11 million people watching at the other end!'

'After a while, I found myself wanting to tell other actors how to do it, which made me think if I was only going to get punched on the nose, I probably ought to make it official! I decided to give up the security and train to become a director, which was a massive salary drop. I think I was earning £140 a week in *Compact*, which was a lot of money in those days. By switching to becoming a director at the BBC, my salary would drop down to £25 a week! We had a small child, with another one the way, so we knew it would be hard financially. But my wife was wonderful and she said, "If it's what you want to do, then you should do it." She was absolutely great. The BBC were also very kind and they let me postpone my director's course for a year and gain experience on *Compact*, whilst I was still in the cast.'

'I was very lucky that we worked with the same camera crew on *Compact* for years, we all knew each other very well. They said, "We're going to make sure we get one director who is properly bloody trained!" Whenever I finished my scenes as an actor, I would go and work on the floor, which made me realise what actually goes on in a studio, from every point of view. I got to operate the camera, I held booms, I pulled cables and I also worked up in the gallery. So by the time I went on the director's course (which was a very good course) I was already very well practiced, thanks to the camera crew, who were great to me. If you're going to be a director, I think it is a very good idea to know a bit about everyone's job, mainly so you know how difficult it can be.'

'One of the first things they did on the director's course was to show you around the gallery, which was well kitted out with a nice carpet on the floor... When they showed us where the director sat, there was always a hole in the carpet, made by the director's right foot nervously stamping and dragging in sheer panic. But like stage fright, you learn how to control it. Also on this same director's course were two names you will recognise: Michael Ferguson and Peter Cregeen. By the time they were making *The Bill*, we were old friends and it was nice of them to invite me to direct these two episodes. The other person I already knew was Eamonn Walker, who I had directed in an episode of *Tales of the Unexpected*. Eamonn is a very good actor who has done so well, going on to play Othello and he is very big in America now. To play Duffy in *All in Good Faith*, I cast another very good actor I worked with on lots of programmes, Leslie Schofield. Leslie is a strong man and an interesting one too, who had served in the Navy before becoming an actor. He's a good man and I liked working with him very much.'

'Directors come in all shapes and sizes. I remember one who was also a writer and said that all an actor had to do was "serve the punctuation..." Actually it's a lot more complicated than that! I've always felt that the actor should believe that the play is theirs and that they invented it, which sometimes a writer can find a bit upsetting... but the actor has to live the part as if those words are his, and that's what I always tried to achieve during rehearsals. As a director, my relationship with the actors was that they needed to know that I was the boss, but I wouldn't boss them around. But they also needed to know that if necessary, I would. You had to give a sense of authority, which they could rally against if they feel like it, which is fine and perfectly right and proper. I also thought it should always be enjoyable if possible, which in my experience it was, mostly.'

'It's nice to have been asked to look back on my career, which is not something I often do, simply because you have to move on. My career ended 25 years ago, when producers were getting younger and didn't want old farts like me around as their directors, which is perfectly understandable. I know some of my contemporaries can't accept that they don't do it anymore, but one really has to. I live in a small village in mid-Wales, surrounded by beautiful countryside, where the fact that I was once a television director means bugger all; it's meaningless and no longer a feature in my life. Sadly my wife died in 2012, but we were together for 55 years after meeting in Leatherhead Rep in 1957, so that's not bad. I've enjoyed my life and I'm more interested now in how our son is getting on, who as well as appropriately being both an actor and director, is also a university professor in America.'

JUST CALL ME GUVNOR

Written by Geoff McQueen

Directed by Brian Parker

Series 4: Episode 6

Broadcast: Thursday 4 August 1988

Case Narrative

Roach isn't best pleased when Burnside is made acting D.I. Burnside is even less pleased with Roach when he blows his undercover operation.

Regular Cast

Sgt. Cryer (Eric Richard), Sgt. Penny (Roger Leach), Sgt. Peters (Larry Dann), Insp. Frazer (Barbara Thorn), D.I. Burnside (Christopher Ellison), Acting D.I. Roach (Tony Scannell), D.C. Dashwood (Jon Iles), D.C. Carver (Mark Wingett), W.P.C. Martella (Nula Conwell), P.C. Edwards (Colin Blumenau), P.C. Haynes (Eamonn Walker), P.C. Smith (Robert Hudson), P.C. Hollis (Jeff Stewart), W.P.C. Ackland (Trudie Goodwin), Ch. Supt. Brownlow (Peter Ellis), Ch. Insp. Conway (Ben Roberts), P.C. Banks (Russell Lewis).

Guest Cast

D.S. Trimlet (Richard Sockett), Lennox (Peter McNamara), Lord Lucan (Chris Chering), Milkman (Bunny May), Dick Turpin (Russell Gold).

Uncredited Personnel

W.P.C. (Denise Powell), CAD Room P.C. (Paddy Murphy), Operation Red Card P.C.s (Derek Lyons, Paul Page-Hanson, Oscar Peck), D.C. (Kevin O'Brien), Press Officer (Rosane Chapman), Accountants (Anne Shields, David Saggs).

Production Team

Stunt Arranger (Andy Bradford), Casting Director (Julia Lisney), Title Music (Andy Pask, Charlie Morgan), Costume Designer (Mandy Harper), Make Up Designer (Gilly Wakeford), Graphics (Jenni Phillips), Videotape Editor (Tom Kavanagh), Lighting (John O'Brien), Camera (Roy Easton), Sound (John Osborne, Alan Lester), Production Buyer (Mike Ashby), Location Manager (Barry Beckett), Floor Manager (Fizz Waters), Stage Manager (Tricia Barnes), Production Manager (Derek Cotty), Production Assistant (Caroline Sutton), Technical Adviser (Wilf Knight), Programme Associate (Valerie Farron), Script Editor (Tim Vaughan), Series

Script Editor (Kenneth Ware), Designers (Robin Parker, Peter Elliott), Executive Producer (Peter Cregeen), Producer (Richard Bramall).

Observation Notes

Just Call Me Guvnor (Production No: D4021, VTR No: THS/45256) was shot between Monday 6th and Friday 10th June 1988.

The Operation Red Card sequence was filmed in West Kilburn, beginning outside 208 Third Avenue, W10. The following scene, where Chief Supt. Brownlow talks to the milkman, was filmed on Oliphant Street, W10. Peter Ellis then enters 118 Sixth Avenue, W10 for the scene where Brownlow inspects the C.S. gas canisters with Edwards and Banks. The final pub scene was shot in the Latimer Arms, 198 Latimer Road, W10.

Just Call Me Guvnor sees Russell Lewis make his debut as P.C. Banks, who would also feature in *Conflict* and *Evacuation*. Lewis began his career as a child actor before beginning a very successful career as a television writer. Lewis would later write 17 episodes of *The Bill*, including iconic episodes *Blue Murder*, *Cry Havoc*, *They Also Serve* and *The Short Straw*. His many credits include *Inspector Morse*, *Lewis*, *Without Motive*, *Taggart*, *Between the Lines*, *The Last Detective*, *Grace* and *Endeavour*.

Trudie Goodwin was erroneously uncredited on *Just Call Me Guvnor*, despite several dialogue scenes. Helping Ackland log all the weapons obtained during Operation Red Card is a W.P.C. played by Denise Powell, who worked regularly as a supporting artist on *The Bill* for the next 22 years and would later play W.P.C. Clarke. Featured in the briefing scene were a number of other prominent *The Bill* personnel: Oscar Peck enjoyed a successful career as an actor with roles in *Get Some In*, *Fawlty Towers*, *Blind Justice* and several credited *The Bill* appearances as a CAD Room P.C. Actor Derek Lyons has appeared in dozens of iconic feature films including *Star Wars*, *Flash Gordon*, *Indiana Jones and the Last Crusade* and multiple Bond films. He worked regularly on *The Bill* and was later credited for his role as P.C. Craig Lovell. Paul Page-Hanson would later be credited for playing P.C. Darryl Hartley and also performed the feet for the end credits sequence in the 1990s alongside Karen England. After a successful racing career, Page-Hanson is now a cycling coach based in San Francisco. Also featured in close-up in *Just Call Me Guvnor* is regular CID supporting artist Kevin O'Brien, who went on to have a successful singing career, performing worldwide tours.

Just Call Me Guvnor was the first episode helmed by Brian Parker, a highly experienced director who began his career as an actor. His many directing credits included episodes of *Play for Today*, *The Wednesday Play*, *Softly Softly*, *Hadleigh*, *Z Cars*, *Crown Court*, *Love and Marriage*, *Inspector Morse* and *Ellington* starring Chris Ellison. Parker directed 46 episodes of *The Bill* between 1988 and 2001, culminating with *Britanniamania* Parts 1&2. Brian Parker passed away in 2020, aged 91.

Just Call Me Guvnor was adapted for an episode of the Netherlands police series *Bureau Kruislaan*, produced by Joop van den Ende TV Productions in 1992. 39 episodes were made across two seasons and the adaption of *Just Call Me Guvnor* was the third episode of the first season. The title, *Operatie rode kaart*, translates as "Operation Red Card" and is a very faithful adaptation, including an undercover officer being headbutted after spitting in a detective's face, as well as the bogus gas inspector storyline. All the regulars were adapted, some keeping similar names: Adjutant Bob Voskuil (Sgt. Cryer), Brigadier Tom Panhuis (Sgt. Penny), Brigadier Alex Peters (Sgt. Peters), Chief Agent Lucy Akkermans (W.P.C. Ackland) and Inspecteur Christine Verwey (Insp. Frazer). Each episode was adapted by Felix Thijssen, a Dutch screenwriter and award-winning crime novelist. Felix Thijssen died in 2022, aged 88.

Just Call Me Guvnor saw Chris Ellison make his regular debut as D.I. Frank Burnside, having appeared as "Tommy" Burnside in three of the hour-long episodes in the first two series. The character notes describe Burnside as being 34 and "known to a number of the Sun Hill personnel as a DS in an adjoining Division... the newly-promoted Burnside is a man who has been involved in a number of "situations" that could have given rise to a belief that he was something less than straight, he might well have actually been working with Countryman. Whatever the truth is, Burnside is, most comprehensively, a man who has learned all the angles and how most effectively to play them; and in his new position will be more than ever prepared to bend rules in order to collar villains whilst keeping a watchful, knowing eye on the men to whom he is now the Guvnor."

Witness Statements

Chris Ellison (D.I. Frank Burnside)
'When the opportunity came along in 1988 for me to join *The Bill* full-time, it was obvious to say, "Yes please" because it was regular

money. Some actors go into the RSC and spend their lives doing quality work, but don't earn very much. I've never been one of those actors. I just used to think, "thank God I'm working" and waited for the cheque to arrive. I have enjoyed working in the theatre, but I've always preferred doing television because I enjoy working with the camera and I get to go home in the evenings!'

'I thought Geoff McQueen wrote Burnside back into the series really well with *Just Call Me Guvnor*, you don't get scripts like that every day as an actor. I always felt Geoff, who unfortunately died unexpectedly when he was still very young, was the main influence in me joining as a regular. I've also got to be very thankful to John Salthouse, because had he decided to carry on with the series, I wouldn't have been brought in as the D.I. Before Burnside, I'd played a bent D.I. in a series called *Wolcott*, where the late Warren Clarke played the villain. My character was called Charlie Bonham and he was not a nice guy. I've always remembered his name, because whenever I used to walk on set, the director would say, "Here comes Cheerful Charlie", because he was a miserable so-and-so. I know Burnside was also a horrible character in a lot of ways, but he was also quite funny and I used to get some great one-liners, which was the most enjoyable thing about playing him. I also think humour helps create a great atmosphere, which is why I didn't understand when they later changed the format when we did the *Burnside* spin-off. It was too black and serious, it lost all the humour which you need to break up the drama. Its like playing an instrument, if you played it all on one note, it would be boring. The great writers we had on *The Bill* all understood that and I got some terrific scripts.'

Barbara Thorn (Insp. Christine Frazer)

'*Just Call Me Guvnor* was the first time I worked with Chris Ellison, who had done a lot more telly than I had at that point, as well as several films. I loved working with him. He was always very solid and I thought the relationship between Frazer and Burnside was lovely because it was understated, and it was left for the audience to make of their past what they wanted. *Just Call Me Guvnor* was directed by the late Brian Parker, who gave me my very first job in television. I had been doing lots of work in the theatre as a young actress, but was getting quite frustrated that I hadn't broken into television. So I wrote Brian a letter, explaining what I had done and that I was keen to work in television. He invited me in to meet him at the BBC and said he had a part that he could offer me, as a nurse in a *BBC Playhouse* he was directing. He explained it was a small part, but it would be a start, for which I was very grateful. It was filmed at Television Centre, which was a fantastic place to work, though I remember feeling quite lonely sat on my own in a little dressing room, waiting to be called onto the set... Brian also cast me in a series called *Love and Marriage* and it was great to work with him again. He was a lovely man and a very focused director.'

Fizz Waters (Floor Manager)

'All the floor managers at Thames were on a weekly roster, and you would find out what you'd be working on a couple of weeks in advance. I had worked on a couple of the hour-long episodes of *The Bill*, one of which was directed by Peter Cregeen, who is the guru of all time - he is such a fantastic bloke. I never saw Peter get in a flap about anything, even when he was directing the episode *Domestics*, on which I was his floor manager and Susan Lewis was the P.A. I don't know how, but after we wrapped, I realised that we had forgotten to shoot a scene! I was so embarrassed and thought it would mean my career was finished... but when I told Peter, he just calmly said that he'd be able to get around it in editing. He was gorgeous!'

'It was a big deal when *The Bill* went into the twice-weekly format. A few of us had been worried that the series might be cheapened somehow, so the thought that it might not work made working on these early episodes a bit nerve-wracking. We'd had two weeks to prep each hour-long story, which was then shot over a fortnight, focusing on one episode at a time. Then when we moved to the half-hours, there were two units working in tandem and we only had one week to prep, followed by a week to shoot an episode. During the prep week, I would read the script and make my notes about what was going to happen in each scene. Then I would put up a big running order on the wall, using the old-fashioned card system, so I could move scenes about when working out the schedule. I remember the first time I saw a group of people using a computer, I pointed to the cards on the wall and said, "Oh those things will never catch on, it's much easier doing it this way!"'

'It was a hell of a lot easier making the hour-long episodes, because you knew that all of the cast were available whenever you needed them. Whereas on the half-hours, we had to liaise with the other unit while we were pulling everything together and you might have to start your schedule again when you found out that one of the actors was tied up with the other unit. Working with two units was hard enough; it would have done my head in later on when they had three or four units on the go! Then you were just hoping to God that everyone was in the right place at the right time on the first shooting day!

'The shot of Chris Ellison coming down the stairs in *Just Call Me Guvnor*, with Burnside "arrested" having been undercover, was the very first shot that he filmed on the half-hours. I think he might have been a bit nervous, as one would be coming down the stairs in your underwear on your first day, but he didn't show it on camera, he did a really good job. I actually remember being in the room, tucked down out of shot, when Chris was being hauled out of bed! Though a sequence wiped from my memory bank was the policemen using a sledgehammer to open the front door, which I thought was odd and I wonder why we didn't use a battering ram? Playing one of the young PCs in that sequence was Russell Lewis, who was very cute and a really good actor! I first worked with Russell, who is now a writer, on a series called *S.W.A.L.K.* I remember once I realised that I hadn't given him his call for the next day and I phoned late at night and woke his dad. Russell got his call time and I think he forgave me...'

Tim Vaughan (Script Editor)
'When I joined *The Bill* in 1987, I knew I was stepping in to something that would be far more challenging than anything I'd done before in my television career. After a bit of work on *The Masterspy* with Colin Shindler, I'd spent eight years as a script editor on *Emmerdale Farm*, where I'd worked on hundreds of episodes, including writing over 100 scripts myself. In truth, *Emmerdale Farm* was dying on its feet by the late 80s, and needed to change, which it did in 1989 when it became simply *Emmerdale*, with Keith Richardson in the executive chair. I'd had a fantastic time at Yorkshire TV, and met many people I would work with again, such as Pat Sandys, Michael Ferguson, Richard Handford, Frank W Smith and Tony Virgo; but coming back to London to meet the likes of Peter Cregeen and John Kershaw felt a bit like leaving the kindergarten for the senior school. The interview with Peter and John was convivial - until Peter asked me why I'd stayed so long up at Yorkshire TV. I just said the first thing that came into my head: "There was work to do, and I thoroughly enjoyed it". I think that might have been what got me the job.'

'There were a few teething troubles. I don't think Ken Ware, the series script editor, ever quite disabused himself of the idea that I was some country bumpkin from up north, and he often voiced his regret at Chris Boucher's departure. It was hard, working with Ken; but I put that down to the stress that we all felt in the run-up to putting scripts together for the new bi-weekly series. The clock was ticking down to the launch, and it was daunting. Chris Boucher himself had resigned because he never thought the bi-weekly show would work, and his sentiments were shared by the pundits. The BBC actually aired a half-hour programme in which various people, including Tony Holland, script editor of *EastEnders*, insisted that a long-running series of the kind we wanted to make, would quickly run out of ideas and hit the buffers.'

'Despite the willingness and enthusiasm of the production team, nobody could be absolutely sure the critics weren't right. But I remember very fondly on the very eve of production, Peter got the whole crew into the office and outlined his entire vision for the show. He spoke for a good forty minutes or more. It kind of galvanised everyone, and when we left that night, it was with a spring in our step. It was a classic Peter Cregeen performance: he was a brilliant executive producer, who kept a light hand on the tiller, let us do what we wanted - within reason - and always backed us up. The late Michael Ferguson and Richard Bramall were also seasoned producers, having already been really good directors on *The Bill*. They were both charming and easy to work with.'

'I remember Ken and I coming back to work the day after the first episode went out, and realising we had a hit on our hands. It didn't mean we could relax, but we could get on with what we wanted to do. The trump card in those early days was Chris Ellison: landing him was a huge coup. *Just Call Me Guvnor* re-introduced Chris as Burnside. Playing P.C. Banks in that episode was my friend Russell Lewis, who'd been an impressive child actor (anyone interested should take a look at John Schlesinger's film *Sunday, Bloody Sunday*, in which a 7 year-old Russell Lewis virtually steals the show - from Peter Finch and Glenda Jackson, no less!). My own long and happy association with Russell Lewis began when I briefly worked with him on *They Also Serve*, which became a little masterpiece thanks to Russell and Gina Cronk, his script editor.'

CAUGHT RED HANDED

Written by Barry Appleton
Directed by Derek Lister

Series 4: Episode 7
Broadcast: Tuesday 9 August 1988

Case Narrative

When a man is viciously stabbed by his pregnant wife for complaining about his soggy cornflakes, how can he not press charges?

Regular Cast

Sgt. Cryer (Eric Richard), Insp. Frazer (Barbara Thorn), Sgt. Peters (Larry Dann), Sgt. Penny (Roger Leach), D.I. Burnside (Christopher Ellison), D.S. Roach (Tony Scannell), D.C. Dashwood (Jon Iles), D.C. Carver (Mark Wingett), Ch. Supt. Brownlow (Peter Ellis), P.C. Smith (Robert Hudson), P.C. Edwards (Colin Blumenau), W.P.C. Ackland (Trudie Goodwin), W.P.C. Martella (Nula Conwell), P.C. Haynes (Eamonn Walker), P.C. Frank (Ashley Gunstock), P.C. Stamp (Graham Cole).

Guest Cast

John Kelsey (Jim Barclay), Jill Kelsey (Chrissie Cotterill), S.O.C.O. (Susan Curnow), Mr. Maple (Sidney Livingstone), Miss Dean (Cazz Scattergood), Dave West (Garry Cooper), Doctor (Shahnaz Pakravan), Landlord (Michael Stainton).

Production Team

Casting Director (Julia Lisney), Title Music (Andy Pask, Charlie Morgan), Costume Designer (Allard Tobin), Make Up Designer (Gilly Wakeford), Graphics (Ethan Ames), Videotape Editor (Tom Kavanagh), Lighting (Allen Harradine), Camera (Jamie Acton-Bond), Sound (Richard Longley, Alan Lester), Production Buyer (Trevor Young), Location Manager (Eddie Mares), Floor Manager (Aidan Boulter), Stage Manager (Ed Stevenson), Production Manager (Derek Cotty), Production Assistant (Susan Lewis), Technical Adviser (Wilf Knight), Programme Associate (Valerie Farron), Series Script Editor (Kenneth Ware), Designers (Robin Parker, Peter Elliott), Executive Producer (Peter Cregeen), Producer (Richard Bramall).

Observation Notes

Caught Red Handed (Production No: D4029, VTR No: THS/45264) was shot between Monday 4th and Friday 8th July 1988, made along with *Runaround* during Derek Lister's second block of episodes.

The scenes set at Mr. and Mrs. Kelsey's home were filmed on the infamous Stonebridge estate, NW10, which has since been redeveloped.

The swimming pool scenes were filmed at the former White City Pools, Bloemfontein Road, W12. The leisure centre was renamed in 1990 as a tribute to Janet Adegoke, the first black Mayor of London, who died of cancer in 1987 at the age of 47. A refurbished leisure centre opened in March 2006, where the swimming pool was also named after Adegoke.

The scene where Carver retrieves the steroids that were flushed down Dave West's toilet was filmed outside 35 St. Charles Square, W10.

Caught Red Handed was adapted for an episode of the Netherlands police series *Bureau Kruislaan* in 1992. The title of the episode *Op heterdaad* translates as "In the Act" and was the ninth episode of the first season.

Witness Statements

Ashley Gunstock (P.C. Robin Frank)

'Thames boxed really cleverly when they made the transition into the half-hour episodes. They wanted something to rival *EastEnders*, which had been running away with the ratings. But they didn't put *The Bill* on at the same time as *EastEnders*, they put it on afterwards in the hope that viewers would switch over and stay with ITV for the rest of the evening, which would please their investors. *The Bill* mushroomed and became a staple for everyone to watch on television. Whilst it might have been the same programme, it was a different format, and doing these smaller self-contained stories was brilliant. I also feel the strength of the show came from so many people who had worked in theatre, which had given us all a good base and foundation of the craft. *The Bill* was still a grassroots show, they didn't get star names in to fulfil the new roles and there wasn't anyone in the cast who was "the big I am." They brought in talented individuals like Barbara Thorn, Nick Reding, Eamonn Walker and Ben Roberts, who were all superb actors and great to work with. Everybody was welcomed into the fold and the whole thing flourished; it was a snowball that kept growing. *The Bill* had a life of its own that just grew organically, which is very rare. Creatives don't get the same opportunity to do that now, because the balance sheet is king and there's very little room for experimentation these days.'

'In *Caught Red Handed,* where Sgt. Penny is still suffering from PTSD, Roger Leach showed what a solid actor he was - by God did he know his stuff. Roger was a really charming man and once he and his wife Brenda invited us to stay at their home in Salisbury, where Roger entertained us all evening. When he got the lead role as Lambert Le Roux in the Salisbury Playhouse's production of *Pravda*, the amazing Nigel Wilson, an organiser non-pareil, hired us a coach and loads of the cast went to watch Roger in the play. He was just loved by everybody, and I was so shocked and stunned when I heard that he had died, because he had such vitality about him.'

Barry Appleton (Writer)

'The stabbing storyline at the beginning of *Caught Red Handed*, over something simple at the breakfast table, was based on another case that actually happened. I had to change some things of course, as in real life this couple had a young kid who had to be looked after by a neighbour. I went home at the end of my shift and I got a call from the station. The Sergeant said that he thought they could let her go because she was sorry... I said, "Are you sure? Its attempted murder." He explained that the husband wasn't worried and didn't want to press charges and that the neighbour couldn't look after the kid overnight. The Sergeant felt she was calm enough to go home. Well you won't believe this, but when he bailed her out, he gave the knife back to her and she did it again that evening!'

'As well as writing interesting cases in the stories, I liked giving the regular cast a chance to show off their acting. *Caught Red Handed* saw the continuation of Tom Penny's breakdown and I thought Roger Leach did a brilliant job playing Penny. I loved writing for him. I read about steroids in the paper and I thought I'd try that idea on Yorkie. I thought Robert Hudson was really good in that scene across the snooker table, saying, "You saw nothing, you know nothing. Nothing at all." He did that really well and it just showed what these actors could do if you gave them the opportunities to play different kinds of scenes.'

'The scene with Carver lifting up the manhole cover and catching the drugs was based on my Flying Squad days. It happened so many times that when the suspect heard "knock knock", we'd then hear the toilet being flushed! Before *Caught Red Handed* was broadcast, I got a phone call from Peter Cregeen, who asked me to go and see one of the big advertising companies in the West End. They wanted to make a small trailer for this episode to go on television. I went to this meeting with 16 people sat around this long table. I told them the story about the manhole cover and I gave them the idea of a car coming over a hill and passing the milkman, to establish it was early in the morning. They all thought it was smashing and they made this trailer, which looked really good... though I never got any money for it!'

Mark Wingett (D.C. Jim Carver)

'Ladbroke Grove was an exciting place to be working. I knew the area well as I'd grown up not far from there and it was my old stomping ground. The studio at Barlby Road was also interesting because not much in that building had changed since the 1950s, when it was the Sunbeam-Talbot factory, manufacturers of some rather fabulous cars. There were still some of the warehouses at the back, and in the summer the cast and crew used to go down to the backlot, passing the old garages where the edit suites were now based, and we would have barbecues by the canal, where everybody was welcome. It was an incredible time. The studio was larger than the old building at Artichoke Hill, though whilst the facilities had increased somewhat, it wasn't such a massive operation that we didn't know everyone inside the building. All the regular male cast shared one dressing room, a bit like the police force really. We had one big room, with lockers and a few sofas, while the girls had a similar dressing room, and there were two more for the supporting artists.'

'We all knew we were onto a good thing when the series went into the half-hours and it became a lot more prevalent to discuss the behaviour of our characters with the new directors coming in, who welcomed our input. *The Bill* was an egalitarian production; we worked together as a cast and closely with our crew and we all cared deeply about the work. We would suggest changing a line if it suited our characters better, or if it helped fix any continuity. Any actor worth their salt actually wants to write their lines themselves, but they must be kept in check and you need to be able to bounce off your director. On *The Bill* we had that latitude and freedom as actors and as a result, a lot of our own personalities as individuals seeped into our characters. There was also no room for ego and nobody got too big for their boots because if you did, you'd just have the mickey taken out of you. There was certainly no glamour, as I distinctly remember in the scene where Carver retrieved the drugs in *Caught Red Handed*. I lifted a manhole cover and went 12 ft down into a drain outside a house. Then a resident in one of the other flats went to the toilet and I ended up with a handful of you-know-what. It was horrible... *that's* the glamour of showbiz!'

Aidan Boulter (Floor Manager)

'The cast became a family on *The Bill*, because they were working so closely together for long hours. Trudie Goodwin and Nula Conwell were both absolutely lovely and fantastic to work with. Jon Iles was a very funny man, who was always cracking jokes and never missed an opportunity to play a practical joke. Mark Powley was also great fun and I am still in touch with Mark Wingett, who is a fellow motorcyclist. Nick Reding was a funny guy and as I was an easily impressionable young man, I was quite impressed by the flash car he got to drive as Ramsey. He worked well with Eamonn Walker, who was a very tall and very handsome young man. I always thought he would go on to great things and I am pleased that he has done well in America. Graham Cole, who of course became quite integral to *The Bill*, had also joined the regular cast by this point. Chris Ellison also made a huge impact as Burnside and was actually quite similar to John Salthouse, in so far as they both had a very dry sense of humour. Chris often had a very stern expression on his face, but then when you were least expecting it, would come out with a really witty line at the drop of a hat. Chris was very professional and stayed in character quite a lot of the time.'

'As floor manager of the Blue unit, I would have to negotiate with the floor manager of the Red unit, about who would have which members of the cast at what point... I remember times when we were going to the producers and saying "We both have this character in our script, can we take that whole section of dialogue and give it to another character, to help us get over our scheduling issues?" The producers were mostly sympathetic to that, because it was the only way that it could work. I have an enormous amount of respect for Peter Cregeen, who was known as 'The Admiral': a very tall man with a beard, which stood out because the rest of us were all clean-shaven. Peter was always very, *very* calm, even when all hell was breaking loose. He had this fantastic way of controlling everything and making sure it all happened. Another great support was our production manager Derek Cotty, who had originally been a location manager at Thames. Derek was very, very organised and hugely hardworking; he was always the first to arrive and the last to leave. I worked very closely with Derek, and latterly Brian Heard when he joined as our second production manager. They were both always there for you, you could knock on their door and ask for help and they would give it if they could. They were both phenomenally professional and I was very grateful to have them around to be honest.'

'My office overlooked the yard, where they parked all the Metros. Whenever you see the officers getting into a car, there were some windows on the left hand side, and our office was the other side of those windows. In my office was Derek Lister, the director and Susan Lewis, the production assistant (now known as a script supervisor). I remember Sue vividly; a lovely lady who I'm very grateful to still be in touch with, especially as she is now an international best-selling author. In those days, it was slightly frustrating because we couldn't get any paperwork out of her; she always seemed to be beavering away at her word processor, but when it came to paperwork for our episodes, there wasn't any. I couldn't figure out what the hell was going on. Then shortly afterwards, I saw the name Susan Lewis on the shelves of my local bookshop and realised *that's* what she'd been typing! I remember Derek Lister being very understanding about this backlog, he just said, "If you can just let me know what I'm supposed to be doing next, I'll shoot it." That was really kind of him, because I hadn't had that much dialogue with him beforehand. He was a brilliant director.'

Derek Lister (Director)

'I went to Central drama school, way back in the 1960s at the start of the 'Summer of Love'. I did a production course, not an acting course. I left after a year, because I was very hippie then and I didn't want to go into provincial repertory theatre, which is what the school was geared for. I just don't like old-fashioned theatre; I was into Captain Beefheart rather than Oscar Wilde. So I went to America travelling and I got picked up by a progressive rock and roll band called Dharma, who were on their way to Chicago for the 1968 Democratic Convention. They were a Cream-type band, right in the midst of the psychedelic era; it was an incredible time. Their first gig in Chicago was at a place called The Electric Circus, where they were actually backing up The Who! The venue had only just been fitted out, but the lights weren't working properly and it was a bit of a mess. Because I was trained theatrically, I went up to the box to see if I could help. I made suggestions about how we could do the lighting and both bands were pleased with the results. I ended up joining Dharma and going back to Detroit with them and becoming their stage director, because they liked how theatrical I made it. I worked with them for just over a year, but then I got arrested and deported because I wouldn't go to Vietnam and I didn't have the right work permit.'

'By the time I came back to England, fringe theatre had grown quite a lot while I'd been away, which was more progressive. So I did some stage management and a little bit of assistant directing at the Traverse theatre in Edinburgh, working on some new plays. I got my first ever directing gig at the Royal Shakespeare Company, putting on a Sam Shepherd play at Stratford, because of my experience working in America. Then I got some directing work at the King's Head, before I got head hunted by the Royal Court in London who gave me a job as an assistant director. I worked with some famous directors, including Lindsay Anderson and Peter Gill. I then got head hunted to Granada TV, where I did the directors course. The industry was heavily unionised then, so I had to stay for a while to earn my ticket; it was like doing my national service at Granada. I got through it and then went freelance and did some plays at Granada, after training on shows like *Coronation Street* and *Crown Court*. I directed some music videos too when they found out I'd been a rock and roller! Then I started to get regular work as a drama director at the BBC, during the era of single plays. There was a wonderful, entrepreneurial atmosphere on the fifth floor of Television Centre; it was a great environment to work in.'

'But when Thatcher came along, single plays disappeared overnight from TV and it became only what the market wanted, which was returnable series like *EastEnders*. I started directing series like *Nanny* and *Rockcliffe's Babies* and *Big Deal*, which is perhaps what led to me working on *The Bill*. I already knew Larry Dann, because he was at Corona at the same time as my wife Ania, who had been a child actress. Larry was on the show a long time and was always reliable, as was Eric Richard, who was always very solid. Eric's a big football fan and he had an Arsenal mug on set, so whenever I came on set I would ask the crew to switch it to a Villa mug! Bob Hudson was very good in *Caught Red Handed* and I liked working with Jonny Iles, Mark Powley and Eamonn Walker, they were all very good. I also thought Tony Scannell was a great actor, though not always the best behaved!'

HOMES AND GARDENS
Written by Christopher Russell
Directed by Derek Lister

Series 4: Episode 8
Broadcast: Thursday 11 August 1988

Case Narrative
Two youths encourage a 30-year-old man with learning difficulties to lose his temper and rage at a car driver who has been forced to a standstill.

Regular Cast
Sgt. Cryer (Eric Richard), Sgt. Peters (Larry Dann), Insp. Frazer (Barbara Thorn), W.P.C. Martella (Nula Conwell), P.C. Melvin (Mark Powley), P.C. Edwards (Colin Blumenau), P.C. Smith (Robert Hudson), D.C. Carver (Mark Wingett), Sgt. Penny (Roger Leach), P.C. Frank (Ashley Gunstock), P.C. Hollis (Jeff Stewart), D.C. Dashwood (Jon Iles), P.C. Ramsey (Nick Reding).

Guest Cast
Mickey Cozens (Stephen Lee), Steve (Mike Smart), Tel (Marc Tufano), Collie (Mark Monero), Motorist (Desmond Cullum-Jones), Motorist's Wife (Yvonne Ash), Jack Fairweather (Anthony Collin), Ede Fairweather (Pamela Pitchford), George Cozens (Brian Peck), Mrs. Ingham (Catherine Clarke), First Neighbour (Marcia Johnson), Second Neighbour (Christopher Tajah), Third Neighbour (Marsha Millar). Passing Woman (Jenny Donnison), Passing Man (Aiden Murphy).

Production Team
Casting Director (Julia Lisney), Title Music (Andy Pask, Charlie Morgan), Costume Designer (Dennis Griffith), Make Up Designer (Gilly Wakeford), Graphics (Jenni Phillips), Videotape Editor (Tom Kavanagh), Lighting (Allen Harradine), Camera (Jamie Acton-Bond), Sound (Stan Lee, Alan Lester), Production Buyer (Mike Ashby), Location Manager (Eddie Mares), Floor Manager (Aidan Boulter), Stage Manager (Marilyn Edwards), Production Manager (Derek Cotty), Production Assistant (Susan Lewis), Technical Adviser (Wilf Knight), Programme Associate (Valerie Farron), Script Editor (Tim Vaughan), Series Script Editor

(Kenneth Ware), Designers (Robin Parker, Deborah Ashforth), Executive Producer (Peter Cregeen), Producer (Richard Bramall).

Observation Notes

Homes and Gardens (Production No: D4018, VTR No: THS/45253) was shot between Monday 30th May and Friday 3rd June 1988.

The scene where Edwards discovers Mickey Cozens and his mates causing a traffic jam was shot outside 7 Leopold Road, Harlesden, NW10. Smith's panda car is parked on the corner of the adjoining Goodson Road, NW10. Most of the shops seen in the background have since been converted into ground floor flats.

Filming for the scenes where Carver investigates Mr and Mrs Fairweather's garden and interviews their neighbours were all shot on the Stonebridge estate, NW10, which has since been redeveloped.

The driving scenes where P.C. Smith is taking Mickey and George Cozens home were shot in Shepherds Bush. Robert Hudson initially drives from The Curve onto the adjoining Hemlock Road, W12. Mickey then spots his mates standing on the corner of Yew Tree Road, W12. The scene concludes outside 5 Tamarisk Square, W12, where Yorkie is assaulted outside. Sgt. Cryer is then seen leaving 2 Tamarisk Square, having interviewed the neighbour, Mrs. Bannister.

The following scene where P.C. Ramsey and P.C. Edwards are searching for Yorkie begins at the end of Abbey Road, North Acton, NW10. Nick Reding then drives onto the adjoining Park Royal Road, NW10. The following scene where Ramsey and Taffy spot the helicopter was shot on Coronation Road, NW10. Nick Reding then drives back down Abbey Road. They spot George Cozens driving past the Plumes pub, which was based at 28 Abbey Road and is now a restaurant, Patisserie Patchi.

The chase continues down Whitby Road, NW10 and the finale was filmed at the gatehouse to the former Guinness Brewery, Cumberland Avenue, Park Royal Estate, NW10. The "Welcome to Guinness" sign was modified to "Gunners & Co", possibly as an in-joke for when Arsenal supporter Eric Richard arrived for filming. The brewery, which was designed by Sir Giles Gilbert Scott and built in 1936, was completely demolished in 2006.

Homes and Gardens was also the first episode of *The Bill* not to feature Trudie Goodwin as W.P.C. Ackland.

Witness Statements

Christopher Russell (Writer)

'The idea for *Homes and Gardens* - that a garden had literally been stolen - was based on something that had happened for real somewhere. I thought, "You can't leave that" when I first read about it and I just had to use it. I love gardening and during my career, the juxtaposition of writing at my desk and then getting outside and gardening was great, because whilst I was turning the soil, the mind was clearing and ideas would come into my head. Some writers spend a lot of their downtime reading, though I only ever read last thing at night, because I still feel guilty if I read a book during the daytime, even though I'm well past retiring age. Whereas gardening is physical and I still go and dig holes in the garden all day long.'

'After you've written your script and got it as good as you can, you submit it to the script editor, who gives their feedback and from that point it becomes a two-way collaborative effort. I have been very fortunate that my wife, Christine, is also a very good script editor, so before I ever sent anything into *The Bill*, it had already been through a script editing process with Christine, who could also help me if I got stuck and always has very good ideas herself. It was on *Homes and Gardens* that I first worked with Tim Vaughan, who was a brilliant script editor and the best I've ever worked with. As well as having great acuity, Tim trusted the writer and, unlike some script editors, never wanted to write the script himself. Tim was just absolutely focused on producing a good script and he left it to the writer to do that.'

Tim Vaughan (Script Editor)

'This was the first time I worked with Chris Russell, who I got to know well over the next few years - and later, when I invited him to write for *A Touch Of Frost*. Chris was one of my top three writers on *The Bill*, along with J.C. Wilsher and Peter J Hammond. You always got compassion and humour in a Chris Russell story — they could be both heartwarming, and heartrending. Most of the time, *The Bill* concentrated far less on "plot" and far more on character; and I think that's what made *The Bill* in its earlier days such a success - and what makes it an object lesson for anyone who wants to write good drama. That's certainly true of Chris's work on the show. In *Homes and Gardens* there's a very moving story about a man and his son, but it doesn't really have an ending: Chris rightly leaves the question of what happened to them afterwards open for the viewers to speculate. As my colleague Barbara Cox famously said, about how to write for *The Bill* – "Start in the middle, and leave before the end": a brilliant mantra that helped a lot of aspiring writers.'

'*Homes and Gardens* is a good example of how packed a good episode of *The Bill* could be. I was astounded, watching it again for the first time in over 30 years, by just how fast and compelling it was. The story time of one episode was actually only 21 and a half minutes long. You couldn't take any prisoners with the storytelling, any spare bits were cut by the time we made it and there were no longeurs anywhere. *Homes and Gardens* was directed by Derek Lister, who I'd met up at Yorkshire and always admired. He was a man of the theatre, and brought a different energy with him. He was a hardworking powerhouse of a man, very forthright, with a clear vision of what he wanted.'

Derek Lister (Director)

'Christopher Russell's scripts were always good and I remember he worked very well with Tim Vaughan. The scripts weren't always up to this standard and the public would never know just how hard it was sometimes to get an episode in on time, especially if the script was demanding. *The Bill* was industrial TV and the eyes were always on the clock. If we didn't finish the episode within our schedule, it would give poor Nigel Wilson – our stage manager and later production scheduler – many logistical problems, and you didn't want to be the director who did that. So quite often, I had to call it quits on things that I wasn't happy with, just to beat the clock. It was a tight schedule, we only had five days to film the running length of 25 minutes, and you always needed to film an extra five minutes of fat to play with in the edit, so on average you were aiming to get six or seven minutes in the can every day.'

'I would spend the first five days preparing very seriously for the shoot the following week. I would write a shooting script, with all my shots detailed in it, which I would give to the crew at the tech recce on the Friday before and explain, "This is what you're going to be shooting next week folks, so get ready." The poor P.A. would then have to type up my shooting script and have copies printed, ready for filming on Monday morning. I'd be perfectly willing to change my shooting script if someone came along with a better idea, but you had to be prepared and go in with a framework so that everybody could do their jobs. You couldn't just go in and wave the camera around and see what might happen.'

'Also because of the time pressures, we didn't have time to properly light the series, we just had to throw the odd light in where we could, though again the producers would have probably preferred if we hadn't lit the station at all. There was always a big debate going on between the directors and the front office about the picture quality, because it was done on old videotape, so it had the same pictorial quality as *Match of the Day* or the *News*. There was technology available to slightly soften the image, which directors were always canvassing for, to give the series a more filmic look, but the producers would not allow it.'

Jamie Acton-Bond (Camera)

'There was no health and safety in those days; it was all done on the hoof. I remember a wonderful instance when we were shooting the car chase for the finale of *Homes and Gardens*. Obviously, when we were shooting driving shots from inside a car, you needed to light the actors. We also needed to hear the actors as well, so we had to find a way for me, the sound engineer and the lighting director to be able to fit in the car. The solution that the vehicle hire company gave us was a mini Metro with a wardrobe built on the back of it! The plan was for us all to get into the back of it and shoot all the forward-facing driving shots from the back of this wardrobe... The three of us climbed in through the wardrobe doors and the batteries for the lights were all attached to the roof rack. We were all ready for the off, but when the director yelled "Action!" the car didn't move... for the simple reason that they hadn't tightened the suspension and the whole car just sat on the floor! We tried taking one person out, but it still wouldn't move, so we ended up with just myself in there. Off we went to film this chase scene, but whenever we went around a corner, the wardrobe doors would fly open! It was quite hilarious.'

Aidan Boulter (Floor Manager)

'When we were trying to figure out how the half-hour format was going to work, we did a number of camera tests in the car park at

Teddington Studios and we even shot a couple of test episodes. Everybody got involved from every department, we all wanted to be part of it, because this was the future of television. We were laying down a set of rules that are still being followed by programmes today. We were also making things up as we went along and a lot of the time we were doing things that you couldn't get away with now. The way we shot the car chase in *Homes and Gardens,* with a camera mount sticking out of the side of the police car, would be illegal now, you would only be allowed to do that on a closed street today.'

'The biggest issue that we had initially when taking the M2 kit out was that they were recording absolutely fine, but if you played back the footage on location to allow the directors to see what had been shot, it damaged the tape and turned everything green! So we realised very quickly that if we wanted to play anything back, we had to then have another piece of kit with us, which was a playback machine. That didn't go down too well, because we were trying to make the unit as lightweight as possible, which we couldn't do if we were wheeling this thumping great trolley covered in cables around with us. We had to build it into our schedule, because it could take 45 minutes to move all the kit, get set up at the other end and pre-light the next location. It wasn't as quick as as I think everybody had assumed it would be initially. We also had to make sure sure that we didn't break our camera crew, because they were working really hard, 10 hours a day. I think it broke a few people along the way and made others fitter.'

'The half-hours were also revolutionary from a rehearsal point of view, because traditionally in those days there would be rehearsal period at an outside rehearsal room, where the director could get to know the cast, who would be developing their characters and the script editor could manage any changes or rewrites that we wanted to make. But each episode of *The Bill* was much more like shooting a miniature feature film, the difference being that we had enormous time pressure. On a feature film, you're expected to shoot around three minutes of on-screen time a day, but with *The Bill* we were expected to shoot more than twice that amount, every day. The pressure was on, particularly for Peter Cregeen, who was taking a huge risk with this new format.'

COUNTRY COUSIN

Written by Barry Appleton
Directed by Sharon Miller

Series 4: Episode 9
Broadcast: Tuesday 16 August 1988

Case Narrative

Burnside is not happy when he has to babysit a visiting Derbyshire policeman who is at Sun Hill to arrest an arsonist.

Regular Cast

D.I. Burnside (Christopher Ellison), D.C. Dashwood (Jon Iles), D.C. Carver (Mark Wingett), Sgt. Penny (Roger Leach), W.P.C. Martella (Nula Conwell), P.C. Edwards (Colin Blumenau), P.C. Haynes (Eamonn Walker).

Guest Cast

D.C. Sanders (Neil Conrich), D.S. Jarvis (John Labanowski), Mrs. Williams (Claire Benedict), George (Andreas Markos), Mrs. Dellow (Nicky Furre), Mr. Harris (Richard Henry), Bus Insp. Doland (Mike Carnell), Guard (Errol J. Edmondson).

Production Team

Casting Director (Julian Oldfield), Title Music (Andy Pask, Charlie Morgan), Costume Designer (Jennie Tate), Make Up Designer (Gilly Wakeford), Graphics (Jenni Phillips), Videotape Editor (Terence E. Badham), Lighting (Allen Harradine), Camera (Jamie Acton-Bond), Sound (Stan Lee, Alan Lester), Production Buyer (Terry Allen), Location Manager (Eamonn Duffy), Floor Manager (Mark Willis), Stage Manager (Nigel J. Wilson), Production Manager (Derek Cotty), Production Assistant (Lynn Gomez), Technical Adviser (Wilf Knight), Programme Associate (Valerie Farron), Series Script Editor (Kenneth Ware), Designers (Robin Parker, David Richens), Executive Producer (Peter Cregeen), Producer (Michael Ferguson).

Observation Notes

Country Cousin (Production No: D4023, VTR No: THS/45258) was shot between Monday 13th and Friday 17th June 1988. The train station scenes were filmed at London King's Cross, which opened in 1852.

The scenes featuring C.I.D. observing and arresting Durham were filmed on First Avenue, Acton, W3. The Art Deco building seen on the corner, behind where Burnside parks his car, was the home of Newman Hire Company, a prop hire facility. The company moved into the warehouse in 1979, before relocating to a purpose-built facility in 2016. The building was converted into apartments in 2021, retaining some of the features.

The exterior scenes of George's bar were filmed outside 37 Malvern Road, Kilburn, NW6. This building would later be used as the location for Panda Pizzas in the 1989 episode *A Little Knowledge* and today operates as a Chinese takeaway. The shots of Martella and Penny driving in response to the fight outside the bar were filmed on Bosworth Road, W10.

The hospital scenes where Edwards and Haynes interview Mrs. Williams were filmed in Hammersmith Hospital, Du Cane Road, White City, W12. The hospital opened in 1902 and played a crucial role in providing care for injured soldiers throughout both World Wars. At the time of filming, the hospital was the home of the Royal Postgraduate Medical School, which in 1997 became part of the Imperial College School of Medicine. The casualty ward seen in *Country Cousin*, with its distinctive woodland backdrop on the wall, appeared in several episodes, including *Blue for a Boy* and *Conflict*. Also seen in the background of this scene as the W.P.C. interviewing some of the injured bus passengers is Karen England.

Country Cousin was the first episode directed by Sharon Miller, whose career began on the classic series *Take Hart* and *Play School*. As well as eight episodes of *The Bill*, Miller's directing credits include episodes of *Casualty*, *Dangerfield*, *Making News*, *All Good Things*, plus several single dramas. For over a decade, Miller has worked as both the lead writer and voice director on hundreds of episodes of *Thomas & Friends*.

Country Cousin was the first episode of *The Bill* not to feature Eric Richard as Sgt. Cryer, and also featured the final appearance of Neil Conrich as C.I.D semi-regular Pete Sanders. Conrich would return to *The Bill* in 1997 as recurring character Gerry Duff, a small-time crook.

Witness Statements

Barry Appleton (Writer)
'What inspired me to write *Country Cousin* was all the kinds of things that could happen to a police officer when they needed to go and

pick up a prisoner. I'll tell you a true story that happened to me when I was a young PC attached to C.I.D. It was Christmas Eve in the late 1950s and I was the only guy who was single in the office, all the others were married. The Sergeant said that they'd like me to go and pick a prisoner up from Bristol, which you'd usually do as a pair, but because it was Christmas they didn't have anyone else available. I then heard the Sergeant say to the D.I. "Barry's going to pick up the gentle giant..." I went to Bristol and sure enough this prisoner was a great big guy, he must have been about six foot five!'

'The only train from Bristol Temple Meads I could take him back on was what they called the milk train, which used to picked up milk churns, and we'd have a carriage all to ourselves. The train was late and I was standing on the platform with this prisoner at 2:00 in the morning and I was dying for a pee... There was nobody else there, just me and this huge guy, who never said a word. On the platform was a big heavy wooden handcart with milk churns on it. I handcuffed the prisoner to the handcart and said "Behave yourself, I'll be back in a minute..." I went to have a pee and all of a sudden I heard this steam train screeching to a halt. I quickly got back out to the platform and I couldn't believe it: this guy had pulled this heavy cart along the platform, down the slope and onto the tracks, forcing the train to stop!'

'I was at another station once when two prisoners were being picked up by two different police forces... and they both took the wrong guy! If you had to go from London out into the sticks to pick up a prisoner, you would want to bring them back straight away. Whereas the officers coming down from the North would want a night out on the town before they took the prisoner back, like D.S. Jarvis in *Country Cousin*. I wanted to keep what he was carrying in the bag a mystery, and I thought it worked well with Burnside always trying to find out what was in it.'

'When I first came to Cyprus, I went to a tavern and they were showing *Country Cousin* on the television, but there was something wrong... It was really short, it seemed to have pieces missing out of it. I came back to check and all the scenes with Burnside and Dashwood in the nightclub were missing. The tavern showing the episode on television was on the Greek side of the island and because those scenes were set in a Turkish Cypriot nightclub and the Turkish flag was in the background, the channel had edited all those scenes out! The second half of the episode didn't make any sense at all, it was ridiculous. All that was left was the bus storyline, which was also based on another true story, where the driver was actually suffering from sickle cell disease and he ended up driving from Muswell Hill to the West End without stopping, he just kept going and all his passengers were being flung around the bus!'

Wilf Knight (Technical Adviser)
Archive Witness Statement, recorded in February 1988.
'Normally officers get two uniforms issued, plus a lightweight, plus a ceremonial, so that's four uniforms. You normally get two jackets, plus a ceremonial, and a lightweight barathea jacket. You get six pairs of trousers and you replace them as and when: if you go over a fence and you rip them, you get a new pair of trousers. If you deal with a dead body and you get covered in blood that you can't wash out... you get a new pair of trousers. They get the uniform through Lambeth. The uniform van comes round to the police station, with a qualified tailor on board who measures you for size, shape, everything. It's rather like a pantechnicon, he drives it into the Met, bringing jackets, trousers, helmets, shirts – you get far more shirts issued than you really need. Now they've got round to asking you to give back your old uniform, but then they only throw them away, so you don't bother. A very lucrative business is run by a guy in the East End buying up the old uniforms... The guy's a millionaire, he drives a Roller.'

Eamonn Walker (P.C. Malcolm Haynes)
'After originally training as a dancer, I started my acting career at the Albany Empire working for John Turner, which was the old-school repertory way of learning to act, doing a play during the day and another at night. I did that for years, a long time before I went anywhere near a camera. My big break came when I was cast in *In Sickness and In Health*, which was a fantastic experience. I got to work with amazing people like Warren Mitchell, Arthur English, Carmel McSharry and Una Stubbs. I was this young actor working with some of the greats of British comedy, so those who say that ignorance is bliss are not wrong! At the audition, they said they were looking for someone "Boy George-ish" to play Marigold. I politely said, "I don't really like Boy George, can I give you my version?" which was based on my mother, who worked in a hospital as a nurse. She was a very funny woman, who used to come home and tell me hilarious stories every night. After that audition, Warren Mitchell took me under his wing and

taught me comic timing. I used to watch him do the warm-up every night before we recorded each episode in the studio and he had the audience in the palm of his hand. He was such a talented man and whilst most people only remember him for Alf Garnett, he was also an amazing Shakespearean actor and had such presence, power and poise. Working with him for two years was one of the best learning experiences of my life.'

'*The Bill* came along after I decided that I didn't want to do *In Sickness and In Health* any more. I knew the type of actor I wanted to be and I was debating with my agent at the time that an actor's career is based on the offers you receive and the decisions that you make as to which ones you accept or not. I explained that it was time I moved on from the series, because otherwise I would only be known for doing comedy and I wanted to avoid doing any more sitcoms for a while. It was as a direct result of that conversation that my agent got me an audition for *The Bill*, which became my opportunity to learn single camera drama, as opposed to multi-camera comedy. I was very lucky to get *The Bill* so soon after leaving *In Sickness and In Health* and even luckier to be joining such a fantastic team of people, who were all hilarious and one of the best groups of people I have ever met.'

'When I joined *The Bill*, I was one of the youngest members of the cast. Now I find myself on *Chicago Fire* as the oldest member of the cast, so there's been a lot of water under the bridge in between. We were working with real fire officers for the sequence with the crashed bus in *Country Cousin*. It is the same on *Chicago Fire*, where the day begins for the cast at 4am. We have to be out of make-up by 4.30am and heading out at 5am to catch first light for filming, which is around the time that the real fire service personnel finish their shift. Some of those serving officers then come on to our set to be part of our show, having just fought fires all night or pulled cars apart to rescue people from whatever mistake they've made on the motorway. It is an honour to work with both serving and retired fire service personnel - if it wasn't for them, we wouldn't be making the show. One of the reasons I wanted to do *Chicago Fire* was to experience a similar sense of camaraderie that I had enjoyed on *The Bill*. Plus the kid in me who wanted to be a fireman is very happy about driving around in a fire engine at 90mph every week!'

Jamie Acton-Bond (Camera)

'My career began back in 1963, when I started in educational television. After that, I joined Thames Television in 1968, which was a big learning ground and where I trained to be a cameraman. Thames was very union-based in those days, so I couldn't play with the engineering side, I was just there to learn how to purely be a cameraman. As a trainee, I spent a couple of years shadowing experienced cameramen, holding cables and learning. Then I started working on programmes like *Magpie* and *Rainbow*, which were the shows we all went on to be trained, before we were allowed to go and assist on dramas like *Callan* and *Armchair Theatre*, back in the days of black and white 405-line resolution. I was also very lucky to work on all the classic light entertainment shows made at Teddington Studios, where we specialised in the art of the pedestal camera.'

'In comparison to the studio cameras, the Panasonics we were using on *The Bill* weren't that heavy, but you had to work out how to move with the actors and keep the crew behind you. If I shot a scene going backwards down a corridor, I'd have my assistant with their hand down the back of my trousers guiding me along. There were times where one tripped up with the camera, there's no doubt about it, but it was always very enjoyable. Each director obviously had a different way of shooting and we camera operators all had our own styles as well. We were each working out different ways of achieving shots like the ones inside the crashed bus in *Country Cousin*. We'd meet fellow professionals at IBC shows who assumed we were using Steadicams and they couldn't believe it when we said it was all handheld. We were reinventing the wheel, we all came up with new ideas together and the laughs we had were amazing!'

'*The Bill* was also wonderful because we started to get credits, whereas on studio shows the camera operators never got one, it would just be the designer, producer and director. It was amazing when my credit started going out on *The Bill*, because I started getting letters with information about my family history! My grandparents started the London School of Speech and Drama and I received letters from some of the students they had taught. My father was an actor, though I decided from an early age that a career on the other side of the camera would be a better and fairly interesting one and it certainly proved so.'

ALARMS AND EMBARRASSMENTS

Written by Christopher Russell
Directed by Sharon Miller

Series 4: Episode 10
Broadcast: Thursday 18 August 1988

Case Narrative

Dashwood attends an off-licence robbery and is surprised to find out that the assistant thinks she can identify the robbers by their teeth.

Regular Cast

Sgt. Cryer (Eric Richard), Insp. Frazer (Barbara Thorn), P.C. Edwards (Colin Blumenau), D.S. Roach (Tony Scannell), D.C. Dashwood (Jon Iles), D.C. Carver (Mark Wingett), Sgt. Penny (Roger Leach), Ch. Insp. Conway (Ben Roberts), P.C. Smith (Robert Hudson), P.C. Haynes (Eamonn Walker), P.C. Hollis (Jeff Stewart), P.C. Melvin (Mark Powley), P.C. Frank (Ashley Gunstock), P.C. Stamp (Graham Cole).

Guest Cast

Derek Pardoe (Jeff Rawle), Paula Chivers (Sallie Anne Field), Bag Lady (Joyce Grundy), Miss Eveleigh (Margot Boht), Mandy Peake (Alison Bettles), Bystanders (Pat Curtis, Frances Tanner, Con Chambers).

Uncredited Personnel

W.P.C. Ford (Vikki Gee-Dare), P.C. (Russell Brook), W.P.C. (Karen England), D.C. (Kevin O'Brien), P.C. (Oscar Peck), Press Officer (Rosane Chapman), Librarian (Bridget Moore), Accountants (Anne Shields, David Saggs).

Production Team

Casting Director (Julian Oldfield), Title Music (Andy Pask, Charlie Morgan), Costume Designer (Dennis Griffith), Make Up Designer (Gilly Wakeford), Graphics (Jenni Phillips), Videotape Editor (Terence E. Badham), Lighting (Allen Harradine), Camera (Jamie Acton-Bond), Sound (Stan Lee, Alan Lester), Production Buyer (Terry Allen), Location Manager (Eamonn Duffy), Floor Manager (Mark Willis), Stage Manager (Nigel J. Wilson), Production Manager (Derek Cotty), Production Assistant (Lynn Gomez), Technical Adviser (Wilf Knight), Programme Associate (Valerie Farron), Script Editor (Tim Vaughan), Series Script Editor

(Kenneth Ware), Designers (Robin Parker, David Richens), Executive Producer (Peter Cregeen), Producer (Michael Ferguson).

Observation Notes

Alarms and Embarrassments (Production No: D4024, VTR No: THS/45259) was shot between Monday 20th and Friday 24th June 1988, made as part of the same production block as *Country Cousin*. The opening scenes where Yorkie attends the off-licence robbery were shot in 82 Burnley Road, Dollis Hill, NW10, which is still an off-licence today.

For the scene where Insp. Frazer encounters the bag lady, Barbara Thorn drives a silver 1987 Vauxhall Cavalier, with the registration E299 WNM. This vehicle was first seen being driven by Yorkie in *The Three Wise Monkeys* and would later be primarily driven by Dashwood and Carver. Jon Iles drove the car in *Country Cousin*, *Save the Last Dance For Me*, *Running Late*, *Paper Chase*, *Old Habits*, *Getting Stressed* and *Taken Into Consideration*; whilst Mark Wingett was behind the wheel for *They Say We're Rough*, *Chasing the Dragon*, *Stop and Search*, *Snout*, *An Old-Fashioned Term* and *Guessing Game*. Also seen driving the car in 1988 were Chris Ellison in *The Trap*; Nick Reding in *Witness* and Tony Scannell in *Duplicates* and *Outmoded*. A few years later, the registration plate was added to a police panda car used in the 1991 *Minder* episode *Cars and Pints and Pains*. The logbook for the car has not been updated since 2001.

Appearing in the line-up scene is Vikki Gee-Dare, who would later join the main cast as regular character W.P.C. Suzanne Ford in 1989. Gee-Dare's other television credits include *The Duchess of Duke Street*, *The Two Ronnies* and *The Little Mermaid*. She started working as a supporting artist on *The Bill* in 1984, whilst learning sign language. Gee-Dare would later qualify as an interpreter and her skills were incorporated into a number of *The Bill* episodes, most notably in *Watch My Lips*.

Alarms and Embarrassments also sees Taffy come to the assistance of Derek Pardoe, which was filmed outside the shops beneath Trellick Tower on Golborne Road, W10. The Character Notes distributed to writers on the series described P.C. Francis "Taffy" Edwards as being 30 years old and that he has "been in the force about four years. He came to London from North Wales and still retains a provincial mistrust of the big city. He is rustic in his humour and his approach to life. Nothing was easy at home, where his family farmed poor land, and Taffy is relieved to have got away. Since escape was his prime motive, rather than ambition, he has readily settled for the constable's lot, keeping out of trouble as much as possible and turning a blind eye to petty offences – not out of indifference as much as pragmatism. He very much resents accusations of indolence, which are sometimes levelled against him by his mates and even senior officers. It is simply that he is not driven by any passionate hates or prejudices. His impulse is to do no more than keep his head above water. Some suspect him or having a slightly devious nature. He is recently married to a home-town girl, Mary, who isn't taking to life in the city."

Witness Statements

Christopher Russell (Writer)

'I am quite astonished about how much we used to pack into these half-hour episodes, there is so much going on in *Alarms and Embarrassments*. The initial idea for this episode came from a friend of mine, who as a police officer had to assist a member of the public with cerebral palsy, which seemed like an interesting basis for a story. The now old-fashioned term used to describe the condition in the episode was how it was known 40 years ago and wasn't used pejoratively in the script. Jeff Rawle gave an incredible performance as Mr Pardoe; I have no idea how he managed to contort himself and change his voice like that. That storyline formed part of an episode which was about everything that a police officer wouldn't want to happen, but could and did, in the space of 25 minutes. A sequence like the one where Frazer is having a nightmare with the old lady and then not being able to get her seat belt on can be quite difficult to get right, but it was well performed by Barbara Thorn and very well directed by Sharon Miller.'

'This episode is an example of the series' original calling card; to open the doors of a police station and watch the officers going about their daily responsibilities. The thing that strikes me the most when watching these episodes back is how open police stations were back then. It's incredible that any one of those officers could have been killed at any moment, because they are just stood there wearing shirts, without one piece of body armour anywhere to be seen. It's striking how much policing has had to change in 30 years, which has been reactive and quite rightly happened incrementally in response to the threats they now face. That's why I don't think you could make *The Bill* now, it would have to lose Geoff McQueen's calling card and be a very different programme.'

Tim Vaughan (Script Editor)

'*Alarms and Embarrassments* is yet another beautiful episode of *The Bill* and one of the funniest ones we ever made. It was the perfect package, being short and sweet, yet still packed with so many sequences. This story was an experiment in Sod's law; a series of misadventures that were hilariously funny, but also truthful. I've got lots of favourite moments from this moment, including Roach's line, "Being disabled is a misfortune Carver, not a frigging privilege!" That scene showed us the best of Carver too, the naïve, kind copper who just wanted to help this man. I laughed the most at the fantastic little moments where literally nothing was going right, such as Frazer not being able to put her seatbelt on, or Taffy having the door bang into his tray and spilling the tea everywhere. Then you had Roach falling around laughing at the woman who has started the fire in her cell, then being really unpleasant to Frazer, who is holding back the tears as she thanks Cryer for standing up for her. Not everything went badly though, because Dashwood got that young woman's phone number! Chris managed to achieve an absence of cliché with this episode and afterwards it was a case of "follow that!" which of course he did time and time again. I loved every script he wrote for us.'

'Giving an amazing performance was Jeff Rawle, who I got to know much later on when he guest starred in a programme called *William and Mary*, where I was the executive producer. Jeff had been cast to play a character who liked to dress up in women's clothing and there was a scene where his character was going to meet all his mates above a pub, where they'd also all be dressed in women's clothes. The producer was complaining that nobody wanted to do this scene and they couldn't find enough people to put a dress on. So I said, "I'll do it, if you do it..." He said, "I'll hold you to that!" Well he didn't do it, but I went and had a fitting at the BBC and wore a dress in the scene, where I was standing next to Jeff Rawle. We got to know each other and we became friends and used to meet for dinner. I had forgotten that he had given this extraordinary performance in *Alarms and Embarrassments*.'

'It brought back a lot of memories seeing Barlby Road again; I can remember where the canteen was and I remember going up to the CID office and talking to the actors. Having the station as a standing set made a hell of a difference for the production, because they always had somewhere they could shoot whatever the weather, as it were. The station was a fantastic theatre in many ways. And working out the logistics for the cast was our stage manager Nigel Wilson, a wonderful guy and a really nice man. He was the person to whom we all went when we had a problem and he'd work out how we were going to get out of it!'

Barbara Thorn (Insp. Christine Frazer)

'*Alarms and Embarrassments* had that scene where Frazer has to help the old lady into her car and then couldn't get her seat belt on, which was just fantastic writing. I used to drive myself to Barlby Road and one morning I had my own funny scene... I was driving through Battersea on a sunny day and there was a policeman stopping drivers. I looked at my watch and hoped he didn't stop me, because I had to be at the studio for 7am. Well, he did pull me over. I had my sunglasses on when I wound my window down, and this policeman said, "Good morning, can I ask you, do you know what the two white lines in the middle of the road mean?" I said "No I'm sorry, I don't. What do they mean?" He explained that I shouldn't drive over them, for which I apologised. He then reached into his pocket and got his little pad and pencil out... I thought, "Oh no, he's going to take my details!" At which point, I took my sunglasses off and he looked at me, stood up straight and said, "Oh I'm sorry, Ma'am!" That happened more than once!'

'When I first joined, we were working on two episodes at a time, either with the Blue unit or the Red unit. There were times later on when some of us would be working on three episodes in one week, which is when they added a Green unit! We had fantastic stage managers like Nigel Wilson and Marilyn Edwards, who would guide us to where we needed to go and shoving the next script in our hand. But once you got used to doing it, you got used to the momentum. We never stopped laughing on *The Bill*, and we still don't now whenever we have a reunion. We were all working long hours, but most evenings when we wrapped, we all went to the pub and continued laughing. Then we started to get invited to fetes, fairs and charity dos and we'd all turn up to those, so we were always with each other.'

Stan Lee (Sound)

'My interest in sound began when my parents bought me a stereo record player, and I was really intrigued as to the sound it created. My career began when I started working as a post-boy for ABC Television at Hanover Square in London. I then got an apprenticeship as a trainee, working across most TV departments at Teddington Studios. ABC and Rediffusion then amalgamated to become Thames Television to cover the London area contract. I worked my way up to Sound Supervisor and made hundreds of different programmes at Teddington; everything from comedies and light entertainment, to drama and children's. Some of my favourites to work on in the studios were *Callan, Rainbow, Magpie, Opportunity Knocks* and *The Benny Hill Show*.'

'I started on *The Bill* in 1988, when the OB department handed the series to the team at Teddington. Sound-wise, each episode had a two-man sound crew, working with a mobile SQN 4-channel sound-mixing device. I remember carrying a LOT of cables, as well as a variety of microphones, OB equipment, batteries and a small TV monitor. We used to rig the cars up with microphones, as the sound team weren't able to be in the vehicles, as it was too tight for space. Then it was always a case of "fingers crossed" as to what the results of the recordings would be! It was quite groundbreaking from a sound and camera perspective. Jamie Acton-Bond was the first cameraman I worked with, who in fact I met up with again one evening a few years ago, with a few other former Thames TV people, who had worked on various shows together.'

'They were long days on *The Bill*, particularly as the unit base at Barlby Road was about 40 minutes from Teddington. We also had to be prepared to record in all weathers – and sometimes we worked at night, if the script required it. The week before each shoot, we had to do a recce of the various locations, to suss out any unforeseen sound disturbances, such as roadworks. I remember on one recce of a pub that we were going to use as a location, there was a big fish tank, which had a pump and filter that really hummed loudly, and I had to ask for it to be switched off as it caused interference with recording the sound!'

'The cast were all great people – they all worked really hard and took it seriously, because it was a tight timescale. I remember Graham Cole, who had started as an extra and ended up as a regular character – we were all pleased for him when that happened. They were a good group of people to work with and we would often all go to the pub together, either at lunchtime or after a day's shoot. I feel quite proud that *The Bill* is still being shown - I still see our names on the repeats sometimes. It was a big part of my career. I've worked on many other programmes, but *The Bill* sticks in my mind. On a scale of 1-10, it's a 10 from me!'

STEALING CARS AND NURSERY RHYMES
Written by Julian Jones
Directed by Paul Harrison

Series 4: Episode 11
Broadcast: Tuesday 23 August 1988

Case Narrative
Smith befriends Jimmy from the local youth club and Ramsey is befriended by a mongrel dog.

Regular Cast
Sgt. Cryer (Eric Richard), P.C. Smith (Robert Hudson), P.C. Haynes (Eamonn Walker), P.C. Ramsey (Nick Reding), Ch. Supt. Brownlow (Peter Ellis).

Guest Cast
Jimmy Nelson (Martino Lazzeri), Youth Worker (Nicholas Donovan), Young Girl (Sabrina Somaroo), Dog Owner (Tom Cotcher), Keith (Jack McNicholl), Mechanic (Aslie Pitter), Mrs. Scott (Patsy Smart), Mrs. Nelson (Sara Clee), Shopper (Christine Kimberley), Mark Brown (Mark Harvey).

Uncredited Personnel
Dog (Benji), Locker Room PCs (Derek Lyons, Oscar Peck), Youths in Car (Patsy Palmer, Jake Wood), Press Officer (Rosane Chapman), Secretaries (Tricia Boyden, Chris Iliffe), Accountants (Anne Shields, David Saggs), Props Chargehand (Alex Bazylewicz), Make Up Assistants (Kate Rudlin, Adam Beck), Floor Assistant (Eleanore Bushnell), ASM (Jinty Coventry).

Production Team
Casting Director (Julia Lisney), Title Music (Andy Pask, Charlie Morgan), Costume (Jennie Tate), Make Up Designer (Gilly Wakeford), Graphics (Jenni Phillips), Videotape Editor (Tom Kavanagh), Lighting (Peter Bower), Camera (Rolie Luker), Sound (Richard Bradford, Paul Langwade), Production Buyer (Mike Ashby), Location Manager (Susan Bradley), Floor Manager (Patrick Vance), Stage Manager (Marilyn Edwards), Production Manager (Derek Cotty), Production Assistant (Janey Mullins), Technical Adviser (Wilf Knight), Programme Associate (Valerie Farron), Series Script Editor (Kenneth Ware), Design (Robin Parker, Deborah Ashforth), Executive Producer (Peter Cregeen), Producer (Richard Bramall).

Observation Notes

Stealing Cars and Nursery Rhymes (Production No: D4026, VTR No: THS/45261) was shot between Monday 27th June and Friday 1st July 1988. The location used for St Marks' Youth Centre was the former rugby club based on Walmer Road, with the back of the building on Portland Road, W11 used for exteriors. The building has since been replaced by the Rugby Portobello Trust and a block of flats.

Ramsey walks the beat along Whitechapel Road, E1. The old Underground entrance closed in 2015 and the area has since been redeveloped.

The scene where Jimmy washes the Aston Martin was shot outside 139 Freston Road, W10 – the former site of Aston Martin specialist Ian Mason.

The Go-kart scenes were shot behind 194 Freston Road, W10 – now the site of the Latimer AP Academy. The following sequence where Yorkie walks Jimmy home was also shot on Freston Road, passing the Harrow Club at No. 187 and meeting Mrs. Nelson on the forecourt of Frinstead House, W10. The ground in front of Frinstead House was redeveloped in 2017 and is now home to the Freston Road Hub, a business unit.

The scene where Ramsey attends to the lady who has been attacked by youths using an aerosol can was filmed outside 71 Barlby Road, W10.

Stealing Cars and Nursery Rhymes was the first of five episodes helmed by prolific television director Paul Harrison, who began his career as a stage manager for both television and theatre, before moving into directing. His first drama, *Come Back Lucy*, was nominated for a BAFTA and his many credits since include *A Touch of Frost, Ballykissangel, Lovejoy, Wycliffe, Ballykissangel, Monarch of the Glen, Casualty, Wild at Heart, Death in Paradise, Agatha Raisin, Trollied* and *Midsomer Murders*.

The character notes issued to writer Julian Jones ahead of writing *Stealing Cars and Nursery Rhymes* detailed P.C. Tony "Yorkie" Smith as being 27 years old and "a Yorkshireman, Smith has a level-headed, honest manner which makes him a sound policeman with evident promotion potential. Reliable in crises, he embodies many of the strong, comforting qualities that folklore tells us could be found in the good old coppers of yesteryear. More right-wing than you would suppose on first meeting him, he has a sense of order, justice and what he sees as the "rightness" of things. He is not a racist or a bigot. Single."

Witness Statements

Julian Jones (Writer)

'When I was trying to get into television as a writer, I met with Peter Cregeen, who said he would see what he could do. A few months went by and I didn't hear anything... so I followed up and I got another meeting with Peter – though this time, I read my pitch for a drama script out loud to him, which he graciously listened to. I remember him briefly interrupting to me to make a phone call, asking his secretary to rearrange his next meeting. He then asked me to continue reading my piece, which was a story set in South America and the Middle East. He explained that my idea was probably a little too ambitious, but he then told me that they were about to start making half-hour episodes of *The Bill* and asked me if I would be interested in submitting an idea. I said "Fantastic!" and I went away and literally wrote an episode straight away! I then submitted my script, called *No Shelter*, to Ken Ware, the script editor who Peter had introduced me to.'

'I then got a phone call from Ken, who asked, "What have you done?" I explained that Peter had said I might be interested in writing an episode, but Ken pointed out that if they had wanted me to write a script, they would have commissioned me – and that if they didn't like the script, I'd have done all that work for no reason... I hadn't written anything before, so I hadn't realised. Ken read the script, which they liked but it wasn't what they were looking for – though it was made the following year when they realised they were running out of scripts! But they did commission me to write a different script and I was given a deadline of two weeks to go away and write a new story.'

'After a week, I hadn't really got anywhere and I was really feeling the pressure. I looked for some advice from a writer I knew called Leslie Stewart, who simply said, "Don't worry, dear boy, I miss deadlines all the time..." He invited me to his house, up near Ely. The first thing he said when I arrived was "Do you want to go for a drink?" Well we were in the pub until 2am! I got up the next day and was even more worried about the deadline, so every day I would stay in Leslie's house writing, while he went to the pub and just kept telling me not to worry about it! By the end of the week at Leslie's, I finished the script and submitted it to Ken, which thankfully he liked and *Stealing Cars and Nursery Rhymes* became my first ever paid writing gig.'

'The idea for the episode came from when I had worked as a youth worker in South East London. I started volunteering at a centre just off the North Peckham estate, which was really rough and I was out of my depth. It was the people who had grown up on that estate who really made an impact, while I ended up teaching the kids some drama and making some films with them. *Stealing Cars and Nursery Rhymes* starts with Yorkie in that traditional position of a police officer thinking these pesky kids are nothing but trouble. But then he gets drawn in and you can sense that he really begins to care and builds a real rapport with Jimmy, who was fantastically played by Martino Lazzeri. At certain points he seemed like a really endearing little boy, which was based on my experiences as a youth worker; one moment you were having a nice chat with the kids, and the next you might spot them in the back of a car with a baseball bat, about to do something terrible! That behaviour was typical of the kids I had known at the club, where it was difficult to gain any kind of respect and you had to be able to take the backchat. I could use *The Bill* to debate whether it was too late to give them a sensitive ear or if all they needed was discipline. I used all my experiences and gave them to Yorkie, who I liked writing for because he was an interesting character who came from a tough background, which meant we could explore two sides of the same coin. He also had a real softness about him and Robert Hudson gave a lovely performance.'

Robert Hudson (P.C. "Yorkie" Smith)

'I remember chatting to Julian Jones, who wrote *Stealing Cars and Nursery Rhymes*, while we were filming. We worked out that he was at RADA at the same time I was at Central, though he decided that he preferred being a writer to being an actor. He told me that he liked Yorkie as a character, and he continued to write me some good episodes, including *Fat'ac* and *Don't Like Mondays*. He also wrote *That Old Malarkey* for me originally, though I didn't find that out until after I'd left and Graham ended up doing it. When I watched *Stealing Cars and Nursery Rhymes* recently, it brought back a lot of memories. The first thing I thought was, why every time I walked into the youth club, did I take my helmet off and run my fingers through my hair? Then I remembered that I didn't want "helmet hair", but talk about posing!'

'I remember the chaos filming the scene where me and Martino Lazzeri, playing young Jimmy, walk around the estate; with all the crew in front of us trying to get through that narrow passageway! There was

Rolie Luker the cameraman, the rigger, the sound man and Paul Harrison the director lurking in the background... I think we had to do it a few times, because they kept banging into the wall as they were walking backwards. As Yorkie, I'm supposed to look like I'm going for a nice, relaxed walk, chatting to Jimmy, whereas all I was thinking was "It's fucking bedlam in front of me, how are they going to pull this shot off?" People who don't work in TV don't realise that its a circus on a film set; there are people everywhere, there's wardrobe people, make-up people, riggers, sparks... all ready to jump in, even on an intimate little scene. The other thing I remember is filming that scene in the underground car park, where I was chasing that lad who'd been sniffing glue. I was trudging through all that shit and water when I said, "Oh yes, filming on location, isn't it glamorous?"'

'I thought Martino was perfect as Jimmy, he was really cheeky and he wasn't bothered by anything going on around him. I liked the scene with him and his mum. You believed their relationship in the episode, that he was really a good lad who loved his mum, who loved him back. He's just got in with a bad crowd and been influenced by his peers, which is what happens to so many young lads. I loved that end shot, when the camera pans down to reveal that he wasn't in the car that had crashed. He was in a car that he shouldn't have been, but he wasn't in the car that got smashed up, so he missed out on the nasty stuff. Jimmy was one of those lads who would always end up on his feet.'

'In this episode, Nick Reding was doing the stuff that I normally did. Yorkie was the one usually dealing with the little old ladies, and so it was a great switch by Julian to have Ramsey doing all that stuff with the dog and the UFOs. Nick, Eamonn Walker and I became really great mates; they used to call us "The Three Cavaleros". We used to go out together all the time and one night, we went to Browns and were standing at the bar, when we looked over at the dance floor and saw this woman dancing the night away. I said, "Look at her, she thinks she's Tina Turner..." Then we got closer and discovered that it was Tina Turner, who had just done a concert earlier that night. It wasn't that busy and we went and joined her on the dance floor. At one point she tripped and Nick caught her and she thanked him. When she went, we all looked at each other and said in unison "We just danced with Tina Turner!" Then when we'd go back to Barlby Road on Monday and Make-up would ask us what we had got up to at the weekend, we'd all say "Oh nothing..."

'The three of us got on so well, then when we got on set, our characters were always at each other's throats, which is the magic of TV. In *Stealing Cars and Nursery Rhymes*, Eamonn and I had that heavy scene in the corridor. I can remember when we first did it, Paul Harrison was saying to me, "Rob, I think you need to get closer..." I said that if I got any closer, I'd be kissing him! I looked at Eamonn and he said, "Let's just do it." He was great and its still bizarre when I watch him as the Chief now on *Chicago Fire* and I think, "That's my mate Eamonn...'"

Paul Harrison (Director)

'Before *The Bill*, I was a studio director. I basically trained on five cameras and the very first thing I ever directed was a show called *The Masterspy*, which was a game show with the wonderful William Franklin as the host. He played an 'M'-like character, with contestants sat across a desk who had to do Mensa IQ tests. I had to make a little five-minute spy film every week and then the last two contestants who made it through would be part of a little drama sequence on film, where they had to solve the clues. We had actors like David Jason and Norman Bowler in those scenes. But because of IBA rules, we had to shoot these 45-minute shows as live, where you would only stop when you got to the commercial break. A baptism of fire because you could never go back and reshoot, but it was enormous fun! Then I was given my first drama production to direct, which was an adaptation of a book called *Come Back, Lucy*. The series got nominated for a BAFTA, so my career has slid downwards ever since!'

'The great thing about *The Bill* was shooting on video. I'd come from ATV Elstree, where every time we went off site, we had to shoot on film, but the unions had strict rules that we could never allow drama to be shot on site using film, because it was an electronic studio. You'll all remember those days in dramas when the actors would rock up outside a building in a nice nicely lit, beautiful film shot, then walk up to the front door, open it and suddenly walk straight into a TV studio. When we did eventually go electronic outside, the cameras were really big and cumbersome and you had to have a scanner and all sorts of technical things to make it work. But when I came to *The Bill*, we were suddenly given these smaller cameras to play with. I remember my very first day and I said to Rolie Luker that I wanted the camera to look right across the office. Rolie just put the camera on a desk and said, "Like that?" And that was it! Then I said I wanted to follow them out the door and he picked the camera up, stuck it on his shoulder and off we went. It was so liberating to suddenly be given that freedom as a director.'

'I loved the scene where Robert Hudson and Eamonn Walker had that set-to in the locker room and then moved out into the hallway. That was such a good moment to be on television at 8pm at that time, with that strong image of a black copper and a white copper nose to nose in the frame, talking about drugs, but really touching on race issues as well. I thought that was such strong writing, with all that tension bubbling under, and it was beautifully played by Robert and Eamonn, who worked really well together. I also liked Cryer's intervention, mediating that moment and gently keeping a lid on it. Eric was so good at keeping the levels right in those moments. We also had a great gang of supporting artists, who were just terrific. You would see the same faces around the station over and over again. Though watching *Stealing Cars and Nursery Rhymes* back, I really felt for those two poor artists who had the scene in Brownlow's office when that bloody dog came to the door. I should have cut away from them sooner, because they couldn't say anything and I left them hanging a bit in the edit, bless them.'

Peter Ellis (Chief Supt. Charles Brownlow)
'I never expected to be in *The Bill* for that long. I was surprised when it came back for the third series, because it had been off for over a year. Then when it went into the half-hours, we were only contracted for six months at a time. The series was also still quite rightly focusing on the officers in the station, rather than the hierarchy. As I was the oldest member of the cast I used to think, "don't depend on this." I always felt lucky every time I was invited to stay for another six months, especially as I had the easiest job on *The Bill*, just sitting behind the desk. The funny thing about *Stealing Cars and Nursery Rhymes* was the dog who came into the station and opened the door to Brownlow's office. The dog was called Benji and as well as being incredibly well trained, he was also a very pampered theatrical pooch, who kept disappearing during the shoot. It turned out he was going off to auditions in a taxi! We'd be filming with him and then his trainer would say "Sorry, Benji's got go now, he's got a call at Elstree!" It was very funny. Our cameraman on this episode and many more was the wonderful Rolie Luker, whose other favourite television job was filming *Sooty*! So once, I got hold of some Sooty and Sweep puppets, hid them under Brownlow's desk and then held them up and waved at Rolie... I think I got into trouble for that!'

HOLD FIRE
Written by Barry Appleton
Directed by Paul Harrison

Series 4: Episode 12
Broadcast: Thursday 25 August 1988

Case Narrative
Melvin suffers burns while attending a serious car accident and Smith is caught in the resultant explosion. Both men are hospitalised.

Regular Cast
Sgt. Cryer (Eric Richard), Insp. Frazer (Barbara Thorn), D.S. Roach (Tony Scannell), D.C. Carver (Mark Wingett), W.P.C. Martella (Nula Conwell), P.C. Melvin (Mark Powley), P.C. Haynes (Eamonn Walker), P.C. Edwards (Colin Blumenau), D.I. Burnside (Christopher Ellison), Ch. Insp. Conway (Ben Roberts), Sgt. Penny (Roger Leach), P.C. Frank (Ashley Gunstock), W.P.C. Ackland (Trudie Goodwin), P.C. Smith (Robert Hudson), D.C. Dashwood (Jon Iles).

Guest Cast
Sadie (Cheryl Hall), Firearms Instructor (Peter Wight), Ward Sister (Jill Damas), Skinhead (Neville Watson), Old Man (Walter Sparrow), S.O.C.O. (Hilary Dawson), F.I.O. (Brian Panton), Doctor (Gene Fode), Roger Davis (Gavin Watson).

Uncredited Personnel
W.P.C. Ford (Vikki Gee-Dare), Porter (Ray Valentine), Press Officer (Rosane Chapman), Secretaries (Tricia Boyden, Chris Iliffe), Accountants (Anne Shields, David Saggs), Props Chargehand (Alex Bazylewicz), Make Up Assistants (Kate Rudlin, Adam Beck), Floor Assistant (Eleanore Bushnell), Assistant Stage Manager (Jinty Coventry).

Production Team
Stuntmen (Peter Diamond, Rod Woodruff), Stunt Arranger (Alf Joint), Casting Director (Julia Lisney), Title Music (Andy Pask, Charlie Morgan), Special Effects (Tom Harris), Costume (Allard Tobin), Make Up Designer (Gilly Wakeford), Graphics (Jenni Phillips), Videotape Editor (Tom Kavanagh), Lighting (Peter Bower), Camera (Rolie Luker), Sound (Richard Bradford, Paul Langwade), Production Buyer (Mike Ashby), Location

Manager (Susan Bradley), Floor Manager (Patrick Vance), Stage Manager (Marilyn Edwards), Production Manager (Derek Cotty), Production Assistant (Janey Mullins), Technical Adviser (Wilf Knight), Programme Associate (Valerie Farron), Series Script Editor (Kenneth Ware), Design (Robin Parker, Deborah Ashforth), Executive Producer (Peter Cregeen), Producer (Richard Bramall).

Observation Notes

Hold Fire (Production No: D4052, VTR No: THS/45260) was shot between Monday 20th and Friday 24th June 1988. The scenes with the exploded car were filmed near St Charles Hospital, W10, with the interior of that building also used for the scenes where Yorkie and Melvin are recovering on the ward.

The scene where the P.C. controls the traffic to allow the police Range Rover through was shot on the junction of Sullivan Road and Brook Drive SE11. The ambulance turns out of Austral Street, SE11.

The scenes where Carver and Martella are undercover, playing video games, were filmed in The Carlton Centre, Granville Road NW6. This building was refurbished in 2018.

The pub scene after Ted's firearms course was filmed at the Latimer Arms, 198 Latimer Road, W10. This scene also featured Cheryl Hall's final appearance as Sadie, the pub landlady who had featured in eleven episodes of the first three series. Hall would later play a further six guest characters in *The Bill.*

Hold Fire was adapted for an episode of the Netherlands police series *Bureau Kruislaan* in 1993. The title of the episode *De peetvader* translates as "The Godfather" and was the 16th episode of the series. *De peetvader* also featured elements of Barry Appleton's 1989 script, *Getting it Right.*

Witness Statements

Barry Appleton (Writer)

'I love *Hold Fire*, this was a really good episode and to me was a great example of how the half-hour episodes could be done. In fact, I remember going to Barlby Road after it went out and I met a young woman who was new to the script department. She handed me a script and said, "This is what we use as a template for training writers on *The*

Bill. This will show you how to write an episode, with a main story and a good subplot..." I looked at the script and it was *Hold Fire.* I said "I know this script..." and she replied "Oh yes it's a good one, they all use it!" She looked rather embarrassed when I pointed out that I had written it!'

'When I was on the Flying Squad at Scotland Yard, there were ten officers on a squad and only three of us were armed. I was a first class shot and I've been involved in quite a lot of shootings. I thought it would be interesting to have one of the characters haunted from a previous shooting and I thought back to *Hostage* in the second series. I'd already established the theme of Ted always being on the booze and in that episode he dropped the bullets on the floor while he was loading his gun and Brownlow asked him if he'd been drinking... It was a good opportunity to follow up on that in *Hold Fire* and Tony Scannell was absolutely brilliant in the scene in the pub, when he had the line "You just squeeze the trigger, almost to the point of no return. Then just that little fraction more... and you blow somebody away for good." He played that really, really well.'

'Another memory I have from when I was a young D.C. on the Flying Squad is a couple of actors turning up, who wanted to be shown around while they were preparing for a series they were about to make. Our guys desperately rushed for the door, falling over each other, making all kind of excuses. "Sorry, places to go, people to see..." But a few of us ended up taking these two actors to "The Tank", a bar in the basement that had a piano. They introduced themselves as John Thaw and Dennis Waterman. I'd never heard of them... "Dennis who?" Lunchtime went into early evening and there was a lot of singing and drinking. I thought we'd be teaching these guys a lot of bad habits, though actually it was the other way around and they drunk us under the table! Soon after, *The Sweeney* was born and the rest is history... Many years later I wrote a two-hour Christmas special for a Yorkshire Television series called *Circles of Deceit*, where Dennis played an ex-SAS officer going undercover. I was disappointed that he didn't recognise me, though I was I was a beatnik in those days, with hair down to my shoulders. I was sorry when he passed away, he was a lovely guy.'

Paul Harrison (Director)

'The subplot of *Hold Fire* was Ted Roach throwing his firearms course. I loved Tony Scannell, he was such a cool guy and a great actor, he was dangerous and it was fun to work with him. And after enjoying working with Robert Hudson on *Stealing Cars and Nursery Rhymes*, I then had to blow him up in the next episode! The back of the car was rebuilt in aluminium and we filled it with explosives. The thing I remember more than anything about that stunt was lovely Mark Powley asking me what exactly would happen? I explained that Rob would be behind the car and that he, Colin Blumenau and Eamonn Walker would run towards the camera and then we'd blow the car up and they'd all fall as close to the camera as possible. Then Mark said, "Oh, OK... And where will you be?" To which I replied "I'll be stood behind that fabulous fireproof box over there with the other camera..."

'My biggest problem with the scheduling was that I loved the East End locations in the early hour-long episodes, and whilst the Barlby Road set was great, the locations around Ladbroke Grove just weren't gritty enough for me. I wanted to shoot *Hold Fire* in and around Whitechapel, so Richard Bramall gave me a payoff situation... If I insisted on filming in Whitechapel, I would lose an hour at the beginning and at the end of the schedule. I had to promise that I could film all the required scenes in that time, otherwise I couldn't go. So I bit the bullet and lost the hour at either end, and we filmed the explosion and all the surrounding scenes around Kennington and Whitechapel. Even though I'd taken a big bite out of my schedule, I still had time for some fun...'

'There's a shot in *Hold Fire* of a young copper running into the road, putting his hand up to stop oncoming traffic and the police Range Rover comes around the corner, followed by an ambulance. That was the last shot we did at the end of this very hot, exhausting day. When we got back to Barlby Road, I took the rushes down to the edit suite and I asked the editor to cut this last sequence first. Tom Kavanagh, the editor, said, "Oh my God, you can't do this!" I went up to Richard's office and said "You'd better come down to the edit suite, something really terrible happened today on the shoot. I'm really sorry, but we're in big trouble..." I explained that it was all caught on camera and by the time he followed me to the edit suite, I was nearly in tears saying, "I'm so sorry, it was such a hard shoot. Show Richard the footage..." Tom pressed play and the young copper came running out and put his arm up to wave the police Range Rover through, and when it screeched around the corner, it hit the copper and he went flying through the air. Richard screamed, "Oh my god! What have you done?" I told him that we'd killed him... Then the camera panned over and there was a dummy lying in the road. Richard was absolutely furious; "You went to Whitechapel, to play??" The effect was fantastic, it was a great stunt!'

Robert Hudson (P.C. "Yorkie" Smith)

'I remember I got on very well with Paul Harrison and Rolie Luker, who was a great cameraman. He and Chas Edwards were the best at doing the handheld camerawork on their shoulders; they were brilliant. For some reason, any time I had something dangerous to do, Rolie was always the one behind the camera. In *Hold Fire*, Rolie was the one filming me getting blown up by that car! It was usually us two being close to danger, followed by the words "everybody back." This time, Rolie was encased in a steel box, while I was stood right next to this thing when it blew up! When the special effects guys rigged up this aluminium car to go flying, they put out a barrier and told everyone not to cross it, as that was where they expected all the debris to land. Well the car blew up and all this metal went flying miles past the safety line... I said to them afterwards, "Wait... was I supposed to survive that?!"'

'If ever you could design a uniform that prevented you from being able to run, we were all wearing them! We always had to hold the helmet while we ran, whilst the big battery packs for the radios were flapping about and banging into our sides, while the truncheon was running down your trouser leg. Whenever we met the real coppers on their beat, who would always come and watch what we were doing, I used to ask them how they ever caught anyone dressed up like that? They agreed that it was a fucking nightmare, because you couldn't run. And trust me, you want to run a mile from an exploding car!'

Colin Blumenau (P.C. "Taffy" Edwards)

'I remember one of the cameramen who joined us for the half-hours was Rolie Luker, who I think was one of the real unsung heroes of *The Bill*. Rolie was a wonderful cameraman, who I later worked with again when he shot a film that I directed. I'll never forget Rolie shooting the car explosion on *Hold Fire*. Paul Harrison told Mark Powley, Eamonn Walker and I that we had to run away from the car and when we heard it explode, we had to jump forwards and land on some mattresses below the camera. Well my memory is that when the car blew up, the next thing I knew was I already on the mattress, because the blast had picked us up and propelled us forward!'

BAD FAITH

Written by Julian Jones
Directed by Frank W. Smith

Series 4: Episode 13
Broadcast: Tuesday 30 August 1988

Case Narrative

Dashwood and Carver must be quick when they try to arrest Warren Michaels. Michaels runs off through the estate and the pair give chase.

Regular Cast

Sgt. Cryer (Eric Richard), D.C. Carver (Mark Wingett), D.C. Dashwood (Jon Iles), D.I. Burnside (Christopher Ellison), P.C. Haynes (Eamonn Walker), P.C. Ramsey (Nick Reding), P.C. Edwards (Colin Blumenau.

Guest Cast

Warren Michaels (Anthony Lennon), Mrs. Keel (Jeillo Edwards), Mrs. Henderson (Sally Sanders), Woman in curlers (Joyce Carpenter), Irish Woman (Maxine O'Reilly), Woman with baby (Carol Harvey), Woman in car (Jayne Tottman), Chester Williams (David Michael Clarke), Boy (Ben Kennedy), Girl (Nina Kennedy).

Production Team

Casting Director (Julian Oldfield), Title Music (Andy Pask, Charlie Morgan), Costume Designer (Mandy Harper), Make Up Designer (Gilly Wakeford), Graphics (Jenni Phillips), Videotape Editor (Terence E. Badham), Lighting (John O'Brien), Camera (Roy Easton), Sound (John Osborne, Alan Lester), Production Buyer (Terry Allen), Location Manager (Adam Kempton), Floor Manager (Tony Tyrer), Stage Manager (Diana Paskin), Production Manager (Derek Cotty), Production Assistant (Valerie Muncey Sanders), Technical Adviser (Wilf Knight), Programme Associate (Valerie Farron), Series Script Editor (Kenneth Ware), Designers (Robin Parker, Pam Blackwell), Executive Producer (Peter Cregeen), Producer (Michael Ferguson).

Observation Notes

Bad Faith (Production No: D4027, VTR No: THS/45262) was shot between Monday 27th June and Friday 1st July 1988. The opening shot shows an Underground train going over the railway bridge on Portobello Road, W11. The camera pans down to show Dashwood's BMW 5 Series car driving underneath the Westway, with the Notting Hill Citizens Advice building to the left of camera.

The following scene begins with Jon Iles driving into Neville Close, Kilburn NW6. The chase scene where Dashwood and Carver pursue Michaels was filmed in Craik Court. The 12-storey building was also used for all the later scenes where Cryer and Edwards find the overdosed parents, as well as the famous scene where Dashwood's car is destroyed.

All the estate scenes featuring Haynes and Ramsey were filmed on the adjacent Peel Precinct, Canterbury Road, Kilburn NW6. The precinct no longer exists and this whole area has been significantly redeveloped.

Bad Faith was the first episode directed by Frank W. Smith, one of the longest serving directors on *The Bill*, helming 23 episodes over the next 13 years. Smith's many directing credits include *The Beiderbecke Affair, Juliet Bravo, Casualty, Howards' Way, Boon, Medics, London's Burning, The Knock, Ballykissangel, Murder in Mind, Heartbeat* and *Byker Grove*.

The HPN 40V licence plate on Dashwood's BMW 5 in *Bad Faith* was borrowed from a Mercedes-Benz, registered in 1980. The destruction of his car sees Dashwood lose his usual cool, which was a characteristic detailed in the Character Notes distributed to writers on the series, which described Mike Dashwood as being 32 years old and "the cool member of the CID team. A Grammar School boy on his way up – not a Cockney, or a rustic or a Northerner with a funny voice, "Dashers" is one of those irritatingly confident young men, who seem to succeed with women, and somehow make more of the money they earn – he's a smart dresser – than other people! He is seen, by most of his colleagues, as a bit of a poser and has the mickey taken – quite often. But he is a conscientious, hard-working officer; not always as bright or imaginative as he might be, but certainly thorough and dependable. Single."

Witness Statements

Jon Iles (D.C. Mike Dashwood)
'You will notice that in the scene in *Bad Faith* where I am talking to the resident with the baby, I am smoking a roll-up cigarette. One of the reasons I always used them on *The Bill* was they were much better for continuity. If we paused a take and an actor was in the middle of a cigarette, it would continue to burn down while we weren't shooting,

which was a nightmare for continuity. Whereas a roll-up goes out straight away, so I could literally pick it up and start again from where I left off. The following scene was one of my favourite one-off moments in *The Bill*. Dashwood has parked his very smart, personal car on a really grotty estate. He is talking to Carver when suddenly a washing machine lands on top of his car! That wonderful moment was beautifully shot and I loved playing Dashwood's reaction, when he completely loses his cool. It harked back to my sitcom days, and the more discerning viewer appreciated what I was trying to do with Dashwood. But then you had people like Charlie Catchpole, the TV critic who once wrote a harsh review that said I was trained at the "MFI School of Acting". I put that down to him not being bright enough to understand the dark humour in Julian Jones' excellent script!'

Julian Jones (Writer)

'The idea of being "trained" as a writer is a very modern one. There were no creative writing courses in the 70's and I doubt that many of the writers on *The Bill* in the 80's had even been to university – nor was that a requirement. All the writers came from very different backgrounds and we were just encouraged to write a story we wanted to tell. When I was at school, we had to fill out a careers form and explain what we wanted to do when we were older. I was quite naïve, and perhaps a little full of myself, when I wrote that my first choice was to be "a superstar", followed by being a playwright. They completely ignored my first choice and then told me that I couldn't even spell playwright and that I'd be lucky to get an English O-Level... They told me I should be an estate agent; I didn't know what this was and assumed they thought I should be taking care of an estate!'

'In *The Bill*, I was writing about a different kind of estate than the one I had imagined working on as a child and often, these estates were out of control. Rather than follow a pumping police investigation, these early episodes were more personal, looking at the community and how their lives were affected by the police and vice versa. The series also had a great palette of regular characters to choose from, each drawing in the audience. Jon Iles was great as Dashwood and it was funny how in *Bad Faith* he went from smoothly interviewing the young mum whilst smoking a cigarette in her flat, doing his level best to pull her; to going outside, reversing his car and finding out that his back wheel has been nicked. Then when he replaces the wheel, they drop a washing machine on the car! I can't take any credit for when he breaks into the old woman's flat and finds her in bed watching *The Third Man*. I don't know who put that in, because it wasn't in the script, but it was an absolutely genius idea!'

'The story of the artist in *Bad Faith*, who was picked up by Dashwood and Carver, was also based on another part of my life, when I'd been living in a flat in East Dulwich. I'd been in bed with a really bad temperature, when suddenly there was a knock at the door and it was the police, who were there to take me down to the station. I had no idea what it was about and when they were driving me around the South Circular, one of them asked the other "So is he going to see the murder detective?" Which is where that line in *Bad Faith* comes from. They took me to Chelsea police station, where their "murder detective" was investigating the Susannah Lamplugh case. They put me in a cell for eight hours and I kept pressing the buzzer, because I was feeling ill with flu, but no one came. I was suspected of bank fraud and was addressed as "Tiger", which I also put in *Bad Faith,* where I had Michaels being interviewed by the horrible Burnside, who was wonderful to write for and brilliantly portrayed by Chris Ellison.'

'Before I got started on *The Bill*, Wilf Knight, the police adviser, arranged for a few of the newer writers to go to Kilburn police station. This was long before the days of Google maps and I was using an A-Z to try and find the police station. It was bucketing it down and I was wearing a big, brown suede coat, which was probably slightly too big for me. I asked a postman on Kilburn High Road, who explained that Kilburn police station was actually near Queen's Park Road. I eventually found it, though I arrived late in this absolutely drenched suede jacket, which had now turned dark brown. I explained at the front desk that I was a writer on *The Bill* and was there to see Commander Wilf Knight, which was how he liked to be addressed. Wilf gave myself and the other writers a tour of the station. Thinking back to my earlier experience, I asked him "What are these buzzers for, Wilf?" He explained that if a prisoner pressed that button, then someone would come and attend to you. I knew a different reality! When we broke for lunch, one of the writers told me that they had been watching the front office through a mirrored-window when I arrived. Apparently when Wilf saw me in my dark brown suede coat, he turned and said, "You see this one... he's a right villain." I had to then work with Wilf, knowing this was his perception of me!'

John Osborne (Sound)

'I first fell in love with radio about 57 years ago, when I was 9 years old. I used to listen to *Round the Horne*, *The Navy Lark* and *The Clitheroe Kid*, but I got really excited when Jack Jackson was on the radio. He used to edit clips from all the shows above, and many more from TV, to create a story interspersed with his dialogue, which made up his show. It was very clever and very funny. At the time, there was no pop radio – it was the Home, the Light and the Third. If you were young, you had to listen to the pirate ships, Radio Caroline, North Sea International or Radio Luxembourg for music, which I was really into, even though we never had a record player. Pirate radio was the curse of the establishment and the government did everything in their power to stop it, but it was so incredibly popular that the government and the BBC decided to join in and Radio 1 was launched on September 30 1967 by Tony Blackburn.'

'Kenny Everett had a live show every Saturday with his inimitable style, which I just loved; similar to Jack Jackson but on another level. Kenny used to record his shows from his recording studio in Wales and send the tape in for broadcast, I guess for management vetting, but it was broadcast every week for years and I used to listen to it and later record it and that's really when my love of sound took off. In those days there was not a great deal of technology around and certainly nothing as advanced as there is today. But Kenny's technical and artistic ability knew no bounds: he would multitrack his voice and harmonise with the music in perfect pitch, making some incredible tracks and jingles for his shows. I brought my own tape recorder, and then another that had 'sound-on-sound', which enabled simple overdubbing and layering up material, or multi-tracking like him (but nowhere as good). I built a console that I used for the school plays, playing in sound effects that I recorded from the BBC sound effects library, which some productions still use today, particularly the lightning effects which are fab.'

'Back in the day, I never really thought much about my career, except that I knew I wanted to do something involving sound. At 15, my economics teacher/careers officer spoke to me at length and I told him about my love of sound and he kindly got me a day at BBC Radio London and that was it. The sight of the broadcast tape machines, all those big faders and jingle machine and sound desks, it was like being in a kid in a candy shop. That was going to be my career! My dad, however, thought I would make a good research scientist and wear a white coat and save the world from some dreadful disease... It was a pivotal moment when I told him that wasn't for me. He wasn't too happy, but he could see how keen I was, so he supported me very well and would often bring me blank tapes so I could record more stuff. I made my first disco console at 16, and I used to play my own radio show to mum and dad, nipping in to take requests as they happily sipped sherry on the sofa. We never really had the sort of relationship that I have with my children, but he was a big fan, albeit silently.'

'I got my first job at LBC radio in Fleet Street when I was 18. A very menial role, but it was radio so I was in. My little glass office overlooked the radio ingest room, where all the reporters would send in their articles for recording and playing into the shows. I would often ask the engineers about sound and what they were doing and I actually met up with two them again at the BBC a few months later. I had already applied to the BBC when I was 18 and was lucky to get offered a job only a few months after taking the job at LBC, so I jumped ship and the rest is history.'

'I did a three-month intensive training course at Evesham. After passing everything, I was put at BBC Broadcasting House in Regent Street. I was incredibly happy as I was working for a proper broadcaster, doing real sound stuff and after a short time, ended up working with the very DJs that I listened to many years before. I think Alan Freeman, or Fluff as he was known, was my favourite, and I would make up his show opening signature and lots of jingles that he called "musical punctuation", that he played in between heavy rock. He had an astonishing style and the perfect radio voice and he was always very appreciative of my efforts. When I got to engineer his show solo for three hours on Saturdays I could barely contain my excitement.'

'Even though I loved working in radio, and the DJs seemed to like what I did as they always played my offerings, it always felt that my efforts were a little frowned upon by the creatives, after all I was only an engineer, so I decided to try my hand in television. That crossover wasn't possible within the BBC at the time, so I reluctantly left in 1974 to join Thames Television, which was the best move of my life. On the plus side I tripled my salary to around £11k per year and my excitement was fired up again because of the shows I got to work on.'

REQUIEM
Written by Peter J. Hammond
Directed by Sharon Miller

Series 4: Episode 14
Broadcast: Thursday 1 September 1988

Case Narrative
A man working to modernise the family flat finds more than he bargained for when he decides that the lounge needs a new fireplace.

Regular Cast
Sgt. Cryer (Eric Richard), D.S. Roach (Tony Scannell), D.C. Dashwood (Jon Iles), P.C. Haynes (Eamonn Walker), P.C. Ramsey (Nick Reding), W.P.C. Martella (Nula Conwell).

Guest Cast
Trant (Anthony Allen), Mrs. Trant (Jane Wood), Debbie Trant (Nicola Jane Scott), Goodhall (Richard Beale), Jenner (Russell Dixon), Mrs. Jenner (Delia Lindsay), Passmore (Ronald Leigh-Hunt), Photographer (Wayne Jackman).

Production Team
Casting Director (Brian Wheeler), Title Music (Andy Pask, Charlie Morgan), Costume Designer (Allard Tobin), Make Up Designer (Gilly Wakeford), Graphics (Ethan Ames), Videotape Editor (Terence E. Badham), Lighting (Allen Harradine), Camera (Jamie Acton-Bond), Sound (Stan Lee, Alan Lester), Production Buyer (Sarah Prebble), Location Manager (Annie Glanfield), Floor Manager (Glynn Purcell), Stage Manager (Diana Paskin), Production Manager (Derek Cotty), Production Assistant (Cherry Crompton), Technical Adviser (Wilf Knight), Programme Associate (Valerie Farron), Series Script Editor (Kenneth Ware), Designers (Robin Parker, Pam Blackwell), Executive Producer (Peter Cregeen), Producer (Michael Ferguson).

Observation Notes
Requiem (Production No: D4035, VTR No: THS/45270) was shot between Monday 25th and Friday 29th July 1988. The episode was the first not to feature any scenes set in Sun Hill station. The scenes featuring the Trant family and a body in their basement flat were all

shot in 29A Millwood Road, W10. The scenes with the neighbours were all shot in the building above, No. 29. Passmore parks his car on the adjoining St Charles Square, W10, outside what was then the Cardinal Manning Boys School. The building has been home to the St. Charles Catholic Sixth Form College since 1990.

Requiem was adapted for an episode of *Bureau Kruislaan* in 1992. The title remained the same and was the seventh episode of the first season. In the remake, the skeleton is revealed much earlier in the story.

Witness Statements

Peter J. Hammond (Writer)

'I went to art school first, though I realised I wasn't very good as an artist, so then I drifted into writing, which was very difficult to break into. No one would take you on unless you had an agent, but an agent wouldn't take you on unless you'd had something produced. I eventually managed to get a radio play done in Canada and that started it all off. My big break in television came in 1968, when I became the script editor on *Z Cars*. At that time, there were a lot of writers at the BBC who had come in from the cold to get a steady job and ended up as staff script editors. They were obliged to take on whatever they were assigned, whether they cared about what they were editing or not. Whereas I felt very lucky to get *Z Cars*, because at that time I'd only had a handful of writing jobs for children's television. I liked *Z Cars* and sent an outline for an idea to my agent, who then sent it to the producer, Richard Beynon, who invited me to meet him...'

'At that time I was driving a baker's van in the mornings, which was helping me supplement my living, in between writing jobs. I parked my bread van around the corner and went to meet Richard outside Threshold House in Shepherds Bush. He invited me to sit down on a wall and simply said, "I read your outline and I don't like it." I wondered why he'd invited me there just to tell me that? But he continued to explain that he liked my approach to some of the ideas and that his script editor was leaving soon. He wondered whether I would like to learn the job from him and then take over? Wow! I would probably have never written anything again had it not been for that moment. Though my friends and relatives were disappointed that I stopped the bakery round, because I used to take them early morning bread and doughnuts!'

'*Z Cars* was a huge learning curve for me and Richard Beynon was a very hard taskmaster, he would take no nonsense and I learnt an awful lot from him. He taught me about the economy of writing, how you should write one line that says a lot, rather than pages and pages of speeches. It was a tough discipline too, because I had to find scripts for 50 episodes a year. After being script editor for two years, I knew how to write for it to some extent and I later wrote 27 episodes for the series.'

'*The Bill* wasn't on my radar, but when I was asked by Ken Ware to write for it, I boned up on the programme and the characters. *The Bill* improved on *Z Cars*, which had been very studio bound, with our police cars stationary with the windscreen cut out in front of a back projection. I was also quite surprised how things had changed with the real police since *Z Cars*, where you could just walk into a police station without all the security. Barlby Road was quite a scary place, they had to have great big barricades up to stop people breaking in. It was a good set-up - and you could park your car there too, which you couldn't do at Merton.'

'For me, the most important thing about writing is to have timelessness, and, if possible, to have no other responsibilities during a writing period. I used to prefer writing in the morning, then enjoying some of the day before carrying on into early evening. But there was a pressure with *The Bill*. It was a fast turnaround show and you had to get the thing done within the time frame given. So it was no use spending hours looking at a blank piece of paper. I was using a typewriter in the early days, and sometimes, on deadline day itself, I would get up at four in the morning to finish the script and then drive it to Barlby Road, stopping to get it photocopied on the way. But the pressure was good. It often brought out the best in one.'

'I got on well with Ken Ware and Tim Vaughan, two very good script editors. If I was too self-indulgent they would tell me. And you couldn't con them. On the odd rare occasion when I was behind with delivery and tried the old trick of asking for an extra day because I wasn't happy with the ending, they knew I was only halfway through the script. But they would receive it, as promised. On a pressure show, script editors need writers who aren't going to let them down. Also, if one had a query, Ken or Tim or a police advisor were always there to help at a moment's notice.'

'The idea for *Requiem* came about when they explained they couldn't use the station set one week, so could I write a story all on location? This was quite a test, but it was a very good way to think of a story within those confines. You have to set the story early and in *Requiem* I kept the audience guessing until the reveal of the hole with the body in the wall. And then I had to wrap the whole thing up in twenty-four minutes, which was quite tricky to do at first. In fact, *Requiem* was originally twenty minutes longer, but they couldn't use it all. There was supposed to be a final scene with Martella pushing the little girl on the swing in the park, but that got cut. We were able to keep some of the black humour in though, like the police photographer who comments on the standing up "stiff" (a word I was later told by the police advisors I could no longer use) making his life easier. I also added the character of Passmore and his old Ford Zephyr as a nod to *Z Cars*.'

'I never really wrote about high-end crime, it was usually events on the edge of crime that I enjoyed writing about and the ordinariness of people, like the family in *Requiem* who felt like prisoners in their own home. That lovely moment when the family all sit down at the same time in unison on the bed was a nice choice by the director, Sharon Miller, I was pleased with that. She and the casting department got it right too, the character actors playing those dreadful neighbours were good, who when asked if they'd like to know why the police are there, they just dismiss them, which is typical isn't it.'

'It's lovely when you get a director who completely understands it from the start. They didn't have readthroughs on *The Bill*, so you didn't get to know people, but Sharon got in touch on the phone beforehand to discuss it, which was good. Once you know that they understand it and they're walking around with your script and that it no longer belongs to you, you know that you've got a good director, it belongs to them and becomes their show. I was very lucky on *The Bill* to get such good actors and good directors who made it all happen.'

'*Requiem* was adapted by a Dutch television company, for a series called *Bureau Kruislaan*, or as I called it, *Van der Bill*. I had forgotten all about it, until I started receiving some mysterious residuals from Fremantle. I enjoyed the Dutch version, they had a great cast and I thought their skeleton was very convincing and I didn't mind seeing it revealed earlier in the episode. I thought the whole show was very faithful to the original, including the pathologist driving an old car, which was an enjoyable moment. I had a Citroen DS way back, from new until rust eventually finished it off.'

TRESPASSES

Written by Christopher Russell
Directed by Brian Parker

Series 4: Episode 15
Broadcast: Tuesday 6 September 1988

Case Narrative

Investigating what he thinks is a cat trapped in a rubbish chute, Ramsey is appalled to find a new-born baby.

Regular Cast

Sgt. Cryer (Eric Richard), Sgt. Penny (Roger Leach), Sgt. Peters (Larry Dann), Insp. Frazer (Barbara Thorn), D.S. Roach (Tony Scannell), D.C. Dashwood (Jon Iles), D.C. Carver (Mark Wingett), P.C. Ramsey (Nick Reding), P.C. Edwards (Colin Blumenau), P.C. Haynes (Eamonn Walker), P.C. Melvin (Mark Powley), P.C. Smith (Robert Hudson), P.C. Hollis (Jeff Stewart), P.C. Stamp (Graham Cole), W.P.C. Martella (Nula Conwell), W.P.C. Brind (Kelly Lawrence).

Guest Cast

Mrs. Turville (Joy Elias-Rilwan), Mrs. Ford (Jeni Giffen), Rev. Ford (Terence Beesley), Nurse (Sabra Williams), Staples (Christopher Whittingham), Wendy Saunders (Julie Neubert), Mrs. Morris (Hazel Bainbridge), Tony (Peter Edbrook), Brignell (Alex McAvoy).

Production Team

Casting Director (Julia Lisney), Title Music (Andy Pask, Charlie Morgan), Costume Designer (Allard Tobin), Make Up Designer (Gilly Wakeford), Graphics (Jenni Phillips), Videotape Editor (Tom Kavanagh), Lighting (John O'Brien), Camera (Roy Easton), Sound (John Osborne, Alan Lester), Production Buyer (Mike Ashby), Location Manager (Barry Beckett), Floor Manager (Fizz Waters), Stage Manager (Tricia Barnes), Production Manager (Derek Cotty), Production Assistant (Caroline Sutton), Technical Adviser (Wilf Knight), Programme Associate (Valerie Farron), Script Editor (Tim Vaughan), Series Script Editor (Kenneth Ware), Designers (Robin Parker, Peter Elliott), Executive Producer (Peter Cregeen), Producer (Richard Bramall).

Observation Notes

Trespasses (Production No: D4022, VTR No: THS/45257) was shot between Monday 13th and Friday 17th June 1988.

The opening scene where P.C. Ramsey reads a newspaper was filmed outside 187 Saltram Crescent, W9. This building is still a newsagent today. The later scene where Ramsey drives the baby to hospital was filmed further along Saltram Crescent and the adjoining Denholme Road, W9. The following baby scenes were filmed at St. Charles Hospital, Exmoor Road, W10. The scenes set at Reverend Ford's church were filmed at St Clement's, 95 Sirdar Rd, London W11.

The closing credits saw Tony Scannell erroneously credited as playing "Acting D.I." Roach – a credit that had been used on *Just Call Me Guvnor*, which was made as part of the same production block as *Trespasses*.

Trespasses was adapted for an episode of *Bureau Kruislaan* in 1992. The title of the episode *Vergeef ons onze schuld* translates as "Forgive us our trespasses" and was the fifth episode of the first season.

Trespasses reveals that P.C. Ken Melvin is a born-again Christian. This aspect of the character was detailed in the Character Notes, which revealed that Ken was 20 years old and "the youngest PC at the station. A Londoner (he grew up in Finchley), he became a Born Again Christian at Sixth Form College and although he lives in Section House, still regularly comes home to visit his mother who lives alone. He is respected and liked by his fellow PCs, but frequently has to be spoonfed on account of his youth and inexperience. He has no difficulty relating his Christianity to his work and sees police work as a chance to witness God. But he doesn't press his beliefs on others, unless asked directly about them. The response to his morality frequently goes one of two ways: either people feel they should tiptoe round him for fear of offending or, as in the case of Ramsey, he unwittingly incites a certain amount of aggression. He has a girlfriend, Michelle, who is a medical student."

Witness Statements

Christopher Russell (Writer)

'You might think that writing a half-hour episode was easier than writing an hour-long story, because it was obviously half the length. Though in terms of script construction, it was a completely different ball game. The stories had to be a lot smaller in scale, but that also seemed to open up a lot of avenues for using material that you couldn't have used in an hour-long story. The whole idea was to show the revolving doors of a police station; the characters come in or go out and they pass people who are either going another way or doing something else. The idea was to mesh all that together, but now, because we only had 25 minutes to tell a story, you had to get going quickly and then keep the story moving. I welcomed this and could certainly see the opportunities with the format. *The Bill* was a terrific job and a fantastic vehicle for writers, because you could write about absolutely anything. As long as you had police officers in it, added a reasonable amount of drama and kept it within the bounds of decency, you could do what you liked, once you were trusted to deliver on time.'

'The idea for *Trespasses* was prompted by a real theft from our local church, where the lectern was stolen. That gave me the quasi-religious title of the episode and then I just needed to add a few more thefts into the story. The baby in the rubbish dump was also actually based on a real case I had read about. Contraception wasn't as good then as it is now and, even in the 1980s, social mores were different then. There were still some people for whom having a baby out of wedlock was a stigma and tough to deal with, and so sadly it wasn't rare at this time for someone to be so desperate as to resort to dumping their own child. The half-hour format was exactly the right length to tell stories about humanity, which was the point of *The Bill*. These officers were ordinary human beings, doing an extraordinary job; none of them were perfect and none of them were totally imperfect. We didn't want beatific goodies or pantomime villains; all the characters had good bits and bad bits, which meant they all had something to rub up against. The drama was intrinsically already there, the writer just had to find a way of including it in their particular short story.'

Nick Reding (P.C. Pete Ramsey)

'It would have been really interesting to explore the corruption storyline further, though the producers lost their nerve, because they were too worried about upsetting the real police. I pushed quite hard to try and develop it, because at the time there were quite a lot of stories coming out in the press about police corruption and it would have been great to explore how you stop it. However, the producers were very good at listening to our ideas, once we'd got hold of our characters. I always remember Michael Ferguson saying, "If you have an idea then go for it!" We were all encouraged to get involved. Though some of the things we did on *The Bill* you could never get away with now. It was during the filming of *Trespasses* that somebody gave me their newborn baby, who was only a day old, at the hospital. I then had to lower this real baby into an old plastic bag, so they could get the close-up shot for when I found the baby in the skip, which was in fact shot in a stairwell at the hospital. We then did another shot of the baby being lifted out of this plastic bag in the corridor. I know people like to get on the telly, but I was so uncomfortable about it. On a happier note, *Trespasses* was when Kelly Lawrence joined the cast as W.P.C. Brind and we became great friends and later travelled around Columbia together.'

Fizz Waters (Floor Manager)

'Thames had a real family feel as a company and, because *The Bill* was made completely off-site, I remember feeling like I was being sent off to Siberia! But of course, they had made their own family feel and I really enjoyed working on the series. When we were setting up shots for filming, the cast would be wandering around and they were all very approachable. Eric Richard was great to work with and I remember Barbara Thorn being fun and very outgoing. Larry Dann was also a brilliant actor and an absolutely gorgeous man. In fact all of them were really nice. It was the whole cohesion of that team that made *The Bill* so successful at that time, and there was definitely a choreography in the way the actors moved with the camera.'

'A certain amount of poetic licence was taken when it came to the rule that every shot should be through the eyes of the police. I was certainly never going to enforce that rule on a director like Brian Parker, who was great to work with and such a hoot! He used to turn up at Barlby Road on his motorbike. One morning, he came in fuming... "A fucking idiot nearly knocked me off my bike, so I kicked his door in with my steel toecaps!" He was a no-nonsense man, which is what we needed on the half-hours, because time was tighter and you needed a director who could get things done. He also trusted his team; when I used to ask him questions, he'd just tell me to do what I thought was best. He was lovely.'

'I was born and bred in Teddington, where the studios were just down the road from where we lived. The mother of one of my school friends worked at Thames in the canteen and got me a Saturday job there, where I was paid £3 a day. I was working part-time until I finished school and I knew I didn't want to work in a canteen for the rest of my life. I saw a notice on the jobs board that read "Call Boy Wanted". I used to take the tea trolley around all the production offices, so I already knew everybody and I used to chat with Harry Lock, the head of the Floor Management department at the time. I used to wake him up in the afternoon with a cup of tea, because he would fall asleep at his desk after lunch! One day, I asked Harry if I could apply for the call boy job, to which he replied, "We've never had a girl do that job..." I politely asked him what difference it made that I was a woman? I wasn't being a screaming feminist, though I understood the problems that women face in the workplace and many have probably experienced worse misogyny than I faced. I fought back and was one of only a handful of applicants, which is bizarre when you think how many people want to work in television nowadays. After all the interviews, he went into the office next door and said that he wanted to give me a job, but didn't know if he was allowed to... and all the women in the office said, "Hire her!"

'Harry didn't actually give me the call boy job directly; he instead gave me a three-month freelance contract, where the first programme I worked on was *And Mother Makes Five*, starring Wendy Craig, produced and directed by Peter Frazer-Jones. I was pooping my pants at first, as you can imagine, because I was only 16 and I didn't know what I would be doing. But Angie Morgan the P.A. took me under her wing and I ended up having a grand old time in my first week of television. I spent the next three weeks in Kent, working on an episode of the Graham Greene series *Shades of Greene*. The episode I worked on was called *Under the Garden* and starred Denholm Elliot and Arthur Lowe, who I later worked with when I became a floor manager on his series *A.J. Wentworth B.A.* Arthur was an absolutely gorgeous man and delightful to work with. He had the condition narcolepsy, which meant that on a couple of occasions when the clock was running to start recording, he would be stood in the corridor, fast asleep. I would give him a little nudge and then he would go straight on and do the performance, which was amazing. And of course I worked on lots of episodes of *Rainbow*, which was a really good Thames programme for training staff and is where I first cut my teeth as a floor manager. It was such good fun and I actually floor-managed the famous "Twangers" episode for the Thames Christmas tape, where we absolutely cacked ourselves laughing!'

'The tide started to change for Thames in the late 1980s, when there were suddenly bean counters everywhere, coming in and telling us how to do a show that we had been making for the last 20 years. The way some members of staff were treated was disgusting. Then programmes gradually started being farmed out to other companies, which we couldn't understand when we'd been making them ourselves for so long. Everything changed as soon as the bean counters made their move and eventually of course Thames lost the franchise. This didn't affect *The Bill* too much, as it had already established its own bubble and remained pretty unscathed. Had I stayed and hung on at Thames for another year or two, I might have walked away with some redundancy money, but that would have been a long time to wait. I went freelance towards the end of 1988 and came back to do Thames shows like *Rumpole of the Bailey*, though that was another show now being made by an independent production company. By then, the bean counters were begrudging every penny that was being spent, even quibbling how many packets of crisps an actor could open in a pub scene... that was the end for me.'

'I did get some nice freelance jobs away from Thames, including some episodes of *Boon* for the BBC and I did the tennis at Wimbledon, which was great. I also did *The Wall* concert in 1990 to commemorate the fall of the Berlin Wall, which was amazing. One of the last jobs I did was a sitcom pilot for a British version of *The Golden Girls*, directed by James Cellan Jones and starring Wendy Craig, who I had worked with on my first week in television. During the filming of *And Mother Makes Five* I had celebrated my 17th birthday and for a present, Wendy Craig gave me a beautiful book of Helen Bradley's painting. Inside she had signed it and written "To Fizz – the girl who always smiles". I reminded Wendy of this and then explained that I had come full circle in my career, having worked with her on my first day in television and then there we were working together again when I had decided to bow out. It was amazing and reminded me how nothing could compare to the old days when Thames would give us a bunch of money to go and make a programme, which they always got back through advertising.'

SAVE THE LAST DANCE FOR ME
Written by Barry Appleton
Directed by Brian Farnham

Series 4: Episode 16
Broadcast: Thursday 8 September 1988

Case Narrative
Chief Insp. Conway is in charge of a stakeout to capture escaped prisoner Terry Bush.

Regular Cast
Sgt. Cryer (Eric Richard), W.P.C. Ackland (Trudie Goodwin), D.C Dashwood (Jon Iles), D.S. Roach (Tony Scannell), Ch. Insp. Conway (Ben Roberts), D.C. Carver (Mark Wingett), Sgt. Peters (Larry Dann), W.P.C. Martella (Nula Conwell), P.C. Ramsey (Nick Reding), P.C. Frank (Ashley Gunstock), P.C. Edwards (Colin Blumenau), P.C. Smith (Robert Hudson).

Guest Cast
Janet Irvine (Elizabeth Seal), Mr. Donaldson (James Duke), Vera (Tamsin Heatley), Joe (Richard Walker), Beastie Boy (Jeff Ward), Pianist (Louis Mordish).

Uncredited Personnel
Props Chargehand (Alex Bazylewicz), Make Up Assistant (Adam Beck), Assistant Stage Manager (Gregory Kinchin), Librarian (Bridget Moore), Press Officer (Rosane Chapman), Accountants (Anne Shields, David Saggs).

Production Team
Choreographer (Christopher Wren), Fight Arranger (Andrew Bradford), Casting Director (Brian Wheeler), Title Music (Andy Pask, Charlie Morgan), Costume (Allard Tobin), Make Up Designer (Gilly Wakeford), Graphics (Ethan Ames), Videotape Editor (Terence E. Badham), Lighting (Peter Bower), Camera (Rolie Luker), Sound (Richard Bradford, Alan Lester), Production Buyer (Terry Allen), Location Manager (Sheila Loughrey), Floor Manager (Quenton Annis), Stage Manager (Nigel J. Wilson), Production Manager (Derek Cotty), Production Assistant (Carol Snook), Technical Adviser (Wilf Knight), Programme Associate (Valerie Farron), Series Script Editor (Kenneth Ware), Design (Robin Parker, David Richens), Executive Producer (Peter Cregeen), Producer (Michael Ferguson).

Observation Notes

Save the Last Dance for Me (Production No: D4032, VTR No: THS/45267) was shot between Monday 11th and Friday 15th July 1988, as part of the same production block as *The Trap*. The episode being shot by the Blue unit at the same time was *Runaround*.

The opening scene shows Jon Iles driving down Acton High Street, before turning into Grove Road W3 and parking outside No. 6. Iles and Trudie Goodwin are then filmed walking down Gloucester Road W3, where Mark Wingett and Larry Dann are sitting in a green 1980 Ford Transit MkII, parked outside No. 21.

Ackland and Dashwood are seen passing a false street sign created by the Design team. Limmer Avenue E1 was in fact Petersfield Road W3. They then enter the former Acton Priory Centre, a Victorian building on the corner of Petersfield Road. Designed by Edward Monson and built in 1896, the building was attached to Priory School, initially acting as offices for the School Board, before becoming a community centre in the 1970s. The building was closed at the time of filming, after 24-year old Alywn Alfred was shot at a Christmas party in the centre on Tuesday 22nd December 1987 and died the following week in hospital. Despite many objections, the building was demolished in 2012 and replaced by residential flats, next to the newly built Ark Priory Primary Academy.

The driving scenes with Edwards and Ramsey were filmed on Acton Lane, while the scenes featuring Conway and Roach parked in a blue Vauxhall Cavalier MkII were filmed near a builder's yard on Bollo Lane, Acton W3.

Back at the station, Ramsey suggests a game of Three Card Brag in the canteen. The Background Information document issued to writers gave some details about the canteen: "During the early relief (6am – 2pm) the canteen is normally at its busiest between 8am and 10.30am and between 12 noon and 1.30pm. Between 1.30pm and 2pm the beat officers should be making their final checks on their beats before the end of the relief." Unfortunately no television for Martella!

Save the Last Dance for Me was the first of 38 episodes of *The Bill* helmed by prolific TV director Brian Farnham, whose 40-year career saw him direct multiple hit television series, including *Armchair Theatre, Bergerac, Rumpole of the Bailey, The Chief, Dangerfield, Heartbeat, Poirot, Bugs, All Quiet on the Preston Front, Where the Heart Is* and *Rosemary and Thyme*.

Save the Last Dance for Me was adapted for an episode of the Netherlands police series *Bureau Kruislaan* in 1992. The title of the episode was *Pasodoble* and was the eighth episode of the first season. The episode has a longer conclusion, with the officers raiding the house under observation and interrupting the gunman having sex with his girlfriend, who is alarmed when the officers discover a gun under his pillow.

Witness Statements

Sheila Loughrey (Location Manager)

'The story behind the building that we used in *Save the Last Dance For Me* was that it had been an arts centre which, as well as having a proper dance studio, also had a photography studio and a recording studio for local youngsters to use. It was a really nice building, but the wrong type of people had started going there, which culminated in tragedy and a young lad was shot in the head in the main hallway. I remember the caretaker of the building pointing out exactly where it had happened and telling me all the grisly details. That's why the building was closed and we were able to film in there. It was later pulled down as part of redevelopment in 2012, which I don't know how they got away with, because it was a beautiful Victorian building.'

'*Save the Last Dance For Me* was directed by Brian Farnham. His P.A. was Carol Snook, who used to call him "Father Farnham." He was a jovial type of chap and he was flexible, which the directors on *The Bill* needed to be, especially with the crews who used to work really hard. When I look at the credits on a television drama today, there are so many more people working on a production. Whereas back on *The Bill*, I was solely responsible for finding the locations and setting them up, briefing the production team and the design department, liaising with the local police and then managing the location on the shoot itself. We also had a lot more contact with the writers in those days and Barry Appleton used to come in and chat to us all. He is a lovely man and wrote such good scripts, perhaps unsurprisingly as he had been a policeman himself. I think that is why the real police used to like the programme so much, because they could see their job realistically portrayed on screen.'

Barry Appleton (Writer)

'I loved *Save the Last Dance for Me*. I had help with this one as it so happens that my wife Pam was a ballroom dancer, as well as being a great cook and a former model. She was a great technical adviser and helped me with the script. When seeing the episode on TV, Pam recognised her friend Elizabeth Seal, who had a long career as an actress, singer and choreographer, playing the dance teacher. This episode was again based on a true story of when I set up an observation in a dance hall with a W.P.C., as we couldn't get any female detectives at the time. We were watching a place over the road, where a suspect was supposed to be hiding out. This guy was a gangster who was wanted for a number of serious crimes and had bragged that he wanted to kill a cop. Then exactly as it happened in the episode, we both ended up dancing to make our cover look good and I tripped the light fantastic. Where real life differed was the guy came out the house and we followed him, but we lost him. We were lucky we did lose him, because when he was eventually caught, he was carrying a shoebox with a hole in the bottom and he had a gun hidden inside it.'

Nigel J. Wilson (Stage Manager)

'By the time of the half-hours, the police had realised that we were no fools and weren't out to get them. Our reputation grew and grew and we were eventually on first-name terms with Peter Imbert, the Commissioner of the Metropolitan Police Service. He had previously been Chief Constable and in 1975 had been the chief negotiator at the Balcombe Street siege involving the IRA. He was probably the last Commissioner who started on the beat and was a fantastic guy, I really liked him and he liked us. This meant we could arrange access for our writers, so if they had an idea and wanted to research a storyline, we could help make that happen.'

'Behind the scenes, Thames was imploding at this time due to the fallout from the *Death on the Rock* documentary. Jobs were on the line and studio cameramen were very keen, despite the opposition from the O.B. department, to get out of the studio and onto *The Bill* if they could. People like Rolie Luker succeeded and we benefited hugely from this, because the O.B. cameramen just thought they could just go from filming Newcastle United against Charlton Athletic on the Saturday, to filming a drama on the Monday in the same way.'

'The landscape of television was also changing at this time and single plays were disappearing, which meant work was beginning to thin out for experienced directors. *The Bill* became something of a haven for them and we benefitted by getting really good directors like Brian Farnham on board, who got the best out of everyone and would come back year after year. Brian directed *Save the Last Dance For Me*, where Jon Iles had to dance with our guest artist Elizabeth Seal, a very famous and fantastic dancer. She was very gracious and hugely professional, teaching Jon the pasodoble, which is not an easy dance to learn, but Jon was very good on his feet.'

Jon Iles (D.C. Mike Dashwood)

'A lot of us had a background in theatre and most of my early television roles had been in comedy shows. I did several episodes of *The Dick Emery Show*, where in one sketch I was dressed up as a knight, standing by a moat at Leeds Castle. Dick Emery was dressed as a medieval lady, taking two Great Danes for a walk. When his character walked past me, I said, "What a fine pair thou hast there, I should dearly love to fondle those two in front of the fire..." which elicited his famous catchphrase, "You are awful, but I like you" and I was pushed into the moat! That was the kind of TV work I had done before I joined *The Bill*, where like many of the cast, I wasn't aware of just how cutting edge the filming technique was and how it affected every aspect of putting the show together. I just thought that was the way all drama was shot and it wasn't until later when I was doing publicity interviews for the show, that I was suddenly made aware of just how much people like Jamie Acton-Bond and Rolie Luker were inventing new styles of camera work.'

'Rolie was our cameraman on *Save the Last Dance for Me*, which was a great episode. The wonderful Trudie Goodwin and I had to learn a couple of dance routines, where we had to time our moves so that we hit our marks at the right time for the camera to see us saying the dialogue. There was one routine where we were all dancing in a circle and Rolie needed to get a wide shot to capture this swirling movement. He found that filming from the window ledge gave him the best angle, though to get everything in frame, he needed to lean back out of the window. What sometimes happens to camera operators is that they are so focused at looking through a lens, they are not aware of the real world around them... As I came into shot, I used my periphal vision to glance over to make sure I was in the right position and I saw that Rolie was falling out of the window - and we were on the first floor of this building! I jumped over and grabbed him by the ankles as he was falling out of the window. He's always said that I saved his life.'

Trudie Goodwin (W.P.C. June Ackland)
'I remember the gap between the third series and the half-hours very well, because I had a baby in between, which was very fortuitous. I actually remember not liking the idea of us making so many episodes and to be honest, I never really liked the half-hour format. I much preferred the hour-long episodes, but that was a luxury. It really got quite confusing early on with the different script colours, and working with more than one unit at a time took some getting used to. Our days were also longer, because the hour-long episodes had been shot by crews who were based in Teddington and so we often had to wrap by 4pm in order for them to get back to base, so we'd had it quite easy in a lot of ways.'

Though one of the half-hour episodes I really did like was *Save the Last Dance for Me*, which was really good fun to make, mainly because of Jon Iles, who is so funny and such good company. We had a really good laugh together and we still do now whenever we catch up. Our cameraman on this episode was the wonderful Rolie Luker, who was brilliant at handheld shooting and was one of the key people for that very identifiable look and style that *The Bill* had early on. Rolie is only a short fellow and there's a 360-degree shot he got in this episode, which he achieved by holding the camera above his head, with his arms fully outstretched and spinning in the middle of the ballroom. He got that fantastic shot without even being able to see what he was doing, it was pure instinct, which I've never seen anyone do before or since. Rolie is still one of my best friends and I am always doubly excited when we meet up, because I am a classic car fan and he drives an Austin 7!'

'I actually studied dance to begin with when I left school. I went straight to Dartington Hall, an arts college that had been recommended to me by a couple of people I knew from youth theatre. They'd both said, "It's the most amazing place, you must go!" So I went with my friend Libby, who is still one of my oldest and best friends, to study Drama, Dance, Music and Art. Dartington is the most beautiful place, just outside Totnes, although the college sadly no longer exists. I felt I was never going to be quite good enough to be a professional dancer, but I might possibly progress in drama... To be on the safe side, I then went to Exeter University and got a teaching qualification. I was very glad I did that, because I did quite a lot of supply teaching earlier in my career when I was out of work. That also definitely helped us get a mortgage, because when you are married to an actor, we were unlikely to get a mortgage if we both said our occupations were actors, whereas I could genuinely say I was a teacher when we applied.'

'I was a terrible teacher to begin with. During my probationary year I was working in a really tough secondary school in Deptford in South London. I was thrown in at the deep end and had my own class from the beginning, which was too much really, especially as I wasn't much older than the kids I was teaching. A lot of the kids were great and I still see some of them around, but I found teaching really quite stressful. I think I got better once I was a bit older. I would go in for a few days in between acting jobs, and I would always go back to the same school, so the kids got to know me. It got more difficult once I got established on television, because that's all the kids wanted to talk about, and by that time I was earning decent money as an actress and so I didn't need to carry on supply teaching. By the time I stopped teaching I think I wasn't too bad at it. I admire teachers massively, I don't know how they do it, especially nowadays, I'd find it impossible.'

Gregory Kinchin (Assistant Stage Manager)
'In the last few years of my secondary school education, we had a new drama teacher join our school. She was young, straight out of college and very enthusiastic, nothing like all the other old codgers that were teaching there. She started up a healthy drama department and I got involved on the practical side of a few productions. Our school used to use a theatre called The Brick Box in New Malden, which was built and run by Kingston upon Thames County Council, who designed and ran the theatre based on The Cockpit in Marylebone. It was open to local drama groups and they ran classes in the evenings, which I got very involved in. That inspired me to go to college at Trent Park in Cockfosters, where I trained as a secondary school drama teacher.'

'In between term time, I used to work at Richmond Theatre when they were crewing up for big shows. I used to frequently drive around the North Circular at the weekends, doing the get-ins and get-outs. I'd be down there on the Saturday night after the show, getting all the sets onto the lorry, ready to go to the next venue. Then I'd help get the next show in next morning. I'd be down there a lot over Christmas, helping on the pantomimes, which was a good source of income. I did a variety of jobs and on many of the shows I was a flyman. Richmond Theatre was a hemp house, which meant it had no counter weights, so when you pulled up the ropes during a scene change, you were lifting the full weight of the flat. Sometimes you'd need six people: two on the top bar, two on the middle and two on the floor and we'd have to use all our weight just to lift the flats off the ground.'

'I completed my teaching course, but I was enjoying the theatre work so much that I took a full-time job at Richmond and spent a year as the deputy stage manager for the in-house crew. From there, I got an Equity card and toured for a year as an assistant stage manager around the country. I made the move to the West End when I got a job at Her Majesty's Theatre as an electrician... don't ask me why, because I'm not an electrician at all! I then worked at the Arts Theatre on Newport Street, near Leicester Sqaure, where I was the only electrician, so I could call myself Chief Electrician on my CV and get away with it!'

'Then I went off travelling for about 18 months and when I came back, I started to get work in TV as a floor assistant on shows like *The Des O'Connor Show*, which was great because he had lots of big names coming on as guests. I also did a few of the hour-long episodes of *The Bill* as a floor assistant. To work in stage management in TV, you had to be in the Equity union and as I had an Equity card, I was able to take a job as an ASM on *The Bill* for a couple of weeks, when they were shooting a pilot episode for the half-hour series. Those two weeks lasted 14 years!'

'Because the actors were always going from one episode to another, usually within the same day, the fundamental job of the ASM on *The Bill* was to be with the actors, preferably ahead of them arriving on set, to run through their lines and help them get the story settled and organised in their head. Then once they were on set, the ASM would keep an eye on the dialogue and help the actors if they needed someone to have a little rehearsal with on the side of the set. It just helped the whole thing flow and helped the actors keep where they needed to be in their head, because once they walked off a set having shot it, they forgot those lines instantly and they'd be moving onto the next scene, especially when they had a really busy schedule. We used to try and schedule the actors so they had the least amount of moves, or if they had a big episode coming up, that they weren't in another story that week, or only had a very little bit to do for the other unit. It was all organised to make it as easy as possible for the actors, which wasn't always easy to achieve, but as a whole I thought it was a very well organised process.'

RUNAROUND

Written by Al Hunter
Directed by Derek Lister

Series 4: Episode 17
Broadcast: Tuesday 13 September 1988

Case Narrative

Martella has to deal with a corpse and a family of excitable Italians, while a drunken bus driver leaves a trail of destruction in his wake.

Regular Cast

Sgt. Cryer (Eric Richard), Sgt. Penny (Roger Leach), P.C. Smith (Robert Hudson), W.P.C. Martella (Nula Conwell), W.P.C. Ackland (Trudie Goodwin), P.C. Haynes (Eamonn Walker), P.C. Hollis (Jeff Stewart), P.C. Stamp (Graham Cole), W.P.C. Ford (Vikki Gee-Dare).

Guest Cast

Janet Simmons (Linda Robson), Daisy Allison (Una Brandon-Jones), Ian Gore (John Challis), Mrs. Borenno (Malya Woolf), Giorgio Caricola (Ian Sears), Isabella Caricola (Patricia Martinelli), Mr. Deegan (Billy Roche), Bus Driver (Joanna Bacon), Doctor (Ève Karpf), Cafe Customer (Len Howe), Mark Bright (Nelson Fletcher), Grant Bright (Winston Crooke).

Production Team

Casting Director (Julia Lisney), Title Music (Andy Pask, Charlie Morgan), Costume Designer (Jennie Tate), Make Up Designer (Gilly Wakeford), Graphics (Ethan Ames), Videotape Editor (Tom Kavanagh), Lighting (Allen Harradine), Camera (Jamie Acton-Bond), Sound (Richard Longley, Alan Lester), Production Buyer (Trevor Young), Location Manager (Eddie Mares), Floor Manager (Aidan Boulter), Stage Manager (Ed Stevenson), Production Manager (Derek Cotty), Production Assistant (Susan Lewis), Technical Adviser (Wilf Knight), Programme Associate (Valerie Farron), Assistant Script Editor (Elizabeth Bradley), Series Script Editor (Kenneth Ware), Designers (Robin Parker, Peter Elliott), Executive Producer (Peter Cregeen), Producer (Richard Bramall).

Observation Notes

Runaround (Production No: D4030, VTR No: THS/45265) was shot between Monday 11th and Friday 15th July 1988. The episode opens with Martella walking her beat on Chapel Market, N1 and visiting the pharmacy based at 70 Chapel Market, which is still in business today.

The scenes set in the Caricola's café were all filmed in the Italian café Alpino, which opened at 97 Chapel Market in 1959. In 2022, the family-run business left the red-tiles behind and relocated to 1 Chapel Market.

The scene where Ackland and Haynes give Yorkie a lift to his beat were filmed on St Mark's Road, North Kensington, W10. Seen in the background behind Robert Hudson is the Kensington Memorial Park.

The scenes at the bus depot were filmed at the Westbourne Park Garage, Great Western Road, London W9, which is still in use today. The bus that Ian Gore smashes up and drives is a DMS-class Daimler Fleetline.

The scenes where Yorkie visits Daisy at her home and observes the Bright brothers were filmed in 23 Treadgold Street, Notting Hill, W11.

The scene where Yorkie radios Ackland to say that the truck is approaching Bushmore Avenue was filmed on Kensal Road, W10. The shot begins outside No. 170, an historic Grade II listed building that opened in 1880 as the Cobden Working Mens Club and Institute.

Runaround was novelised by author John Burke for "*The Bill 3*", the third in a series of tie-in books. This edition was published in 1989 and also featured adaptations of *Light Duties, Homes and Gardens, Alarms and Embarrassments, Community Relations, Home Sweet Home, Trespasses, The Three Wise Monkeys* and *Just Call Me Guv'nor*. There were six books released in the series between 1989 and 1992, all penned by Burke, who adapted many film and TV scripts for novelisations over a 30-year period, including *UFO, Strange Report, Jason King, The Protectors, King and Castle* and *London's Burning*. John Burke passed away in 2011, aged 89.

Runaround was adapted for an episode of the Netherlands police series *Bureau Kruislaan* in 1992. The title of the episode *Dienst en wederdienst* translates as "Service and Return" and was the first episode of the series.

Runaround was the first episode of three episodes of *The Bill* written by Alan Hunter, who later worked under the name Al Hunter Ashton and enjoyed a successful dual career as an actor and a writer. On screen he is perhaps best remembered for his role as Pit Bull in six series of *London's Burning*, with other TV roles in *Mr Bean, The Brittas Empire, Tales from* the Crypt, Minder, Inspector Morse, Juliet Bravo, Murder in Mind and film appearances including A Fish Called Wanda, From Hell and Gladiator. His extensive screenwriting credits include The Firm, Casualty, The Broker's Man, Holby City, See How They Run, New Tricks and the BAFTA winning single-drama Safe. Al Hunter Ashton passed away in 2007, aged 49.

Runaround opens with a stoic Martella on her beat whilst suffering with hayfever. The Background Information document issued to writers features a section about Beats, explaining that "the ground is split into 20 BEATS... grouped into fours, to make 5 HOME BEATS." An officer like Martella would "normally stay on the same HOME BEAT for two years."

Martella also explains in Runaround that whilst her grandfather was Italian, she doesn't speak a word of it. In the Characters Notes, Viv is detailed as being 22 years old and described as "an attractive, dark-haired girl who went into the police force purely because it is such a male-orientated society. While she is a person of few words, she has a pithy, Cockney wit. She is not particularly ambitious about the job. She'll do what she's asked to – but it is only a job, after all. She has no social ideals or political convictions; no driving sense of justice, or law and order. She happens to be on one side of the fence rather than the other. No one ever worries about Viv. She has an instinct for self-preservation which appears to cloak her, quite securely. Viv is single."

Witness Statements

Nula Conwell (W.P.C. Viv Martella)
'It wasn't until The Bill went into the half-hours that Martella really became a regular character; they must have been hedging their bets until then! By this point the ratings were doing very well and we all started to get recognised. Fame comes with the job and there are good bits about that and others that can be quite difficult. That comes with the territory when you are in a high profile programme and I mostly embraced it, because the people who wanted our autographs were the people who were watching us twice a week and without that audience we wouldn't have had a show. We had to be quite discreet when we went on holidays if we wanted privacy, so we would choose places where we thought the target audience might not go. Though I don't really remember anyone invading my privacy and people were mostly complimentary about the programme and it was a happy time for me.'

'Guest starring in *Runaround* was my old friend Linda Robson, who I had known since our days attending drama workshops with Anna Scher. Anna's children's theatre was a charity organisation, full of young people who liked doing drama and expressing themselves from within. Anna herself was a primary schoolteacher, who had set up a performing arts club after school. When it grew, we moved over to the council hall in Bentham Court and then to the theatre in Islington. It was a very different approach into the business than the traditional drama schools, where, with all due respect, the students are generally only able to attend because their parents have the money to be able to send them there, which wasn't the case for any of us who went to Anna Scher.'

'Anna always used to tell me that I would come into my own when I was much older, as she felt I am more of a character actress. I have always loved playing with accents and I do love to watch people and study their behaviour. It also becomes more exciting for me when I can play someone completely different, where I can hide under make-up and not look like I do in real life. An example of that was my first job after I left *The Bill*, playing Annie Wilkes in a theatre production of *Misery*, opposite Ray Lonnen. It was an enormous challenge, particularly as it was a two-hander, but a wonderful opportunity that I grasped with both hands. I worked with a voice coach and I looked much older with the costume and make-up. My husband actually cried when he first came to see it, because he couldn't believe that was his wife on stage. I feel really proud of that performance, especially as we only had three weeks to rehearse it before we opened. It was one of the finest pieces of work I've ever done and very liberating, I'd love to do something like that again.'

Derek Lister (Director)
'The editing process, as per any drama series, is that while you were shooting, the footage would go back to the cutting room and the editor would do an assembly cut. Then once I had done my five days, I would go in the next week and look at the rough assembly and give the editor my feedback. But I always shot in a way that is was fairly obvious what I wanted, like John Ford used to shoot his movies in a way where they could only go together one way. The editors didn't mind of course, because it made their life very easy!'

'Reviewing these episodes again has been a bit of a lesson to me, because at the time I saw *The Bill* as routine TV and quite often something to pay the mortgage. The idea that they are still coming out on DVD and the public are still enjoying them is lovely; I never in a million years would have anticipated that. I later returned to *The Bill* when Pat Sandys and Michael Simpson were producing and I became the senior director on the series. Pat and Michael were great to me, because I'm also a writer and when I was trying to move into films, they would give me a block on *The Bill* whenever I was broke. I'm a full-time writer now, which is thanks to them for funding me throughout the 1990s while I made that transition. I still miss them both.'

'I had been directing for a very long time and after 150 productions I was getting bored with the mechanics of directing and I hadn't been given anything that required any deep stylistic interpretation in a while. I also realised that as a writer, I'd no longer have to be on a street corner at 8:00 in the morning, trying to make a bad TV script work. Instead people were paying me to write what I wanted to write, which was great! Writing is a very different life, mostly for my poor wife who married a director, but is now married to someone who sits in a room with his eyes in front of the Mac all day. I'm also a producer and spend a lot of my time finding funding for my very ambitious scripts. I'm currently working with Simon Callow on a fun screenplay about what Orson Welles might have got up to whilst making *The Third Man*.'

John Challis (Ian Gore)

'Derek Lister had seen me in something else and asked me to come in and read for the part of Ian Gore, to see what I would be like playing a different kind of character. At this time in my career, I was being increasingly identified with Boycie, even though we were only making one Christmas special a year by this point. So I was delighted when I got the part, because I genuinely loved *The Bill* and I used to watch it a lot. It was a step up from *Dixon of Dock Green* and I thought it was terrific the way they got all those stories and subplots together and made it work in half an hour. I remember talking about *The Bill* with Nula Conwell when we worked together on *Only Fools*, which she couldn't be in for longer because she couldn't do both series, which was a shame for us. Nula is a very good actress and was excellent in *Runaround*.'

'Ian Gore was a fantastic character to play because he was going through a bad time. Bus drivers are very vulnerable, particularly at night, which is why he didn't want to go out again, but they weren't listening to him. There was no rehearsal for the scene in the depot where I smashed up the bus, I just had to get in there and do it. I suggested coming around the outside and smashing up the panelling, but I was only allowed to attack the windows - I think they were looking to mend the bus and get it back on the road again as soon as possible!'

'I was really looking forward to the scene where he drives the bus into someone's garden, as I thought I'd get to do that myself, but because it was quite complicated and they could only do it once, they had to use a stuntman who was insured and could get it right, particularly for the owners of the location. Though I didn't have a double for the scene where I jumped over a wall and legged it up the street. It was whilst I was running uphill that I suddenly felt a twang in the calf area and realised I'd pulled a muscle! I then had to try and disguise it, which I think I just about got away with. Whilst I felt sorry for Ian Gore, his behaviour did make me laugh. That last scene in particular was funny, when they spot him just standing there in a crowd. It wasn't resolved either, you never saw him get caught and banged up. That was the only thing I was disappointed about, I thought there was an ongoing story to be told there... But then I would think that!'

'I feel very lucky to have been part of *The Bill* and whilst I know fashions change, I never understood why ITV took it off. Earlier in my career, I was thrilled to play Sgt. Culshaw, a semi-regular in *Z Cars*, which was a smashing show and the first of the grittier police series. I don't know why there isn't an ongoing police drama on television anymore, because I think people are fascinated by the police and have a great affection and thankfulness for what they do. Of course, it all goes wrong sometimes, but we still rely on them and need them to help us feel secure. I'm a big fan of *Police Interceptors*, which also makes me laugh because of some of the things they have to deal with. I really admire the patience of the people doing that job, I don't know how they do it.'

Aidan Boulter (Floor Manager)

'I initially went to the London Nautical School in Waterloo, as did my brother, who was a very successful seaman. He got his master mariners ticket and went to serve with the Royal Fleet Auxiliary. I went in completely the opposite direction, because I was dismal at exams and couldn't cope with logarithms or anything like that. By sixteen, I didn't have a clue about what I wanted to do... My mother was an opera singer and member of the BBC Singers, as was my father, who for a very long time was one of the leads in the *Black and White Minstrel Show*, which I know isn't politically correct nowadays. My mum suggested I write to the stage manager of the local theatre in Richmond. I met a chap called Cyril Booth, who was the technical director of the Richmond Theatre. He needed casual staff for the pantomime that year, *Cinderella* starring Liz Fraser and Arthur Askey. In those days, pantomimes ran from early December until April, so we had a fantastic run and it was absolutely brilliant. I had great fun moving props and scenery and doing anything that needed doing. By the end of it, I thought, "This is what I want to do with my life..." I got a full-time job at the theatre and worked there from 1976 until 1979.'

'I was living in Teddington and I used to go to the pub next door to the Thames Studios, called The Tide End. I got to know a chap who drank in there called Ronnie Nicholas, who was the scenes chargehand for Thames Television. He became a bit of a friend, because obviously we were working in similar businesses. One day, I said, "Ronnie, how can I get a job in television?" He told me I should get a job as a floor manager. I didn't have the foggiest idea what a floor manager was, but he gave me a telephone number for the Head of Floor Managers. I had an interview with John Wayne, who asked me if I had any days off from the theatre? I worked six days a week at Richmond, but I had every Tuesday off. So John gave me a job as a freelance floor assistant on Tuesdays and the very first job I did was *The Benny Hill Show*! I just had to do fetch teas and coffees and help people with whatever they need help with. That gave me the opportunity to work my way around the site, which was massive. I think it covered over a square mile across three or four floors, so you could get some steps in during the day!'

'I did that job on and off for a year, just going in and doing a day here and there. Then in March 1979, John said they were looking to take on a new staff floor assistant. I had an interview and got the job! I worked at Teddington as a floor assistant for about five years, where I got to work on light entertainment shows like *The Morecambe and Wise Show* and *The Des O'Connor Show*. In the days before autocue, I used to write out Des' idiot boards, which were about three foot long and I had to write all of his lines on these boards in one-inch felt-tip pen. One particular live show, I had to write out about 90 of these cards, including one that said, "Good evening, my name is Des O'Connor!" The floor manager, Tony Tyrer, was getting quite nervous, because I was still writing out the cards as they were preparing to play the opening bars of the music... I got them finished just in time, though when I went to lift these 90 cards onto a huge steel trolley, I suddenly felt all woozy... Of course, I'd been breathing in the fumes from this felt tip pen for about four hours and was as high as a kite!'

'I also worked on dramas like *Mr. Palfrey of Westminster* and *Rumpole of the Bailey* as a floor assistant, before getting a nine-month trainee floor manager's job, which was fascinating because I was sent to work for every department in the studios. I worked on children's programmes like *Button Moon, Magpie, Rainbow* and *Rod, Jane and Freddy*. After my training, my first drama as a junior floor manager was on an afternoon soap opera called *Gems*. The lead director on this series was Mervyn Cumming, who became a mentor to me (and subsequently many years later to the author of this book). Before Mervyn became a director, he had been a floor manager at Yorkshire Television, so as a consequence he utterly understood what it was like for me coming in as the new boy. He was of tremendous help to me and made my job so much easier, he was ever so kind.'

'Over ten years later, we were reunited when I was working on *Family Affairs* as first assistant director. One day, a director didn't turn up for work. It turned out that he'd fallen out of bed on the wrong side and broke his arm on the radiator! As the clock was ticking, I started directing. When the producer arrived, she asked me what I thought I was doing... when I explained what had happened, she called in Mervyn, who was prepping for an upcoming block of episodes. We used to direct *Family Affairs* from the floor, but Mervyn went up to the gallery and said to me on talkback, "Aidan, I won't interfere because you are already directing from the floor, but if you need any help, I'm here."'

'We cracked on and by the end of the day we'd dragged the schedule back and caught up a bit. It put my mind at rest knowing that Mervyn was there. I did ask for one note, which was about passing a prop from one artist to another. They were doing it so quickly that it was difficult to follow on camera, so Merv quietly said, "Just ask them to slow it down..." It was such a simple note, but very effective and I was just so grateful to have him there. He was an angel.'

THE TRAP

Written by Jonathan Rich
Directed by Brian Farnham

Series 4: Episode 18
Broadcast: Thursday 15 September 1988

Case Narrative

Burnside sets a trap for an old antagonist, while an overheating CAD room sends Sergeant Penny into a crisis.

Regular Cast

Sgt. Cryer (Eric Richard), D.S. Roach (Tony Scannell), D.C Dashwood (Jon Iles), D.I. Burnside (Christopher Ellison), D.C. Carver (Mark Wingett), P.C. Melvin (Mark Powley), Insp. Frazer (Barbara Thorn), Sgt. Penny (Roger Leach), Ch. Insp. Conway (Ben Roberts), Chief Supt. Brownlow (Peter Ellis).

Guest Cast

Julian Pembridge (Robert Addie), Electrician (Julian Griffiths).

Production Team

Casting Director (Brian Wheeler), Title Music (Andy Pask, Charlie Morgan), Costume (Mandy Harper), Make Up Designer (Gilly Wakeford), Graphics (Ethan Ames), Videotape Editor (Terence E. Badham), Lighting (Peter Bower), Camera (Rolie Luker), Sound (Richard Bradford, Alan Lester), Production Buyer (Terry Allen), Location Manager (Sheila Loughrey), Floor Manager (Quenton Annis), Stage Manager (Nigel J. Wilson), Production Manager (Derek Cotty), Production Assistant (Carol Snook), Technical Adviser (Wilf Knight), Programme Associate (Valerie Farron), Series Script Editor (Kenneth Ware), Design (Robin Parker, David Richens), Executive Producer (Peter Cregeen), Producer (Michael Ferguson).

Observation Notes

The Trap (Production No: D4031, VTR No: THS/45266) was shot between Monday 18th and Friday 22nd July 1988. The scenes where CID set the trap with the van were shot in St James' Gardens, W11. The location used for the exterior of Julian Pembridge's home was 27 Penzance Street, Notting Hill, W11.

The Trap sees Sgt. Penny cause a power outage after spilling tea over his CAD console. The Background Information document gave a detailed description of the Computer Aided Despatch room: "Two officers sit at a console of VDUs. One of them is performing the function of the officer who used to sit at Comms Desk, the other is taking and sending messages to and from the 'Yard' – requests to deal with 999 calls, for example." The document also mentions that there was to be little paperwork seen in the CAD room as "the forms that require filling are available ON SCREEN and when filed they go on record at the central computer at HENDON." The document also explains that the CAD Sgt. "supervises the handling and distribution of incoming and outgoing information; and any action taken as a result of that information. He sits at another console, matching that of the PCs, so that he is aware at all times, from the screens in front of him, of exactly what the operators are reading, recording and filing through their computers. He can override any action they take, if necessary, through his own keyboard."

The character notes distributed to writers on the programme described Penny as being 43 years old and explain that he has returned to Sun Hill "after recovering, physically anyway, from a gunshot wound (stomach). He is a man frustrated by the need for regular medication and constant screening, anxious about his job future... a man who will become increasingly embittered and angry - not only with the Fates, but with those around him - as the uncertainty continues and absolute clearance and a return to pre-trauma normality eludes him. He is married to Wendy and in the past we have been aware of marital problems. He practises yoga, which he believes gives him "control of mind and body", and has been known to adopt the lotus position on a C.A.D. Room desk."

The Trap was the first of 24 episodes of *The Bill* written by Jonathan Rich between 1988-2009. His many writing credits include episodes of *Perfect Scoundrels, Stay Lucky, Wycliffe, London's Burning, Casualty, The Royal Today* and *Postman Pat*. Rich now works as a voiceover artist.

Witness Statements

Jonathan Rich (Writer)

'*The Trap* was within a whisker of not happening. If it hadn't happened, I would never have written for *The Bill*, nor would I have ever written for television. I had written a play called *Sell Out!* – a comedy that went to the Edinburgh Fringe Festival, before playing at the Latchmere Theatre in Battersea, which is now Theatre503. In December 1987, towards the end of the run, someone approached me at the interval and asked me if I was the writer... He introduced himself as John Kershaw, a script consultant from Thames TV. He asked me if I would like to write for *The Bill*... I was completely stunned!'

'Embarrassingly, I had never seen an episode of *The Bill*. I was aware of the hour-long episodes, but I had never watched a single second. I had heard lots of positive things about this gritty, earthy police procedural series, so I was very keen to write for it, even though I knew nothing about it at all. I thought I had been personally selected, but what I didn't know was that John Kershaw had been sent out to trawl around all the fringe theatres in London, looking for new writers to feed the very hungry machine of the new bi-weekly format of *The Bill*.'

'I was very lucky that the script editor I was dealing with was Ken Ware, who was Peter Cregeen's right-hand man. Ken looked like the unhealthiest man on the planet; he was a chain-smoker in his mid-fifties, built like a sparrow and always had his feet on the desk. He hated directors, and would snarl if one walked past his office door. Ken would get irate when, after delivering a script, the director would want to make changes to it. He used to say, "They've got a perfectly good blueprint, all they need to do is follow the instructions!" But Ken loved writers and it was thanks to him that *The Trap* happened.'

'At the time I was working as a reporter for the *Bookseller* magazine, so I had to phone in sick to be able to go to this first meeting at Barlby Road. I was given a set tour by a very bored secretary, who must have been doing it for the hundredth time. Then I had a chat with Ken, who gave you the impression that he was always in a bad mood. I was dreading him asking me who my favourite character was... I thought if I told him that I'd never seen the series, he'd tell me to get out of there! Thankfully he didn't and after giving me a copy of the series bible, he invited me to go away and come up with a storyline...'

'They needed writers who could come up with lots of ideas, because not every storyline submitted would be used. You could do anything, as long as it used the central characters and fitted the format of having a main "A" story, focused around a plausible crime, with a "B" story, both wrapped up in 24 and a half minutes. Anything could happen, it was wide open... the problem was, I had no idea what to write about!'

'I did all the standard research; I read Roger Graef's book *Talking Blues*, as well as the *Police Gazette* and all the crime pages in the newspaper. I thought if I pulled a story out of the tabloids, then the Police Adviser couldn't say, "That wouldn't happen." I sent in my first idea... and it was a "No". Second idea... "No". Third idea... "No". Fourth idea... "No". These were taking me a week at a time, because I was still doing the day job. I could see a pattern emerging; either my ideas weren't very *Bill*-like, or when I found one that was, Ken would say, "Sorry mate, we've just commissioned a similar story." Because I hadn't started right at the beginning, there was already a stack of episodes building up.'

'I'm not really an "ideas" writer and by the time I got to the end of my fifth submission, also a "No", I had no ideas left. I didn't know what to do and I ended up doing something very unlike me and I phoned Ken to tell him that I was sorry, but I'd run out of ideas... But then I asked, "Is there anything that you *need* to happen in the series?" That was a stupid question, because there was no storylining on *The Bill*, which was the agony and the ecstasy of the format. But I felt I needed guidance...'

'On the other end of the phone, I could hear the plume of smoke being blown out of Ken's mouth... what was he going to say? "That Roger Leach... he's got himself a fringe theatre engagement. We need to write him out for four weeks..." Ken absolutely hated theatre and couldn't understand why anyone would want to leave the joyous world of television. He then muttered, "the stupid bastard." I jumped in and said, "Ken, that's just what I need! Please let me write something to write him out for four weeks?" I thought as long as he hadn't said the same thing to somebody else (which did sometimes happen) and if I could just come up with the goods, it might get commissioned...'

'The characters were very well described in the bible and I knew that Sgt. Penny had a breakdown after being shot in the stomach. I also knew from visiting real police CAD rooms, that they all had notices telling the officers not to have drinks in there. I noticed that they were always overheated, because the old-school equipment in those days just generated masses of heat. I thought, "What if Penny loses it in the heat?" I always thought Penny looked rather febrile; he wasn't a wise Yoda figure like Sgt. Cryer, or the happy-go-lucky Sgt. Peters - Penny was a bit like the Ken Ware of the Sergeants, a bit snarly. I loved what each of those actors brought to their characters. Then the idea of Penny being sent off for counselling would allow Roger to be able to go off and do his play. In police terms, the idea of an officer going off for counselling at this time was quite a radical one, which is why I had Inspector Frazer make this suggestion. She was a character who went against the grain; a strong woman in a sea of men, who was more likely to say something different than old-school coppers like Brownlow and Conway.'

'When I met the cast, there was hardly anyone who I thought, "You're nothing like your character!" That was because they wanted very naturalistic actors, so the audience believed in these characters. A lot of the dialogue was written in a very neutral way, it was then the actors who would turn their lines into the way their characters talked, through their performances. That was the key to it for me; actors don't like to be told how to say a line in a script and the actors on *The Bill* knew how to to find the nuances in the text and bring it to life. I also couldn't resist giving them some funny dialogue, because all the serving officers I had met had quite dark senses of humour, which sometimes was the only thing that got them through a difficult job.'

'For the second storyline, I had read a little snippet about police entrapment, that Scotland Yard were looking into. I remember Wilf Knight saying that they didn't really do "corruption" storylines, but I said, "I'm not in favour of it, but I've just read it in the paper, so it does happen..." Then I said, "Burnside would do it!" That was the answer for anything "dodgy"; Burnside was the magic card we could play whenever we wanted to try and get anything through, because that character could, and would, do anything to get a result. I had my storyline and was commissioned to write my first TV script. I then had to do what Ken Ware used to call "joining the dots." I realised I needed a cliffhanger to the end the first part, and I was running out of plot. I knew it couldn't just be a villain and then I thought, "What if he's a solicitor?"'

'I blew all my savings and bought myself an Amstrad PC, with a dot matrix printer. I'd written the script in A4, but in order to format it before I could post it off, I had to manually shift the margins so that the text was centralised in a smaller widthed column, taking up only a half page. What I didn't realise, as I was moving everything across, was the shift key on an Amstrad was a repeating key... Suddenly the whole script shifted to the right-hand margin, creating a million pages of text only one character wide. After all the struggle of getting my first TV commission,

I yelled, "Fuck, it's gone!" My girlfriend at the time was Rachel Wright; a future script editor and story producer on *The Bill* (though never on my episodes). Rachel found me facedown in the carpet, pummelling the floor. Being much wiser than me, she asked, "Have you saved it? If you switch it off, it might go back to how it was..." With huge trepidation, I put the floppy disk back in and with huge relief; the script was back! I very carefully shifted the text back across, printed it off and posted it.'

'The moment you hand a script in, you think about how you should have written it differently. Your doubts grow and as soon as you don't hear anything, you think everyone is sat around in the office, doing rock-paper-scissors to see who is going to phone you up and tell you that they hate it. A week went by and I didn't hear anything. By the end of the second week, still nothing. I couldn't bear it any longer and so I phoned Ken to ask him if the script was OK. After the smoke cleared, he said, "Yeah, just made a few tweaks. It's in production." I said "But it's a first draft?!" I think he just cut out a few of my gags, because it was too long. That gave me completely the wrong impression about television writing, because I never had it as easy as that ever again!'

Wilf Knight (Technical Adviser)
Archive Witness Statement, recorded in February 1988.
'When an officer uses their Personal Radio (PR) to call up the station, it's very casual. They will start off by saying "Sierra Oscar, Sierra Oscar from 101." And then the Station will answer, "Go ahead Taff", because they know that 101 is Edwards or 643 is Ackland and so on. Then they'll say "Can you show me 'off watch' at 32 Commercial Road, just going in to deal with an old lady who's stuck in the toilet..." "Okay, Taff." Off he goes and 'off watch'. And then when he calls back, he'll come through to CAD and he'll say "Sierra Oscar from 101." "Yes, Taff?" "Show me back 'on watch', she pulled the chain and flushed herself away..." and off we go. Technically speaking, they'd go 'off beat'. You never switch your radio off, but you go 'off your beat'. Going into a house 'on your beat', you still have your radio on, but you've got to be on the road walking, to be 'on your beat'. But if Taffy came in here now and sat down to have a cup of coffee with me, his radio (his little parrot) would still be going. He'd turn it down, but it'd still be going and he'd keep it going all the time and he'd be half listening to me and half listening to the radio. And if he suddenly heard "101 from Sierra Oscar", he'd pick it up and say, "101, go ahead" and that'd be it.'

Sheila Loughrey (Location Manager)

'We used to make a block of two episodes in a six-week turnaround. In the first week I would read the script and find the locations. As a staff location manager, Thames gave me a leasehold company car. At Barlby Road, I remember being given a brand new BMW, which was red with a cream interior. I'll never forget taking Michael Ferguson on a recce on the first day I had that car. I said to Michael, "please be very careful, as I have only just picked this car up..." He said, "Of course I will, Sheila"... then he spilt his coffee all over the cream interior! I said, "I'm not clearing that up!" and I made him do it!

'Sometimes I would get in that car and just drive, with no idea how I was going to find a certain location. I used to say, "Please God, take the car somewhere undiscovered..." and I'd just drive around until I found somewhere worth stopping for a look. It was whilst driving around that I suddenly came across the really nice little square that we used in *The Trap*, which was on the borders of Notting Hill. Whilst it was close to a council estate, it was very nice and people like Sir Robin Day and Cynthia Lennon had houses on that square.'

'One good bit of advice I'd been told by a senior location manager during my training was that it could sometimes be sensible to do your recces in the evening, because if you were looking for a specific type of house, you'd have a much better chance of seeing inside people's houses when they had the lights on! And thank goodness for people who don't draw their curtains! I have been known to peer into people's living room windows or look through their letterboxes, even when I was looking for something grotty. If someone opened their front door, I would launch into my spiel, explain that I was looking for locations for *The Bill* and give them my card. I would know within 30 seconds if it was the right location or not. I still look through people's windows now out of habit and bemoan anyone with net curtains.'

'The cast were all really nice people, which was the beauty of the series at this time. I can't think of anyone who acted like a "star"; everyone just mucked in and we'd all sit in the pub together in the evenings. Larry Dann and Roger Leach were great guys and they were spot on for their roles. Jon Iles was also a gentleman and lovely to work with. Then you had the likes of Eric Richard, Trudie Goodwin, Mark Wingett, Nula Conwell, Ashley Gunstock... they were all brilliantly cast and lovely people. I also became good friends with Barbara Thorn, who I met when she came into Barlby Road for her interview. They used to have the tea and coffee station on the first floor, outside a row of offices that were filled with each production team, consisting of a director, floor manager, production assistant and location manager. I remember going out to the corridor and seeing this lovely blonde lady smiling at me. We got chatting and she explained she was being seen for the new Inspector. I asked her if she'd like a coffee and we had a lovely chat. I was living in Blackheath then and it turned out that Barbara was living down the road in Catford. I remember going back into the office and saying, "She seems really nice, I do hope she gets the part..." and she did of course!'

Barbara Thorn (Insp. Christine Frazer)

'Because there were only 22 of us playing regulars in the series, along with the fact that we were all so different, there was no envy between any of us about who we were playing. We all brought what we each had to our characters and then just delivered on the writing. And then of course, the writers started to get to know our personalities and write for us. I had my first big scene with Ben Roberts in *The Trap*, who I already knew because we went to Webber Douglas together. We didn't know that we had both been cast in *The Bill* until we first saw each other on the set, which was great, because we had known each other for so long and had been very good friends. So all the arguments we had as Frazer and Conway didn't really matter and we used to joke, "No I'm in charge!" We were having a blast and we knew we were very lucky!'

'Before I actually started filming, they sent me off to Notting Hill police station, where I used to go out with one of their patrols on weekends. It was so thrilling to be in a police car when the siren was going! I used to listen carefully to what the officers were saying and what was going on over the radio. My first introduction got exciting when suddenly, the officers I was with had to respond to an incident, where a man had been assaulted at a pub and hit over the head with a hammer. No sooner had they heard the words "the assailant has fled the scene", they had raced the car over there! The two policemen in the front told me to stay and look after the injured man, while they pursued the suspect... I could hardly look at his head, which was bleeding. Then a whole load of police cars screeched up. I had helped the injured man into the back of the police car and the officers who had just arrived said, "Who are you?" To which I replied, "Hello, I'm an actress and I'm going to be in *The Bill*..." I think they thought at first I was the one who had put the hammer in this poor man's head!'

'No matter how many police dramas we have seen on the telly, nothing compares to being that close and witnessing the stuff that happens. You cannot not respect what they do in the situations they have to put themselves in, it is their job and as an actor, you have to look like you have been doing that same job for the last 15 years when you are portraying it. I always found that side of *The Bill* hugely interesting, where we were very privileged as actors to be given the opportunities to work with the real officers, who also loved being part of it, it was a two-way thing. *The Bill* had an in-house police adviser called Wilf Knight, though I also made contact with another very good police adviser called Jackie Malton. If I had any questions, I could pick up the phone and speak to Jackie and ask her what she would do in a certain situation. As soon as I understood their police psyche, I knew how to approach the scenes I had to play. In real life, police officers are very cool and hugely understated about how they do the job.'

Chris Ellison (D.I. Frank Burnside)

'I didn't feel any pressure joining *The Bill,* because it was an ensemble piece. Whilst some of the actors were more well-known, there were no stars, which was how they wanted it. We were all young then. I was in my early 40s and had so much energy, I was flying. We were also very silly and I can't tell you how much Mark Wingett, Jon Iles, Tony Scannell and I used to laugh. It was always deadly serious when it came to the take of course, but in between we were always giggling and must have annoyed some of the directors! We used to sit around in cars on location and because we were wired up, all the sound men could hear was us laughing. We had a lot of fun, though we also worked extremely hard and it could be exhausting. We used to get called very early, because we were always chasing the daylight for filming. We were shooting two episodes a week at this point and then on the Saturday you'd read your next two scripts and learn those lines. It got more confusing later on when we started filming three or four episodes at a time, which was when they started segregating C.I.D. so we rarely worked with uniform. After some great early scenes together, I hardly ever worked with Eric later on, sadly.'

COMMUNITY RELATIONS
Written by Christopher Russell
Directed by Frank W. Smith

Series 4: Episode 19
Broadcast: Tuesday 20 September 1988

Case Narrative
Ramsey and Melvin use a garden shed as an observation post when they are tasked with keeping an eye on a lock-up garage.

Regular Cast
P.C. Ramsey (Nick Reding), P.C. Melvin (Mark Powley), Ch. Insp. Conway (Ben Roberts), Insp. Frazer (Barbara Thorn), P.C. Smith (Robert Hudson), P.C. Edwards (Colin Blumenau), Sgt. Peters (Larry Dann), W.P.C. Martella (Nula Conwell), W.P.C. Ackland (Trudie Goodwin).

Guest Cast
Mrs. Kirby (Joan Hooley), Mrs. Garwood (Maria Warner), Mr. Garwood (Jim Findley), Rogers (David Beale), Hopkins (John Channell Mills), Estelle Gambrill (Leila Bertrand), Marion Moxon (Shirley Dixon), Fleck (Roger Monk), Gomes (Leonard Hay), Abrahams (Trevor Harris), Dot Broadberry (Juli Castell), Alice Askew (Anthea Holloway), Shafique (Paul Anil), Kendry's Father (Tommy Eytle), Kendry's Brother (Roy Lee).

Uncredited Personnel
P.C. (Russell Brook), P.C. (Oscar Peck), Press Officer (Rosane Chapman), Accountants (Anne Shields, David Saggs), Librarian (Bridget Moore).

Production Team
Casting Director (Julian Oldfield), Title Music (Andy Pask, Charlie Morgan), Costume Designer (Dennis Griffith), Make Up Designer (Gilly Wakeford), Graphics (Jenni Phillips), Videotape Editor (John Sharland), Lighting (John O'Brien), Camera (Roy Easton), Sound (John Osborne, Bill Rawcliffe), Production Buyer (Terry Allen), Location Manager (Adam Kempton), Floor Manager (Tony Tyrer), Stage Manager (Diana Paskin), Production Manager (Derek Cotty), Production Assistant (Valerie Muncey Sanders), Technical Adviser (Wilf Knight), Programme Associate (Valerie Farron), Script Editor (Tim Vaughan), Series Script Editor (Kenneth Ware), Designers

(Robin Parker, Pam Blackwell), Executive Producer (Peter Cregeen), Producer (Michael Ferguson).

Observation Notes

Community Relations (Production No: D4028, VTR No: THS/45263) was shot between Monday 4th and Friday 8th July 1988.

The episode features the earliest mention of the infamous Jasmine Allen estate, when Yorkie radios the CAD Room to ask for urgent assistance on the estate, which would become synonymous with *The Bill* for the next 22 years.

The shots of Ch. Insp. Conway driving and listening to LBC Radio were filmed on the Hammersmith flyover. Ben Roberts then parks the car down Nigel Playfair Avenue, W6. The rest of Conway's scenes were shot in Hammersmith Town Hall, King Street, W6 9JU, with the residents' meeting being filmed in the Council Chamber. The Neo-Georgian style building was designed by Ernest Berry Webber and opened in 1939. An extension was added to the Grade II listed building in 1975, which was demolished in 2019 as part of significant redevelopment to the area.

Conway is described in the Character Notes as being 42 years old and "the man who runs Sun Hill. He is no politician – he has tried and failed at that game. He is, however, very much a thinking policeman and, even more so, a policeman's policeman – as conscious of the developing them/us problem as he is of the need for favourable PR. Never forgetting – occasionally reminding himself – that "real" police work begins and ends on the street (in amongst it), he is concerned that the flipside of the no-go mentality is a para-military force. 25 years service plus – he must do 30 years for retirement pension".

Conway's home life is also detailed and reveals that Conway will have driven to the meeting in *Community Relations* from his home in Chigwell in Essex and that he is "happily married to a hairdresser, with three children (two boys and one girl). One boy, aged 19, goes to Royal Holloway and Bedford New College, London University; one boy, aged 16, goes to the local comprehensive. One daughter, aged eight (possibly a mistake – or "try again for a girl"). Played MIAR rugby until 1973, when a knee injury forced him out. Now plays a bit of social squash." The Character Notes also explain that Conway was "a former member of the Round Table, is now out of it and into a Masonic Lodge", details which were dropped.

Witness Statements

Christopher Russell (Writer)

'*Community Relations* is an example of why the half-hour format of *The Bill* was a great job for a writer, because it gave a greater opportunity to focus on the main characters. It was an interesting idea to make Ken Melvin a born-again Christian, which is not something you might expect from a policeman. Thematically, I felt an interesting way to go was to have him in a confined space, being needled by somebody who obviously has completely opposite views. It was a way of exploring the characters and letting them propel the action in an understatedly dramatic way. It's a lot easier to create drama in a small space, because Melvin couldn't just walk away and they could have been interrupted at any moment. They also couldn't really thump each other in a shed, though they come close to trying.'

'I don't really have a favourite episode, but I liked the shape of *Community Relations* and Frank W. Smith's direction added some gravitas to it. This was also the episode where I came up with the name of the Jasmine Allen estate, although I can't take credit for the architecture of the edifice itself. This was in an era where public buildings and social housing were named after local councillors who had worked hard on their committees. Jasmine Allen was a lady who worked tirelessly for the impoverished and deserved to have something named after her, and a block of flats in *The Bill* seemed as good as anything. I also later came up with the name of Canley Fields, though I didn't realise when I wrote them that different writers would be featuring these places in the programme for the next 20 years.'

Mark Powley (P.C. Ken Melvin)

'Our producer, Richard Bramall, was a very charismatic Christian and had a lot of input into the development of the character of Ken, who was a very useful character to have knocking around, because his faith meant that he handled situations very differently to the other characters. Whilst later in my career I played a lot of villains, I actually think it is much easier playing a nice character, rather than a nasty one. Playing Ken meant that I generally got a nice reaction from the public and I even used to get letters inviting me around to their houses for dinner and meet their mothers!'

'*Community Relations* saw me working in a shed with a camera man, a sound man and Nick Reding. I used to knock around socially quite a lot with Nick, we had a lot of mutual friends in Camden and Shepherd's Bush. The fun in making *The Bill* was often down to the camera and sound boys, because a good crew could make any filming conditions a good laugh. And a lot of the jobs I got later in my career were from people who I'd worked with on *The Bill*, so there's a lot to be said for turning up on time, knowing your lines and getting on with people.'

'I remember when we moved to the half-hours, they asked me to be in the opening titles. They wanted a shot of Melvin chasing a suspect down the street, which they scheduled for the start of a day's filming. I thought it would just be a case of running 50 yards towards the camera outside the station after breakfast... But I was wrong and we filmed about ten takes of me running as hard as I could down from the bridge on the Golborne Road. After the eighth take, I threw all my breakfast up everywhere and felt like such a prat. Though as a whole, I look back very fondly at this time.'

Tim Vaughan (Script Editor)

'I think the idea for Melvin being a born-again Christian was developed by Richard Bramall, who was a very committed Christian, as well as being a nice guy and superb producer, who did his job very well. *Community Relations* was a very interesting episode, it still feels new and fresh and was always was one of my favourites of Chris' work. I didn't have to do a thing with this script when I first read it: all I had to do was to sit back and admire it. Sparing Chris' blushes, I think *Community Relations* is up there with some of the best television writing I've seen. It was hilarious in places, outrageous in others and tragic, as well as tense, in others.'

'The three locations in this story — the tedious machinations of the council committee, the two bored, antagonistic cops on observation duty, and the attack on Sun Hill nick following a death in custody — sort of summarise why *The Bill* was so good in those days: Along with the best writers on the show, Chris somehow managed to give us realistic and completely believable insights into every one of those places, and the characters in them, in the space of twenty one minutes of screen time. From a directorial point of view, considering how much variety is packed into the episode, I think *Community Relations* must have been very challenging, but Frank W. Smith, who I first met at Yorkshire Television, did a great job getting those performances and maintaining that energy. Again, you can't help but marvel at the speed at which the production had to go, to get all that material into the can in a matter of a few days.'

'Once a week at Barlby Road, and later in the Merton offices, the production got a visit from the "main man", Lloyd Shirley, Thames TV's controller of Drama. I think I only met Lloyd twice myself, but his reputation was huge and, inevitably, the producers were always slightly on edge before the great man arrived to review the two programmes that had been assembled the previous week. Lloyd Shirley was a giant in the industry and his track record was exemplary: a Canadian ex-advertising man who moved to London at the age of 25 in 1957, just two years after independent television was set up, back in the days when independent television was dubbed a "licence to print money". Lloyd's credits included, but were no means confined to, *Callan, Van Der Valk, The Sweeney,* and *Minder,* and he was a founder of Euston Films. Ken Ware often used to try to intimidate me by invoking him, describing Lloyd's "take no prisoners" attitude in hopes of making me believe that he and Lloyd were bosom pals (I can't believe they were, but to be fair to Ken, he had been a script editor on *Z Cars,* so he probably had some respect for that).'

'Whenever Lloyd was expected at Barlby Road, an air of febrile apprehension descended on the office. People smartened themselves up and strutted about the place pretending to be purposeful; coffee and biscuits appeared – unknown on any other working day – and younger producers especially had the jitters. Later on, our immediate boss, the great Executive Producer Michael Chapman, knew Lloyd Shirley of old and shared none of the other producers' anxiety about him, and I got the impression Michael thought him a confounded nuisance. Michael sometimes used to come out of those meetings in a kind of fury, usually muttering about Lloyd's constant habit of jingling loose change about in his pockets as he sat through a programme. Other producers sometimes complained that Lloyd hadn't paid the programme he was reviewing enough attention – but if Lloyd saw something he really didn't like, he'd tell you – and would do so in no uncertain terms.'

A DOG'S LIFE
Written by Graeme Curry
Directed by Brian Parker

Series 4: Episode 20
Broadcast: Thursday 22 September 1988

Case Narrative
Brownlow pressures Cryer into speeding up his fly-tipping investigation when he is tackled on the subject by a local councillor.

Regular Cast
Sgt. Cryer (Eric Richard), D.S. Roach (Tony Scannell), W.P.C. Ackland (Trudie Goodwin), P.C. Edwards (Colin Blumenau), P.C. Haynes (Eamonn Walker), P.C. Smith (Robert Hudson), W.P.C. Martella (Nula Conwell), P.C. Hollis (Jeff Stewart), D.C. Carver (Mark Wingett), P.C. Ramsey (Nick Reding), Ch. Supt. Brownlow (Peter Ellis).

Guest Cast
Archie Watts (Robert Putt), Callaghan (Ronald Herdman), Killby (Barry Woolgar), Mrs. Lane (Jacqueline Beatty), Mrs. Jacobs (Cleo Sylvestre), Mrs. Collins (Brenda Cavendish), Mr. Dixon (Leo Dove), Danny Collins (Danny Adams), Neville Jacobs (Michael Mascoll), John Dixon (Scott Lane), Walker (Paul Innocent).

Uncredited Personnel
P.C. Lovell (Derek Lyons), P.C. Bradley (Russell Brook).

Production Team
Stunt Arranger (Clive Curtis), Casting Director (Julia Lisney), Title Music (Andy Pask, Charlie Morgan), Costume Designer (Dennis Hogan), Make Up Designer (Gilly Wakeford), Graphics (Ethan Ames), Videotape Editor (Tom Kavanagh), Lighting (John O'Brien), Camera (Roy Easton), Sound (John Osborne, Alan Lester), Production Buyer (Trevor Young), Location Manager (Barry Beckett), Floor Manager (Debbie Vertue), Stage Manager (Marilyn Edwards), Production Manager (Derek Cotty), Production Assistant (Caroline Sutton), Technical Adviser (Wilf Knight), Programme Associate (Valerie Farron), Series Script Editor (Kenneth Ware), Designers (Robin Parker, Debbie Ashforth), Executive Producer (Peter Cregeen), Producer (Richard Bramall).

Observation Notes

A Dog's Life (Production No: D4033, VTR No: THS/45268) was shot between Monday 18th and Friday 22nd July 1988. The scene where Martella and Ramsey meet Archie Watts in the pub was filmed in The Carlton Tavern, 33 Carlton Vale, Maida Vale, NW6. Shortly before the historic pub was due to be announced as Grade II listed status, its owners demolished the building without permission. Westminster City Council ordered the owners to rebuild an exact facsimile of the pub "brick by brick." The recreated pub opened in April 2021.

The scene where Haynes arrests John Dixon was filmed on Andover Place, W9, to the rear of Dibdin House, North Maida Vale. The following scene with Haynes and Ackland apprehending Neville Jacobs at his flat was filmed at the nearby Torridon House, Randolph Gardens, W9.

A Dog's Life features a lengthy scene in the Collator's office. The Background Information document issued to writers features a section about the Collator's role: "His main work is to sift through all the Charge Sheets and the Station's Books, extracting useful and relevant information, which is transferred to microfilm at Scotland Yard." The guide does not name Hollis as the Collator, though perhaps planted the seed in the writers' imagination: "It could reasonably be the job sought after by the station's 'Federation' man, since it gives him more opportunities – being in the station all day – of finding the time to pursue 'Federation' issues. The section concludes that the collator's office is "normally used for relief parades." The document also notes "The parade room is now redundant and has fallen into disuse." The Collator's office was furnished with the following by the Designers and Stage Management: "a desk for Hollis and a spare unoccupied desk, Index drawers containing Collator's cards, a Microfax ('Microfish') machine, Police Federation information and computer print-outs on noticeboard."

Playing the PC in Archie Watts' interview scene is Derek Lyons; while appearing in the background of the other interview scene is long-term supporting artist Russell Brook. Brook's many TV credits include *Doctor Who, Blackadder Goes Forth, Hi-de-Hi, No Place Like Home* and *One Foot in the Grave*, as well as feature films including *Who Framed Roger Rabbit, Superman III, Krull, Chariots of Fire, Octopussy* and *Return of the Jedi*. He would later have several dialogue scenes and was credited for playing P.C. Bradley in the 1990 episode *Blue Murder*.

A Dog's Life was the only episode of *The Bill* written by Graeme Curry, whose breakthrough came after winning a writing competition with *Over the Moon*, a radio play about racism in football. This led to him penning a controversial *Doctor Who* story called *The Happiness Patrol*, where anyone feeling unhappy was liquidated. As well as *EastEnders*, Curry wrote radio plays *PS I Love You, The Mantle of the Earth* and for Radio 4's *Citizens* series. Graeme Curry passed away in 2019, aged 61.

Witness Statements

Diana Bramall (Widow of producer Richard Bramall)
'I would describe Richard as a people person; he had a very good moral compass and always saw the best in people. We met when I was 17 and he was 20, on a caravan holiday in Aldeburgh, Suffolk. I lived in West London and he lived in Twickenham, so it all worked out rather well! I went into nursing while Richard was training as an actor at the Guildhall. There had been no one in his family who had worked in the business; his parents were both very political and his father was Sir Ernest Ashley Bramall, a Labour M.P. and Leader of the Inner London Education Authority (ILEA). Richard had loved drama since school, though after graduating from the Guildhall, he got a teaching diploma at Trent Park, which he thought would be sensible just in case he couldn't make it in the business, which is what he really wanted to do.'

Richard Bramall (Producer)
Archive Witness Statement, written in November 1995
'I trained as an actor and qualified as a specialist teacher of Speech and Drama at London University. I worked in the theatre for over two years as a stage manager, an actor and stage director, before at the age of 23, I became one of four directors selected out of 1000 applicants to be trained by ATV as a television director. After a number of successful years as a staff director and producer at ATV, during which time I was responsible for directing such classics as *Hunters Walk, Love Story* and *The Foundation* and producing and directing ATV's children's drama output for two years, I went freelance.'

'As a freelance, I have directed and produced a wide range of mainstream drama for the BBC, ITV and the independent sector. I have been fortunate to direct everything from musicals through one-off plays and film series to soap operas. They have been period, stylised, modern and very contemporary. In 1988, with co-producer Michael Ferguson, I developed *The Bill* in its half-hour format for Thames TV, producing the first 18 months of the acclaimed half-hour series. After *The Bill*, I was commissioned by the BBC to revitalise the then ailing *EastEnders*. During my 18-months at the helm with my co-producer Corinne Hollingworth, the soap regained the number one slot in the ratings. I then produced two series of the BBC drama *Growing Pains*, starring Ray Brooks and Sharon Duce. I produced *Pigeon Summer*, a Channel 4 Schools drama, which was so successful that it was transmitted at Christmas on Network.'

'As an independent TV producer, I have had many years in team management and administration. I have been successful in motivating and envisioning a team. I am good at delegation and encouraging the best from people. I enjoy scheduling and finding and directing practical solutions to administrative problems. I am experienced in the selection and employment of staff, the setting of goals and the management of large budgets. I am a good team member and well used to leading people with both an artistic temperament and those from a more secure clerical, financial and administrative background. I am used to public presentations and supporting and representing institutions. My passion is for drama and my mission is to make drama more accessible to all. At certain times in my career I have specialised in children's drama, which I regard as a tremendous responsibility, in that one is nurturing the audiences of the future.'

Trudie Goodwin (W.P.C. June Ackland)
'My teaching qualification helped me get my Equity card, which was very important in those days. When I was starting off as an actress, I was writing thousands of letters and sending them off with my photograph. But when I explained that unfortunately I didn't have an Equity card, it meant that I wasn't being seen for auditions. Eventually, a friend told me not to tell anyone that I didn't have an Equity card, which started to get me auditions. Although, when I was asked what my number was, I felt I couldn't lie and I'd confess that I didn't have one... which meant I didn't get those jobs. It was when I was working behind the bar at the Greenwich Theatre that one of the actors showed me an advert for a job in Theatre in Education. He urged me to apply, because I had a teaching background as well as drama experience from college. But he also told me that I must not tell them

that I didn't have an Equity card, because he knew that they might have some spares...'

'One of the very first things they asked me in my interview was "Are you a member of Equity?" and I had to lie, which I hated doing. I then went through all the auditions, though to be honest I think they were more interested that I had a clean driving licence, rather than my acting ability. I got offered the job and then I came clean and explained I didn't have an Equity card... Thankfully, they told me they had an allocation and so I finally got my Equity card. I was a professional actress, yay! I worked for that company for two years and my clean driving licence meant I drove the van as we toured all over the country. It gave me fantastic experience and a really good discipline, because I learned that you can never be late and you can never not be on the ball. I played every sort of part under the sun and even did some directing as well, which stood me in really good stead for everything I did afterwards in my career.'

Robert Putt (Archie Watts)
'I hadn't seen *A Dog's Life* since it was first shown in 1988. Archie Watts was a loveable rogue and a nice part to play. Unusually, I didn't have to audition – the director, Brian Parker, knew my work and just cast me, which was lovely. The atmosphere was frenetic for the regular cast; I recall that Tony Scannell was doing pick-up scenes for various episodes where they had run out of time. I enjoyed working with Eric Richard again, who I first worked with years back in the theatre, which is my first love as an actor. Eric was lovely to me on *The Bill*; before I shot my first scene, he put his head around the door and said, "Be careful with him, he's bloody good!" It was really nice of him to welcome me to the set and make me feel comfortable. Another actor who always did that on *The Bill* was Graham Cole; a very nice chap who would bring the guest actors in to meet the regulars for a chat before they filmed their scenes. After Archie Watts, I came back to play an antiques dealer, an ex-policeman and a second-hand bookseller. And every time I came back, Graham Cole greeted me with a hug and made me feel part of it. *The Bill* was brilliant for all us jobbing actors who could pop in and out, playing different parts over the years. Every actor I know has been in *The Bill* – it was a very important programme that helped us all put bread on the table for our families. It was always a joy to work on.'

John Osborne (Sound)

'Working on so many episodes of *The Bill* and for so long, I was fortunate to work with some fantastic and distinguished directors. It was also very easy to spot them as well, because they just *looked* like the director, having such calmness about them, engaging with the whole crew. They appreciated that it was always a joint effort – there was no point in having a great shot if we can't hear the artists or see them. That said, if a silhouette was needed against a burnt out window in full sun, if the story warranted it they got it.'

'I do have a funny anecdote about one director, who was always so engrossed in his script and had such a warm voice when he spoke to you. He used to chew on his fingers when he spoke and sounded exactly like Rob Wilton ("I remember the day War broke out"), but knew exactly what he wanted... Mr Brian Parker. He'd arrive on a motorbike and carried a small brown leather briefcase with everything in it. He is actually responsible for one of my recording techniques, which I've used ever since, and that is of the 'clean of dialogue' background recording. Without getting too technical, *The Bill* was shot like film on single camera, so if you imagine recording a scene at 10am on a building site, which I had to do with Brian on *A Dog's Life,* there would obviously be lots of different noises across a few hours of recording. These noises could also be quite different, so editing the different takes together would be quite problematic. Having a separate recording of the noises, without the dialogue, gives the editors a better chance to smooth things over.'

'However, that same building site caused me to almost fall out with Brian in the same breath... The two brilliant equipment trolleys were not very building site friendly, so I chose to take all the sound gear off and build it in a bag, so we could easily walk around the site. When we had to move a few hundred feet to the next set-up, my bag made it easy for me to do, but my dear friend and colleague, the lighting director John O'Brien, hadn't done so. To be fair he had bigger monitors and a recorder, but I can remember watching him struggling over the rubble taking some time to get to where we were shooting. When I asked Brian Parker for a few seconds to put his advised FX mic out, he told my boom op Phil Colman to "stop faffing about". I was annoyed, as was Phil, so I made a label up saying "FAFF Kit", stuck it on my sound bag and put in front of him at every opportunity and tell Phil to stop faffing about.

Somewhat childish I know, but I was trying to make a point... Sadly, I don't think Brian ever realised, but it didn't really matter in the end as he was such a nice man, if a bit eccentric. I still work with Phil to this day, and when we reminisce about *The Bill* he still remembers that day and he often tells me to stop faffing about... I mean really!'

Derek Cotty (Production Manager)

'Around this time we also brought in Brian Heard as our second production manager, who like me had been a location manager on the hour-long series. Brian was a great mate of mine and our interaction was endless, because the key was to constantly make sure that both our teams were where they should be and that our handovers of cast from unit to unit went smoothly. We were also doing this within the constraints of union rules, which made our lives really quite difficult. I knew the rulebook very closely, but my attitude was you either wanted to read a book, or make programmes. We achieved what we did because at the end of the day, we had a team of people who wanted to do it, no matter what. Our busy production secretaries were splendid and kept the whole production together. Working with me was the brilliant Adele Steward, for whom I have the greatest admiration and has gone on to great things, recently working on the latest James Bond film.'

'As a very arrogant young man, I wanted to be a film producer, because I thought that was the top job. I got a job with a company called Green Park Productions, who used to make a lot of very successful documentary films. I was fortunate enough to get put on a picture called *The Shadow of Progress*, which was about international pollution and won multiple awards, including a Golden Rose. I was the assistant director and got to go around the world working on this film, which was sponsored by BP. The writer/director Derek Williams had identified areas of high pollution in the world, as well as some beautiful places as a contrast. My job first of all was to go to these places and explain what we were doing, and then set up our 12-week shoot. It was also very helpful for me because the film ran every afternoon on BBC Two, replacing the afternoon test card. There were only four of us on the titles, so it was a very apt way of promoting myself. I could say, "If you want to know what I've done, put on the box at 2 o'clock..." I worked as a freelancer for about ten years before I got a full-time job at Thames, where the Teddington Studios were only a short walk from where I lived along the river.'

TROUBLE & STRIFE
Written by Julian Jones
Directed by Brian Parker

Series 4: Episode 21
Broadcast: Tuesday 27 September 1988

Case Narrative
Ramsey and Haynes are called to a domestic – Mrs. Mancini has beaten up her husband with a motorbike chain.

Regular Cast
P.C. Haynes (Eamonn Walker), P.C. Ramsey (Nick Reding).

Guest Cast
Joanna Mancini (Kay Adshead), Antonio Mancini (Brian Capron), Wayne Mancini (Miles Eady), Grey-Haired Man (Lester White), Teenage Son (Ricardo Degruttola), Neighbour (Jo Warne).

Production Team
Stunt Arranger (Denise Ryan), Casting Director (Julia Lisney), Title Music (Andy Pask, Charlie Morgan), Costume Designer (Dennis Griffith), Make Up Designer (Gilly Wakeford), Graphics (Ethan Ames), Videotape Editor (Tom Kavanagh), Lighting (John O'Brien), Camera (Roy Easton), Sound (John Osborne, Alan Lester), Production Buyer (Trevor Young), Location Manager (Barry Beckett), Floor Manager (Debbie Vertue), Stage Manager (Marilyn Edwards), Production Manager (Derek Cotty), Production Assistant (Caroline Sutton), Technical Adviser (Wilf Knight), Programme Associate (Valerie Farron), Series Script Editor (Kenneth Ware), Designers (Robin Parker, Debbie Ashforth), Executive Producer (Peter Cregeen), Producer (Richard Bramall).

Observation Notes
Trouble & Strife (Production No: D4034, VTR No: THS/45269) was shot between Monday 25th and Friday 29th July 1988. The episode opens with a shot of Queen's Park train station in the distance as Eamonn Walker drives into Claremont Road, Queens Park, W9, where the entire episode was shot in and around No. 27. On the brick wall that Mrs Mancini drives the 1979 Alfa Romeo Sedan into, an advertising sign

reads "Cotty's Scrap Metals" – created by the design department, as a nod to production manager Derek Cotty.

Witness Statements

Marilyn Edwards (Stage Manager)
'We had been a small team when we were making the hour-long episodes, so it was very interesting when the crew expanded massively for the half-hours. Everything was doubled up, including the number of stage managers. I was initially concerned about how we would make two episodes in two weeks, but it worked really well. What I remember most vividly about *Trouble & Strife* is the house where most of the action takes place. When we first saw the location on the recce, we were absolutely appalled. Apart from the horrendous décor, it was the most chaotic and filthy house I'd ever been in. There was a thick layer of dog hair on top of all the mess and the dirt, in every single room. I also vividly remember that there was even dog poo on the stairs. We could not believe that there were people actually living there. Debbie Ashforth, the designer, didn't have much to do at all to make it look as awful as it did on camera. Nevertheless, it was actually a very enjoyable week, shooting this episode. Nick Reding and Eamonn Walker were good fun and Brian Capron and Kay Adshead were a delight to work with. They both relished playing such dreadful characters.'

Julian Jones (Writer)
'The Mancinis in *Trouble & Strife* were based on the parents of my first girlfriend. When my girlfriend used to call me on the landline, the cable was long enough that she could move it into the downstairs toilet under the stairs. She'd talk to me in there, while in the background all I could hear was shouting. She once looked out from under the stairs and said, "Oh my brother's in my dad's car and threatening to drive it into a wall... Hang on... Oh now my dad's hanging out of the window yelling at him and threatening to smash up his stuff." It was like getting a news report on the radio, although she would always tell me not to worry, because these kind of things happened all the time... I remember they had a Formica table in the kitchen where everyone ate, on which her parents used to write messages to each other on the table in felt tip... "Your meal is in the oven". They would do this even when they were in the house at the

same time, rather than talk to each other. Their relationship became the basis of *Trouble & Strife*, which I also married with what I'd learned from spending time with the real police, where often in situations like this, the woman finds it very difficult to prosecute the man. I wanted to explore how difficult it is for police officers to be thrown in between two people who love each other, but are also unfortunately hurting each other.'

'Peter Cregeen was a fantastic executive producer, who never seemed under pressure, although he must have been. He is such a lovely man and so well respected and good to work with. We got really good directors on *The Bill*, who were allowed to do their own thing, in the same way the writers could. That attracted people like Brian Parker, because it wasn't like going to do an episode of *EastEnders*, where the directors could see all the marks on the floor from where the previous team had done all those shots before. On *Trouble & Strife*, Brian Parker got to do something very different and effectively make a little movie in this house, which was a squat filled with Colombians! God knows who owned that house and because the location manager was dealing with the people who were squatting there, I think a blind eye might have been turned in terms of permissions. We chose that location because we needed a wall to crash the car into, though we had more problems arranging that with British Rail, because the wall belonged to them.'

'I loved the moment in the front room where Ramsey is dared by Wayne Mancini to take a shot on that little snooker table, covered in peanuts, and if he misses it, he's not a man... and of course he takes it on and misses! When I first started writing for *The Bill*, the character of Ramsey hadn't been cast yet. Whilst I was writing my first submission, I got a call from Julian Oldfield the casting director, who asked me if I would be interested in reading for Ramsey. I had originally trained to be an actor at RADA and after some initial work in the theatre, I did a *Play for Today*, a few episodes of *The Tripods*, and I played a skinhead in an episode of *The Gentle Touch*. By this time I had given up wanting to be an actor, though Julian was really keen about me coming in to read for Ramsey, who I knew from the breakdowns was a fantastic character. But Peter Cregeen had also given me this opportunity as a writer, so I contacted him and said I didn't know what to do. Peter is a very liberal and open man, who is never going to tell anyone what to do, but he gave me some really good advice and said that he could see me as Ramsey, but that would only be one part, whereas he felt I had a talent as a writer and could go on to have a career as one...'

Nick Reding (P.C. Pete Ramsey)

'I thought Ramsey was a prat when I read the first script and originally I intended to play him as a racist and wanted everyone would hate him. What I hadn't counted on was that the kids who watched the show loved him, so I had to backpedal on the idea of playing him as a racist really fast, especially when the writers had the brilliant idea of pairing me with Eamonn Walker, who I got on with so well from the get go. I think that helped create a really good partnership on screen. We became best mates and I later introduced Eamonn to his wife. We are still super close and he is doing tremendous work on *Chicago Fire* in the states. We started to get loads of scripts that centred around Haynes and Ramsey and perhaps the most memorable was *Trouble & Strife.*'

The episode opens with us arriving in a little panda car, which makes me realise now that we were making *The Bill* a really long time ago... This was the first episode where Ramsey and Haynes had to deal with the warring Mancini couple. We had a blast working with Brian Capron and Kay Adshead, who are both such lovely people. I remember whispering something rude into Brian's ear before I put his head down the toilet and pulled the chain! That house was a squat when we were filming in it and that was a nasty old toilet, though the props guys scrubbed it so clean that you could have eaten your dinner off it! The director Brian Parker was great fun too and encouraged us to be doing as much as we could for real, though you could never get away with the kind of stuff we did in this episode now. I remember being dropped through the ceiling for real, without a stunt double. Then the ceiling gave way and Eamonn caught me as I fell!'

Eamonn Walker (P.C. Malcolm Haynes)

'As an actor, I was just in learning mode at this time. I was concentrating on my single camera technique and what was fantastic was being able to share that experience with Nick Reding. We used to have a lot of conversations about the craft of being in front of the camera, because we were both taking our acting very seriously. We knew that *The Bill* was a stepping stone in the right direction for the type of actors we wanted to be. We used to share our dreams and aspirations with each other in between racing around the streets of London in our panda car. We had so much fun together... half of which, I can't tell you!'

'What I can tell you is *Trouble & Strife* was the funniest production I have ever been in. I was having so much fun, running around in a police uniform with my best mate, yelling at Kay Adshead racing up and down in that car, with Brian Capron throwing stuff at us out of the window. They couldn't use half of the takes, because we genuinely could not stop laughing. Brian Parker would be telling us to stop laughing while the props guys were picking all that stuff up and taking it back upstairs. Kay Adshead was amazing and I'll never forget her yelling "MANCINI!" at the top of her voice. You also have to realise that half of what she and Brian did in that opening scene wasn't in Julian Jones' fantastic script; they were just kicking off at each other. Nick and I were watching these two fantastic pros in awe and so a lot of the time the shock on our faces in those scenes is real! When you consider that we had no rehearsals or any plan before we arrived, the way we collaborated together was a big learning process for me. Many of my episodes of *The Bill* blend together, but thanks to Kay and Brian and the alchemy that Nick and I shared with them means *Trouble & Strife* has always stuck out for me.'

Tim Vaughan (Script Editor)

'There was a glorious anarchy about *The Bill* at this time, and Julian Jones' *Trouble & Strife* is an example of how experimental we were allowed to be in those days. I wasn't actually Julian's script editor at this time – Julian was under Ken Ware's supervision then, and after Ken left, Barbara Cox took him. But I somehow got to read Julian's script for *Trouble & Strife* – it surprises me now that Ken ever invited me to look at it, as he liked to keep his writers to himself. Anyway, Julian was always very careful and concise about his stage directions, and when I read the script, I came upon one of my favourite Julian Jones moments.... Describing the child's snooker table that Ramsey was to play on, Julian wrote that it should be "covered with salted peanuts". Julian is a lovely man and I remember how much his early episodes amazed me - I've never forgotten his very funny line in his next episode, *Here We Go Loopy Lou*, when the woman who has been pushed in the canal is asked to describe her attacker and she responds "He was definitely circumcised." I always enjoyed working with him and eventually we worked together on the episode *Dead Man's Boots*, where Eric Richard and Larry Dann gave marvellous performances.'

RUNNING LATE

Written by John Milne
Directed by Sharon Miller

Series 4: Episode 22
Broadcast: Thursday 29 September 1988

Case Narrative

CID have an area of the Dock Industrial Estate under observation after being tipped off about a robbery on a security van.

Regular Cast

Sgt. Cryer (Eric Richard), D.I. Burnside (Christopher Ellison), D.C. Carver (Mark Wingett), D.C Dashwood (Jon Iles), W.P.C. Brind (Kelly Lawrence), P.C. Smith (Robert Hudson), Insp. Frazer (Barbara Thorn), P.C. Edwards (Colin Blumenau), Ch. Supt. Brownlow (Peter Ellis), Sgt. Peters (Larry Dann), P.C. Frank (Ashley Gunstock), P.C. Stamp (Graham Cole).

Guest Cast

Sgt. Straw (Nigel Harrison), Jane Woods (Melissa Wilks), Helen Woods (Angela Catherall), Jim Woods (Robin Summers), Prisoner (Charles Baillie), Van Driver (Kraig Thornber).

Production Team

Stunt Arranger (Clive Curtis), Casting Director (Brian Wheeler), Title Music (Andy Pask, Charlie Morgan), Costume Designer (Jan Rowell), Make Up Designer (Gilly Wakeford), Graphics (Ethan Ames), Videotape Editor (Terence E. Badham), Lighting (Allen Harradine), Camera (Jamie Acton-Bond), Sound (Stan Lee, Alan Lester), Production Buyer (Terry Allen), Location Manager (Annie Glanfield), Floor Manager (Glynn Purcell), Stage Manager (Diana Paskin), Production Manager (Derek Cotty), Production Assistant (Cherry Crompton), Technical Adviser (Wilf Knight), Programme Associate (Valerie Farron), Assistant Script Editor (Barbara Cox), Series Script Editor (Kenneth Ware), Designers (Robin Parker, Pam Blackwell), Executive Producer (Peter Cregeen), Producer (Michael Ferguson).

Observation Notes

Running Late (Production No: D4036, VTR No: THS/45271) was shot between Monday 1st and Friday 5th August 1988. *Running Late* was the first of 20 episodes written by the late screenwriter and novelist John Milne, whose published novels include *London Fields, Tyro, Out of the Blue, Dead Birds, Shadow Play* and *Alive and Kicking*. Milne's many television credits include episodes of *Bergerac, Lovejoy, A Mind to Kill, Silent Witness, Wycliffe, Pie in the Sky, Waking the Dead, Taggart, Maisie Raine, Holby City* and *Heartbeat*.

The Dock Estate scenes in *Running Late*, where CID are expecting a security van raid, were shot on what is now known as the Wembley Stadium Industrial Estate. The Partscity building that CID are observing was demolished as part of the area's redevelopment and is now the Pink Car Park for Wembley Stadium, South Way, London HA9. The building on the opposite site of South Way, where Kelly Lawrence filmed her scene as W.P.C. Brind apprehended Jane Woods, still exists and is the rear of Access Self Storage, First Way, Wembley HA9. The later scene before the raid, where P.C. Frank says he has more to live for than D.C. Carver, was filmed at the end of Second Way, Wembley, HA9.

The vehicle used for Sgt. Straw's squad is a 1987 Freight Rover Sherpa 350, while Eric Richard is seen driving a 1984 Rover 2600 hatchback. This same vehicle was used in *The Bill* until the 1991 episode *The Chase*, where it was written off when P.C. Steve Loxton is involved in a POLAC.

The scenes where Brind and Yorkie visit the Woods family were filmed on Becklow Gardens on the White City Estate, W12. When they return to the station, Kelly Lawrence and Robert Hudson pass Karen England and Oscar Peck as they walk through the doors into the custody area, while Russell Brook and Vikki Gee-Dare can be seen in the charge room.

Insp. Frazer signs out the firearms at the back of the Front Office in *Running Late*. This room is described in the Background Information document: "PCs write up reports on this desk. Books on shelves – crime, etc. Hatch to PC behind counter. Duty State Book kept on desk. A few nearly dead plants on window-sill. Gun Cabinet. RT batteries."

Running Late also establishes that the four Sun Hill officers who hold a firearms 'pink card' are D.I. Burnside, Sgt. Cryer, D.C. Dashwood and P.C. Stamp. Graham Cole had now joined the series as a full-time cast member, with the Character Notes describing Stamp as 24 years old and "brought up in Slough, but chose The Met and London rather than the Thames Valley and his home town for the excitement of policework in the big city. He's not a man who thinks too much about his future – he's not looking for promotion. He enjoys life as a beat copper, and if climbing up the ladder meant taking him away from the sharp end of things, he wouldn't be interested. It's a view that can express itself in criticisms of his superior officers – sometimes over-conscientious. He can lack a certain tact and diplomacy when dealing with the public. It could be said that policing for him is more about making arrests than it is about protecting the community. Stamp has a girlfriend, with whom he shares a flat. He's a keen sportsman with an interest in the martial arts."

Witness Statements

Graham Cole OBE (P.C. Tony Stamp)

'I had been getting great feedback from the producers about all the little bits I'd been doing in the first few series, doing fight scenes or being naughty in the CAD room, whatever they'd wanted me to do. After lots of meetings and brainstorming ideas with the writers, I was excited when Tony Stamp was propelled into the regular cast in 1988 and I was signed up for a six-month contract! Though TV productions assume they are the only world for an actor, whereas I was constantly in and out of the West End doing musicals. So I'd had to explain to Julian Oldfield the casting director that I had just agreed to play the Lieutenant in a national tour of *Guys & Dolls*! Fortunately *The Bill* was able to get me out of the tour and the rest, as they say, is history.'

'It was absolutely crazy when we started making two episodes a week. One crew might be filming with uniform in the custody area, while another unit might be filming above us in CID. Sometimes we would hear the other crew say "Action" and start running our scene before our camera had rolled! We also rarely filmed the episodes in order, let alone our scenes, so you had to constantly think about your character's journey. Also with the half-hours came the question "Is *The Bill* a soap now?" I used to say, "Who cares when 18 million people are watching us?!" Our audience was a great gift and no matter which supermarket you walked in, everyone would come up to you, whether you were in Tesco or Waitrose... other stores are available!'

Eric Richard (Sgt. Bob Cryer)

'I think there was some concern when we made the split from the hour-long stories that we might be moving away from "proper drama" and going into "soap land". But that wasn't the case when we made the transition to the half-hours and there was absolutely no reason for me not to continue when the opportunity came along. My decision was simple, because I loved playing the part. I also loved the process of making *The Bill*, which was like a moving train that moved at a steady old lick. I also enjoyed the expansion of *The Bill* cast and the new members of the team who joined us in 1988 all had to jump on that moving train and get to work straight away. I loved the way we were working together as a team, which reminded me of my work with a small theatre company called Plaine's Plough, where a small band of us were on the road together for a few years and very much became a unit. All those ingredients made it the right decision for me.'

'In *Running Late,* we showed Sgt. Cryer carrying a gun. I am only an actor, I am not a gunsmith, nor am I the armourer. Other than the scenes where I am seen holding it, I never touched that gun, because it is not a toy to be played with. I am not a fan of guns; a friend invited me to try firing a shotgun at clay pigeons and I get nothing out of it, there is nothing about it that excites me. That all added to how I approached playing Sgt. Cryer and fed into what I felt *The Bill* excelled at during this period, which was telling stories about men and women who were going to work every day. On this particular day at work, Sgt. Cryer is issued with a gun, because he has the authority to use one. In every scene where Cryer had to point a gun at a suspect, my thought process in performance was, "If this goes wrong, you pull the trigger." And because you do that in character, it reads perfectly on screen, which helps bring the audience into that position and they then wonder what it must be like to be in that position.'

'One of my favourite encounters with a real police officer was in Northern Ireland, when I was doing some work for Ulster Television, covering a motorcycle race. I was talking to a bobby, who was being very kind about the programme. He explained that when the Police and Criminal Evidence Act came into Northern Ireland, their Inspector had said to the troops, "I'm not going to tell you how to use PACE, just watch *The Bill*..." Another encounter more recently was when I was doing some work in the garage and I nipped round to the supermarket. As I was getting back on the bike, a man came over to me and said, "Excuse me, Mr. Richard, I need to thank you because I have just done 21 years as a police sergeant because of you." That has happened on more than one occasion and I'm sure that all my mates from the programme have their own versions of that as well. That is quite a responsibility when you think about it and shows the impact *The Bill* had on people's careers!'

Wilf Knight (Technical Adviser)
Archive Witness Statement, recorded in February 1988.

'Sun Hill has a couple of pandas, which are Metros at the moment and are your day-to-day general purpose cars, they take people round the beat and go out on non-emergency calls. Sun Hill also has a straightforward Bedford Sherpa van, marked as a police vehicle. The job is becoming much more cost-conscious in the size of vehicles and the size of engine capacity. Sun Hill in theory is only six miles long by two miles wide and it's mostly built-up roads, so you don't need a car that is heavy and juicy. You need something light and fast to get round the streets. The old Area cars, the big 3.5 Rovers, are being replaced by Montegos. A patrol car is the Area car, which has one blue light on the top. They answer all the emergency calls, from suspects on premises, through to police under attack. And then you've got your traffic cars, which have two blue lights on, and they deal with all the traffic accidents on your particular ground, and there are BMW motorcycles to supplement them. The CID cars are Vauxhall Cavaliers (sometimes Carltons) and they do all the general CID work. A CID officer may use his own vehicle for what's called a mileage allowance, which is paid so much a mile for doing so many miles in his vehicle on the terms of wear and tear. If production needed a lot of vehicles, you would hire them from Godfrey Davies, in which case you'd have a variety of makes.'

Chris Ellison (D.I. Frank Burnside)

'Before Burnside I was always being cast as gangsters and awful characters. I remember playing a bank robber in an episode of *The Gentle Touch*, where two of us got cornered up an alley in South London, next to a Mecca bingo hall. I had a stocking mask on, which I wore a lot in those days, and I was using a baseball bat in a fight scene with Derek Thompson, where I fell against the double doors of this bingo hall. The doors flew open and I went crashing into the middle of a bingo session, with all these women who all turned round in unison, to see this man wearing a stocking mask and holding a baseball bat, and they all whispered "Ssshhhh!" That is a true story, which I reminded Derek Thompson about when I did a Christmas special of *Casualty*, which was the first time I'd seen him since filming that fight scene 40 years ago!'

THEY SAY WE'RE ROUGH
Written by Douglas Watkinson
Directed by Frank W. Smith

Series 4: Episode 23
Broadcast: Tuesday 4 October 1988

Case Narrative
Stolen Army surplus brings the military police to Sun Hill, while Hollis has to try and deal with two angry motorists.

Regular Cast
Sgt. Cryer (Eric Richard), D.S. Roach (Tony Scannell), D.C. Carver (Mark Wingett), Sgt. Peters (Larry Dann), Ch. Insp. Conway (Ben Roberts), P.C. Melvin (Mark Powley), W.P.C. Martella (Nula Conwell), P.C. Smith (Robert Hudson), P.C. Hollis (Jeff Stewart), W.P.C. Ackland (Trudie Goodwin).

Guest Cast
Davis (Robert Gary), Searle (Marcus Eyre), Armstrong (David Fielder), Frobisher (Paul M. Meston), Manners (Peter Jonfield), Gloria (Imogen Bain).

Production Team
Casting Director (Brian Wheeler), Title Music (Andy Pask, Charlie Morgan), Costume Designer (Dennis Griffith), Make Up Designer (Gilly Wakeford), Graphics (Ethan Ames), Videotape Editor (Terence E. Badham), Lighting (Christopher Davies), Camera (Chas Watts), Sound (Robert Newton, Alan Lester), Production Buyer (Sarah Prebble), Location Manager (Tom Adam), Floor Manager (David Cherrill), Stage Manager (Nigel J. Wilson), Production Manager (Derek Cotty), Production Assistant (Valerie Muncey Sanders), Technical Adviser (Wilf Knight), Programme Associate (Valerie Farron), Series Script Editor (Kenneth Ware), Designers (Robin Parker, Stuart McCarthy), Executive Producer (Peter Cregeen), Producer (Michael Ferguson).

Observation Notes
They Say We're Rough (Production No: D4039, VTR No: THS/45274) was shot between Monday 8th and Friday 12th August 1988. Appearing alongside Mark Powley and Derek Lyons in the opening locker room scene is Bryan Jacobs, who worked as a supporting artist on hundreds of episodes of *The Bill* until the series ended in 2010. Jacobs' other

television credits include *Dempsey and Makepeace, Eureka, Bluebell* and *The Comic Strip Presents*.

The army surplus store scenes were shot in 20 Station Terrace, NW10. This building has since been home to several restaurants and is situated on the corner of Dagmar Gardens, NW10. The then unoccupied building was redressed and would later appear as the café in *The Assassins*.

The traffic jam scenes were all filmed on Threshers Place, W11, beginning with Robert Hudson walking down from the adjoining Runcorn Place. The following scene where D.S. Roach tips off Gloria the traffic warden was filmed on Avondale Park Road, the other end of the L-shaped Threshers Place. Gloria is then joined by Local Intelligence Officer Reg Hollis. The Character Notes described Hollis as "one of life's persistent moaners. He enjoys the gossip round the station, true or false, and is always ready to initiate alarm and despondency, even where there is no justification. Reg is also a hypochondriac, suffering variously from headache, backache, and neckache; aside from an occasional stomachache, no doubt caused by food poisoning acquired in the nick's canteen. He is the station's Federation man – initially because no one else wanted the job. But he becomes even more of a pain in the neck when he begins to take the job very seriously. Not surprisingly, Hollis is a loner; neither popular or married."

Witness Statements

Nigel J. Wilson (Stage Manager)

'I remember *They Say We're Rough* as an example of a "day in the life" episode of *The Bill*, while the series was still settling into the half-hour format. I remember Frank W. Smith as a very hard-working and committed director, who went on to direct many episodes for us. This episode also showed Reg Hollis, despite the apparent clowning and the ever-present potential for comedy, as an effective working copper, who was not always appreciated. Jeff Stewart's work on the series was often underestimated; he played the scripts and more often than not instinctively hit the right dramatic notes along the way. As Conway, Ben Roberts gave new meaning to the adjective "irascible". *They Say We're Rough* also included a measured contribution from Tony Scannell – it was easy to take for granted how good an actor he was. Eric Richard was also at his best in this episode.'

Eric Richard (Sgt. Bob Cryer)

'The manner in which I go about my job means that I do as much research as I can. I spent a lot of time with real police officers, I went out in cars with them and I went out drinking with them. The other thing that I always do for every character I play is draw my own backstory. I decided that before he became a police officer, Bob Cryer would have been in the Army and served in Northern Ireland. During his service, he will have seen people killed and he knew the reality of taking someone's life. I also decided when I started playing Sgt. Cryer that because he had been in the military, and to show what a precise human being he was, his boots would always be shiny and his cap would never have any fingerprints on it. Similarly, I always had Cryer's sleeves rolled up to present him as a worker who always had his arms deep in the muck. This was based on my own experiences working in factories as a fifteen year old, where you didn't want to get your shirts mucky. As an actor, I feel all those tiny details and little touches help make your character's behaviour more natural. After conversations with the producers and the script editors, we started incorporating Cryer's army background into the stories, which led us to episodes like *They Say We're Rough.*'

Douglas Watkinson (Writer)

'I can't remember when I wasn't a writer; I've always done it. I went to drama school and when I realised I wasn't going to be much cop as an actor, I bit the bullet and started writing plays there, which were produced. Then I started hammering the BBC with half-hour plays, which were all the rage then. Eventually one got done, a two-hander called *Click* starring Ray Brooks and John Paul. Television was the medium for everyone and it was the one that I really, really loved and I went straight for it. While I was at drama school, I paid my way by working in Barnet police station for three years, which was very much like Sun Hill. I worked on 'late turn' Saturdays and Sundays on a switchboard that was so ancient, it was divided into two with a civilian on one side and a copper on the other. I learned so much that stood me in good stead for eventually writing police dramas, as well as script editing *Z Cars*, which I did for a couple of years once I'd got my foot in the door at the BBC.

'By the time *The Bill* came along, things were going well in my career and I was invited by Peter Cregeen to write an episode for the new half-hour format. I found it strange that all of a sudden they had turned the show from 50 minutes a week to two episodes of 30 minutes.

I was sent off with a brief, but found myself flailing in the dark at first, because I wasn't quite sure exactly what Peter wanted, except a script that was fast moving and funny. For me, the great key was Ken Ware, who was a very experienced, very clever and very skilled script editor. I think Ken was the great driving force behind *The Bill* at that time, which was then a very credible and believable police drama. What I liked mostly about that period of *The Bill* was that it was about the coppers in the station and the problems that they were coming across, and the crimes that they were dealing with, large or small. It only minimally went into their private lives then. Later I thought the series tended to let the private lives of the coppers take over most of the scripts; you were left wondering whether you were watching a soap opera or a police drama.'

'I don't personally have a military background, but my father went into the army, as did his brothers, and all the girls in the family went into the Royal Nursing Corps. My father was killed in Palestine, so I didn't really know him and that is perhaps why I was lucky to escape going into the military, because it was never mooted to me. My uncles didn't like the army, yet they wouldn't allow anyone to criticise it. It's like in my house, I'm the only one allowed to criticise the BBC; if anyone else does I go berserk! I can't see an episode of drama without wanting a memorable line and it's usually a back chatty, witty line. I can neither write an episode that doesn't have one in it, nor can I stand watching a drama if everyone's dialogue just rolls on without anybody making a quip. Though I was a bit ashamed watching back *They Say We're Rough*, as I had given my old friend Peter Jonfield, playing the military policeman, a line that I've used far too many times. When Sergeant Cryer tells him his name, he replies "Cryer? I'd have had that changed." That's the end of that line, I've flogged that one to death!'

'It took me about two weeks to write *They Say We're Rough*. I write quite slowly and I actually do most of it when I'm not facing a piece of paper. Since I was about five years old, I have always written in an A5 notebook, using an H2 pencil. I then transfer it to the computer. I've always done that and always will, because I can't actually communicate directly with the screen. So during the transferring of it from the paper to the screen, I edit and elaborate my own work as I go along. I've got a whole stack of those notebooks somewhere in my house, there must be over a hundred filled with my ideas written in scratchy old pencil. The late great Peter Terson used to send his scripts to the BBC handwritten in an old exercise book, written in biro. I don't think anyone dared ask him to use a typewriter, because they were absolutely superb scripts.'

Chas Watts (Camera)

'Thames management had decided that the first three series of *The Bill* should be filmed by the Outside Broadcast department, because the series was being shot on video and outside of the traditional studio set-up... Back at Teddington, we were envious of our friends from Hanworth, because up until that moment we had shot all the productions for the Drama department. As well as studio dramas like *Rumpole of the Bailey*, we were also honoured to be working with the likes of Morecambe and Wise, Tommy Cooper and Benny Hill. But we didn't become cameramen just to solely work in Studios 1, 2 and 3 at Teddington... we also wanted to see the world! So when we heard that *The Bill* was coming back to fill two half-hour slots a week on ITV in 1988, we wanted to shoot it. There was a perception that we wouldn't be able to work with the smaller, handheld cameras, which had proved easier to rig and use in the outside world, though they weren't specifically being used for handheld shooting and certainly not on drama productions. We enlisted the help of the Union, who were interested in supporting us, because they could see that more drama was being shot on video and away from the confines of the studio. The Drama department also helped make the change happen, because they were used to working with us. I was sorry for the Hanworth boys who had enjoyed working on *The Bill* – we had nothing against them at all, we just had to increase our drama output.'

'Jamie Acton-Bond, Roy Easton, Rolie Luker and I, along with our Teddington camera assistants, the Sound department and Lighting directors from Teddington, started work on the half-hours and we all enjoyed it immensely. Barlby Road was a great place to work; the canteen used for filming was the same one that the cast and crew ate our meals in. We'd tell the Blue unit that they'd have to be out soon, because we'd be shooting a scene in there soon, and they'd say, "Oh blimey, I've just ordered pudding!" There was lots of joking around; I got locked in the cells once, after the boys said, "Chas, we thought we'd do a shot from inside the cell looking out, what do you think..." Then I'd walk in and boom, the door was locked and they all went off for lunch! Then the shutter came down and a tray slid in with a solitary bun on it... We all loved being part of the gang on *The Bill*.'

It's not *Z Cars*, it's legendary writer Barry Appleton! Pictured in his uniform before he joined Special Branch. Barry wrote nine episodes in 1988 and 50 scripts in total for *The Bill* between 1984-1992. © Barry Appleton

Eamonn Walker, Kevin Lloyd and Mark Wingett play dice games with members of the production team as they await their call onto set. © Richard Marson

Kelly Lawrence and Nula Conwell ready for filming in the ladies' dressing room at Barlby Road. © Richard Marson

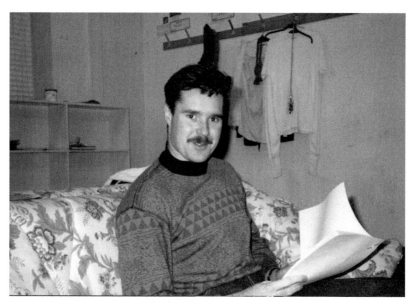

Robert Hudson reads through his script in the dressing room that all the male cast shared at Barlby Road. © Nigel J. Wilson

Nick Reding behind the scenes at Barlby Road. © Nigel J. Wilson

Director Paul Harrison (centre) discusses the car explosion in *Hold Fire* with stunt arranger Alf Joint. © Paul Harrison

Stunt performer Rod Woodruff being fitted with a flame retardant balaclava, ahead of filming the car explosion in *Hold Fire*. © Paul Harrison

Nick Reding as P.C. Pete Ramsey   Eamonn Walker as P.C. Malcolm Haynes

Mark Wingett as D.C. Jim Carver   Mark Powley as P.C. Ken Melvin

1988 location photos © Richard Marson

1988 costume photos of new recruits Chris Ellison and Ben Roberts.
Returning for duty: Roger Leach and Peter Ellis © Nigel J. Wilson

Producer Michael Ferguson, Nula Conwell, Trudie Goodwin, Roger Leach and Barbara Thorn relax at a *The Bill* charity match, while Eamonn Walker prepares to deliver one of his legendary "fast" bowls. © Nigel J. Wilson

Graham Cole and Robert Hudson in action at one of *The Bill* charity cricket matches organised by Larry Dann. © Nigel J. Wilson

Mark Wingett, Larry Dann, Mark Powley and Colin Blumenau take a shower after playing in one of *The Bill* charity cricket matches. © Nigel J. Wilson

Writer Julian Jones (right) amuses fellow writer Christopher Russell and his wife Christine at one of *The Bill* Christmas Parties. © Nigel J. Wilson

Eric Richard and Jon Iles relax after a day's filming. © Nigel J. Wilson

Nick Reding as an undercover Pete Ramsey during filming of
Chasing the Dragon in August 1988. © Nigel J. Wilson

Legendary camera operator Chas Watts mounts a camera and lighting rig
to one of the police Metros. © Chas Watts

The Bill gave opportunities to young directors like Niall Leonard, who directed seven episodes between 1988-1992. © Niall Leonard

Brookside director Terence Daw was invited by Peter Cregeen to direct *The Bill* in 1988, beginning with the episode *The Assassins*. © Terence Daw

Camera Operator Rolie Luker

Stage Manager Nigel J. Wilson

Location Manager Sheila Loughrey

Floor Manager Aidan Boulter

Stage Manager Greg Kinchin

Floor Manager Isboel Neil

Rebels *with* a cause... Polaroids from a caption competition © Nigel J. Wilson

Larry Dann, Kelly Lawrence and Chris Ellison join in the fun backstage.

Continuity Polaroids of Robert Hudson and Tony Scannell

Nick Reding falls victim to a prank!   Sound Supervisor Stan Lee

Polaroids © Nigel J. Wilson (1-5) and Stan Lee (6)

Richard Bramall directed the hour-long episode *Skipper* in 1987, before producing 30 episodes of *The Bill* between 1988-89. © Diana Bramall

BLUE FOR A BOY
Written by John Foster
Directed by Paul Harrison

Series 4: Episode 24
Broadcast: Thursday 6 October 1988

Case Narrative
A domestic argument provokes a clash between Burnside and Frazer –
and a crisis for Sun Hill.

Regular Cast
Sgt. Cryer (Eric Richard), D.I. Burnside (Christopher Ellison), Insp. Frazer
(Barbara Thorn), D.C Dashwood (Jon Iles), P.C. Edwards (Colin Blumenau),
W.P.C. Martella (Nula Conwell), Sgt. Peters (Larry Dann), P.C. Haynes
(Eamonn Walker), P.C. Frank (Ashley Gunstock), W.P.C. Ackland
(Trudie Goodwin), P.C. Melvin (Mark Powley), P.C. Stamp (Graham Cole).

Guest Cast
Brenda Knight (Gerry Cowper), Sam Rice (Robert Glenister), Martha Rice
(Joanna Phillips-Lane), Henshaw (Paul Bradley), Neighbour (Vicky Ogden),
Shopper (Christine Edmonds), Blonde Girl (Nadine Wilson).

Uncredited Personnel
Press Officer (Rosane Chapman), Secretaries (Tricia Boyden, Chris Iliffe),
Accountants (Anne Shields, David Saggs), Make Up Assistants
(Kate Rudlin, Adam Beck), Props Chargehand (Alex Bazylewicz).

Production Team
Stuntman (Stuart St. Paul), Casting Director (Julia Lisney), Title Music
(Andy Pask, Charlie Morgan), Costume Designer (Dennis Hogan),
Make Up Designer (Gilly Wakeford), Graphics (Ethan Ames), Videotape
Editor (Tom Kavanagh), Lighting (Peter Bower), Camera (Rolie Luker),
Sound (Richard Bradford, Paul Langwade), Production Buyer (Trevor Young),
Location Manager (Susan Bradley), Floor Manager (Tony Boyle), Stage
Manager (Susan Shattock), Production Manager (Derek Cotty),
Production Assistant (Janet Mullins), Technical Adviser (Wilf Knight),
Programme Associate (Valerie Farron), Script Editor (Tim Vaughan),
Series Script Editor (Kenneth Ware), Designers (Robin Parker,
Neil Thompson), Executive Producer (Peter Cregeen), Producer
(Richard Bramall).

Observation Notes

Blue for a Boy (Production No: D4037, VTR No: THS/45272) was shot between Monday 1st and Friday 5th August 1988. The opening scenes with Edwards and Martella walking the beat were filmed on Neville Close, NW6. They then discover "Grandad" outside Merle Court on Carlton Vale, NW6. The following scene where they break up the row between Brenda Knight and Sam Rice begins on Peel Precinct, before Colin Blumenau and Nula Conwell continue onto the Carlton Vale end of Neville Close, NW6. This area has since been significantly redeveloped.

The scenes where Haynes and Frank watch a lady undressing down Pope Road were filmed on Stoneleigh Street, Notting Hill, W11. The real street sign was covered by a fake one created by the design department.

The scene where Dashwood meets Mr Dewhurst was filmed on Station Terrace, Kensal Rise, NW6. Dashwood then discovers that Brenda Knight's baby has been snatched on the adjoining Chamberlayne Road.

The scene where Dashwood investigates Brenda Knight's flat was filmed on the South Kilburn Estate, Rupert Road, NW6. The building seen in the background is Winterleys House. This area has also been redeveloped.

The scene where Stamp stops Henshaw was filmed on Sutton Way, W10.

The sequence where Burnside, Dashwood, Martella, Haynes and Edwards investigate Rice's home was shot on the Heath Road, Wandsworth, SW8.

The scene where Ackland finds Sam Rice was filmed at Hammersmith Hospital, Du Cane Road, W12.

Witness Statements

Sue Shattock (Stage Manager)

'I had been working as an assistant stage manager at Thames for three years, on lots of programmes like *King and Castle* and *Ladies in Charge*. I then got the job on *The Bill*, and *Blue for a Boy* was the first programme where I hit the ground running as a stage manager, which was really exciting. I liked how fast-paced the production was; it wasn't like working in the theatre, where you had the same script every night. On *The Bill*, you prepped each scene and after it was in the can, you put those pages in the bin and moved on. That was the beauty of it for me and once we had finished each scene, I wouldn't even remember it – it was onto the next set-up. Whilst I would only be working on one episode at a time, there was always another unit working around us and so I was always meeting different members of the cast. One of the jobs stage management did whenever we could was sit with the actors in the make-up van and go through their lines with them. We also used to have amazing afternoon teas, with sandwiches, cakes and doughnuts. It was a great show to work on and to be part of such a close-knit team. All the stage managers shared a room together and people like Marilyn Edwards, Greg Kinchin and Nigel Wilson were all well established on *The Bill* and very supportive to me. I also liked working with Paul Harrison, the good looking director of *Blue for a Boy*.'

Paul Harrison (Director)

'From a director's point of view, the thing that I loved most about *The Bill* was the restrictions on the writers, that nothing could happen until the police arrived, we could only see their point of view. That was a unique selling point and as a director you had to engineer your show around that rule. I loved that we would never see robbers planning or domestic situations in their home lives, which stopped *The Bill* turning into a soap. The biggest challenge for me with *Blue for a Boy* was that we see Robert Glenister driving the car away from the scene of the crime, so we know it can only be him. Where we had to build the tension was in making the audience wonder what he had done with the child? We also had that scene with Jon Iles and the pram, which was a nod to *Battleship Potemkin*. If only I'd had a staircase! Imagine if we'd been allowed music in that scene, we could have really ramped up the tension, because it was quite hard to cut that sequence without it.'

'My favourite shot in *Blue for a Boy* is when the police pull up behind Paul Bradley's car. Graham Cole gets out of the car and the camera goes with him, in one shot. I remember the prop guy saying I couldn't do that and I said, "I want that shot, take the back door off the car." And that's what we did! Rolie was in the back with the camera and when the car came to a halt, we were standing in a doorway and the camera assistant ran out, grabbed the camera from Rolie and carried on the shot, it worked really well.'

'*Blue for a Boy* opens with Colin Blumenau and Nula Conwell walking the beat through an estate. When we were doing a recce of that location, we were standing in a line and somebody above emptied a urinal off a balcony from one of the tower blocks. Our script supervisor was Janet Mullins, who was very tall and elegant, a beautiful woman. Because Janet was taller than everybody else, she was like a lightning rod and the contents of this urinal landed right into her script, it was shocking. It got worse on that estate because when we were filming that sequence, it was a very hot day and I was really ill. I had a bucket beside me and I was literally throwing up before saying "Action!" all morning. Then when the catering guys came out to set up a table for teas and coffees, they put it down over this big piece of cardboard on the pavement. This little old lady came out and said, "I wouldn't put that there... Have a look underneath." They lifted up the corner of the cardboard and there was blood all over the pavement. "That's where he landed yesterday! They're always bloody jumping off this building!" Well that was me back in the bucket!'

'I've always been a storyteller and I had an interesting childhood. When I was four years old, my parents came home one day to find that I'd cut all my mum's mint in the garden, laid it all on the wall and flogged the lot for three farthings and a ha'penny. Mum worked in musical theatre and Dad was a prop man who started at the BBC and worked on the very first broadcast. Then after the Second World War, he went back to the BBC and progressed to doing the title sequence for *Andy Pandy*, turning the letters! He was then asked to help set up Elstree Studios with Bill Ward and Lew Grade.'

'Dad couldn't take me to Elstree until I was twelve, because of insurance. As soon as I was allowed, he took me to see a promotion for *The Golden Shot* being made, with Jackie Rae who presented the first series. Dad had been to Holland to see the original version of the show, to decide whether it was viable for our studio or not. Basically *The Golden Shot* was a crossbow bolt attached to the front of a studio camera and the cameraman operated the bolt from instructions by the contestant and shot an apple off a dummy's head. I got there in the morning and I sat there and watched them rehearse it over and over again. It was a 90 second promo and it was broadcast live! I was told to sit very quietly and suddenly the studio lights went down and it went out live, then 90 seconds later it was off and everybody cheered and clapped and jumped up and down. I just remember thinking "This is bonkers, I want to do this..."

Tim Vaughan (Script Editor)

'Being a script editor could sometimes be quite taxing. I once remarked that it was a bit like delivering a baby: with an easy birth you only have to give the mum some gas and air, sometimes an epidural... and then other times it's a caesarean. It wasn't taxing in the case of my three closest writers, Chris Russell, J.C. Wilsher and Peter J Hammond. When they came in for a meeting, we used to just sit and talk creatively about things that they wanted to write about. Sometimes they'd have read something in the paper or seen a documentary on telly that inspired them — and they'd go away and come back with something loosely based on what we'd been talking about. It was a good creative collaboration.'

'John Foster came with a brilliant reputation, and I had the pleasure of working with him a second time, on *A Death in the Family* — although due to some error or other, I never got credited as script editor on that one, despite having worked quite hard with John. *Blue for a Boy* resembled *A Death in the Family* in that both stories were about children - a missing child and a dead child, respectively. *Blue for a Boy* is a favourite of mine, partly due to the superb performance of Nula Conwell. I always loved her work on the show: her character as Martella comes over as guarded - sceptical and slightly dead-pan, which has always struck me as completely believable, but you know that, however indifferent Martella may appear, she has a heart, and is thoroughly committed to the job of policing.'

'I first met Paul Harrison in 1979, when I walked onto a TV set for the first time, on a series called *The Masterspy*, starring Bill Franklyn and Jenny Lee Wright. I remember my first day, I was walking down the long corridor at Elstree Studios, and Lew Grade noticed me and came over. I recognised him immediately. He said, "Excuse me, do I know you?" I told him who I was and he said, "Nice to meet you, Tim. My name's Lew Grade, and I run this place. Now, I want you to know that any time you've got an idea for a programme, just come and see me, my door is always open." I thought I'd struck gold... Until a couple of weeks later, when Grade saw me again, came over, and delivered exactly the same spiel as he had before! But nevertheless, having come from the confines of BBC Radio, it was still a joy to be working at ITV.'

CHASING THE DRAGON

Written by Brendan J. Cassin

Directed by Frank W. Smith

Series 4: Episode 25

Broadcast: Tuesday 11 October 1988

Viewing Figures: 11.10m

ITV Chart Position: 9

Case Narrative

In the course of closing down a drugs ring, Haynes and Ramsey are involved in a car crash that seriously injures a child.

Regular Cast

P.C. Haynes (Eamonn Walker), P.C. Ramsey (Nick Reding), D.S. Roach (Tony Scannell), D.C. Carver (Mark Wingett), D.C Dashwood (Jon Iles), Ch. Insp. Conway (Ben Roberts), Sgt. Peters (Larry Dann), Sgt. Penny (Roger Leach), W.P.C. Brind (Kelly Lawrence), P.C. Melvin (Mark Powley), W.P.C. Martella (Nula Conwell), P.C. Hollis (Jeff Stewart).

Guest Cast

Ace (Robert Phillips), Squire (Terry Sue-Patt), Alec (David Doyle), Kristos (Kenneth Coombs), Liz (Norma Dunbar), Eileen (Jean Hastings), Mrs. Carter (Gabrielle Cowburn), Doctor (Jenny Robbins), Pirate (Shango Baku), Monica (Cindy Milo).

Production Team

Stunt Arranger (Roy Alon), Casting Director (Brian Wheeler), Title Music (Andy Pask, Charlie Morgan), Costume (Allard Tobin, Dennis Griffith), Make Up Designer (Gilly Wakeford), Graphics (Ethan Ames), Videotape Editor (Terence E. Badham), Lighting (Christopher Davies), Camera (Chas Watts), Sound (Robert Newton, Paul Langwade), Production Buyer (Sarah Prebble), Location Manager (Tom Adam), Floor Manager (David Cherrill), Stage Manager (Nigel J. Wilson), Production Manager (Derek Cotty), Production Assistant (Valerie Muncey Sanders), Technical Adviser (Wilf Knight), Programme Associate (Valerie Farron), Series Script Editor (Kenneth Ware), Designers (Robin Parker, Stuart McCarthy), Executive Producer (Peter Cregeen), Producer (Michael Ferguson).

Observation Notes

Chasing the Dragon (Production No: D4040, VTR No: THS/45275) was shot between Monday 15th and Friday 19th August 1988. The opening shot features a train pulling into Marylebone Station. The camera then pans down onto the Lisson Green estate. The drug dealing outside the garages was filmed outside Lavendon House, Paveley Street, NW8. Roach observes the drug deal from the walkway connecting to Horwood House, which has since been demolished. The Lisson estate was built in the early 1970s and has since been regenerated, with some of the garages converted into flats. The music heard on the car radio during this sequence on original broadcast was The Police track "Roxanne". For subsequent repeats and UK DVD releases, this track was replaced by another track by The Police, "Message in a Bottle".

The following scene with Haynes and Ramsey in the panda car was filmed on Capland Street at the junction of Frampton Street, NW8. The chase continues down Capland Street. Eamonn Walker then drives the panda car down the adjoining Orchardson Street. The chase concludes outside what was Bledlow House, which has since been redeveloped and is now 53 Capland Street. The ramp that Haynes' suspect runs up to escape used to lead onto the adjoining Salisbury Street, but has since been demolished.

The scene where Brind and Melvin attend the dispute at the laundrette was filmed at 71 Barlby Road, W10, just over the road from the Unit Base. The building has since been converted into a convenience store.

The scene with Haynes and Ramsey undercover in plain clothes begins on the footbridge that crosses the Grand Union Canal and leads to Tickford House, Casey Court, NW8. The rest of this sequence was filmed on the Lisson Green estate, which has since been significantly redeveloped.

On *Chasing the Dragon*, Eamonn Walker became only the second actor, after Eric Richard, to top the credits of the bi-weekly episodes twice, having first done so in *Trouble & Strife*. The Character Notes distributed to writers in 1988 describe his character of Malcolm Haynes as being 28 years old and "born-n-raised in the Notting Hill/Ladbroke Grove area of West London and has pounded the bricks in some of the more volatile of the Met's divisions, a career that includes having been stationed at Brixton during the Summer of '81. Haynes is street-smart in a way only those who've been at the sharp end and survived can be... and has a sense of humour that matches the colour of his skin."

Witness Statements

Peter Cregeen (Executive Producer)

'For the bi-weekly episodes, Ken Ware became our series script editor. I had worked with Ken before, as had our Head of Drama, Lloyd Shirley, who was very keen for Ken to join the show. Ken was probably the best script editor I've ever known. Apart from being a very good writer himself, he had a wealth of experience and really loved writers; although he was very intolerant of any who he thought were messing around and not getting the job done. Some script editors would give hundreds of notes all over the place, whereas Ken was much like the best directors in that regard and would find a way of giving the minimum of notes to the maximum effect. He knew how to give a specific note that would trigger off other thoughts in the writer's mind.'

'When we were looking for new writers, we we put the word out that nobody had ever needed to have written for television before, but if they thought they could write for *The Bill*, then we'd see them. The only condition was that they had to come in with an idea, there was no point in them just coming in for a chat. We could tell them who all the characters were, but they had to come up with something that they wanted to write. Then if we thought they had some talent and potential, we would put them in touch with the police, which was made possible by our police advisor, Wilf Knight, who was great friends with the then commissioner, Peter Imbert. After the writer had gone and done some research, they would come back and pitch the idea for the script to us. We would then either say, "Sorry, try again" or "That's a great idea, go ahead and write it." We also told new writers not to worry about how we were going to do it, just write it and leave that to us...'

'That was based on a philosophy which Tony Garnet had used earlier with *Play For Today*, where he introduced writers like Jimmy O'Connor, who became quite a successful writer under Tony. Jimmy's claim to fame was that he had been on a raid on a stall in London, where a man called George Ambridge was shot and killed. Jimmy was put on trial for murder, at a time when people were still being executed in this country. He got reprieved, not long before he was due to be hanged, and subsequently married his lawyer, Nemone Lethbridge, which is a story in itself! A few years later, Tony Garnet picked him up as a writer and encouraged him and told him, "You just write what you like and we'll find a way of doing it..." We adopted a similar philosophy when we moved to the bi-weekly series of *The Bill*, which was how we found writers like Julian Jones and Brendan J. Cassin. Then quite often what happened was the new writers would hinge onto certain characters that they had liked watching. Brendan wrote around Eamonn Walker, who gave an absolutely terrific performance in *Chasing the Dragon*, which showcased the great double act he had formed with Nick Reding.'

Derek Cotty (Production Manager)

'When *The Bill* was based in the East End, our early stories were all based around robberies and general thuggery, which reflected that these tough coppers and tough criminals had all probably been at school together. The Notting Hill area had different issues from the East End. As a production, we were imposing ourselves on a new set of policemen, whose main problem in those days was drugs, which was a very serious issue. The writers started to reflect the tone of this new terrain in stories like *Chasing the Dragon*, which showed how drugs were much more prominent on these streets. We also tried very deliberately in the half-hours not to have too much violence, because it wasn't as if the real police get beaten up every week. Also it saved Make-up from applying cut lips every week, especially when the episodes might be shown out of sequence. Though this episode showed that we had not lost our desire to do car chases every so often. We were working at the same time as *London's Burning*, a programme enjoying similar success for London Weekend. I was regularly in touch with their production team, to make sure we didn't go on each other's patches, as they were always burning stuff down while we were blowing stuff up! We had a good relationship with them - in fact I once organised a prank on two of their cast members and sent a couple of our coppers down their to arrest them and bring them back to Sun Hill - they thought they'd been nicked for real!'

Chas Watts (Camera)

'The recces were great on *The Bill*, everyone would work together and come up with ideas. A sound recordist might make a brilliant suggestion for where the camera could go, which would also be better for their recording. The designer might also ask us to avoid shooting a street sign, because they might have ran out of East London signs that they'd made to hide the fact we were filming in Shepherd's Bush. Another important part of the recces was to work out where would be "safe" for the rest of the crew to stand, because I liked to pan around and show as much of the world that these officers were policing as I could. Jamie Acton-Bond, Rolie Luker, Roy Easton and I each developed our own styles of shooting. I always wanted to achieve an energy with the camera movement and I brought it to every episode that demanded it.'

'I enjoyed *Chasing the Dragon*; it had a good pace and was well directed by Frank W. Smith, who was an excellent director. Filming in the Metros was a joke, because there wasn't room for any of us! We asked the car boys to strengthen the parcel shelves in the Metros, because they would have bent from the weight of the camera. They added a chipboard surface with a hole in, so we could add a "quick fit" pan and tilt head on. Then we would set up the shot and go for a cup of tea, while the artists would go for a drive around the block. Sometimes they would come back and the camera had been knocked and was shooting diagonally, so we'd have to go again. The chase sequence finished with that poor girl with the skipping rope being run over. The people in the tower block on the estate above where we shot the crash, started yelling and chucking stuff at us, which was very trying. Our floor manager, David Cherrill, got fed up with all this stuff raining down on us. He got the megaphone and announced in his rather posh voice that they might be interested in the episode of *EastEnders* that was about to begin... We thought he was going to get murdered, but it worked and in they all went!'

'Whether on foot or in cars, the chases were all good fun to do, though very hectic and energy sapping. Working as my camera assistant on a couple of episodes was Simon Harding, who was a strapping lad and very fit. Simon decided he was going to look after me and would not allow me to pick the camera up or put it down - instead, he would cradle it and pass it to me when everyone was ready to go for a shot. I never asked him to do that; he just wanted to make sure that I wasn't using my energy on anything that wasn't connected to the shot itself. Simon was clearly going places and is now a leading Steadicam operator based in New Zealand and worked on *The Hobbit* trilogy. Even though he is a big cheese now, we still catch up on the phone once a year.'

Eamonn Walker (P.C. Malcolm Haynes)

'The schedule on *The Bill* was one of the hardest for any show I have ever been on, to this day. To shoot two episodes a week - and later three episodes - every week for a year, was nuts. It hadn't really been done before and shows like *EastEnders* started watching how we were doing it. The production team had vans that would ship us from one unit to the other, so keeping up with what episode we were in was a challenge, because none of them were consecutive. On the odd occasion they might follow on from each other, but as a whole they were separate entities. What helped me get up to speed were amazing people like Trudie Goodwin and Nula Conwell, who were both so nice to me when I arrived. Those two women helped me so much, they are beautiful human beings.'

'When I started on the series, someone else was playing Ramsey. Then after a couple of days, Nick came in to replace that actor, who later ended up joining *EastEnders*... I remember at the end of our first day working together, Nick and I sat in my car and asked whether or not we thought they liked what we were doing. Back then, I drove around London in a navy blue Capri, much like the one we chase in *Chasing the Dragon*. We continued our debrief chats throughout our time on *The Bill*, asking each other how we thought it was going... By the time of this episode, we could see what the writers were trying to do with our characters and we were really enjoying playing our scenes, which is why they started pairing us together more and more. Nick and I used to spend time working out how we were going to play the 'good cop/bad cop' relationship in the interview scenes.'

'We actually had a little unexpected reunion when we were both playing roles in the series *Strike Back*. Even though we didn't share any scenes together, we both ended up in the same hotel in South Africa, on the same day and we didn't even know we were going to be in the same show. It was incredible when I got a call in my hotel room from Nick, who said, "Step out onto your balcony and look up..." and he was in the room above! Nick is an incredible human being, who has taken ginormous action in helping make the world a better place. I remember when he was looking for a new challenge away from acting and the idea for S.A.F.E. was floating around in his mind. He went out to Kenya and helped build an AIDS hospital and he has been working really hard out there ever since. For such a long time, he has been trying to get rid of bad thinking towards people who have AIDS. Reacting to people terribly for having AIDS and ostracising them is as harmful as them having it. People with AIDS have died lonely and nobody should die like that. When I think about all the lives Nick has helped and changed, it makes me very, *very* proud to be his friend. S.A.F.E. Kenya has my support for life.'

THE COOP

Written by Garry Lyons
Directed by Graham Theakston

Series 4: Episode 26
Broadcast: Thursday 13 October 1988

Viewing Figures: 12.20m
ITV Chart Position: 7

Case Narrative

Ackland and Edwards are put off their takeaway when they uncover a shed full of rotting chicken corpses.

Regular Cast

P.C. Edwards (Colin Blumenau), W.P.C. Ackland (Trudie Goodwin), Sgt. Peters (Larry Dann), Sgt. Penny (Roger Leach), P.C. Smith (Robert Hudson), P.C. Melvin (Mark Powley), P.C. Stamp (Graham Cole), CAD Room W.P.C. (Karen England).

Guest Cast

Ian Stokes (John Rees), Man with Model Helicopter (John Dallimore), Van Driver (Erik Collinson), Woman with Toddler (Karen Scargill), Lady Pedestrian (Angela Saul).

Uncredited Personnel

Press Officer (Rosane Chapman), Secretaries (Diane Boland, Tracy Sinclair), Accountants (Anne Shields, David Saggs), Props Chargehand (John Walkham), Make Up Assistants (Carolyn Wills, Kate Rudlin), Floor Assistant (Emma Cowan), Assistant Stage Manager (Annie Scott).

Production Team

Casting Director (Julia Lisney), Title Music (Andy Pask, Charlie Morgan), Costume (Allard Tobin, Maggie Chappelhow), Make Up Designer (Gilly Wakeford), Graphics (Ethan Ames), Videotape Editor (Dave Lewinton), Lighting (Bill Minto), Camera (Adrian J. Fearnley), Sound (Bill Rawcliffe, Paul Langwade), Production Buyer (Trevor Young), Location Manager (Garance Rawinsky), Floor Manager (Mike Hook), Stage Manager (Marilyn Edwards), Production Manager (Derek Cotty), Production Assistant (Sonia Hampson), Technical Adviser (Wilf Knight), Programme

Associate (Valerie Farron), Script Editor (Tim Vaughan), Series Script Editor (Kenneth Ware), Designers (Robin Parker, Peter Joyce), Executive Producer (Peter Cregeen), Producer (Richard Bramall).

Observation Notes

The Coop (Production No: D4041, VTR No: THS/45276) was shot between Monday 15th and Friday 19th August 1988. The opening scene with Edwards and Ackland at the café was filmed on Old Oak Common Lane, Acton W3. The café is now a kebab shop. They then spot Sgt. Peters' panda car exiting Foliot Street, which in reality is slightly further along the other side of the road. Larry Dann then drives the panda down Old Oak Common Lane as we see Trudie Goodwin and Colin Blumenau walk down the side of Photo Hire (David French) Ltd's premises. This business, now operating from Kent, also loaned props to Thames to be used in *The Bill* over the years.

The following scene was filmed on Gypsy Corner, beginning with the skateboarder passing Ackland and Edwards on the entrance to Jenner Avenue, W3. In the background on Wales Farm Road is the former Remploy factory, which closed in 2012 prior to being demolished. Trudie Goodwin and Colin Blumenau then walk further down Jenner Avenue to the entrance to the former Acton Council yard, where all the helicopter and chicken shed scenes were filmed. This area was redeveloped in the late 1990s and is now Garrett Close and Lister Close respectively.

Filming then moved to Kilburn, where Larry Dann filmed the scene where a van performs an emergency stop because of the helicopter. This was shot at the end of Malvern Road, on the junction of Carlton Vale, NW6. The shops have since been demolished, though Kilburn House, seen behind Peters' panda car on the corner, still stands.

Whilst Kelly Lawrence does not appear in *The Coop,* the end credits saw Karen England, who has dialogue in the CAD room scenes, credited as W.P.C. Brind in error. England would later be credited for playing W.P.C. Taylor in *Favours* and P.C. Dobey in *When the Snow Lay Round About.*

The Coop was directed by Graham Theakston, who had helmed the hour-long episodes *Blind Alleys and Clogged Roads* and *Overnight Stay* in 1987. He had not been available to work on the half-hour episodes prior to *The Coop* as he was directing two episodes of *Casualty.* Theakston directed 22 episodes of *The Bill* in total, including the iconic *Trojan*

Horse, and his later credits included *New Tricks, A Touch of Frost, The Inspector Lynley Mysteries* and *The Politician's Wife,* for which he won a BAFTA. Graham Theakston passed away in 2014, aged 62.

Witness Statements

Garry Lyons (Writer)

'I can't remember ever not wanting to be a writer; it was what I wanted to do from a very early age. Although I was acting and directing through school and university, it was a writer that I really wanted to be. I did an English degree and then trained as a journalist, becoming a local newspaper reporter for a few years in the early part of my career. But I always had the desire to become a playwright and dramatist, with television being a natural extension of that. *The Coop* was my first episode of *The Bill.* I'd been invited to join the programme by Tim Vaughan, who I'd made a play with called *Mohicans* up at Yorkshire Television. The idea for *The Coop* came after I'd been inspired by a BBC documentary series called *Animal Squad,* which followed an RSPCA Inspector called Sid Jenkins. In one episode, he found himself going into this appalling battery farm that was being run in a desperate way, with the chickens being terribly abused. So, when Tim invited me to write an episode for *The Bill,* this image had obviously stayed with me. I thought it would be interesting to write something a bit different from the normal police caper, to see a couple of officers find some chickens being treated appallingly, which then turns into a hostage drama. My first story outline had *The Coop* set on an allotment, before Wilf Knight pointed out "There's no allotments on the Isle of Dogs mate."'

'I needed something for the opening of the episode that was going to get June and Taffy away from the High Street and into the coop. The original idea that popped into my head was a model airplane, as I have childhood memories of one buzzing around Epsom Downs when I was a kid. But very close to production, I got a phone call from Tim Vaughan to say we were going to have to lose the model airplane, because they couldn't get permission to fly one in a built up area. Bearing in mind I was relatively new to television, I remember asking, "What am I supposed to do about that?" Fortunately, someone in the production team resolved the last minute panic and got permission to use a model helicopter instead.'

'I was completely naïve and remember going to the production office at Barlby Road for the first time and walking into what looked like an airport departure lounge, with these great big boards up on the wall above your head, listing all the different episodes in various stages of development and production. I remember thinking "How am I going to survive in something this big?" I'd come from running a small theatre in Bradford and had worked in small-scale touring theatre, so the idea of writing quite a small confined piece, which was effectively about three characters stuck in one place for half an hour, was something I felt confident enough to be able to do. But in order to make that kind of story work, you have to develop character and give them something that you feel is important to say. Looking back at it now, I think some of it was terribly overwritten, but at the time it was the best that I could do.'

'I never got to know the actors very well, I was mainly responding to what I saw on the screen and what was detailed in the writer's briefs. I was generally more interested in characters who were not typical of the canteen culture and could bring a different perspective to the stories. Ackland drives *The Coop* and there was something about the character of Taffy that always struck a chord for me. Taffy never felt quite comfortable being a policeman and he had a vulnerability about him, which appealed to me because he came across as an outsider, both in terms of his character and also because he was a Welshman in London. That was quite an interesting dynamic, which extended through to his character to me. It was fun writing for Burnside and Roach, but they were rogues and to an extent they didn't think too much about the morality of what they were doing. Whereas characters like Taffy and Ackland were more thoughtful and those were the kind of characters I liked writing for. I would have enjoyed a chance to work with the actors face to face; I think some good stuff might have come out of that. But the factory nature of the production didn't really create space for that.'

'Whereas the research and development for my new play *Blow Down* was heavily reliant on an extensive interview process with members of a particular community. *Blow Down* works like a drama documentary and tells the story of the community who lived behind the Ferrybridge Power Station in Yorkshire. With the shift to green and nuclear energy, the coal-fired station was closed and over the last 18 months, all the huge cooling towers have been demolished. What gives the story an emotional weight is those cooling towers were the one piece of architecture that acted as a landmark for that industrial town. Symbolically for the community, their demolition was a really big deal for them. It was a good hook to hang a story on and explore what has happened to towns all over the North and the Midlands, which have been in decline for 30 years and nobody has really paid them much attention.'

Marilyn Edwards (Stage Manager)

'Right at the beginning of production on *The Coop*, Graham Theakston held a meeting with Peter Joyce and myself to ask us how we felt about this episode, because a lot of the script was set in a horrible, battery chicken place. I explained that I was thinking about coming off the episode, because I am a vegetarian and was really not happy about the idea of shooting with real chickens in such conditions. Graham and Peter both felt the same, so the plan was to use live chickens only where we had to, but to find ones that looked as if they were in a bad state, but actually weren't... Phone calls were made and somebody found a farmer who reared free-range chickens and at that particular time of year, there had been lots of mating going on... part of the mating involves the cock pulling a lot of feathers out of the female chickens. So we were very lucky that these chickens actually looked quite bedraggled, but only as a result of having had a good time and not cruelty!'

'The farmer was happy to bring the chickens out to us, so as well as the poorly conditioned coop needed for the story, Peter Joyce also built a bigger coop for the chickens to live in on location, because we were going to be there for several days and to have moved them backwards and forwards would have been stressful. The point of the story was for June and Taffy to discover a knee-high pile of chicken carcasses. To provide these dead chickens, we got a load of rubber toys and a tonne of feathers. There were a couple of prop men, along with Peter and myself whenever we could spare the time, sticking feathers onto these rubber chickens, which took quite some time!'

'On the second or third day of the shoot, the first shot of the day involved the live chickens, who we had to get from their coop into that horrible shed that was full of the rubber chickens. We had an early call, but the chicken handler didn't turn up! Bearing in mind this was before mobile phones, we only had a great big unit phone with a wind-up handle, which the location manager was in charge of. We kept phoning the farmer's landline, but there was no answer. Time was getting on and

Graham Theakston was obviously pacing up and down... I suggested that we could try and move them ourselves. Graham asked me if I'd ever caught a chicken before? I said, "No, but how hard can it be?"

'I had two good prop men with me who were up for the challenge... The rest of the crew watched on as the three of us were running around trying to catch these chickens, who did not want to be caught! It was pandemonium at first and I didn't know whether to laugh or cry. Then we realised that there is a technique! You don't run or grab them, you just approach them very quietly and hold them around their wings to stop them flapping, so they aren't so stressed. It was then I realised how lovely it is to actually hold a chicken, because they quite like it if you stroke their head. I was quite sad when the chicken handler finally turned up and we didn't have to do it anymore.'

Peter Joyce (Designer)

'On a long-running series like *The Bill*, it was usually cheaper to buy props, rather than hire them. I saved the production considerable money by persuading them to buy the chairs for the CID office, rather than hiring them for 52 weeks a year, which would have been ridiculously expensive. But *The Coop* was an episode I remember very well, because as well as hiring a model helicopter; we also had to bring in a load of rubber chickens. This caused some creative differences, as the producer Richard Bramall thought it would be easier and cheaper to get a load of real dead chickens from the supermarket. Our stage manager was Marilyn Edwards and she was very much in favour of animal rights. Like many of us, Marilyn thought it was totally wrong to suggest using real dead chickens and there were a few arguments in the office about this.'

'I got to know Graham Theakston very well, who had initially planned on a career in architecture before becoming a director. He was definitely aspiring to be a filmmaker and we had lots of talks about films and other directors. Graham was very particular about what he wanted and wouldn't really take no for an answer. One of the most difficult problems for him on *The Coop* was filming the model helicopter, because they're quite difficult things to control. We worked on other episodes together as well and when later on at Merton there were some people on the crew who were getting a bit lazy or fed up with the show, Graham would get quite angry about that, as he wanted to keep the enthusiasm going. I certainly fed off that and enjoyed working with him.'

Colin Blumenau (P.C. "Taffy" Edwards)

'I have this really clear memory of thinking, "Why are they writing an episode about The Co-op?" Then of course when I read it, I thought "Oh my God, we're going to have to do some work here, because it's only the two of us and I have more lines to learn than I normally have in three or four episodes!" Joking aside, I really loved the texture of the script and the focus of it. I also like to think that when people were asked to do episodes that were slightly different to what *The Bill* normally did, they quite often involved Taffy, because he was the character that the writers liked to fall in pig shit or swim across the Grand Union Canal. If a story went slightly off the beaten track, Taffy usually got something interesting to do, presumably because they found him a character that they could write for, which was nice for me. Graham Theakston got that lovely shot early in the episode, where Taffy and June stumble across the pile of dead chickens. I was supposed to pick up this chicken, which you could see was so clearly made of rubber because the leg went up in a very strange angle. But even though they were made of rubber, I still remember it being very smelly in that shed! But what made it all worthwhile was working with Trudie, who is just a delight and one of the best people in the world!'

Trudie Goodwin (W.P.C. June Ackland)

'It was always very pleasant working with Colin Blumenau, because we became good friends and socialised outside of the programme and we remain good friends to this day. Though we had a really close call on *The Coop* when the Alsatian dog got off its chain! The dog had been deliberately allowed to sniff our uniforms and then encouraged to bark at the sight or smell of us. We had to walk very closely past this aggressive dog to make the shot work. The dog was on a chain, with the trainer on the other side of the wall. We did the shot a couple of times and by the third take this dog was ready to kill us, because Graham wanted it to be really fierce in the scene. Well, the chain broke off the wall and the dog handler screamed "FREEZE!" at us. I remember looking at Colin, who simply said, "Oh shit." The dog got so close to us before the trainer managed to get it back... I've never been so scared in my life.'

'Aside from that, it was a nice few days for us as actors, because it was quite a privilege on *The Bill* in those days to be given quite a lot to do, as opposed to being part of the larger team. *The Coop* was pretty much a three-hander between myself, Colin and John Rees before Larry comes to rescue us. I don't think the series had done too many stories like this at that point and not everybody was lucky enough to get one. That meant the pressure was on us a bit, but that's what you want really and I do remember enjoying it enormously, apart from being boiling hot in my uniform! We shot *The Coop* in August when it was very hot and I remember it being extremely hot in that chicken coop. Thank goodness most of the chickens were made of rubber, because I don't think we could have stood the smell if it had been much worse! I was actually back at work quite quickly after having my second child a few months earlier. I was still breastfeeding, which was probably making me feel a bit hot as well! One of the huge problems was that I was expressing milk throughout the whole week making *The Coop*. I would go off into a little van and express the milk, which would be sent home and given to the baby. My bust size actually went up and down throughout this whole episode, so wardrobe had to give me two costumes to wear for the whole of that week!'

Larry Dann (Sgt. Alec Peters)

'*The Coop* was very close to my heart, because I have always been opposed to factory farming of any kind. It was horrible for Trudie, Colin and I to be captured and surrounded by all those dead chickens, even though they were made of rubber. Playing the gunman was the late John Rees, a good actor who I had worked with years before. I always enjoyed Garry Lyons' scripts, he later wrote *Close Co-operation*, which was one of my best episodes. I also liked working with Graham Theakston, or "Old Peculiar" as we used to call him. He was a good director, though he could be a bit naughty sometimes, because he wanted his episodes to be absolutely perfect, so he could do up to ten takes on a scene until he got what he wanted! But he also spent time with the actors, so he was good to us. I remember it was bloody hot in that shed in *The Coop,* so in between takes Colin Blumenau and I stood outside to cool down. We looked over the wall and in the yard behind us, there was a guy fly tipping. He looked up and saw us in our uniforms and he did a runner, which was brilliant! I got mistaken for a real police officer again whilst filming the driving scenes for *The Coop* in Acton. I was sat in the panda car with the radio, waiting for the call to drive around the corner, when this woman ran up and started banging on the window, telling me someone had collapsed at the station and I needed to come and help!'

THE QUICK AND THE DEAD
Written by Christopher Russell
Directed by Philip Casson

Series 4: Episode 27
Broadcast: Tuesday 18 October 1988

Viewing Figures: 11.90m
ITV Chart Position: 8

Case Narrative
There's a whisper of mortality when the physical training officer visits Sun Hill and finds fitness levels below par. Things don't improve when a corpse goes missing from the local undertakers!

Regular Cast
P.C. Ramsey (Nick Reding), P.C. Frank (Ashley Gunstock), Sgt. Peters (Larry Dann), W.P.C. Ackland (Trudie Goodwin), P.C. Melvin (Mark Powley), Ch. Insp. Conway (Ben Roberts), P.C. Smith (Robert Hudson), P.C. Haynes (Eamonn Walker), P.C. Stamp (Graham Cole).

Guest Cast
Morrissey (Michael O'Hagan), Shaun Rydel (Garry Roost), Mr. Bond (Philip Fox), Mrs. Bond (Lindy Whiteford), Darren (Steve Fletcher), Mr. Covington (John Rolfe), Mr. Talbot (Henry Moxon), Mrs. Talbot (Stella Tanner), Bruce Purdy (Raymond Witch), Babs Purdy (Betty Turner), Gilbert (George Ballantine), Cantello (Frankie Novak), Fryer (Tony Stephens).

Production Team
Stunt Arranger (Stuart St. Paul), Casting Director (Brian Wheeler), Title Music (Andy Pask, Charlie Morgan), Costume (Allard Tobin, Maggie Chappelhow), Make Up Designer (Gilly Wakeford), Graphics (Ethan Ames), Videotape Editor (Colin Bocking), Lighting (Bill Minto), Camera (Adrian J. Fearnley), Sound (Dave Evans, Alan Lester), Production Buyer (Sarah Prebble), Location Manager (Brian Bilgorri), Floor Manager (David Downing), Stage Manager (Nigel J. Wilson), Production Manager (Brian Heard), Production Assistant (Susan Lewis), Technical Adviser (Wilf Knight), Programme Associate (Valerie Farron), Script Editor (Tim Vaughan),

Series Script Editor (Kenneth Ware), Designers (Robin Parker, Stuart McCarthy), Executive Producer (Peter Cregeen), Producer (Michael Ferguson).

Observation Notes

The Quick and the Dead (Production No: D4043, VTR No: THS/45278) was shot between Monday 22nd and Friday 26th August 1988. The opening van scene with Ramsey driving and Frank on the radio was filmed on Barlby Road, W10, with Nick Reding initially driving the van past the Pall Mall Deposit at No.124-128. The following van scene where Ramsey and Frank discuss the fitness test was filmed on Chesterton Road and Golborne Road, W10.

The scene where Ramsey and Frank first encounter the robbers leaving the newsagents was filmed at junction of Golborne Road and Wornington Road, W10. The Rainbow Newsagents is still in business today. Nick Reding then drives the van over the bridge and pursues the 1981 Morris Sedan down Southam Street, W10, continuing down Adair Road.

For the following sequence where P.C. Frank pursues the suspect on foot, Ashley Gunstock runs down Munro Mews, W10. The conclusion of the chase was filmed outside Watts House, 105 Wornington Road, W10.

The funeral parlour scenes were filmed at John Nodes Funeral Service, 181 Ladbroke Grove, W10. The business was established in 1828.

The scene where P.C. Frank drives the police van and Ramsey questions Conway's fitness was filmed at the Ladbroke Grove end of Barlby Road, beginning outside the Admiral Blake pub, which was demolished in 2012. Ashley Gunstock then performs a u-turn around a mini-roundabout and drives the van back down Barlby Road as they continue the scene.

The following scene where Ramsey and Frank break up the fight between the mechanic and the yuppie and are then sprayed by the mortuary van joyriders was filmed on the Sutton Estate, Dalgarno Gardens, W10.

The Quick and the Dead ends with Ashley Gunstock getting the drums as P.C. Robin Frank, who is described in the Character Notes as being 26 years old and "Cheerful and dependable, Frank gets on easily with colleagues and the public. A school teacher's son from Bethnal Green, he worked in office jobs for a while before joining the Force. He is married to a nurse (Angela). While not visibly pushing for promotion, he will probably proceed steadily – a future Bob Cryer?"

The Quick and the Dead was adapted for an episode of *Bureau Kruislaan* in 1992. *Tegen de lamp* was the second episode of the series and also featured story elements from *Good Will Visit*, opening with new recruit Piet Haarman parking his sports car in the Chief Inspector's space.

Witness Statements

Christopher Russell (Writer)

'The idea for *The Quick and the Dead* came from *Police Review*, the magazine of the Metropolitan Police, which often contained lots of snippets about strange cases. I read a report about a hearse that had lost its coffin, which seemed a good starting point for a story. I like to listen to how people talk to each other and then try to accurately portray that in my scripts. I liked to inject plenty of black humour, as that is part of everyday life, particularly in a job like the police, where the banter was essential to how the officers formed their camaraderie. The only thing I needed to tone down was the language, but I think the actual humour is realistic and reflects how the officers get through the day.'

'Broadly speaking, I always prefer a slower pace of storytelling. I will always choose an interrogation scene over a car chase, because I think human interaction that gradually unfolds is more satisfying than crash-bang-wallop. On *The Bill*, you had the opportunity to do both and I could juxtapose those different types of story at the same time, as I did in *The Quick and the Dead*. Part of the fun was also to use the chemistry between the different cast members, though this became a rather more prosaic, logistical exercise when making the half-hours, because we wouldn't always know which characters we could have, due to the actors now filming more than one episode at a time. Though to be given restrictions as a writer was a nice challenge and we were fortunate to have such a good mix of characters to play with in this era. It is nice to know that the actors all enjoyed their time on the series and I think *The Bill* must have been a good series to be in, where if they could keep up with the pace, they would be guaranteed a variety of storylines.'

Tim Vaughan (Script Editor)

'It was great seeing Ben Roberts on his exercise bike in *The Quick and the Dead*. He was a lovely guy and I was surprised when I found out he was only five years older than me, because when I first met him, I thought, "This bloke's been around the houses" and I felt just a wee bit intimidated by him, to be honest — but that was probably because he was so often in character, behaving like an inspector, rather than an actor. Off set, I quickly discovered he was hilarious, kind and relaxed. The cast, though, were always great fun. There was a great buzz with them, and you knew whoever you put in an episode would be wonderful, — as Ashley Gunstock proved when we gave him a leading role in this episode.'

'One of the things that amused me about *The Quick and the Dead* was that Chris used it to have a good dig at Ramsey. Chris and I later worked on episodes that had a lot to do with PACE and interrogation techniques. In this episode, Ramsey was getting it completely wrong and making a total pig's ear of it, which was very funny — and slightly scary — to watch. It used to puzzle us all where Chris got his ideas from, but he kept on coming up with them. It was after this episode that I read a book explaining in detail how to interrogate a suspect and I gave a copy to Chris, which inspired another episode of his, *Greig versus Taylor*, which was a stonking episode.'

'I never had to do very much whenever Chris delivered any of his scripts, whereas I had to work quite hard with some other writers. Directing *The Quick and the Dead* was Philip Casson, who is one of the most amazing men I've ever met in my life. I first met him at ATV, and then at Yorkshire Television. He had an amazing career, directing everything from *The Muppets* to Trevor Nunn's adaptation of *Macbeth*, starring Judi Dench and Ian McKellen. He was still directing *Emmerdale* when he was 80 years old and away from television had been a round-the-world yachtsman. He is an exceptional man, charming, generous and very funny; one of the best people I've ever met in TV.'

'Philip will have absolutely got Chris Russell's sense of humour and I don't know why we didn't use him on more of Chris' episodes, because he was the perfect fit. One of many favourite moments in *The Quick and the Dead* was a classic bit of directing by Philip, who added that terribly funny moment when Ackland goes up to Mrs Purdy's flat and she passes this group of residents in the care home, who are quietly sat watching a boxing match on the telly, with two blokes slugging each other in the face. That was a characteristically hilarious little touch from Philip that helped bring to life the world that these pensioners were living in. The missing corpse, though, is what does it for me: especially the argument between the undertaker and his hapless apprentice: that was priceless casting.'

Philip Casson (Director)

Archive interview by Andrew T. Smith, November 2011.

'I trained as a classical ballet dancer when I was about eighteen, so it was late training. I joined a couple of ballet companies - Ballet Montmartre and Anglo Polish - where I danced classical roles. After a while, I really rather got into modern dance, which took me into American musicals. I then went abroad several times with those companies, taking me to many places. When I came back to England, I went into programmes for television as a dancer. Then I became a choreographer in television, working on lots of light entertainment shows. The last choreographic job I did was a year's contract on a weekly Granada series called *Song Parade*, which was a very popular and well-known programme in its day.'

'Rather than choreographing dancers, I worked with a whole collection of singers, telling stories through movement for all the Top Ten pop songs. For instance, I'd turn the singers into tiny figures and use great big cups and saucers on set, or put them in a gymnasium; all sorts of different storylines that I had to dream up the ideas for. The American executive who was with Granada at the time then asked me if I was interested in becoming a director. It was because of him that I was doing these programmes, so I said, "Of course I want to be a director. I want to do everything! I want to design the sets!" Foolish youth! So I went up to Granada and did my first set of training as a director. The reason they asked me if I wanted to direct was because they knew that I did my own camera scripts when I was doing the choreography. If they didn't shoot off my camera scripts for those programmes, they didn't have anything to shoot, because there wasn't anything else! I purposefully made it so that they could only do it one way.'

'I did lots and lots of musical stuff at Granada and worked with so many people in that period of time. I worked with The Beatles and did a one-hour programme with John and Paul called *Lennon McCartney*. I did lots of pop concerts for television, including something called *Pop Proms*, which were three one-hour programmes. They were done with a big orchestra and a lot of pop artists. We did it like *The Proms*, but instead of being classical music, it was pop. I once did a big audience concert with Jerry Lee Lewis in the studio. I had an idea for a set and managed to get about a week's output of motorbikes. I had scaffolding built all the way around the set, and had motorbikes put up on them. I based the whole idea on it, so the audience was sitting on motorbikes. We started the programme off around Manchester, with motorbikes driving around the city at night. I was tracking them with cameras and took it right into the studio, where the motorbikes all around the walls had their lights on and hooters going, with Jerry Lee Lewis blaring away! I must have done hundreds of programmes for Granada.'

'When I was a dancer, I'd worked on an MGM film, made at Elstree, called *Invitation To The Dance* with Gene Kelly. I understudied him a little bit, because he was directing at the same time. There were some long scenes on the big high Atlantic camera, so he was up there and I doubled for him. You could never tell; he was a clown and so I had on all the clown makeup and all kinds of things that were hanging from this ladder that was on me. Years later, I directed Kelly when he came to do *The Muppet Show*, though I didn't tell him I had once understudied him. But when we were up in the rehearsal room I laughed at some of the things the puppeteers were doing and he whipped his head around and said, "I know that laugh." So I confessed! He was a lovely man. I got a single frame from the 35mm print of *Singing In The Rain* and had the set built exactly. The puddles were the same; the water came down exactly in the right places, you couldn't tell the difference in the set. I knew Kelly wouldn't dance – he was a bit too old for that. But he did do a little walk up and down the kerb for me. As he came out of the shot, he said, "That's for you Philip." It was a lovely moment.'

Ashley Gunstock (P.C. Robin Frank)
'Watching *The Quick and the Dead* again brought back some amazing memories. It was so evocative seeing those streets as they were and fabulous to see all the other actors again. It was a real joy for me when I first read the script and saw what Chris Russell had handed to me, for which I'm very grateful for to this day. This was a rollercoaster of an episode that gave us all so much to do. The kaleidoscope of events leapt off the page, cutting from one story to another, but with such laser-like precision that it was easy to keep up with. It was a fabulous episode to participate in and you can see people on the estates watching us filming, because they knew the show by this point, which generated an excitement. People would ask when they were going to be able to watch it on the telly! The atmosphere around us when we were shooting on location had a real buzz, which as an actor I felt and fed off too.'

'Nick Reding was lovely to work with and his screen persona could not have been more further removed from the man himself. I'm a bit of an environmentalist, and one of the things that sticks out in my mind during a filming break was Nick talking about the destruction of the Amazon rainforest, way back before many people were even aware of it. He described it as like taking out the hairs from your nose; the trees are the filters for the Earth that stop all the rubbish going through. Nick is a very gentle man, so what you see him doing on screen as Ramsey is just the other side of the coin. The beauty of *The Quick and the Dead* for me is that Ramsey gets his comeuppance at the end, when after all the grief he's given Robin throughout, he's then told that he can't even do the fitness test because of his high blood pressure, which was so on the money. At the end I wanted to register on my face that Robin knew that Ramsey had screwed up and had performed even worse than Sgt. Peters! I knew I was getting the drums too, which was the perfect ending.'

'Robin Frank was the "bobby on the beat", pure and simple, whereas there were new and more exciting characters being written for in the half-hours, which was the direction the show was going in. When *The Quick and the Dead* came along, I just thought, "Right, I'm going to put my heart and soul into this", as I had done with all the other smaller little parts I'd been getting in episodes. It was sad for me, because by that time I had already made the decision, with a heavy heart, to leave the series. I hadn't seemed to be making any headway in the show and if more writers had written for me earlier like Chris did, then I would have undoubtedly stayed in *The Bill* for longer. It is still a pleasant surprise for me when people occasionally contact me to say how much they still enjoy the series, it is really rewarding.'

Nick Reding (P.C. Pete Ramsey)

'When Ashley and I were filming the opening chase scene for *The Quick and the Dead*, we got pulled over by the real cops! Ashley and I did all our own driving in this episode and I was hurtling that van down the Golborne Road and around the streets under Trellick Tower, when suddenly the real police came racing up after us. They ran out and stopped us, because they thought it was a real chase and they just dived in. That was excellent, though you could never get away with filming like that now; there was no health and safety. It is a million miles away from the restrictions on a film set now, especially since the pandemic.'

'Over the last 20 years, I have directed several feature films through my work with S.A.F.E. – a non-profit organisation in Kenya that uses theatre, film and education to inform, inspire and deliver social, health and environmental change. We work in hard to reach and vulnerable communities, focusing on sexual health, gender-based violence, clean water and sanitation. We were very lucky during the pandemic that our donors stood by us and helped while we adapted our programming. For our Maasai and Samburu projects, we usually do live theatre performances in crowded marketplaces, which for obvious reasons was not possible during the pandemic. Thanks to our donors, we were able to adapt our shows and turn them all into little films, working with a film crew who came in and very kindly worked within our budget, once restrictions had eased. For one of these films, after we all did Covid tests, the entire crew moved into this house together, like the Big Brother house. There were 22 of us, 12 boys and 10 girls, sharing two bathrooms, which was a little bit of a challenge. But it was such an extraordinary relief in the midst of the pandemic, for us all to be hanging out in our own little bubble and making life feel a bit more normal again. As a result, I feel we created something quite special, which was partly down to the joy that everyone felt being back doing something creative.'

'This latest film looks at family planning options for young girls in Mombasa. There's a lot of pressure on girls in poorer parts of the community, where sex is semi-transactional. Often they get what is known as a "sponsor", who provides them with a SIM card or sanitary products, but in return they're having sex. These girls are often getting pregnant by 16 and by the time they are 23, they've got four kids, all with different sponsors. And of course, as a result they never finish their education, they never get any vocational training and they're struggling to put food on the table. Many end up selling things on the side of the road, while their kids are running wild. It's a growing problem. We work with two drama groups in a place called Mtwapa, just north of Mombasa, and we developed a play which tells the story of five sisters, who basically fall asleep under a tree and dream this terrible future, which you don't realise is a dream until they wake up and then they have a chance to live their life in a different way. Funding from The Rosita Trust in the UK allowed us to turn this play into a little film. I love directing these absolutely brilliant Kenyan actors. They are incredible at on the spot improvisations, and when I throw them ideas, they always execute them so well.'

WITNESS
Written by Christopher Russell
Directed by Graham Theakston

Series 4: Episode 28
Broadcast: Thursday 20 October 1988

Viewing Figures: 12.90m
ITV Chart Position: 5

Case Narrative
P.C. Ramsey isn't pleased to be given witness protection duties: "When it comes to feeling collars, I'm there, right? None better. But this is just another Mickey Mouse job, innit? Housemaid to a plonker."

Regular Cast
P.C. Edwards (Colin Blumenau), P.C. Ramsey (Nick Reding), P.C. Smith (Robert Hudson).

Guest Cast
Andrew Pike (Rick Stone), Percy (Bill Moody), Graham Sudbury (Paul Ridley), Nicholas Martin (Martin Turner), Court Police Inspector (Bunny Losh), Bullivant (Gary O'Brien), Mrs. Fox (Kate Dunn), Mr. Fox (Neville Watchurst), Chairwoman (Margaret Stallard).

Uncredited Personnel
Props Chargehand (John Walkham), Make Up Assistants (Carolyn Wills, Kate Rudlin), Floor Assistant (Emma Cowan), ASM (Annie Scott).

Production Team
Casting Director (Julia Lisney), Title Music (Andy Pask, Charlie Morgan), Costume (Allard Tobin, Maggie Chappelhow), Make Up Designer (Gilly Wakeford), Graphics (Ethan Ames), Videotape Editor (Dave Lewinton), Lighting (Bill Minto), Camera (Adrian J. Fearnley), Sound (Bill Rawcliffe, Paul Langwade), Production Buyer (Trevor Young), Location Manager (Garance Rawinsky), Floor Manager (Mike Hook), Stage Manager (Marilyn Edwards), Production Manager (Derek Cotty), Production Assistant (Sonia Hampson), Technical Adviser (Wilf Knight), Programme Associate (Valerie Farron), Script Editor (Tim Vaughan), Series Script Editor (Kenneth Ware), Designers (Robin Parker, Peter Joyce), Executive Producer (Peter Cregeen), Producer (Richard Bramall).

Observation Notes

Witness (Production No: D4042, VTR No: THS/45277) was shot between Monday 22nd and Friday 26th August 1988. The opening shot sees Nick Reding park on Dalgarno Way, W10, next to the north entrance of the Peabody estate, where all the scenes in and around Andrew Pike's flat were filmed.

The courtroom scenes were all shot at Acton Magistrates Court, 56 Winchester Street, W3. Built in the early 1900s, the Court closed in 2011 and has since been converted into several luxury flats.

The greyhound track scenes were filmed at the Hackney Wick stadium, Waterden Road, E15. The stadium opened in 1932, closed in 1997 and was demolished in 2003. The redeveloped site was later used as the Media Centre for the 2012 Summer Olympics and Paralympics.

Witness Statements

Christopher Russell (Writer)

'My main source for most of my ideas on *The Bill* was a friend who was a P.C. in South London. He was always willing to share subversive stories and he'd actually done some witness protection, so I took his experiences and embellished them somewhat using our characters. I had forgotten that *Witness* was a very violent episode, with a lot of fighting, though I am pleased to learn that the actors enjoyed filming these scenes. With the ensemble of actors we had in this era, you were confident that whoever you picked for your episode would do a fantastic job. If I wanted to write an "Eeyore" story, then I would always pick Colin Blumenau as Taffy, who was a very mordant character. If I wanted some solid Yorkshire grit, I would pick Rob Hudson as Yorkie. And if I wanted someone to stab one of their colleagues in the back, I would pick Nick Reding as Ramsey. It might be a cliché, but they were all a pleasure to work with and you just knew that whatever you came up with, as long as it wasn't complete tripe, they would do a great job and those three guys always did.'

Robert Hudson (P.C. "Yorkie" Smith)

'Every time I see Yorkie in his civvies now, I just think it screams 1980s. I don't know what look I was going for in *Witness*, some kind of *Miami Vice* bollocks, with my sleeves rolled up and my floppy hair. Oh my God, it looks a bit dated! My memory is that when I originally read the script for *Witness*, it had a sequence set on the Dockland Light Railway, but the production team said they couldn't stop the train, and so getting on and off would have been a nightmare. So instead, Chris wrote in the dog track, which I loved doing. Nick and I had such a laugh. I'd forgotten about the big fight we had outside the track. We roughly talked through what we were going to do, but nine times out of ten it is better when you just suck it and see. In real life, fights are messy - they aren't choreographed! It looks more realistic when you have blokes kicking and pushing each other, not doing Bruce Lee moves. We talked about what we were going to do, blocked it out slowly for the camera and then we just went for it. Graham Theakston was a great director and he knew how to make the most of the handheld camera, which made the fight look more real and it worked so well.'

'When I thought back to *Witness*, my memories were obviously about the scenes that me and Nick did. But when I watched it again, I saw the absolute nightmare that Colin's character was going through, where it just kept going from bad to worse all the way through! I thought, "No wonder Taffy was always a bit hacked off!" I visited Kilburn nick once, which is where they got the idea for the C.A.D. room, and all the coppers I spoke to said the same thing, that the amount of paperwork they had to do was a complete nightmare and they couldn't get anything else done. I thought the juxtaposition in this episode worked really well, with Yorkie and Ramsey "protecting" the witness and getting involved in all the kicking and punching; counterpointed by all the bureaucracy and the nonsense that Taffy was buried in, which a lot of people don't realise that coppers have to go through at court. Taffy was doing police work, but not what the public perceive as police work.'

'A lot of different writers on *The Bill* had their favourite characters and wrote episodes based on what happened to them. I was lucky that writers like Chris and Julian Jones both liked Yorkie and they gave me some really good episodes. Chris gave me my big break in *Home Beat* and later wrote *A Good Result*, where Yorkie went undercover with football hooligans. I also think Chris wrote really well for each of our characters and that Colin, Nick and I couldn't have played each other's parts in *Witness*, because our characters were so well defined. I was absolutely amazed when I found out that Colin wasn't really Welsh, which just proves how good he was as Taffy. Colin was one of the actors, along with Eric, Trudie and Mark Wingett, who when they were working, I would sit and watch them, because they had all done a lot more telly than I had, so I would just listen and learn.'

Colin Blumenau (P.C. "Taffy" Edwards)

'It was really interesting watching *Witness* again and seeing how Graham Theakston used the single camera to follow individual people around, which was really marked and quite advanced for the 1980s. Graham was one of my favourite directors and I remember him spending time with me, especially on this episode, where I had the comparative luxury of being able to talk about the words and the performance, rather than "Colin, can you do an emergency stop and hit that mark?" I really enjoyed working with him and for a young director, he seemed very assured and experienced.'

'However much trouble Taffy got in would depend on which writer was behind the episode. Chris Russell certainly wrote more trouble for me than others, which went all the way back to *This Little Pig*. I was reminded whilst watching Taffy pick up all his ruined paperwork from the toilet floor that it was when we started *The Bill* that PACE had first come into use, which according to the real coppers we were speaking to, had changed everything out of all proportion. All that paperwork suddenly landed on their shoulders, which hitherto they'd never had to do. It was fascinating to watch that bureaucracy happening back in those days. Also at this time, they were burning houses in Wales that belonged to second homeowners and I used to get a steady trickle of mail, saying "How dare you take jobs from our boys!"

'I gave up acting very soon after I left *The Bill* and started writing and running theatres. Now, I run a charity which looks after early career performers, who we support as they try and make a career in this business. The theatre industry was decimated during the Covid pandemic, though it has started to come back now. The TV and film industries are doing really well and there's masses of work, thanks to the proliferation of streaming platforms like Netflix and Amazon Prime, who are all making original drama, which is fabulous. The trouble is, whilst there's lots and lots of work, there's also so many actors out there, all competing for the same work.'

'But people have suddenly started asking me to do stuff as an older actor, which is really bemusing though also quite flattering. I hadn't acted since 1990 and had sworn off doing it again, because I didn't enjoy it after leaving *The Bill*. But in the last couple of years, people have weirdly started knocking on the door again, which has tickled my fancy and now it's fun when I do it. Over 30 years after *Witness*, I returned to a courtroom to play a barrister in an episode of *EastEnders*. Though this was a completely different experience, because we shot that during the pandemic, where the rule on set was that nobody could be within two metres of anybody else, which they were mega strict about. That meant we had to shoot every scene far more times than you would normally, because you couldn't use the usual three cameras at the same time. I was acting with tennis balls on sticks in front of me and because I never stopped talking, that quite lengthy court scene took three days to film, which is unheard of on something like *EastEnders*.'

Tim Vaughan (Script Editor)

'The first scene at the dog track in *Witness* was very subtly directed by Graham Theakston. You can actually see the two blokes coming out of their van and following them, but you have to look really carefully to see that. Graham was a wonderful director and such a fun man to be with. I'll never forget one afternoon with Graham – we had a free afternoon, and he'd been given a Formula 1 driving course by a girlfriend, so he took me for a spin, from the Merton Studios up to Wimbledon Common – probably the most hair-raising car journey I've ever had! It was terribly sad when the phone stopped ringing for Graham in 2007, as it did for a lot of people at that time – me included, as I was made redundant the following year and had to go back to freelancing. We were fairly close neighbours, both living in Wimbledon at the time, and we used to meet at the Hand In Hand pub, but as work dried up for him, Graham became increasingly bitter about it all. For a long time, I tried to persuade him to take any job, no matter how mundane – anything to stop him from sitting there festering. In the end he got cancer and died very quickly, which was just awful.'

'These were the glory days of *The Bill* for me, where all the characters were written to such a high standard and we had great actors playing them. Colin Blumenau, Nick Reding and Bob Hudson were all great in this episode, but then again they were always rock solid. Another thing about *Witness* that I loved were the little touches, like the woman in court wearing the neck brace, or the empty can that Colin kicks on his way out after all his papers got chucked down the lavatory.

It's those details that make it so interesting and helped create that big slice of reality that I think we are all proud of.'

'I thought Rick Stone was good as poor old Andrew the witness. I liked the way he finally had enough of Ramsey and stood up for himself. I loved the tension that developed between Yorkie, who was an example of a good police officer, and Ramsey, who whilst being handy in a fight was about as far away from being a model officer as you could get. Nick's character quickly became the show's bête noire; you knew he was going to say something really stupid, which combined with Nick's marvellous performance made him so popular. Nick Reding is a fascinating man and you really have to doff your cap to him for his charity work in Kenya. It's not easy what he is doing out there; he's put himself out on quite a ledge in order to challenge some of the issues that he's trying to help people will — AIDS being around the top of the list. It's such an extraordinarily brave thing to do, because it's not without risk, but he seems to be making a difference, which is wonderful, even though he's much missed back here in Blighty.'

Nick Reding (P.C. Pete Ramsey)

'Some episodes I can't even remember filming, because they were more of a standard investigation. I've never forgotten how much I enjoyed making *Witness*, which was one of the real golden nuggets and one of my absolute favourite episodes. It was beautifully written by Chris Russell, who gave me some great lines, and fantastically directed by Graham Theakston, who loved to do really long takes. So all those scenes with me and Rob Hudson at the beginning of *Witness*, where we leave the car, walk through the car park, up the stairs to the flat, meet the witness in the kitchen and then take him back down to the car, were all played in a series of long takes. If a director was going to do those really ambitious shots, they had to keep the cast and crew with them, because everybody knew that one mistake would mean going right back to the beginning. So many things could go wrong, but Graham was brilliant at keeping spirits high and created such a good, positive energy on set.'

'Then we had a lot of fun at Hackney Wick, which was still a functioning greyhound track. That meant we could film in amongst a real crowd, because everyone was so focused on the dogs, no one gave a toss about what we were doing. I had to run down those stairs and launch straight into a fight scene, where I was being picked up and kicked. Then

Graham said, "We nearly got that, we're just going to go one more time..." Which we did again, and again, and again... I thought I was gonna throw up! It was hard work, but the result was a really cracking episode. It felt like we were making really good entertainment, which was what *The Bill* was all about. It was a joy to do.'

'It makes me really chuffed that people are still talking about Pete Ramsey and I'm really proud to have been part of *The Bill*. Whilst I would never want to return to it full time, I'd still like to do some more acting. Because it is no longer my primary pursuit, I take a lot more pleasure from acting when I occasionally do some bits and bobs. I recently recorded a podcast with Rob Hudson, who was just about to go on tour with a play, which made me realise how much I'd love to do a good play in a really nice repertory theatre back in the UK. Although, the work I am now doing at S.A.F.E. Kenya has a much stronger purpose. Using street theatre, films and community programmes to educate, inspire and deliver social change is a real privilege.'

'I think the biggest example of that change is the work we do on Female Genital Mutilation/Cutting abandonment with the Maasai. This is a very, very difficult thing to talk about and it took two years for the Council of Elders to agree that we could even discuss it publicly. To help try and tackle the subject, we created a theatre performance where there's a group of men and women who sing in favour of FGM/C and a group of men and women who sing against it. It doesn't matter what the audience's opinion is, or what their beliefs are, because their argument is presented on stage in a culturally appropriate way, that is both respectful and non-judgmental. Though the performers singing against FGM/C have got the best song and the best singers and gradually, people start to defect. Then at the end, we just say, "Let's talk about it..."

'When we started that programme, 100% of the girls were being cut with type 2 circumcisions, which involves the removal of the clitoris and labia. Whereas now, 60% do a small symbolic cut and 30% do no cut at all and have an alternate rite of passage. There was such stigma around it before, people wouldn't talk about it, but suddenly they could talk about characters they had seen on stage. That shift could not have happened without the creative industry and those world-class performers and the support we receive through safekenya.org. Together we are making a real impact on people's lives.'

HERE WE GO LOOPY LOU
Written by Julian Jones
Directed by Brian Farnham

Series 4: Episode 29
Broadcast: Tuesday 25 October 1988

Viewing Figures: 11.50m
ITV Chart Position: 10

Case Narrative
Cryer, Edwards and Brind look into reports of a man wearing a flowing white robe – and are caught in a deadly game of hide and seek.

Regular Cast
Sgt. Cryer (Eric Richard), P.C. Edwards (Colin Blumenau), W.P.C. Brind (Kelly Lawrence), P.C. Stamp (Graham Cole).

Guest Cast
McGregor (Kevin McMonagle), Poodle Owner (Marcia Ashton), Worried Woman (Violetta Farjeon), Young Woman (Juliette Grassby), Van Driver (Ricky Garrett), Foreman (Phil Horsley), Workman (Terry Duran), Nurse (Race Davies), Porter (Vince Rayner), Doctor (Mellan Mitchell).

Production Team
Stunt Arranger (Stuart St. Paul), Casting Director (Brian Wheeler), Title Music (Andy Pask, Charlie Morgan), Costume (Allard Tobin, Dennis Hogan), Make Up Designer (Gilly Wakeford), Graphics (Ethan Ames), Videotape Editor (Terence E. Badham), Lighting (Graham Jaggers), Camera (Peter Edwards), Sound (Richard Longley, Paul Langwade), Production Buyer (Sarah Prebble), Location Manager (Eddie Mares), Floor Manager (Peter Price), Stage Manager (Gregory Kinchin), Production Manager (Brian Heard), Production Assistant (Krystyna Wojciechowska), Technical Adviser (Wilf Knight), Programme Associate (Valerie Farron), Series Script Editor (Kenneth Ware), Design (Robin Parker, Colin Andrews), Executive Producer (Peter Cregeen), Producer (Michael Ferguson).

Observation Notes
Here We Go Loopy Lou (Production No: D4047, VTR No: THS/45282) was shot between Monday 5th and Friday 9th September 1988. The

graveyard scene where the officers are looking for the cross was shot in Kensal Green Cemetery, W10. The cemetery runs parallel to the Grand Union Canal, which featured in several sequences, notably when Edwards dives in after McGregor.

The following scene where Cryer climbs up to the roof and chats to the builder was filmed on the top of Bramley Gardens, 123 St Ann's Road, W11 – a retirement home that was under construction and opened in 1989.

The scene where the poodle owner almost crashes into the panda car was filmed on the junction of Wrentham Avenue and Tiverton Road, NW10.

The sequence where Brind and Edwards are trying to catch Raymond the dog was filmed on the former roundabout at Kilburn Park Road, NW6, on the junction of Carlton Vale. This area has since been redeveloped.

The following sequence where Edwards fails to notice the green filter begins on Latimer Road, W10. Colin Blumenau then turns left onto the adjoining North Pole Road, where they are stopped by the pedestrian.

The sequence where Cryer is driving and Edwards spots McGregor was filmed on Barlby Road, W10, with Eric Richard parking opposite 69-71 Barlby Road. The following searching sequence, where Cryer is exorcised by McGregor, was filmed in the gardens of Hill Farm Road, W10.

The scene where McGregor tries to escape standing on a lorry was filmed on Freston Road, W10. Cryer and Edwards then pursue McGregor up the building site of the extension to the Phoenix Brewery, Bramley Road, W10.

The scene where P.C. Stamp responds to the call for assistance was filmed on the junction of Notting Barn Road and Barlby Road, W10.

The final ambulance scene was shot outside St Charles' Hospital, W10.

Witness Statements

Julian Jones (Writer)
'What was wonderful for the writers on *The Bill* was that the house style was fairly eclectic. It was a fairly permissive writing world and we could go away and do our own thing. I feel very fortunate that my writing career started on these half-hour episodes, which were quirky and had little bits and pieces of my life squashed in there. And it was great that *The Bill* allowed me to tell stories that had no real

structure, which was partly down to my inexperience. Something I wrote in *Here We Go Loopy Lou* gave us a big problem. We couldn't find a bridge for McGregor to jump off, because we needed permission from Thames Water and they didn't want us to show people jumping into the water and behaviour that could be imitated. I can't remember how we got around it, but it was one of those problems you get as a writer, where you have written a key scene that you might then have to change if the production team can't get permission.'

'Before I watched *Here We Go Loopy Lou* back after all these years, there were things I remembered, like the cross and the line about McGregor being circumcised. Whilst I was watching Edwards and Cryer go up the scaffolding, I realised this was the episode where the stunt man went down the rubbish chute! When I wrote that, I thought, "Will anyone be able to do this?" but then I thought, "fuck it" and wrote it anyway and a stunt man did that for real! But there were so many lines that I'd forgotten about, that you wouldn't be able to get away with now, like Taffy describing the vehicle that overtakes him as "a paddy wagon". These were observations of how the police talked and behaved at that time, though it is surprising now to be reminded about some of the language that was considered permissible back then. I was also surprised by the swearing and the dark humour that we were allowed to show before the watershed, like the end scene with the finger. *The Bill* feels quite radical looking at in today's television landscape, which is much more puritan and anything that is likely to offend will be pushed to a later slot.'

'I also hadn't remembered all the stuff in *Here We Go Loopy Lou* talking about mental health and how people with problems should be treated. What was also great was exploring Edwards' relationship with Cryer, where he feels he is disliked and unpopular. For me, that exemplified what was so good about *The Bill*, in that I could pick up the character of Taffy and expand his relationships in the series, whilst also giving the audience something to discuss about mental health... This could be the only day of the year where McGregor behaves like that, in which case they can't just lock him up forever. *The Bill* was always good at giving writers the chance to discuss social issues, which could be wrapped in a great piece of entertainment with moments of comedy. That's what motivated me to want to write for television and I had a desire for the world that I knew to be shown. You have to be in a very privileged position now to be able to use a drama programme to voice a piece of social commentary, whereas *The Bill* gave writers like me the chance to do that from the very start of our careers.'

Colin Blumenau (P.C. "Taffy" Edwards)

'*Here We Go Loopy Lou* was an extraordinary episode by Julian Jones which saw Eric, Kelly and I chasing a madman across London. I'll never forget the scene where he jumped off the bridge and I had to swim across the Grand Union Canal. I had my police boots on, they filled with water and consequently I couldn't swim and I just went down and down, which sums up the kind of dangers we sometimes let ourselves in for on *The Bill*. Another danger I was always wary of was the idea of "celebrity", because that can potentially be very disruptive to your life. Even worse than that is the fact that "fame" can distort an actor's self-image and when you start believing your own publicity, bad things can happen. For me, acting was never about fame, only fortune – and so the move to the half-hours and having employment for 52 weeks a year was great and I enjoyed my work. Though during the week this episode was transmitted, three things happened that made me realise that the programme had become big...'

'It started when I tried to take my children to the zoo and we couldn't get in, because there were so many people who wanted to talk to me. Then mid-week, I was shopping in a supermarket on the Harrow Road and a lady started going on and on, asking me questions about her husband and whether or not I thought he was going to be OK... I had to explain that I had no idea what she was talking about, to which she replied "You sound different..." It turned out that her husband was a policeman and she thought I was from his nick. It was very odd, because she had got totally confused between reality and make-believe. And then on the Friday of that week, Trudie and I were on the front of the TV Times with the words "laying down the law for a safe bonfire night", which was the following week. I never thought I was famous, because I wasn't, and as a whole it was never problematic, but I just remember that week feeling a little bit of an intrusion into my life.'

Gregory Kinchin (Stage Manager)

'One of the beauties for a stage manager working on *The Bill* was we worked to a four-week turnaround. We did two weeks prep, followed by two weeks of shooting. The designers would do an extra week on a block and the floor managers and location managers would do another couple of weeks on top of that. We did two episodes every four weeks, which meant that every month we'd be working with a different crew and different members of the regular cast. Some of the actors might coincide with your next block, or others you might not have worked with before or seen for a while, which was quite nice for us, we got to know lots of different people. *The Bill* was also great for the industry; it was employing so many people, more so than something like *EastEnders*, which was pretty set with who was working on it. We also had two or three guest actors coming in all the time for every episode.'

'We also always had new directors coming onto *The Bill*; some were established, while others were less experienced. They all had their own different styles of shooting, but the first thing I used to think about was whether they could stick to the schedule or not. Whether you were going to finish shooting on time partly depended on how efficient the director was. Some of the less experienced directors were not thinking about schedules, they were thinking on a purely creative level. But on *The Bill*, the director had to be able to tell a good story in a limited amount of time, which some found harder than others. Brian Farnham obviously knew what he was doing on *Here We Go Loopy Lou*, he was a very experienced director and a lovely man who was very easy to get on with. He picked locations that were close to Barlby Road as "closest is cheapest" was always the rule. We rarely did anything more than half an hour away, because it would have been too expensive in time.'

Graham Cole OBE (P.C. Tony Stamp)

'As actors we are only as good as the words and in what other programme could you pick up a script and read that you are going to find the lost finger of a man dressed as Jesus Christ? These early episodes were magical! It is also fascinating to watch episodes of *The Bill* through the 27 years that the series was on, because you will see the London skyline change almost with each episode. Sometimes the location manager would tell us about the atmospheric location they had found, with an amazing building to act as a backdrop to a scene, only to discover when we arrived for filming that it had been knocked down after the recce! It would be pretty tough to find a cobbled street in London to do those end credits on now. We were all desperate to play the feet, which is the number one question I get asked by fans, "Are they your feet?" and I always say "Yes... in the tights!"'

STOP AND SEARCH
Written by Geoff Mcqueen
Directed by Terry Marcel

Series 4: Episode 30
Broadcast: Thursday 27 October 1988

Viewing Figures: 12.50m
ITV Chart Position: 7

Case Narrative
Special Constables Ronnie Defoe and Mary Kilnair are an engaged couple
learning the ropes at Sun Hill – but there is one fact that they would
rather not have to face.

Regular Cast
Sgt. Cryer (Eric Richard), D.I. Burnside (Christopher Ellison), D.C. Lines
(Kevin Lloyd), D.C. Carver (Mark Wingett), Insp. Frazer (Barbara Thorn),
Ch. Supt. Brownlow (Peter Ellis), P.C. Edwards (Colin Blumenau),
P.C. Smith (Robert Hudson), P.C. Haynes (Eamonn Walker), Sgt. Penny
(Roger Leach), Sgt. Peters (Larry Dann), W.P.C. Ackland (Trudie Goodwin),
W.P.C. Brind (Kelly Lawrence), W.P.C. Martella (Nula Conwell), P.C. Hollis
(Jeff Stewart), Ch. Insp. Conway (Ben Roberts), D.C Dashwood (Jon Iles),
D.S. Roach (Tony Scannell).

Guest Cast
W.S.C. Kilnair (Noreen Leighton), S.C. Defoe (Chris Samsworth), Doctor
(Daniel Moynihan), Mr. Baxter (Ray Mort), Liz Barnescroft (Elsa O'Toole),
Kingsley 1 (William Vanderpuye), Kingsley 2 (Sylvano Clarke), Male
Junkie (Chris Pitt).

Production Team
Casting Director (Julia Lisney), Title Music (Andy Pask, Charlie Morgan),
Costume Designer (Dennis Griffith), Make Up Designer (Gilly Wakeford),
Graphics (Ethan Ames), Videotape Editor (John Sharland), Lighting
(Allen Harradine), Camera (Chas Watts), Sound (Robert Newton,
Paul Langwade), Production Buyer (Trevor Young), Location Manager
(Quenton Annis), Floor Manager (Barry Beckett), Stage Manager
(Susan Shattock), Production Manager (Brian Heard), Production Assistant
(Sylvia Rumney), Technical Adviser (Wilf Knight), Script Editor

(Tim Vaughan), Series Script Editor (Kenneth Ware), Designers (Robin Parker, Jill Reedman), Executive Producer (Peter Cregeen), Producer (Richard Bramall).

Observation Notes

Stop and Search (Production No: D4045, VTR No: THS/45280) was shot between Monday 29th August and Friday 2nd September 1988. The sequence where Yorkie and Edwards, along with Special Constables Kilnair and Defoe respectively, perform their stop and searches were filmed on Crowthorne Road, W10. This area has since been redeveloped and is now the site of The Westway Sports Centre.

The scene where Haynes and Edwards reprimand the two young men for illegal parking was filmed outside 56 Chiswick High Road, W4.

The driving scene where Lines and Carver discuss Baxter was filmed on Bramley Road, W10. The following scene where Lines deduces that Mrs Baxter's body must be under a high-rise tower block was filmed outside Dixon House, Darfield Way, W10, which was constructed in 1970.

The final pub scene was shot in The Earl Derby, Southern Row, W10.

Stop and Search was adapted for an episode of *Bureau Kruislaan* in 1992. *De naald* ("The Needle") was the tenth episode of the first season.

Stop and Search was the only time that Special Constables Defoe and Kilnair appeared in *The Bill*. S.C. Defoe was played by Chris Samsworth, whose other television credits include *As Time Goes By, Dangerfield, Saracen* and the 1991 *The Bill* episode *Night and Day*. W.S.C. Kilnair was played by Noreen Leighton, whose other television roles include *Casualty, Rebus, The Professionals, Taggart* and the 2000 *The Bill* episode *Beyond Conviction*. Leighton also worked as a successful voiceover artist and children's novelist. Noreen Leighton passed away in 2017, aged 60.

Stop and Search saw Kevin Lloyd make his debut as D.C. Alfred "Tosh" Lines. The Character Notes issued to writers in 1988 featured a breakdown of Lines, beginning with the words "To Be Cast". The description of the character makes it impossible to imagine another actor playing Tosh, who is described as standing "just five feet seven inches tall, is a little on the chubby side, has a wife and five young kids (three girls, two boys), a mortgage he can't afford, owns one suit, one pair of cheap shoes and has a habit of making one shirt last from Monday through to Friday. In short, Tosh is a right scruff. He is also a good copper – and always has a steady smile that goes right up into his eyes."

Stop and Search was also the first of 13 episodes helmed by feature film director Terry Marcel, whose big screen directing credits include the cult classics *Hawk the Slayer, Prisoners of the Lost Universe* and *Jane and the Lost City*. His television directing credits include *C.A.T.S. Eyes, Bergerac, Heartbeat, The Castle of Adventure, The New Adventures of Robin Hood* and *The Dark Knight*, which he created, wrote and produced.

Witness Statements

Sue Shattock (Stage Manager)

'During the prep for each episode, we would all go out on a recce, where the location managers had found atmospheric areas that were already "dressed" to an extent, because the series aimed to be as true to real life as possible. The designers would then beautifully handle any additional dressing required, while the stage managers dealt with all the props that would be handled by the actors. I would make a list of what was required for each shoot and then our lovely prop men would load the props that we needed onto a lorry in a big cage. Then on location, they would unload the cage. They were the only ones allowed to go inside it, so I would ask them to get the props we needed for each scene, like the junkie's needle seen in *Stop and Search*. If we needed to do more than one take, the prop would be 'reset' and ready to go again before being handed back to the actor. I remember that Terry Marcel was an amazing director, who always liked to have something unusual going on in the background to make it more interesting. For example, it was his idea in *Stop and Search* to have workmen up ladders mending the ceiling. I thought those little touches made the series more realistic and gave everyone motivation.'

Terry Marcel (Director)

'At this time in my career, I was well established as a film director and had been taking projects as they came along. The one I'm most proud of is *Hawk the Slayer*, which is still being played, and I've recently been involved with a new comicbook sequel, which looks fantastic. After my fifth picture, *Jane and the Lost City*, my feature career wasn't really going anywhere and I started to get offered directing work in television. I thought, "What the hell..." The good thing about *The Bill* was they had a team who would back you, led by Peter Cregeen, who I consider to be one of the best executive producers we've ever had; he was always game for his directors to try different things. I used to love doing a tracking shot that developed into an over the shoulder shot, which then moved into a reverse on someone and that was the scene covered. I was able to do those shots because they had a great camera crew and a team of fantastic actors, who all knew their lines and how to find the camera, there wasn't a dud among them.'

'There were some good scripts and some not-so-good scripts, but if you could get your hands on a Geoff McQueen script you were lucky. *Stop and Search* was also a controversial script, because of the scene with W.S.C. Kilnair getting stabbed by the junkie's needle and we had to work out how to do that. It had plenty of speed too, with over thirty scenes in twenty-five minutes. Ken Ware was a very clever man, he could be a grumpy old sod, but once you got used to him you realised he was a really good script editor. I was always driving him mad with my ideas, "Can we try this? What about that?" That's why in *Stop and Search* you see decorators in the corridor painting the ceiling and the woman who has found a monkey; I wanted to add anything I could think of that would make my episodes different. I had another idea when we introduced Tosh Lines, who I felt should be quite a scruffy character. I gave Kevin Lloyd this old plastic bag to carry around, which you see him holding in his very first shot in the car park. It helped make it all real.'

Tim Vaughan (Script Editor)

'*Stop and Search* was a great script from Geoff McQueen, directed by Terry Marcel with his usual aplomb: every time Terry came to work on the show, you knew you could expect a packed Sun Hill, filled with some really unexpected little moments — such as, in this episode, a woman walking through shot carrying a chimpanzee! But mostly, looking back on this one, I'm reminded of what a joy it was to work with Geoff. In the early days, he used to come into my office and natter, usually anxious to know how well I thought the show was going, and whether it would survive in the competitive world of ITV. He'd already had a few successes, with *Give Us a Break, Stay Lucky*, and *Boon* — and had had the idea of *Woodentop*, the first ever episode of the show, while painting and decorating a police station, standing on a ladder listening to all these coppers talking. The scripts he sent me were usually late and always haphazardly arranged — I remember ringing him once in a panic to get a script and and was fobbed off with the excuse — "I've just got to go out and get a new typewriter ribbon, and it'll be with you!" That was one of his many gambits, used far too often for me to buy it! He was terrible at spelling, punctuation and so on, and his ideas often seemed to come out of the blue, but when the scripts at last arrived, and you'd figured out what he was trying to say, and how to put all the ideas in it together, the end result was just pure gold.'

'Along with *An Old Fashioned Term* and *Yesterday, Today, Tomorrow, Stop and Search* was one of his best, I think: a lovely story for the newly-arrived Kevin Lloyd, whose performance always reminds me of an English Peter Falk: brisk, but painstaking and thorough as he imparts some of his detective wisdom to Carver — and coming up with the means by which Ch. Supt. Brownlow can see off the solicitor, Ms. Barnscroft (who, in keeping with the period, uses the "N" word as she denounces the harassment employed by Sun Hill officers). We get that story, as well as the investigation of the "confession" from Mr. Baxter (a tremendous performance from the late Ray Mort), the striking predicament of Special Constable Defoe and his fiancee WSC Kilnair — and D.S. Roach's attempts on Insp. Frazer. As always, Geoff packed the episode with incident, insight, humour and tragedy - so I never really had to worry that much about Geoff's typewriter ribbon!'

'Geoff McQueen soon became fairly wealthy as the show continued to grow and prosper. I was chewing the cud with him one evening in the office some time later when the janitor at Barlby Road came in to ask him to move his car, as it was blocking the driveway. I can't remember now what car Geoff had, but it was snazzy, an Aston Martin, I think. The janitor was really chuffed when Geoff invited him to move it himself, as we were busy, and when he'd gone, Geoff said, "it wasn't blocking the drive: I'd parked it. He just wants a drive in it." Twenty or so minutes later, the janitor came back, crestfallen. He'd not only driven Geoff's car — he'd pranged it, and bent the bumper, or grille, or whatever. Geoff reacted — I was expecting an explosion — but Geoff took a deep breath — looked at him a moment — and just said, "Oh, never mind, mate, these things happen". That was Geoff McQueen for you — liberal, humane, easy-going, kind — a wonderful writer, and a great guy to be with. It was a terrible tragedy when he died, still in his 40s, only a couple of years later. He is much missed.'

SPOOK STUFF

Written by Geoff McQueen

Directed by Terry Marcel

Series 4: Episode 31

Broadcast: Tuesday 1 November 1988

Viewing Figures: 11.40m

ITV Chart Position: 10

Case Narrative

D.S. Ted Roach gets lucky when he meets an informer at the dog track. But with D.I. Frank Burnside to work with, luck isn't the only thing Roach will need...

Regular Cast

Sgt. Cryer (Eric Richard), D.I. Burnside (Christopher Ellison), D.S. Roach (Tony Scannell), Insp. Frazer (Barbara Thorn), Ch. Insp. Conway (Ben Roberts), W.P.C. Martella (Nula Conwell), P.C. Stamp (Graham Cole), Ch. Supt. Brownlow (Peter Ellis), D.C Dashwood (Jon Iles), D.C. Lines (Kevin Lloyd), D.C. Carver (Mark Wingett), Sgt. Peters (Larry Dann), P.C. Hollis (Jeff Stewart).

Guest Cast

Ch. Insp. McBride (Andrew McCulloch), Sinbad (Daniel Peacock), C.I.A. Man (Ray Thompson), Mrs. Gary (Gay Baynes), Mr. Gary (Blain Fairman), Supermarket Employee (Tracy Hyde), Supermarket Manager (Tom Karol), Dolly (Joan Turner), Abby (Astley Harvey), Terry (Jonathon Jackson).

Uncredited Personnel

W.P.C. Ford (Vikki Gee-Dare), D.C. Baker (Victor Gallucci), P.C. Lovell (Derek Lyons), Floor Assistant (Richard Marson).

Production Team

Casting Director (Julia Lisney), Title Music (Andy Pask, Charlie Morgan), Costume Designer (Dennis Griffith), Make Up Designer (Gilly Wakeford), Graphics (Ethan Ames), Videotape Editor (John Sharland), Lighting (Allen Harradine), Camera (Chas Watts), Sound (Robert Newton, Paul Langwade), Production Buyer (Trevor Young), Location Manager (Quenton Annis), Floor Manager (Barry Beckett), Stage Manager

(Susan Shattock), Production Manager (Brian Heard), Production Assistant (Sylvia Rumney), Technical Adviser (Wilf Knight), Script Editor (Tim Vaughan), Series Script Editor (Kenneth Ware), Designers (Robin Parker, Jill Reedman), Executive Producer (Peter Cregeen), Producer (Richard Bramall).

Observation Notes

Spook Stuff (Production No: D4046, VTR No: THS/45281) was shot between Monday 5th and Friday 9th September 1988. The opening scene where Martella and Stamp respond to a shoplifter was filmed at 114-120 Notting Hill Gate, W11. This supermarket is now a Tesco Metro. The market scene in which Chief Insp. Conway introduces Insp. Frazer to Dolly was filmed outside 232 Portobello Road, Notting Hill, W11. The dog track scenes where Roach meets Sinbad were filmed at the Hackney Wick Stadium, which had also featured earlier in *Witness*. The scene where Burnside sets a trap for Sinbad was filmed under the railway bridge on the Scrubs Lane end of Mitre Way, W10. Burnside and McBride are observing from the end of the adjoining Bracewell Road. As with *Stop and Search*, the final pub scene featuring Roach, Cryer and Burnside was shot in The Earl Derby, on the Southern Row side of the building, W10.

Spook Stuff sees Roach, as so often, trying to get a result and coming up short. The Character Notes described Ted as being 41 years old and "Not exactly a slob, Roach relies on getting the job done with the minimum of real effort – though, when being watched, he disguises this with a show of blood, sweat and tears, tie loose at the neck, hair unruly, and whatever other instinctive tricks of the art he can improvise. The demands of his work, like his life, seem always to be running just ahead of him. His manner is like that of a man who can't quite control an over-powered car. But for all that, he is, at most times, genial and placid. However, when hounded by superiors or when his failings catch up with him, he occasionally shows a flash of Gaelic temper. His normal way of dealing with stress, though, is to resort to the bottle. He keeps some Scotch in his desk, which everyone, including the Chief Superintendent, is aware of. And he is constantly in trouble because of it. He has a young girlfriend whom, we suspect, he needs more than she needs him. Roach knows all the dodges, all the angles, yet seems likely to crash at any moment. In spite of his faults, he is, as his previous boss Galloway admitted, "a good old-fashioned policeman and catcher of villains.""

Witness Statements

Peter Cregeen (Executive Producer)

'I thought Tony Scannell brought something very positive to the series and he was very popular with the public, even though the rather shambolic Roach was certainly not a favourite character amongst senior police officers. Before *The Bill*, police officers had always been played by older actors on British television, whereas our police force was actually much younger than how it was being represented. We always tried to cast younger actors to reflect that, though I always thought Tony looked slightly older than he actually was. He had very good chemistry with Jon Iles; they were like chalk and cheese, but they worked so well together. Tony wasn't somebody who ever came to see me to complain that his part wasn't big enough and he never talked to me at great lengths about the rationalisation of his character. I think Tony really created the character of Roach and the writers loved writing for him, because they had a character they could really develop and could react to what he gave them. You never quite knew what Tony was going to come up with next; he had a danger about him and I've always liked dangerous actors. He was an invaluable member of the cast.'

Terry Marcel (Director)

'When I got a script, I would first work with Ken Ware to clear up any story points I was unhappy with. Then I would work out all the shots in my mind and break the script down into its different components and assess their feasibility. Next, you would work with your team to find the locations and sort a schedule. *The Bill* also had a very good casting team; very rarely did they get any of the guest parts wrong. I'm also very keen on background, which goes back to my love of those early 1930s movies, where all the supporting artists were working their arses off in the background, hoping that someone might spot them and they were going to become the next Gary Cooper. They had such a good team of supporting artists on *The Bill*, who were always on board for getting involved. For example in *Spook Stuff*, I added the birthday party going on in the canteen, because in workplaces people are always doing things like that and it helped the station feel alive. I also brought Vic Gallucci onto *The Bill*, who had been in a couple of my movies and was always great to work with. He's a good guy and we have stayed in touch.'

'The one thing that's a shame about *The Bill* is that many of those very fine actors haven't enjoyed the same level of success since leaving the series. That doesn't apply to them all of course, but they all deserved to go on to do fantastic stuff and I would have loved to have been in a position to work with them all again. *Spook Stuff* ended with that pub scene between Tony Scannell and Eric Richard, followed by Chris Ellison. They were really good actors, so from a directing point of view there was nothing I could teach them in terms of acting, but I could certainly hope to bring out the best in them and they delivered. I'm also pretty square in terms of how I liked to set my camera up and here I liked how that scene played out, on one good master shot for two minutes. Chas Watts was a good cameraman and he'd come up with great ideas as well. If you've got the right people and the scripts are good, you can't go wrong. I loved working there, it was a great place to work.'

'It wasn't actually my idea to work in the business. I grew up near Slough and after leaving school, my dad, who was a bookmaker, suggested I should try and get a job at Pinewood Studios... so I just got on my bike and rode over there. When I got to the gate, standing there was a man called Maurice, who was dressed up like a sergeant-in-arms in his uniform. He said, "What do you want, son?" I explained I'd like to get a job in the studios. He let me in and told me to go and find a man called Seth Harris, who explained the whole studio system to me. But he then showed me a piece of paper, which had 21 names on it. These were the names of sons and daughters of people already working at Pinewood, who were waiting to get in. I asked him if he could put my name on the list and he put mine on the bottom. I rode back home and about 15 minutes later, the phone rang and it was Seth. Someone had pulled out at the last minute and he asked me if I could come in tomorrow? I did and I got a job as a mailboy... true story!'

'This was in 1960 and in those days when you joined the mailroom, there were three mailboys and you started as number three. Then gradually, as the others moved up, you became number one. At that point, you'd have the discussion about where you wanted to go. I decided I wanted to go to production and when the chance came to go up to the next stage, I became a runner, where again you had to work your way up to number one. Then I got a very good break and started to work for Disney when they were using the studios. Then, when the studio system broke down and they decided they weren't able to keep people on regular wages anymore, we all went freelance. I became a third assistant director and then moved up to second assistant and then first assistant.'

'I worked on some big features, including *Straw Dogs* with Sam Peckinpah and Ridley Scott's first movie, *The Duelists*. I also made several movies with Richard Fleischer, who was technically brilliant. But the one I admired most of all, in terms of working on the floor, was Blake Edwards, who I made several *Pink Panther* films with. He was one of the big Hollywood directors and the only one I ever worked with who would walk onto the set and it would go quiet automatically. He was a giant of a man and a big presence, but he also made it fun and we couldn't stop laughing at times. He liked to work in a very calm environment, where he allowed his actors to breathe and didn't put them under any pressure. He was my idol and helped shape the way I later directed.'

Tim Vaughan (Script Editor)

'One of the most astonishing experiences I had whilst working on *The Bill* happened after work one night, when I popped in for a pint on my way home in Hammersmith. Sitting in this pub was a bloke who was clearly a fairly serious villain. He was wearing an awful lot of bling, round his neck and all over all of his fingers, and various cauliflower-eared bruisers, evidently his minders, were getting his drinks, fetching and carrying for him, and and paying him obsequious homage. I'd met plenty of cops by then, but never a villain, so I decided to talk to this chap. We talked for a good ten minutes and he was perfectly friendly and affable...'

'Then half an hour later, when I went to the loo, I was followed in there by one of this man's minders, who cornered me and said, "Here. That bloke out there's a face, and very dangerous. He thinks you're Old Bill. He's told me that if you can't prove you're not Old Bill, me and a couple of the others are going to have to break both your legs..." He told me that he didn't personally relish the thought of breaking my legs, but if it had to be done, he'd do it. I told him not to worry. We went back into the lounge bar and I sat next to this "face", and said, "I hear you think I'm a police officer?" I proved to him that I wasn't by taking him through every one of the principal cast of the show, their real names, where we filmed it, and so on. One of the minders was still suspicious and asked, 'What's the name of that pub you all drink at?' I gave him the name of the North Pole Pub, favoured by cast and crew and just down from Barlby Road. The "face" relaxed and apologised for having suspected me.'

'The minder then piped up with, "I know that pub! I was in there about four months ago, tooled up. I was going to kill someone - I had a sawn-off in my coat, ready to do him. I bought a drink and had a look around for the target: he was there - and I was just about to pull my shooter out when they all came in - Sergeant Cryer, Burnside, Roach, Conway, Ackland, the lot of them. I thought, fuck me, the place is crawling with coppers, so I left. It was only when I got half way home that I realised it was all those cunts off the fucking telly!" It was then that I realised that *The Bill* was evidently as popular with the villains as it was with the police...'

Richard Marson (Floor Assistant)

'My dad was a lawyer who occasionally worked for London Weekend Television and would sometimes take me with him. This was pre-safeguarding, so he would literally go into a studio and say to the floor manager, "Can I park my son here for the next hour while I go to a meeting?" LWT was very much a family company, like a lot of the TV companies were in those days; it wasn't exactly cosy, but it was friendly and everyone knew everyone else. I will never forget how vividly I was struck by the smell of the studio, that combination of electricity and paint, mixed with adrenaline and fear. I remember thinking how glamorous the floor manager's job was, "Shot 42, very quiet please!" I just wanted to be involved and that never deviated from the age of 12.'

'My first taste of the BBC came when I was writing for *Doctor Who Magazine*, which I had started doing when I was 17, thanks to help from a friend who got me an interview with the wonderful Louise Jameson. My mother had been a journalist and she helped me format my manuscript and I submitted this interview. What started out as a hobby soon became official and I was being invited to go and watch studio recordings at Television Centre and record interviews. It was incredible, though at the time I don't think I realised how lucky I was! I very quickly became aware that *Doctor Who* was regarded with a lot of stigma at the time, and my being associated with it, even very peripherally, wasn't necessarily going to be helpful when I started applying for jobs.'

'To become a floor assistant, you had a probationary period, where one of the first things you did was the BBC version of The Knowledge, which London cab drivers have to do in their training. You had to very quickly learn all the ins and outs of Television Centre, because you would often be picking up an artist or a contributor from reception, to then take them anywhere in the building. You might be told to go to production office E567, which you needed to know meant East Tower, 5th floor, room 67… You would be tested in front of a BBC board, which was very scary because you'd have four people behind a table staring at you, asking questions. It took me three goes to get the job, which was standard at the time, whatever your background. Television Centre was an amazing place to work and I loved that the BBC was fully subsidised, so you could eat really cheaply at any time, or you would get a "soft-sole shoe allowance" of £5.22, to buy footwear for the studio. You had to know what you were entitled to beyond your miserable little pay packet.'

'How *The Bill* came along was thanks to a weird reciprocal arrangement, almost like a gentleman's agreement, between Studio management at the BBC and the much smaller version they had at Thames Television in Teddington. As a BBC floor assistant, you could offer yourself to Thames during a contract break and see if they could use you on any of their programmes. I did *Rod Jane and Freddy*, which was a classic show, and then I did *This Is Your Life* with the unbelievably wonderful Michael Aspel, probably one of the nicest men in telly. Then I was seconded to go and do four episodes of *The Bill* in 1988, which was a kind of spin-off empire in its own world at Barlby Road, though they all still reported back to Teddington.'

'I joined the Blue unit and I was incredibly impressed with how they made *The Bill*, it was very pioneering for the time. I think the way they were making television, using the kit that was available, was really groundbreaking. It was an incredibly energised production and very exciting to be around, because there was always so much going on. I remember being warned really early on by a wardrobe guy, "Don't let the young actors handcuff you to the set, because it's one of their favourite games…" Well on my second day, I did get handcuffed to a radiator in Barlby Road, about 10 minutes before the coach was setting off! Because of the way it was organised, once the coaches left there would be almost nobody back at base, so I was yelling for help at the top of my voice. It was almost like my initiation and luckily this same wardrobe guy heard me, rolled his eyes and said, "You didn't listen then!"'

'There was a lot of creative traffic between these young actors, who were all interesting and stimulating company. It was up to the regulars to keep in their head where they were, in relation to the story. If any of them wanted to establish or build up their character, they had to do their homework in their own time, because there wasn't a rehearsal room where they could all sit around and discuss it over coffee. There were no rehearsals at all; once they came on set, they would block a scene and then shoot it, which meant that sometimes they could be in and out in 90 minutes! It was an incredible pressure, but the younger actors seemed to love the challenge of how little time they had to do their scenes; you could see them really getting an energy from it, especially if it was an action scene or one that relied on a bit of tension.'

'I love it when an actor or a member of a production team knows what they've got and that they're onto a good thing and are therefore appreciative. Jeff Stewart was someone who was enjoying his work and wasn't moaning about not being at the National. I never remember him ever being like that, I think he was really happy to be working. He was also someone who had a long wait for his own storyline in *The Bill* and I think his hunger as an actor and the part of Reg were a perfect collision and he created a great character. I also think he liked to wind up and subvert some of the slightly grander members of the team, who perhaps considered themselves to be more serious actors. I liked Jeff a lot, even though he was one of the naughty people who handcuffed me to the radiator during the making of *Spook Stuff*.'

'I remember getting a cup of coffee for Wilf Knight, the Police Advisor and we had a quick chat. I asked him how realistic *The Bill* could be. He said that the toughest thing to get right in a police drama was the "shady morality" around a lot of police work, where in order to get results, coppers sometimes had to do things that were quite suspect. He said characters like Burnside or Roach weren't corrupt, but they sometimes had to bend the rules in a situation, where if they didn't they wouldn't get a result. He explained that in real life, particularly when it goes wrong in detective work, that's when you end up with a scandal. But when it goes right, no one is actually going to say that the reason it went right was that they turned a blind eye here or did something dodgy there... I found those human politics quite interesting and I also remember finding out what all the acronyms like FATAC meant. I loved learning, which as a floor assistant, you were doing all the time.'

EVACUATION

Written by Edwin Pearce

Directed by Terry Green

Series 4: Episode 32

Broadcast: Thursday 3 November 1988

Viewing Figures: 13.20m

ITV Chart Position: 4

Case Narrative

P.C. Smith makes a discovery that causes severe disruption at Sun Hill – and which could have fatal consequences.

Regular Cast

Sgt. Cryer (Eric Richard), P.C. Smith (Robert Hudson), Insp. Frazer (Barbara Thorn), W.P.C. Martella (Nula Conwell), Ch. Insp. Conway (Ben Roberts), P.C. Edwards (Colin Blumenau), W.P.C. Ackland (Trudie Goodwin), P.C. Haynes (Eamonn Walker), D.I. Burnside (Christopher Ellison), P.C. Ramsey (Nick Reding), D.C. Lines (Kevin Lloyd), D.C Dashwood (Jon Iles), D.S. Roach (Tony Scannell), Sgt. Penny (Roger Leach), Sgt. Peters (Larry Dann), P.C. Hollis (Jeff Stewart), P.C. Frank (Ashley Gunstock), P.C. Banks (Russell Lewis).

Guest Cast

Wassermann (Jim McManus), Gloria (Debbie Wheeler), Norris (Matthew Scurfield), Filbert (Eddie Tagoe), Gertie (Valerie Lilley), Sandra (Tilly Vosburgh), Yuppie Man (Jeffrey Perry), Yuppie Woman (Jane Hayward), Weak Minded Man (Paul McCleary), Bill Farmer (John Hug).

Production Team

Stunt Arranger (Peter Diamond), Casting Director (Julia Lisney), Title Music (Andy Pask, Charlie Morgan), Costume (Allard Tobin, Dennis Hogan), Make Up Designer (Gilly Wakeford), Graphics (Ethan Ames), Videotape Editor (John Sharland), Lighting (Graham Jaggers), Camera (Peter Edwards), Sound (Alan Norman, Alan Lester), Production Buyer (Trevor Young), Location Manager (Douglas Macdonald), Floor Manager (Aidan Boulter), Stage Manager (Marilyn Edwards), Production Manager (Brian Heard), Production Assistant (Caroline O'Reilly), Technical Adviser (Wilf Knight), Assistant Script Editor (Elizabeth Bradley), Series Script Editor

(Kenneth Ware), Design (Robin Parker, Peter Joyce), Executive Producer (Peter Cregeen), Producer (Richard Bramall).

Observation Notes

Evacuation (Production No: D4049, VTR No: THS/45284) was shot between Monday 12th and Friday 16th September 1988. The final pub scene was then filmed in The Earl Derby, this time on the Bosworth Road-facing side. The rest of the episode was filmed in the base at Barlby Road, where future regulars Susan Majolier (Marion) and Vikki Gee-Dare (W.P.C. Ford) appear uncredited, as does Russell Lewis as P.C. Banks, who was missed off the credits despite a lengthy dialogue scene in the canteen.

Evacuation concerns a mysterious package being left in the front office. This entrance to the station is described in the Background Information document issued to writers: "The Front Office at Sun Hill consists of a waiting area for the public, with a small counter. A PC, on his/her own, sits at a desk behind the counter, in a small room, probably shielded from the customers by a glass screen, to give them time to take a look at them as they come in. Then when he is ready, he goes forward to deal with them. But only ONE AT A TIME. (There is almost always a notice in the public waiting area, warning people of this restriction)."

Evacuation was the first of six episodes of *The Bill* directed by Terry Green, a TV veteran who made the jump into directing after success as a designer on iconic programmes such as *The Avengers, Red Cap* and *Armchair Theatre*. Green became a specialist at directing crime drama, helming multiple episodes of *The Sweeney, Special Branch, Target, The Chinese Detective* and *Bergerac.* He was also one of the longest-serving directors on *Minder.* Terry Green passed away in 2013, aged 77.

Evacuation was adapted for the Netherlands police series *Bureau Kruislaan* in 1993, though Christopher Russell was erroneously credited for the original story, rather than Edwin Pearce. The title of the episode, *De Bom* translates as "The Bomb" and was final episode of the first season. The episode is a faithful adaption, including the singing prisoner. The finale differs after the station is evacuated and in a dramatic twist, Agent Ron Smit (their version of P.C. Tony Smith) accidentally sets the bomb by using his police radio, which triggers the explosion. After 26 episodes broadcast between 1992-93, *Bureau Kruislaan* returned in 1995 for a final season of 13 episodes, all adapted from *The Bill* scripts.

Witness Statements

Peter Joyce (Designer)

'I went to art school at a very early age when I was 13, because I failed the 11-plus. I studied at the Ealing School of Art, where I was in the same form as Pete Townshend of *The Who* and I designed various record covers and sleeves for him. When I left college, I did various jobs, including working as graphic designer on *Reader's Digest Magazine*. Eventually there was an ad in the newspaper, the cutting of which I still have, that read, "Spacecraft designer needed in Slough Trading Estate". I got the job and my television career started off working on *Thunderbirds*, where I designed the spacecrafts and various sets for the puppets. Then I didn't work for a little while, because you get pigeonholed in the business and in those days the phone never used to ring unless it was somebody wanting a spacecraft designer. The next job I got was working on Stanley Kubrick's *2001: A Space Odyssey*.'

'Eventually I broke out of the spaceship mould and one of my first big movies was *Where Eagles Dare* starring Clint Eastwood and Richard Burton, which was a good film and made a lot of money. I then worked on a few horror movies, though working on films ruined my first marriage, because I was always on location and never at home. I worked on a film called the *Rise and Fall of Idi Amin* where I worked in Kenya for nine months and I didn't see my family at all. I tried to save the marriage by going into television, where you had a different lifestyle because you were at home in the mornings and when you get home you could read the kids a bedtime story. I made the move back into television and I eventually became the series designer on *The Professionals*. I then got a job at Thames Television, where I designed the sets for all sorts of programmes like *This Is Your Life* and *Home James!*'

'Then I got a job on *The Bill* and worked on the series for the next 14 years, eventually ending up as the Head of Design at Merton. When I started in 1988, Robin Parker was in charge of the department. Robin had a very short temper and was the sort of person who broke pencils and slammed doors, though I worked well with him. Robin was very fond of the police; I think he wanted to be a policeman in many ways. He loved going for lunch with them at Scotland Yard and would come back with lots of ideas. Robin would assign a different designer to each alternate episode. Traditionally in television, you would have a stock set in the studio that you used every week and then the rest of the scenes would be shot on location. Whereas on *The Bill*, our "stock" station set was also our location, which worked particularly well on *Evacuation*, where most of the action takes place entirely in the station.'

'When you work on a movie you get to know people slightly, but then you never see them again. When you join a show like *The Bill* and work on it for 52 weeks a year, you get to know people quite well and they become friends. There was lot of camaraderie between cast and crew and everybody used to go to the pub at lunchtime in those days. I always loved working with Trudie Goodwin, who is fantastic. Eric Richard is also a very nice chap who would always talk to the crew in between takes. Peter Cregeen was a very good executive producer; he was a drama person and had a talent for picking up a good script. I think he chose what stories were told at this time quite carefully. Peter was very involved with the detail of *The Bill*, because he had spent a lot of time with Geoff McQueen, whose brainchild the series was.'

'The director of *Evacuation* was Terry Green, who came from the East End of London and was very good with the crews. You were always guaranteed lots of laughs with Terry; the amount he used to drink was amazing! I remember I went to his house once to go through the script and his phone was ringing, but he didn't appear to hear it. I told him his phone was ringing, but he said, "Oh don't worry about it..." It turned out that when he'd had a new wooden floor installed into his house, the phone had slipped between the joists in the floorboards and the phone was still down there! It was people like that who made the job enjoyable. Sometimes us old timers meet up for a drink and recount all the old stories and get reminded of some of the problems and stresses we used to have, because things did go wrong along the way, but we always have a good laugh about it all now.'

Caroline O'Reilly (Production Assistant)

'I was the youngest of five children from a poor, working-class family. My parents had come over from Ireland before I was born and moved into a council house in Kennington, South East London. We lived in 4 Pownall Terrace and years before us, Charlie Chaplin had lived next door with his mother, who was a servant in number three. From a very early age, we used to have film crews down our street filming outside the house. We'd be hanging around asking questions, as kids do... "Hello

Mister, are you from the BBC or ITV?" They would pay us money either to get rid of us, or for us to help out in general. I remember my sister got asked to be in a shot, where she was skipping outside our house and then she passed Charlie's house. I used to love watching the film crews, who all wore really nice clothes and ate lovely food and drove expensive cars. I remember one executive producer in particular driving a yellow Rolls Royce! I'd had no idea what I wanted to do as a career until I saw those groups of media people and thought, "That looks like a good life."'

'My ambition became to work in the media and I geared all my school exams towards media production. I then went to college and after I earned my diploma, I got offered two secretarial jobs, one with Thames TV and the other with the BBC. I chose Thames because they were using electric typewriters, whilst the BBC were still using manual ones, which shows you how long ago it was! I started working in the office at Teddington and then began helping with the scripts in the office. That's when I realised I wanted to work as part of the crew on the floor. Luckily for me, especially in terms of encouraging people to move up in their careers, Thames TV was a really fantastic company to work for. They ran great training schemes every year that you could apply for. They paid you while they trained you and once you completed your course, you would then be guaranteed that job! I applied and got to train as a production assistant, which is the job I still do today as a freelancer, though we are now called script supervisors.'

'During my nine months training, I worked in all the departments at Thames: Light Entertainment, Sport, Documentaries, Children's TV and Drama. *Rumpole of the Bailey* was the first drama I worked on and then I was sent up to Barlby Road to work on *The Bill*, which was mostly crewed by freelancers. Because we were Thames staff, we were never going to be sent home on standby whenever there wasn't a big drama production being made at Teddington, because *The Bill* was running all year round. *Evacuation* was my first episode and it was a great programme to work on, not just because you were on friendly terms with everybody, but it was a good training ground for everyone at all grades.'

'An ITV half-hour is actually 24 and a half minutes of programme time, to allow for the commercial breaks. The general rule of thumb is that a page of a script runs at a minute on screen. But you can't assume that because a script is 24 pages long, it will run to 24 minutes on screen. A page from a scene where two coppers were having an argument with each other would be played fast and would likely be quicker than a minute. But if you had a page from an interview scene, or a victim talking about being raped, that one page of dialogue would last much longer than a minute. One of my responsibilities as production assistant was to time the script by acting out each scene in my head.'

'On average we would shoot about six minutes a day on *The Bill*, which is a lot. By comparison, on *Doc Martin* we shot four and a half minutes a day. On a feature film, you might not even shoot a minute a day, especially if there's a big stunt sequence. If I timed a script of *The Bill* and it was running at 30 minutes, we would cut scenes before we started shooting, because television is an expensive business and there was no point shooting material that would end up being cut. Equally. if the script was under running when I timed it, we would ask the writer to add some more scenes to the script. Then on the shoot itself, I would time each scene as we shot them and update the director at the end of each day, explaining whether the scenes were longer or shorter than anticipated. We would always shoot an extra three minutes on average, so they had footage that could play with and trim down in the edit, but any more would have been a waste of time and money.'

'Also as part of my prep for each episode, I would write a story breakdown that I would issue to each department. This would detail which characters were in each scene, any props they needed and what happened in the scene. If for example someone got a black eye, then I would write "Black Eye" next to that character's name in the breakdown for all the following scenes. This was very important for maintaining the continuity of the story order, because we always shot out of sequence. I also noted which shift patterns the characters were on for each episode, so the floor manager could make sure they had the correct actors on each set. If we had a CAD scene with Peters talking to Ackland and Stamp and we then moved onto a later scene where Hollis comes in to talk to Peters, we still had to make sure Ackland and Stamp were there, even if they didn't have dialogue in that scene because we have established their shift pattern.'

Aidan Boulter (Floor Manager)

'It was on *The Bill* that many of us made the jump from being a floor manager to becoming assistant directors. At this time in television, floor managers would traditionally look after the studio aspect of any production. But if there was any outside filming to be done, such as inserts for situation comedies or dramas, they would be shot on single camera film, usually on a little 16mm Arriflex. The location manager would actually act as the first assistant director on these shoots, which was always a bit odd for us, because we would do all the preparation work and then hand it over to somebody else to go and run the shoot on location. Those poor location managers were already rushed off their feet; they were not only running the set, but also looking after the location and any issues or problems that arose with that. They were also thinking ahead and planning what came next; there was too much work for them to do.'

'That all changed when *The Bill* came along, because as floor managers we had been managing the location filming when it was done as an outside broadcast on the one hour series. When the production made the move to single camera for the half-hour episodes, we felt that we should continue managing the location shooting. This meant learning a whole new set of skills and working as an assistant director with single camera, rather than floor managing a multi-camera television studio. It was a different way of working, because obviously you would be repeating the same action over and over within a scene, so that the editor can then choose from several different angles. Therefore you had to have your mind on background continuity and what a supporting artist was doing at a certain time. It was at this point that our credits changed on *The Bill* from floor manager to first assistant director.'

'It was definitely a great time to work in television, and it is only since the 1990s that people have become pigeon-holed into one specific area of television, which is a huge shame. There are plenty of multi-talented people who don't get the same opportunities today, which means an awful lot of wasted talent. Another difference, thanks to accountants and insurance companies, is that crews don't go for a drink together at lunchtimes anymore. Back then *everybody* went to the bar, which was where all of the business took place! Thames had three bars at Teddington Studios: on the top floor was The Club Bar; on the next floor down was the Terrace Bar and moored up against the riverbank was the MV Iris, which was the executive dining room (and bar!) Then next door we had the Anglers pub; and next door to that we had The Tide End Cottage. Then over the road was the British Motor Yacht Club, which also used to open its bar for Thames staff. It was great fun!'

PERSONAL IMPORTS
Written by Kevin Clarke
Directed by Brian Farnham

Series 4: Episode 33
Broadcast: Tuesday 8 November 1988

Case Narrative
P.C. Melvin is injured in a desperate raid at a chemist's shop, Carver conducts a surveillance, and Martella and Roach look into a strange case of truancy.

Regular Cast
D.S. Roach (Tony Scannell), D.C. Carver (Mark Wingett), W.P.C. Martella (Nula Conwell), D.C Dashwood (Jon Iles), D.C. Lines (Kevin Lloyd), Sgt. Peters (Larry Dann), P.C. Melvin (Mark Powley), P.C. Stamp (Graham Cole), CAD Room P.C. (Oscar Peck).

Guest Cast
Auntie (Christine Collins), Mrs. Kemp (Cherith Mellor), Roxanne (Paul O'Grady), Morris (Robert Ralph), Fylde (Stevan Rimkus), Fiona (Sarah Woodward), Mr. Kemp (Ronald Markham), Omir (Joel Samuels).

Production Team
Casting Director (Brian Wheeler), Title Music (Andy Pask, Charlie Morgan), Costume (Allard Tobin, Dennis Hogan), Make Up Designer (Gilly Wakeford), Graphics (Ethan Ames), Videotape Editor (Terence E. Badham), Lighting (Graham Jaggers), Camera (Peter Edwards), Sound (Richard Longley, Paul Langwade), Production Buyer (Sarah Prebble), Location Manager (Eddie Mares), Floor Manager (Peter Price), Stage Manager (Gregory Kinchin), Production Manager (Brian Heard), Production Assistant (Krystyna Wojciechowska), Technical Adviser (Wilf Knight), Programme Associate (Valerie Farron), Assistant Script Editor (Barbara Cox), Series Script Editor (Kenneth Ware), Design (Robin Parker, Colin Andrews), Executive Producer (Peter Cregeen), Producer (Michael Ferguson).

Observation Notes
Personal Imports (Production No: D4048, VTR No: THS/45283) was shot between Monday 12th and Friday 16th September 1988. The pub seen on the corner as Mark Powley runs into the opening shot was the Kensington

Tavern, which was writer Kevin Clarke's local pub. The chemist shop where Melvin is attacked was filmed in 1 Russell Gardens, Holland Park, W14. The shop was chosen as a location as a reward to the owner, who showed his drugs safe to Kevin Clarke whilst he was writing the script.

The scenes featuring Carver's observation from Mrs. Kemp's house were filmed on Northumberland Place, Notting Hill, W11. The following scene where Roach picks Carver up was filmed on Bevington Road, W10. Roach is then attacked in the public toilets under 2-4 Bevington Road, W10, which still remain today. Carver pursues the suspect down the adjoining Golborne Road, where the design team have masked the street sign above the Portobello Road Post Office, which is still open today.

The scene where Roach meets Roxanne outside the Earl of Monmouth pub was filmed outside what in reality was The Tavistock Arms, 41 Tavistock Crescent, W11. The pub was demolished in 2010 and replaced by flats.

The scene where Carver is ordered to break off his pursuit was filmed on the corner of Artesian Road and Needham Road, Notting Hill, W11. The Star Tavern seen on the corner is now called The Cock & Bottle.

Lines and Dashwood set the trap for Fylde on the Lancaster West Estate, pursuing him through Barandon Walk, W11. Grenfell Tower was used to capture overhead shots of the pursuit and can be seen in the distance.

Personal Imports was the first of seven episodes written by Kevin Clarke, an acclaimed playwright and prolific writer of over 150 episodes of television drama. Before writing feature film screenplays, his many credits included *The Last Detective, The Inspector Lynley Mysteries, Doctor Who, Wycliffe, Minder, Casualty* and boxing drama *Ellington* starring Chris Ellison.

Witness Statements

Kevin Clarke (Writer)
'When the bi-weekly episodes of *The Bill* started, I hadn't been writing for very long. I got into television via a play I had written and directed called *The Jackpot*, which fortunately attracted some interest and was seen as being a little bit dangerous. A year or so later, when the team at *The Bill* were drawing up a list of new writers they might like to see, I was lucky enough to be on it. By then I had a little telly experience, having written half a dozen scripts, and I was invited down to Teddington Studios, where I had never been before, for an interview.'

'I was meeting the script editor Ken Ware, who is sadly no longer with us. Ken was a small man who feared nobody and I had been pre-warned that he could be irascible and wasn't afraid to tell people where to get off. But I just talked to him like I would talk to anyone and I actually found him to be quite friendly and very encouraging. He said very nice things about *The Jackpot*, which he'd read. He then asked me if I had any ideas for *The Bill*... Well if you've got any sense as a writer, you should always have an idea to offer. In my case, I'd spent every minute, of every hour, since getting the phone call, thinking about an idea. I then did my best to deceive Ken and make it sound like I had just casually thought of the idea on my way to the interview...'

'At the time, I was going out with a social worker and the bones of the idea for *Personal Imports* were drawn from a real case she had been involved in, where a little boy was being sexually exploited. In real life they were African, though in *The Bill* I made them Turkish immigrants because I didn't think the programme had done that before and I thought it would make a change. I explained to Ken what my girlfriend had been working on and how it might make a good idea for a story. I've never forgotten how he responded to my pitch... "Little boys getting screwed... I like that!" He was of course meaning the narrative idea and the fact that nobody had suggested it before, rather than anything sexual.'

'Ken commissioned me and said "This is a good show to get on, because there will be a repeat on Friday afternoon, so you'll get an hour's worth of money for a half-hour script." I hadn't realised this beforehand, so to come away with a commission, plus an amazing deal where I'd get 100% of my fee a week later in residuals, was just fantastic! Ken shook my hand and said, "If this first one works well, there will be more to follow..." I thought to myself, "Bloody hell!" We then walked to the door and Ken said, "Mind you, the show's only going to last a year, so make the most of it." I asked him why he thought it would only last a year and he said, "Well think about it, if it's on twice a week, that's 104 episodes a year... and there aren't 104 crimes!"'

'I was made to feel welcome on *The Bill* in a way I never had been before, nor since. Barbara Cox, who became my script editor, once told me that, "the writers have the run of the place." That was true and if I'd wanted to, I could have turned up at Barlby Road whenever I liked for a chat. Whilst I never turned up unannounced, what I was intent on doing throughout the early part of my career was going to all the filming of my scripts. I'd had no formal training as a writer, so I'd learned how to format scripts through trial and error and had no understanding of cameras or lights. By attending my filming, I could find out very quickly about how technical the medium of television is, and appreciate how highly skilled the people who would be making my scripts were in their roles on the production. At the first production meeting, when I asked Brian Farnham, who directed *Personal Imports* superbly, if I could come to the filming, he was very pleased and said I'd be very welcome. I learned an enormous amount from Brian, who is an extremely nice man.'

'I watched every minute of *Personal Imports* being filmed and Brian told me that he thought it was marvellous that I was so interested. He also liked the fact that I laugh at my own jokes, though quite often it was because I'd forgotten them by the time they were being filmed! And as all of those actors on *The Bill* were so damn good, it was a treat hearing them perform my dialogue, which I can assure you isn't always the case. There wasn't one weak member of that cast and you could give them absolutely anything to do and they could turn it on a sixpence. They would only usually do two takes on a scene, and often the second was only to have a back up in case something went wrong technically. The cast also all arrived word perfect, which again wasn't always the case when I worked on other programmes in the future.'

'In my interview, Ken Ware had said to me that he wanted "lots of action". I took him at his word and created four different strands in *Personal Imports* to keep it moving. At the end of the second day's filming, Brian Farnham came up to me looking really exhausted. He said, "71 scenes in 22 and a half minutes... don't ever do this to me again." I explained that Ken had told me to write "lots of action", to which Brian laughed and said "Lots of action means lots of set-ups!" Because I was so inexperienced, I hadn't thought about the fact that not only does every shot need to be set up, but it also needs to be dismantled before they can move onto the next one - and all that needs to be scheduled. If it hadn't been for Brian and his absolutely crack team, that episode wouldn't have been filmed in five days.'

'I clearly remember when they filmed the scene where Dashwood, Lines and Stamp hold Fylde over the metal railings of that balcony. When I wrote that scene, I put myself in the position of those detectives and thought, "What would I do to get this guy to talk?" Well what they did on screen is what I would have done. The cameraman, Peter Edwards, got that fantastic shot from below and really captured the height and the danger. I was standing down below and when Brian yelled, "Cut!" the actors stood back and it went really quiet... there was a silence and nobody moved... I asked the P.A. "What's wrong?" She said, "We've never done anything like that before. This could be really controversial..." Of course, I later met police officers who told me they loved that scene!'

'Before I started writing *Personal Imports*, Barbara Cox asked me which of the characters I responded to. I hadn't thought about it before, but I immediately said, "Ted Roach." At the time, I couldn't rationalise why I picked him, but one of the things I have since learned as a writer, is that in order to effectively write for any character – even those I "borrow", rather than create – they have to be an aspect of your own personality. And whilst I didn't consciously know it, I identified in the character of Ted Roach – and perhaps more so in the case of dear Tony Scannell himself – an older version of myself that I feared I might become. So in some ways, I wrote Roach as a nightmare version of myself. I put him in that t-shirt with the revolting slogan "I've done it in Corfu", which I'd seen someone else wearing before. I thought it was marvellous having Roach wearing that T-shirt, which was all they'd had lying around in Sun Hill lost property, whilst interviewing someone for immoral behaviour in a public place.'

'Perhaps most memorably, *Personal Imports* saw the introduction of Roach's informant, Roxanne. When I was writing the scene, originally I had a prostitute clattering down the pavement in high heels, who Roach was going to pull into his car and get some information. As I was writing the scene, a line came into my head that I liked and wanted to use... "Mr. Roach, where do you get those ties from?" But as I was writing Roach pulling this woman into the car, I thought, "this feels familiar..." We'd all seen scenes like this in *The Sweeney*, with Jack Regan getting information from tarts. But I liked the line about the ties, so how could I use that line, but make the scene different? At that moment, I remembered seeing a documentary about Buster Keaton, where Keaton had solved the problem of being trapped in a cabin, with a bear on the other side of the door, trying to get in and kill. Keaton thought of the brilliant illogical gag of spinning the door around, so that the bear was then on the inside and he was free. How could I spin this scene around? "What if Roxanne is a man dressed as a woman?" Which worked because a transvestite would know about the gay scene... So off we went!'

'A few weeks later, we were filming the scene on a cold evening near Westbourne Park. Brian had told me beforehand that he'd got "Lily Savage" for the part... "She's very big on the drag scene in London." I watched them film the first take outside the car and I nearly fell over when I first heard Paul O'Grady's accent... When they were sat in the car between takes, I ran over and asked Paul if he was from Liverpool. "Near there yeah... Birkenhead." I said, "I'm from Birkenhead!" We were of a similar age and we started comparing what schools we'd gone to, it was a remarkable co-incidence! The house rule at the time was that there should be no returning guest characters in *The Bill*. But because the chemistry between Paul and Tony was so powerful, I got a message through from Peter Cregeen, saying they needed another episode...'

Mark Wingett (D.C. Jim Carver)

'*Personal Imports* was the beginning of Tony Scannell's storyline with Paul O'Grady as Roxanne, which hinted that they might have had an affair with each other, which was extraordinarily ahead of its time. I worked closely with Tony for many years and we later shared a dressing room at Merton, where we were like *The Odd Couple*! Tony was one of the people who laid the foundations of *The Bill*; he was passionate about the character of Ted Roach, who he really made his own, and he was absolutely fundamental to the original cast having input into our characters. He was a very, very good actor, who was always fully committed and acted with an intensity, which brought an inner life to every scene he played. He was very inventive and would often do something quite spontaneous in a take, which was great for me as an actor doing scenes with him, because you wouldn't quite know what you were going to get from him and he got my juices going. We locked horns occasionally, because as the more experienced actor he had strong views about how a scene should be played, but we would usually meet halfway.'

'His like has disappeared from the acting profession now; the proud Irishman who worked hard and drank hard, who hated bullies and fought for what he believed in. I used to come into work in the morning and Tony would still be dressed in his tuxedo from the night before! His nickname on *The Bill* was "Tony Scandal", because he was always in the newspapers, for one reason or another! He was no angel, but he was a charming man when he wanted to be and I can still remember some of the jokes he used to tell us on set. He even wrote a cookery book, called

"Drunk and Dish Orderly", which only contained meals that could be cooked with alcohol! We had some wild times together.'

Oscar Peck (CAD Room P.C.)

'I went to stage school and got off to a great start when I was cast in a comedy series called *Get Some In!* where I played one of the regular "Erks", opposite people like Robert Lindsay. That was great because it went on for a few years. I also got a couple of nice parts early on, including the very first episode of *Fawlty Towers*, playing the son of Terence Conoley's character Mr Wareing, who famously orders "a gin and orange, a lemon squash and a scotch and water." I found it tough trying to make a living as an actor and when I was 20 I started doing temp work for an agency, who then offered me a full-time job.'

'When you go to work, you want to do something that you don't dread going in to do and whilst I was earning money, I wasn't enjoying it. After a couple of years, I remember getting out of bed and thinking, "I can't do this again." To get back into working in film and television, I joined a number of agencies as a supporting artist, which I was able to do because I was already an Equity member, which was a requirement in those days. Some casting directors didn't look too kindly on actors working as supporting artists, even though we were all actors, singers or dancers. I actually started to get more cameo roles and speaking parts than I'd got before as an actor, whilst also making a really good living and having a lot of fun. I'd be working on massive movies like *Superman* one day and a Bond film the next, which was a really great way of earning a living and still be associated with the art of acting.'

'I also started to do a lot of television work, again with occasional cameo parts, on programmes like *Doctor Who, Only Fools & Horses, The Silver Chair* and a regular stint on *The Paul Daniels Magic Show*. Then there was a nice period where I would do two days a week on *EastEnders* and another two on *The Bill*, where because there were so many regular cast members, they didn't need many supporting artists. A small group of us got regular work wandering around in the background, playing cops and robbers. The wardrobe department would put our uniforms out ready for us each time we turned up, which were always our own and weren't shared around. We all had our own epaulettes too and my number was 858. The uniforms in those days were so different to what police officers wear today, where they have stab vests and Tasers, whereas what we used to wear was more like a suit, with shirt and tie.'

'You never knew what you were going to do until you turned up, which was the fun of it. Some days there wouldn't be much going on, so we'd sit in the dressing room all day playing cards or Scrabble and the highlight of the day would be when the tea wagon came around! On other days you would be working all day, either getting involved in a scuffle or taking part in a long scripted scene. Because there were only five or six of us who were in regularly, we got to know the first assistant directors and Angela the casting director, who in turn got to know us and knew if we could do a line or two. That was how opportunities like the CAD Room scene in *Personal Imports* came along for me.'

'I knew the CAD set well because I had sat in there many times. We didn't have any audio coming through those headphones; that was all added on afterwards. I was very pleased to have a couple of lines in this episode, though it was still a little nervewracking sharing a scene with someone from the main cast. Larry Dann was such a friendly guy and and he made it all very relaxed. Larry lived quite close to us at the time and often used to say hello to us in the high street. I still felt the pressure, because it was a fast-moving show and they wouldn't want to be doing take after take. I was also sat next to another regular supporting artist, a really nice guy called Peter Gates-Fleming, though if I'd got my dialogue wrong in front of him, I'd have been in trouble going back to the dressing room with all my mates!'

'We were always invited to go to the Christmas parties that *The Bill* threw. One year they showed a spoof video, where the supporting artists played the main parts, and the regular cast were in the background. I played the Sergeant giving out instructions, while the main cast were asking me when their tea break would be. It was very funny and whilst it was never to be released, somebody must have a copy of it somewhere... All of the supporting artists on *The Bill* were pursuing other careers and around this time I started to do some work for an events company. This inspired me to form my own promotions and events agency, which has now been ticking over for more than 30 years. It surprises me when I get reminded about *The Bill* because it was a long time ago, but it's fantastic that these episodes are still being watched. I had a lot of fun and have great memories of working on programmes that have such an amazing following and people are still so fond of.'

PAPER CHASE
Written by Barry Appleton
Directed by Niall Leonard

Series 4: Episode 34
Broadcast: Thursday 10 November 1988

Viewing Figures: 13.55m
ITV Chart Position: 5

Case Narrative
A schoolgirl is kidnapped with a half-million pound ransom demand. For Burnside and the Sun Hill detectives, the chase is on.

Regular Cast
D.I. Burnside (Christopher Ellison), D.C Dashwood (Jon Iles), Insp. Frazer (Barbara Thorn), W.P.C. Brind (Kelly Lawrence), Ch. Insp. Conway (Ben Roberts), D.C. Lines (Kevin Lloyd), P.C. Frank (Ashley Gunstock).

Guest Cast
Technical Officer (Ewen Cummins), Celia Hortman (Christine Kavanagh), Mr. Hortman (Robert Morris), Joella Hortman (Angie Davies), Mrs. Downes (Theresa Streatfield), Paula (Becky Smith), Headmistress (Sally Faulkner), Secretary (Melanie Parr).

Uncredited Personnel
Press Officer (Rosane Chapman), Accountants (Anne Shields, David Saggs), Props Chargehand (John Walkham), Make Up Assistants (Carolyn Wills, Kate Rudlin, Adam Beck).

Production Team
Casting Director (Brian Wheeler), Title Music (Andy Pask, Charlie Morgan), Costume (Allard Tobin, Peter Roberts), Make Up Designer (Gilly Wakeford), Graphics (Ethan Ames), Videotape Editor (Colin Bocking), Lighting (Allen Harradine), Camera (Chas Watts), Sound (Robert Newton, Alan Lester), Production Buyer (Sarah Prebble), Location Manager (Rob Champion), First Assistant Director (David Cherrill), Stage Manager (Diana Paskin), Production Manager (Brian Heard), Production Assistant (Caroline Sutton), Technical Adviser (Wilf Knight), Series Script Editor (Kenneth Ware), Design (Robin Parker, Kyz Kistell), Executive Producer (Peter Cregeen), Producer (Michael Ferguson).

Observation Notes

Paper Chase (Production No: D4051, VTR No: THS/45286) was shot between Monday 19th and Friday 23rd September 1988. The recce of the locations took place on Monday 12th September. The school scenes were filmed at Oxford Gardens Primary School, W10.

The scene where Dashwood observes Hortman using his car phone was filmed on the junction of Eric Road and Church Road, Willesden, NW10. The following driving shots of Dashwood looking for Hortman were filmed on Latimer Road, W10. Lines then spots Hortman further down Latimer Road, from the junction of the adjoining Oxford Gardens, W10.

The scene where Hortman drops off the case by a bench was filmed in Gladstone Park. Dashwood observes from Park Side, Dollis Hill, NW2.

The surveillance van is initially parked at the end of Freston Road, W10. At the other end of the road and just around the corner is the empty "gaff" that Burnside and the team raid: 7A Bramley Road, W10.

Watched by 13.55 million viewers, *Paper Chase* attracted the highest audience for *The Bill* in 1988. This episode saw the job title of Floor Manager retitled to First Assistant Director on the end credits.

Paper Chase was adapted for *Bureau Kruislaan* in 1992. *Kind Ontvoerd*, ("Kid Abducted") was the fourth episode of the first season. The episode also features a different conclusion and shows the father being arrested after the officers have discovered the tracking device. His wife is held back from assaulting him, revealing that she had no idea of the scheme.

Witness Statements

Barry Appleton (Writer)

'*Paper Chase* was based on a major case that I can't go into because it remains unsolved. But the thing that I remember was being under a car on a car lot, watching the briefcase being put down. I saw a car go by slowly and then I saw it come back again. But the thing that I remember most is a dog walking by and peeing on the case, so I put that in the script. It was surprising how many people walked by and saw the case, but didn't know whether to pick it up or not, though this was before we had bomb scares. I thought *Paper Chase* worked well as a half-hour; there was some good stuff in it and it was well shot and directed.'

Niall Leonard (Director)

'I grew up in Northern Ireland in the 1970s, watching the TV shows of the day. For a while I thought every drama was made like *I Claudius*, in a multi-camera studio, which of course as a drama format is almost dead now. I was so locked into the idea that this was how all television was made, with very rigid choreography and artificial movements as the actors walked themselves into the right position for the camera framing. But I never thought of it as a career until I saw a locally produced play about two teenagers talking in a derelict Belfast lot. I remember thinking "I don't know any teenagers who talk like that... I could write better than this!" So I started trying to write screenplays...'

'I studied English at the University of York and after I finished my degree, a friend of mine at the National Film School asked me to write a script for him. When the Film School saw the script, they invited me to apply as a writer, because as always they had a million students wanting to do the glamorous jobs like directing or camera operating, but no writers. I turned up as was one of two writers on the course, along with ten trainee directors. During the course, I realised that some of the directing students couldn't actually direct to save their lives - they could never talk to actors or decide where to put the camera and the less time they had, the more indecisive they got. I used to think, "it's really not that hard!" To me there's a particular set of skills that a director needs and one of those is decisiveness - you need to make a decision, *any* decision is better than no decision. I felt that while I might never be Spielberg, I could make a competent director.'

'After graduating from Film school, I got my first directing work on a comedy show for Channel 4 called *Arthur and Phil Go Off*, though looking back I wasn't really ready for that show. Then after a year of directing corporate videos, I got a job on *The Bill*, where there was a cameraman called Chas Watts. Chas was slim and athletic and just loved the job, he used to stay on at the end of a shoot unpaid if he needed, just to get the right shot. He was one of the best teachers ever, showing me how developing shots work and how we could find actors with the camera, rather than them walk into a static shot. I learned more on that first week working with Chas on *Paper Chase* than I'd learned in a year at Film School. Every day was just so exciting, I'd wake up and think "What am I going to learn today?" or "What extraordinary shot are we got to pull off?"

'*Paper Chase* was a nice script by Barry Appleton about a businessman who - spoiler alert - claimed that his daughter had been kidnapped, but all along it was an insurance scam. The line that always comes back to me is Burnside's "We've been stuffed!" I loved the way Chris Ellison delivered that line. We had Chris and Barbara Thorn in a surveillance van tracking the case; Jon Iles and Kevin Lloyd following from different cars, and Ben Roberts listening in from the station. The action kept cutting between all three locations, which was actually logistically really difficult, because each scene would only last for a couple of lines, so I had to take the whole script apart and record all these mini scenes together in the various locations. But this caused problems in the cutting room, because the editor struggled to put everything in the right order and the first cut was absolutely unintelligible. I'll never forget taking that rough cut home at the end of my first week on *The Bill* and sitting down with my wife and a bottle of champagne to watch it for the first time... It was just awful, it literally gave me nightmares and I sweated buckets all night fearing this episode was going to be a disaster. But I went back in the next week and we recut it and got it in the right order.'

Chas Watts (Camera)

'I remember Niall Leonard very well. We could tell from the planning meeting and the recces that this young and talented director had great ideas, even though he hadn't had a lot of experience in how to achieve them. But there was absolutely nothing wrong with that and I loved the opportunity to help Niall and therefore help the show. A cameraman has to be very sympathetic to what the director is trying to achieve within each scene, because one shot can make or break that story. I used to love doing the shots where we found the actors, rather than have them walking into a shot and hitting a mark. I used shorthand when working closely with the actors and if I had a tight enough shot, I would actually reach forward and cue them, either in or out of a shot. If I was doing an over the shoulder shot, the next part of the scene could be dictated by something going on in the background, so I would cue the actor in the foreground to move at the right time, to help me move onto the next part of the shot. I remember cueing Kevin Lloyd once, but I must have tapped him in the ribs, because he suddenly laughed out loud and said "Chas tickled me!" That started us all off laughing! Kevin was a lovely man and it was dreadful that he died so young.'

'The Vauxhall Cavaliers that CID drove were a challenge, because the back windows were designed to only go halfway down, which was a safety precaution to stop children from falling out. But we were stuck with these cars, because we had to use what the real police used. We asked the car boys to modify the windows, so that they could go all the way down and get a shot we all loved. I devised a method where the camera was rammed against the door pillar, with the windowsill acting as a shoulder mount, and with a soft black cloth used to stabilise the camera. I could then get what I called a "backward over-shoulder" of our two artists on the move. Those shots were great, not only for saving valuable set-up time, but also for showing off some good visuals of London, whilst the actors delivered their dialogue.'

'The artists all knew to turn their head when they talked to each other, so we could see their eyes clearly. We would reposition and do some tighter over the shoulder shots of each artist. That worked very well as a time-saving shot, especially if we had a driving conversation scene to film late in the day. If we wanted to put a mount to the outside of the car, that would take half an hour. Then if we wanted to position it on the other side of the car, it would take half an hour to de-rig and reposition. Then if the artists go off and have a cup of tea while they wait, they would then need make-up when they came back, so that might be another quarter of an hour. That would all be a terrible waste of time, which we could ill afford on a schedule like *The Bill*.'

'My television career began thanks to the paper round I did when I was fifteen years old. One day, the owner of the newsagent kindly mentioned my interest in photography to a customer, who worked for ATV as a graphic designer, who recommended that I apply for a vacancy. I went for an interview and got the job as a Dark Room Assistant. ATV made a series called *On The Braden Beat*, a Saturday night consumer affairs show, presented by the Canadian Bernard Braden. During discussions, they showed stills instead of footage, because it was cheaper. They once needed some shots of Marble Arch tube station, which was around the corner from our office. I was deputised to go to the station, where I was apprehended by the transport police, because I didn't have permission to take photographs. I pretended I hadn't taken any, then went back and printed my photographs and had them biked up to the studios at Elstree. My photographs of tube trains appeared that night on *On The Braden Beat* and my parents were so impressed by their young son's first work in television. I also worked as a photographer's assistant at ATV, covering big press evenings for *Sunday Night at the London Palladium*, working right at the heart of entertainment.'

'I then started doing some photography at Elstree, which was fantastic. There I got to know some of the television camera assistants, because we all ate in the same canteen. I applied to the ATV Camera department three times, but got turned down every time. It was a tough interview process, where you were asked questions by ten people from different departments, all silhouetted by the light coming in through a large window behind them, which was quite intimidating. They had a minimum height requirement of 5'10" and would ask you questions like "Are you strong enough to swing the camera crane?" A doctor would then measure and weigh you in front of the panel... Imagine that today!'

'It was a very busy time in television and ITV was changing out of all recognition. When Thames Television started in 1968, I applied for a camera assistant position and went for an interview at Teddington Studios. The setting was much more intimate than I had experienced at ATV and I had a fantastic interview. I had a feeling that it was going well and after chatting to the four people interviewing me, I was given a test... They presented me with some black and white prints of various pieces of television equipment, which I had to identify. As luck would have it, I had printed two of the photographs at ATV! I remember not only identifying a proctor dolly, but also describing how it worked, who designed it and who manufactured it... That went down very well and I was one of only two successful applicants!'

'Working at Teddington was fabulous. I started in Studio 3 on programmes like *Magpie* and *Rainbow*, which is where I learned how to be a camera assistant and would occasionally be allowed to do a shot. Then you moved to the larger Studio 2 and then onto Studio 1. There was a central corridor where all the sound booms were stored, which was known colloquially as "boom alley." This was the main entrance to all the studios, dressing rooms and the canteen and so you would have Morecambe & Wise bumping into Bungle the Bear and cracking gags! This was before the cult of "celebrity" and all the artists treated the crew as equals. Benny Hill once heard me singing "The fastest milkman in the West", from his record "Ernie", while I was putting equipment away. He said "Very nice... though I prefer my version!" I apologised, but he was pleased to know that the tune was catchy. Then at the after show party he brought me a drink over. It was a fantastic place to work.'

INTRUDER
Written by Roger Parkes
Directed by Graham Theakston

Series 4: Episode 35
Broadcast: Tuesday 15 November 1988

Case Narrative
A single unarmed policeman bravely takes on a man with a knife, and the assailant is arrested. But what really happened? Haynes, Cryer and Frazer have different views.

Regular Cast
Sgt. Cryer (Eric Richard), P.C. Edwards (Colin Blumenau), Insp. Frazer (Barbara Thorn), P.C. Melvin (Mark Powley), P.C. Haynes (Eamonn Walker), D.C. Lines (Kevin Lloyd), Sgt. Peters (Larry Dann), Ch. Insp. Conway (Ben Roberts), W.P.C. Brind (Kelly Lawrence).

Guest Cast
Martin Horton (Rob Dixon), Duty Solicitor (Terence Wilton), Psychiatrist (Richard Addison), Miss Billington (Alison Groves), C.P.S. Prosecutor (Iain Rattray), Dr. Green (John Arthur), Stipendiary Magistrate (Martin Matthews), Shopkeeper (Ali Baba), Rowdy (Paul Venables), Drunk (Nick Cursi), Decoy (James Pertwee), Runner (Ben Losh).

Uncredited Personnel
Press Officer (Rosane Chapman), Secretaries (Diane Boland, Tracy Sinclair), Accountants (Anne Shields, David Saggs), Wardrobe Supervisor (Carolyn Maddocks), Make Up Assistants (Carolyn Wills, Kate Rudlin, Adam Beck), Props Chargehand (John Walkham), Floor Assistant (Eleanor Bushnell), Assistant Stage Manager (Annie Scott).

Production Team
Casting Director (Julia Lisney), Title Music (Andy Pask, Charlie Morgan), Costume (Maggie Chappelhow, Carolyn Maddocks), Make Up Designer (Gilly Wakeford), Graphics (Ethan Ames), Videotape Editor (John Sharland), Lighting (Bill Minto), Camera (Adrian J. Fearnley), Sound (Dave Evans, Alan Lester), Production Buyer (Trevor Young), Location Manager (Garance Rawinsky), First Assistant Director (Geoff Lewis),

Stage Manager (Susan Shattock), Production Manager (Brian Heard), Production Assistant (Sonia Hampson), Technical Adviser (Wilf Knight), Script Editor (Barbara Cox), Series Script Editor (Kenneth Ware), Designers (Robin Parker, Neil Thomson), Executive Producer (Peter Cregeen), Producer (Richard Bramall).

Observation Notes

Intruder (Production No: D4053, VTR No: THS/45288) was shot between Monday 26th and Friday 30th September 1988. The opening shot was filmed outside 1 Crowthorne Road, W10. The garage seen in the background has since closed down and this area is now the Westway Sports & Fitness Centre. Melvin chases the youth further down Crowthorne Road, with Robinson House in the background, which is where the following sequence where he apprehends the coach thief was filmed. This block of flats has since been refurbished. The sequence continues with Eamonn Walker running out of Cambridge Gardens, W10 and into St. Helen's Gardens for the scene where Haynes tackles the man with a knife.

The later scene when Melvin and Haynes go back out on the beat begins on Kensal Road, W10. Behind them is The Village Inn pub, situated at 265 Kensal Road. The building was a bar called Frames at time of its closure in 2016 and remains unoccupied. The suspects are then seen leaving an off-licence based at No. 277, which is today Kensal Food & Wine. Melvin then pursues his suspect down Adela Street, which has since been redeveloped.

Intruder was the only episode of *The Bill* written by Roger Parkes, a prolific writer who began his television career as a script editor at the BBC, working on programmes such as *The Old Wives' Tale*, *Menace*, *The Paradise Makers* and *Out of the Unknown*. His first script was an episode of the iconic Patrick McGoohan series *The Prisoner* and he went on to write for dozens of cult series, including *Z Cars*, *Strange Report*, *Warship*, *Man in a Suitcase*, *Doomwatch*, *The Onedin Line*, *Survivors*, *Return of the Saint*, *Angels* and *Blake's 7*. Roger Parkes passed away in 2008, aged 75.

Witness Statements

Sue Shattock (Stage Manager)

'When I left school with my O-Levels, I didn't really know what I wanted to do. I got a job in a travel agency, where I was told it would be three years before I would be allowed to talk to customers! I then met a friend who worked at London Weekend Television and they invited me to the LWT bar for a drink, which was full of exciting, creative people! I had so much fun and thought how much I'd love to work there. I got a temp job on World of Sport with Dickie Davies over the Christmas period, where I don't recall doing much work, but I attended some unbelievable parties! I then got a job in Drama working for producer Jack Williams, where the first programme I worked on was *Within These Walls* starring Googie Withers. As the producer's secretary, I would sit behind the production team in the control room and bring them tea and coffee. It was watching them at work that inspired me to want to work on the studio floor and be part of the production.'

'I wanted to become a stage manager, which meant making the difficult decision to leave my job and go to drama school in order to get my Equity card, which was a requirement. I was lucky enough to get a scholarship to the Guildhall School of Music and Drama as an older student. After my two years' training, I got a job in the Swan Theatre in Worcester, which got me my Equity card. I had great fun making all the props; it was so much more interesting than being a secretary. I then got a job as an assistant stage manager at the Chichester Festival Theatre and was eventually made up to deputy stage manager. I worked there for two seasons and had a wonderful time working on a touring production of *The Sleeping Prince* with Omar Sharif and Debbie Arnold.'

'As a stage manager in the theatre, after the first night, every show becomes very repetitive. The actors obviously have the audience to bounce off, but I felt very bored after a while sitting in the wings turning the lights on and off for a handful of cues. I love the theatre, but I loved television more and so after taking the curtain up at the Theatre Royal Haymarket, I decided to walk away and not take another job unless it was in television. I wrote letters to many companies, but the main one I wanted to work at was Thames Television. I wrote to John Wayne, who was in charge of recruiting stage managers and floor managers, and I must have sent him a letter every day for six months. Then one day, my letter must have been at the top of the pile, because I got a call asking me to come in and work as an ASM on a new afternoon soap called *Gems*, about the fashion industry. I happily accepted and that was the start of my TV career in stage management.'

'*Intruder* was directed by Graham Theakston, who was a very good director and very thorough. When members of the public used to see us filming, they would often ask, "Why is everyone just sitting around?" Well there is a lot of sitting around in television, but one of the reasons for that is everyone involved with pre-production has done most of their job beforehand. People don't realise that from our perspective, the filming is actually the final bit of the jigsaw for us, so you will only really see people from the production team rushing around like a blue-arsed fly on set if they haven't done their job properly.'

'I used to drive in from Surbiton every day and because we had to get to work really early in the morning, I beat most of the traffic, though even back then parking in London could be a challenge. When you work on a series like *The Bill*, it becomes all encompassing; there were lots of early mornings and late evenings and you didn't have much time for anything else, because you became very caught up with the whole thing. You also don't tend to sleep very well when you work on in television, because you know you *have* to be there, which is what I had instilled in me when working in the theatre. Being late or not turning up is simply not an option, which meant you would often leave two hours earlier than you normally would, just to make sure you were there on time. It's not that the show can't go on without you, but we were all part of a wonderful machine and even if you are just a small cog, that cog still makes a difference. On *The Bill*, the producers treated everyone like an integral part of the machine. I remember sitting next to Peter Cregeen on the bus going to a location and having a nice chat with him, which was great. The producers created an atmosphere that made it very easy for everyone to get on with each other.'

Barbara Thorn (Insp. Christine Frazer)

'*The Bill* was brilliant for me and I was learning all the time. I was working with fantastic directors, who would talk to you at the end of filming and invite you to view the rushes, where they'd give you feedback. I first met my late great friend Graham Theakston in 1982, when he filmed a show I did for a company called The National Theatre of Brent, which was set up by Patrick Barlow. The idea was we would take huge, epic events and turn them into a show. I starred in *The Black Hole of Calcutta*, where the audience was encouraged to take an active involvement in the show, which we took all over the UK. It was a dream job! Graham then gave me one of my first television roles when he offered me a part in an episode of *The Tripods*, which was a series that went on to become a cult. I was still quite new to television and I felt quite overawed by the technology of it, so I just kept quiet, watched and learned and got on with it. I had a near escape on the set that they built at the BBC, where my character Dorrie, had to put her foot out and trip over a baddie on this huge staircase. I put my foot out and sent this stuntman tumbling down the staircase, then I realised that I had been standing on the very edge of the set, with a sheer drop behind me!'

Eamonn Walker (P.C. Malcolm Haynes)

'There were no performers in my household growing up; my family is full of doctors, teachers and workers. There are several from the next generation now who are interested in acting, so I guess I've been an inspiration for them to follow their dreams. The acting bug got me when I was nine years old and I saw a film called *In the Heat of the Night*, starring Sidney Poitier and Rod Steiger. That dynamic story of a black policeman from New York, who happened to be passing through a town in the South where there had been a murder and everyone assumes the killer was a black guy. That movie changed my life, particularly the scene in the green house where a white plantation owner slaps Sidney Poitier's character in the face, because he thinks he can, but Sidney Poitier slaps him straight back. That single moment sparked my whole life, because it was reminiscent of things that were happening to me on the streets of London as a nine-year boy. That film showed me an option about how I could survive and that I didn't have to take whatever was coming at me. Somewhere deep inside, my brain started putting together the idea that through the power of good writing in television, film and theatre, you could change the idea in somebody's head, which is basically what I have tried to do throughout my whole career.'

'I later met Mr. Poitier, when I had the privilege of playing Mark Antony opposite Denzel Washington as Brutus in *Julius Caesar* on Broadway. Because Denzel knows everybody, all these huge, massive stars attended our opening night. After the show I was backstage, covered in fake blood and freaking out having just done my first night on Broadway. One of the people who came backstage to see Denzel was Sidney Poitier. I was wiping this blood from my hands, when I looked up and instantly recognised this very tall, older man. I was trying to speak, but was speechless. He realised I was having something of an apoplectic moment and he just put his arms out and said, "Come here." He hugged me and he whispered some very complimentary things in my ear. I got to tell him that he was the reason I am an actor.'

CONFLICT
Written by Al Hunter
Directed by Graham Theakston

Series 4: Episode 36
Broadcast: Thursday 17 November 1988

Viewing Figures: 13.20m
ITV Chart Position: 8

Case Narrative
An observation on a suspect develops into an ugly domestic incident – and proves a clash between Burnside and Cryer.

Regular Cast
Sgt. Cryer (Eric Richard), P.C. Ramsey (Nick Reding), D.C. Lines (Kevin Lloyd), D.C. Carver (Mark Wingett), D.I. Burnside (Christopher Ellison), W.P.C. Ackland (Trudie Goodwin), Ch. Insp. Conway (Ben Roberts), W.P.C. Brind (Kelly Lawrence), P.C. Stamp (Graham Cole), P.C. Banks (Russell Lewis).

Guest Cast
Joe Daniels (Rory Edwards), Patsie Kemp (Kamilla Blanche), Dr. Howard (Alex Kingston), Dealer (Jon McKenna), Traffic Cop (Rodney Cardiff).

Uncredited Personnel
Press Officer (Rosane Chapman), Secretaries (Diane Boland, Tracy Sinclair), Accountants (Anne Shields, David Saggs), Wardrobe Supervisor (Carolyn Maddocks), Make Up Assistants (Carolyn Wills, Kate Rudlin, Adam Beck), Props Chargehand (John Walkham), Floor Assistant (Eleanor Bushnell), Assistant Stage Manager (Annie Scott).

Production Team
Fight Arranger (Colin Skeaping), Casting Director (Julia Lisney), Title Music (Andy Pask, Charlie Morgan), Costume (Maggie Chappelhow, Carolyn Maddocks), Make Up Designer (Gilly Wakeford), Graphics (Ethan Ames), Videotape Editor (John Sharland), Lighting (Bill Minto), Camera (Adrian J. Fearnley), Sound (Dave Evans, Mike Fairbairn), Production Buyer (Trevor Young), Location Manager (Garance Rawinsky), First Assistant Director (Geoff Lewis), Stage Manager (Susan Shattock), Production Manager (Brian Heard), Production Assistant (Sonia Hampson),

Technical Adviser (Wilf Knight), Assistant Script Editor (Elizabeth Bradley), Series Script Editor (Kenneth Ware), Designers (Robin Parker, Neil Thomson), Executive Producer (Peter Cregeen), Producer (Richard Bramall).

Observation Notes

Conflict (Production No: D4054, VTR No: THS/45289) was shot between Monday 3rd and Friday 7th October 1988. There was usually an eight-week buffer between the filming dates and transmission, though this episode was brought forward by two weeks in the running order and broadcast six weeks after being filmed.

The scene at the traffic lights where Carver's cover is blown by the traffic cop, was filmed on Hazlewood Crsecent, W10. The following scene sees Lines and Carver turn out of Kensal Road, W10 and parking outside Our Lady of the Holy Souls Church, Bosworth Road, W10.

Conflict then features a rare sequence where the action is not seen from a police officer's point of view, as several shots show the character of Joe Daniels driving his red Datsun 280ZX into the hospital, after he has lost Carver and Lines. This Nissan car was registered in 1981 and has not been taxed since 1997.

The hospital scenes were filmed in and around Hammersmith Hospital, Du Cane Road, W12.

Witness Statements

Trudie Goodwin (W.P.C. June Ackland)

'*Conflict* was directed by Graham Theakston, who became a friend outside of the programme. All the actors really liked him because he was good fun and a bit anarchic; he didn't like the bosses too much because we were always short of money and he liked to spend a bit on his episodes. Even though he was young, he had already done quite a lot of television before *The Bill* and I thought he was a really good director. His first aim was always the actor's performance and not everything else that was going on around him. Quite often for directors on *The Bill* it would be the opposite of that and it would be more about the action than the acting. Graham's philosophy was if we got the acting right, usually everything else would follow, whereas if the acting isn't right, it doesn't matter how good your stunt is, the story is not going to work.'

'Filming on location in and around Notting Hill was more difficult than when we'd been in the East End. For me it was a longer commute, but also, because the show had got so popular, we were all much more recognisable when we were out filming. We suddenly needed security, not because we were in danger of being attacked, but because people wanted to see what was going on. They were interested in the best possible way, but that did mean that some people got in the way or ended up in the back of shot. I can't remember the first time I was recognised for playing June, but once it started it really didn't stop. Things like going out for a meal or even going on holiday became quite difficult, because I was being stopped all the time.'

'No one was ever horrible, but of course people might have thought they were the first person to ask you for an autograph that day, when in fact they might have been the 50th. It really did hit new heights when we went to the half-hours! That was only a slight downside, because people were very positive about the programme. June was also a sympathetic character, so they were always very nice to me, whereas poor Chris Ellison used to get it in the neck sometimes. Blokes would literally try to pick a fight with him so that they could say they'd got one over on Frank Burnside. Nobody ever did that to me, thank goodness.'

Russell Lewis (P.C. Banks)

'Acting was something I was put to when I was a kid. I started when I was three years old. I was lucky enough to get quite a lot of work while I was at stage school, but then when I got into my teens, it became a different kettle of fish. I wanted to be playing parts like Travis Bickle in *Taxi Driver*, but I ended up being cast as people's sons or the boy next door. Writing has always been my first love and was how I spent my summer holidays when I was a kid.'

'I'd more or less signed off on wanting to be in front of the camera anymore by the time *The Bill* came along, which I fancy was very much down to Richard Bramall, who I first worked with when I was nine years old on a series called *The Kids from 47A*. Later I did *S.W.A.L.K.* with Richard, a drama for C4 when the channel first began, written by the great Paula Milne. I remember him as having a pretty light touch as a director, which I suspect is what you need with kids. I remember going for tea to the house he and Diana lived in with their kids in Edgbaston.'

'Richard was producing *The Bill* when our paths next crossed, where he was instrumental in getting me onto the rolling roster of spare coppers, who would come in and say the odd line. As P.C. Banks, truncheon carrying was my speciality. During the making of *Conflict*, Graham Cole and I were sat in the police van, in our uniforms waiting to go for a take. A guy came up to us and asked us if we were real police officers... When we explained we weren't, he then tried to sell us some dope! It must have looked quite amusing for anyone nearby, seeing some bloke trying to sell drugs to two coppers in a police van. Whilst my compass by then was set for the other side of the camera, it was typical of Richard Bramall to do something nice for an old soldier and I was very sorry to hear he had gone ahead, he was a sweet chap.'

Richard Bramall (Producer)

Archive Witness Statement, written in November 1995

'I have been an "Actor's Director" and during my work, I have discovered how much I have been able to help actors better express their talents, just by showing them openly what I have learnt about "The Business". It has been this experience that has enabled me to be, I believe, a helpful teacher of aspiring actors. I have taught voice, improvisation acting and acting for camera. I have developed three courses called "Acting for the Camera", "Performing for the Recorded Media" and "The Pro-Active Performer". These prepare actors for the many different techniques needed by artists in the film and TV world; they introduce them to the many areas in the media where their training is prized and used; and they encourage actors to become intelligent thinking professionals who are more in control of their own work and less liable to be used as performance fodder.'

'My desire is that actors should be better prepared for the real worlds of theatre, radio, sound recording, television and film. I believe that in the past, Drama Schools have neglected to teach about the information, techniques and technology used by actors to earn their major source of income. These areas include Corporates, Commercials, Voice Overs, Voice Recordings, Post Synching, Dubbing, Camera Work etc. The skills of being able to perform with adaptability, naturalism and a confidence in the wide-ranging demands of media, is something that helps actors to be better prepared for every area of their profession. I therefore see it as a time for a change in the emphasis of our training of actors in Drama Schools.'

Diana Bramall (Widow of producer Richard Bramall)

'Richard had really enjoyed working as a director on *The Bill* when it was in its original hour-long format. He then worked very hard to help establish the twice-weekly format with Michael Ferguson and Peter Cregeen, who he got on very well with. The three of them were true friends and we all knew each other well, because we all lived in the same area in and around Twickenham, where we lived for 30 years and had a very happy time. Richard enjoyed his time on *The Bill* and he was given posters of Trudie Goodwin as June Ackland, Eric Richard as Bob Cryer and Tony Scannell as Ted Roach, which we put up on the wall at home.'

'As a freelancer, Richard never wanted to do any one programme for more than a couple of years and so after 18 months on *The Bill*, he moved on when he was asked to produce *EastEnders*. We had to do flash cards of all the characters, because we had never watched an episode before and needed to get up to speed with all the storylines! *EastEnders* wasn't really his cup of tea because the stories were all so depressing, but he was proud to regain the number one slot in the ratings.'

'Richard and I were married for 51 years and had been together for three years before that. In that time, he did masses of television, some of which I had forgotten about until I recently read his CV. As a freelance producer/director, it was feast or famine, but he only ever had two really bad patches of being out of work, because he was always looking for work and very proactive. He loved working in television, but it came to the point where he had done an awful lot of it and had been away so much whilst working on productions. After more than 25 years in television, Richard started thinking about doing something else...'

'We had become Christians in our late 30s, attending a very charismatic church called The Vineyard. This was the direction Richard decided he wanted to go and so, at the age of 52, he gave up television and became a minister. He loved his pastoral work, which he did for the next seven years, until we were nearing 60 and we wanted to have more of a life together. Though Richard never really "retired" and after we moved to Chichester, he retrained as a life coach and also taught a "Writing for Film" course at Portsmouth University. He was such a diverse man and left a very rich history of work. I am delighted that Richard's episodes of *The Bill* are still being enjoyed... He would be too.'

DUPLICATES
Written by Simon Moss
Directed by Niall Leonard

Series 4: Episode 37
Broadcast: Tuesday 22 November 1988

Case Narrative
W.P.C. Brind re-enacts the last known movements of a missing girl. Roach and Carver find grisly evidence of illegal boxing.

Regular Cast
Sgt. Peters (Larry Dann), W.P.C. Brind (Kelly Lawrence), D.S. Roach (Tony Scannell), D.C. Carver (Mark Wingett), D.C Dashwood (Jon Iles), W.P.C. Ackland (Trudie Goodwin), P.C. Ramsey (Nick Reding), Sgt. Penny (Roger Leach), P.C. Frank (Ashley Gunstock), P.C. Stamp (Graham Cole), P.C. Hollis (Jeff Stewart).

Guest Cast
Emma Wintour (Maggie Saunders), Bentley (Leon Eagles), Mr. Viggers (Michael Lees), Mrs. Viggers (Shirley Cain), Churchill (Steve Knowles), Newsreader (Bill Bingham), 1st Boy (Danny-Joe MacDonald), 2nd Boy (Danny Wooder), Passerby (Peter Beverley).

Uncredited Personnel
W.P.C. Ford (Vikki Gee-Dare), P.C. (Paul Page Hanson), Press Officer (Rosane Chapman), Accountants (Anne Shields, David Saggs), Librarian (Bridget Moore), Props Chargehand (John Walkham), Make Up Assistants (Carolyn Wills, Kate Rudlin, Adam Beck).

Production Team
Stunt Arranger (Graeme Crowther), Casting Director (Brian Wheeler), Title Music (Andy Pask, Charlie Morgan), Costume (Allard Tobin, Peter Roberts), Make Up Designer (Gilly Wakeford), Graphics (Ethan Ames), Videotape Editor (Colin Bocking), Lighting (Allen Harradine), Camera (Chas Watts), Sound (Robert Newton, Paul Gartrell), Production Buyer (Sarah Prebble), Location Manager (Rob Champion), First Assistant Director (David Cherrill), Stage Manager (Diana Paskin), Production Manager (Brian Heard), Production Assistant (Caroline Sutton), Technical Adviser (Wilf Knight), Script Editor (Barbara Cox), Series Script Editor

(Kenneth Ware), Design (Robin Parker, Kyz Kistell), Executive Producer (Peter Cregeen), Producer (Michael Ferguson).

Observation Notes
Duplicates (Production No: D4052, VTR No: THS/45287) was shot between Monday 26th and Friday 30th September 1988. The reconstruction scenes were filmed along Neasden Lane, NW10, with the police van parked in front of No. 265, next to the junction of Birse Crescent NW10. Nick Reding filmed the scene with the youths outside the Laundercentre at 287 Neasden Lane, which is still open.

The scenes at the video shop were filmed at 282 Harrow Road, W2, underneath Oldbury House. The following chase scene was filmed in the alley behind Oldbury House, with the suspect being apprehended by P.C. Frank on the adjoining Senior Street, W2. Ashley Gunstock jumps over the wall and down into the front yard of 2-16 Senior Street.

Duplicates was the first episode of *The Bill* written by Simon Moss, who wrote 38 episodes for the series over the next 20 years. Moss' other credits include episodes of *EastEnders*, *Casualty* and *Streetwise*.

On Wednesday 23rd November 1988, the evening after *Duplicates* was broadcast, Eric Richard, Larry Dann and Barbara Thorn appeared as special guests on *Des O'Connor Tonight*, watched by 10.6 million viewers.

Witness Statements

Mark Wingett (D.C. Jim Carver)
'I'm delighted that these episodes, which are nearly 35 years old, are still being enjoyed. Without blowing our own trumpets, *The Bill* was quite a pioneering series, because at the time the BBC were still making dramas in television studios, whereas *The Bill* was 100% on location, including the station at Barlby Road, which added to the quality of the production. We got even more flexibility when we started using the lightweight, on-the-shoulder cameras, the "wobble cam" as we affectionately called it! Of course what was groundbreaking then is nothing compared with the technology today, where anyone can make a film and then edit it in their kitchen. The really great thing today is that the business is more democratic and there are a lot more outlets for people to show their work. Fantastic platforms like Netflix have disrupted the business and allowed directors to make some

extraordinary series. Whereas the terrestrial channels have been very slow to catch onto streaming, the BBC should be miles ahead of the game, but they're not. There is so much scope now for individuality and for a filmmaker to put their stamp on things.'

Niall Leonard (Director)

'The biggest challenge of the half-hour format was you had to have real economy in storytelling, you couldn't hang around and could only afford to tell a tiny bit of the story. Occasionally you'd have episodes that were a little too neat, where everything was tied up with a little bow at the end. The better writers would actually create a story that didn't have a happy ending and *Duplicates* was one of those, where you just got a glimpse of a much bigger story. It also had a lot of emotion, especially after Brind does the reconstruction and then meets the parents of the missing girl. That was a nice little moment and built a lot of really good realistic texture, which is the storytelling I like. I get impatient with very glossy cop shows that have beautiful casts, set in beautiful cities, with a different murder of the week. We didn't have time for pretty shots in *The Bill*, but that's not what people watched the show for – they watched for the energy and these early episodes had such vigour – it was action, walk, walk... action, walk, walk. We were *The West Wing* before *The West Wing.*'

'I thought Ladbroke Grove was a fantastic location and the textures around there were so varied and interesting. I loved the Barlby Road set, the thing I liked about that station was it was supposed to be slightly crumbling, which meant you could have characters fixing the lights and painting the walls in the background. I was given an amazing train set to play with and the actors were a massive part of that – they knew their lines and they hit their marks. At that age as a young director, I was immensely cocky and just having a great time, but occasionally it was a bit intimidating. Tony Scannell could be a bit prickly, and I remember in *Duplicates* after the big scene where Roach and Carver have arrested the organiser of an illegal boxing match. I had them standing outside watching the injured fighter being taken out to an ambulance. Tony Scannell turned to me and said, "What am I doing at the start of this scene? I'm just standing here!" I said the first thing that came into my head: "You're blowing your nose." That's why he has a hanky out at the start of the scene, blowing his nose. All he wanted was a bit of business and he was perfectly right to ask me, because I too get bored with actors who stand with their hands by the sides, just saying the lines. Scannell wasn't one of those actors, and after we shot that scene, I heard him say to Mark Wingett, "He's good this guy, isn't he?"'

'One of the things I learned as a director on *The Bill* was how hard and fast you had to work to meet the schedule. Sometimes you'd think about an earlier scene and think you had shot it last week, then realise you had shot it earlier that morning! We were hammering through it and one minute you'd be really engrossed in a scene and then bang, it was onto the next one. The buzz was electric! Though there was a moment on *Duplicates* when Roach is chasing a suspect and calls Dashwood a pillock. On location, someone questioned whether or not we were allowed to say "pillock" at 8pm... I rang Michael Ferguson, the producer, back at base to ask him. Michael was a very friendly guy and launched into a long conversation about the cumulative effect of rude words, while all the crew and actors are standing around waiting to go for a take and the clock was ticking. In the end I had to interrupt him and ask, "Michael is that a yes or a no?!" In the end he said it was fine.'

'*The Bill* was one of the best shows I could have worked on as a young director, because everybody knew their job so well. It was a privilege to be working with a really good team of people. I made these first two episodes on time and on budget and they kept inviting me back to direct two episodes a year for the next three years, until eventually I moved out of directing and into full-time writing. I realised that being a writer would mean I didn't have to get up at 5am anymore and I could spend more time with my kids and my wife - who at that time I didn't know would go onto become the worldwide phenomenon, E.L. James! It's fun looking back on my directing days on *The Bill*, I'm proud to have worked on the show and the fact that the work we all did in the 1980s is still being enjoyed is just wonderful.'

Chas Watts (Camera)

'We had mixed weather on the *Duplicates* shoot, one minute we had pouring rain, the next we had sunshine, which proved a challenge for continuity. This was why we also did Second Unit shooting on *The Bill*, when pick-ups were required for both Units. In fact, my very first shot on *The Bill* was an "up and passed" shot of a police car going down Worple Road in Wimbledon. I have no idea why we shot it there, but that was several years before we moved to the nearby Merton Studios.'

'In *Duplicates*, there's a shot where Roach and Carver pull up and park on a yellow line, which works fine in the story, because they are policemen. But in real life, our location managers will have had to call up the council and get permission to suspend that line for the time we were filming. They all did a fabulous job on *The Bill*. Then at the end of that scene, Tony Scannell says the word "pillock", which was the latest in many attempts to find swear words that we could get through the censor. We all enjoyed trying outs loads of different swear words on each other and I remember Chris Ellison asking one of the scene hands, "What do you say when you drop a tin of paint?" which was very funny. Though without saying a word, Tony Scannell could also give looks that could kill as Roach – he knew how to use his eyes to give a someone a frightening look, which was scarily effective!'

'*Duplicates* wasn't the most exciting episode in terms of action, but it was a chance for the actors to shine. I liked the way that Larry Dann and Jon Iles played the sequence where Sgt. Peters (the old hand), has set up Dashwood (the handsome and ambitious detective) for the TV interview. Larry walks away laughing through frame, while Jon is anxiously sorting out his tie for the interview... The characters were so well written and backed up by such good acting. The reconstruction scene was also interesting, because it was a different way of shooting. I had to think about how an ENG (Electronic news-gathering) crew would film it... They would have had Brind walking sulkily down the high street and Jon Iles talking off-camera to an unseen reporter. They would have used a tripod, rather than handheld, because they would have had another report to do straight after filming this one. Then you had that scene at the end of the episode with all that banter as the relief watch the television in the snooker room.'

Ashley Gunstock (P.C. Robin Frank)

'I loved doing all the chase scenes, because during that era I was probably about the fittest I've ever been. I used to play a lot of football and go to the gym, so running around the streets of London was great for me, because it was an extra workout, especially after the lunches we used to get! It was also great any time I got to share a scene with Tony Scannell, who was a fabulous actor. One of my favourite memories of Tony is on one of our *The Bill* cabaret nights, he performed an hysterical monologue about a drunk butler, his technique was just top notch. I also liked to make light of situations and whenever we worked together, in between takes we used to tell a joke or two and he loved hearing new gags. If anything, I was honing my comic timing with him, because if I could make him laugh I could do anything. He was a loveable rogue too, he had a wild side and we had some great nights out! He was an Irishman with a lust for life and he went for it, all with a twinkle in his eye. That showed in his acting too, where he had a real energy and spark! The world is a sadder place without him.'

'Years after I left the show, I took part in an excellent workshop that Michael Ferguson gave at The Actors' Centre. As an actor, I always want to keep myself in touch and be doing something positive to work on my craft. I was actually one of the first members of The Actors' Centre, before it even had premises, and we used to do workshops in the YMCA when it started. I remember attending a workshop by Sheila Hancock and, in later years, another by Richard Wilson. The centre eventually found a home in Shelton Street, Covent Garden and then in Chenies Street on the corner with Tottenham Court Road. I remember when I went to re-enrol at Chenies Street the receptionist asked me if I'd been there before. I explained that I was one of the early members, but that every time I rejoined, I would get work that meant that I couldn't stay for all the courses. When I said it was probably a coincidence, she said, "I don't think it is... you are putting out positive energy by getting involved in something and that is why you are being picked up for parts."

'During Michael Ferguson's workshop, he said something that really has stayed with me. He explained that actors have four components: Intellectuality, Vulnerability, Sensuality and Danger. He said, "If you look at the top actors, you will find they either have a balance of all four, or they excel in one particular area." The prime example is Laurence Olivier, who had them all. Then someone like Alec Guiness had intellectuality, vulnerability and a certain sense of danger... but was he really sensual? Marilyn Monroe might not have excelled in danger or intellectuality, but she certainly had lots of vulnerability and her sensuality was above and beyond! Michael told us that if an actor doesn't feel they can give any of those four components to a role that demands them, then they shouldn't even bother to go for the part. I said that I felt a fifth component to add to the list was Timing, which every actor needs to have an understanding of. I distinctly remember saying to him afterwards that I wished that I had known of his approach to actors while we were working together, but I found him quite aloof. To be frank, pun intended, Michael was one of the few people on *The Bill* I couldn't get on with and I don't really know why. I wouldn't say he was dismissive of me, but he wasn't approachable and I got the feeling he didn't think as highly of me as an actor as the directors and my fellow actors did. Whereas our other producer on *The Bill*, Richard Bramall, was so easy to talk to, a very congenial man who was affable and amiable. I wish I had built a similar relationship with Michael, but he kept more of a professional distance. I am sad that they are both no longer with us.'

Jon Iles (D.C. Mike Dashwood)

'I remember the scene in *Duplicates* where Dashwood has to be interviewed on camera by a local news crew. Poor Kelly's character is worried stiff about doing this crime reconstruction, while Dashwood's only concern is about how good he looks – which is very like me! Then at the end when the relief are watching the reconstruction, someone yells, "It's James Bond!" The irony of that is a couple of years after I left *The Bill*, I was meeting Barbara Broccoli in the Hilton Hotel on Park Lane, being interviewed for Bond. That sounds wonderful, though every actor in that age range was being hauled in, especially if you'd been on the telly and had a good profile. It didn't go past us having sandwiches – and very nice they were too – but it's a nice tie-in to this episode and perhaps demonstrates the impact that *The Bill* had on all of our careers.'

'Another interesting impact, once the series was being shown twice a week, was that we were all recognised much more by the public. At first, I got a bit up myself to be honest and the friends that I had at that time would probably say that I turned into a bit of an arse. But that happens to some actors when they suddenly get a bit of recognition thrust upon them, for which there is no training. That's when you need to rely on your family and really good friends to be able to tell you not to behave like that and bring you back down to Earth. Not everyone is that lucky and we've all seen the actors who are surrounded by people who only suck up to them and make them believe their own press. I then grew into it and realised that if it wasn't for the people who watched the series, I wouldn't have had the wonderful life I lived for eight years, doing a job that meant I could afford some nicer things in life and having a real laugh. Now, I really enjoy interacting with the fans on social media and have made some lovely friends. It's really heartwarming.'

SNOUT

Written by Arthur McKenzie
Directed by Paul Harrison

Series 4: Episode 38
Broadcast: Thursday 24 November 1988

Viewing Figures: 12.75m
ITV Chart Position: 6

Case Narrative

There are days when working with D.I. Burnside is something you wouldn't wish on your worst enemy. This is one of those days.

Regular Cast

Sgt. Cryer (Eric Richard), D.I. Burnside (Christopher Ellison), P.C. Edwards (Colin Blumenau), Sgt. Peters (Larry Dann), D.C. Carver (Mark Wingett), D.C Dashwood (Jon Iles), Ch. Supt. Brownlow (Peter Ellis), W.P.C. Ackland (Trudie Goodwin), P.C. Hollis (Jeff Stewart), P.C. Smith (Robert Hudson), W.P.C. Brind (Kelly Lawrence).

Guest Cast

Alfie Dobbs (Desmond McNamara), Prisoner (Karl James), Drunk (Willie Ross), Arawaz (Tony Wredden), Burnside's Girlfriend (Linda Regan).

Production Team

Casting Director (Julia Lisney), Title Music (Andy Pask, Charlie Morgan), Costume (Dennis Hogan), Make Up Designer (Gilly Wakeford), Graphics (Ethan Ames), Videotape Editor (Tom Kavanagh), Lighting (Peter Bower), Camera (Rolie Luker), Sound (Richard Bradford, Paul Langwade), Production Buyer (Trevor Young), Location Manager (Susan Bradley), Floor Manager (Tony Boyle), Stage Manager (Susan Shattock), Production Manager (Derek Cotty), Production Assistant (Janet Mullins), Technical Adviser (Wilf Knight), Programme Associate (Valerie Farron), Series Script Editor (Kenneth Ware), Designers (Robin Parker, Neil Thomson), Executive Producer (Peter Cregeen), Producer (Richard Bramall).

Observation Notes

Snout (Production No: D4038, VTR No: THS/45273) was shot between Monday 8th and Friday 12th August 1988, plus a remount later in August.

Filming for the opening shot took place at the end of Dagmar Gardens, looking out onto Chamberlayne Road, NW10, with Burnside driving in from the adjoining Station Terrace. The action then jumps to the corner of Bramley Road, W10, for the scene where Burnside picks up Alfie Dobbs, outside the Bramley Arms pub, which closed earlier that year and is now used as offices. The scene concludes with Burnside dropping Dobbs off under the railway bridge on Freston Road, W10. The later pub scene was filmed at The Latimer Arms, 198 Latimer Road, W10.

The music featured on Burnside's car radio in these scenes on original broadcast was "Every Breath You Take" by The Police, with Chris Ellison singing along to the lyrics. This track was replaced on repeats and UK DVD releases by "Message in a Bottle", another track by The Police. As well as overdubbing the scene, subsequent versions saw the removal of a close-up shot of Chris Ellison singing the lyrics "I'll be watching you" as his eyes scanned the streets.

Snout was the first of 17 episodes of *The Bill* written by Arthur McKenzie, who prior to his writing career served as a police officer in Newcastle upon Tyne for 31 years. Rising up the ranks from beat officer to Detective Inspector, McKenzie received 27 commendations on the force. Along with his work as a playwright, McKenzie's writing credits include *Casualty, Sam Saturday, Wycliffe*, and the feature film *Harrigan*.

In *Snout,* Sgt. Peters is the Custody Sergeant, dealing with a drunk covered in vomit and tipping Burnside off about a "punter on the boil". The Background Information document details that the custody officer deals with "all charges and with the care and welfare of all persons in custody. This is his sole job. He works from the charge room. He has to ensure that every charge, whoever the officer involved, is an acceptable, appropriate charge, worthy of being sent up to the CPS at court."

The character notes that writer Arthur McKenzie received prior to writing *Snout* detailed that Alec Peters was 47 years old and describe him as a "solid, reliable, good-humoured man who gets on with the job with the minimum of fuss. Peters, like Cryer, has settled quite happily for his role. He has always enjoyed the camaraderie of police life, though does admit that it isn't what it used to be. He's also ready to admit that his reservations may have something to do with the generation problem. Most of his colleagues are a good deal younger than he is. He has a sneaking feeling that the real problem, though, lies in a fundamental change in society. Peters would rather not think about it all too much. And then goes home to his wife and allotment. His one daughter left home three years ago and is now married, with a young baby. Peters is the only grandfather in the station, and he doesn't mind people knowing!"

Witness Statements

Larry Dann (Sgt. Alec Peters)

'I wish I'd got to get out of the station more, which is sadly where I spent most of my episodes, saying "Come on son, empty your pockets", which got a bit repetitive after five years. I like to be challenged as an actor and with respect, doing the half-hours was mainly about learning your lines, not bumping into the furniture, then moving onto the next episode. Unbeknown to many, we had quite a lot of spare time hanging around. Jon Iles and I had a fun idea to do our own version of *It'll Be All Right On The Night* and show some out-takes, with Jon doing his brilliant impression of Denis Norden. The out-takes were never allowed to be shown on TV – a directive I agreed with, as it could have deflected from the strength of reality that *The Bill* had. But I got the go ahead to direct this video, as long as I promised they would go no further than being shown at the Christmas party – a promise I have kept to this day, some 35 years later! I still have the tape somewhere... I was given a cameraman and the PAs gave me some reels of out-takes, which took some time to go through, but I think it was worth it!'

'As well as shooting Jon's pieces to camera, I asked our producers, Michael Ferguson and Richard Bramall, if they were willing to fake a car crash in the car park... unbelievably, they agreed! I got two basically derelict cars from the props boys, used normally as dressing for street scenes where a staged incident was shot. We cleared a space in the car park, where Michael and Richard would be going for the same parking space. It had to be done in one take... and they did it! They then both acted as angry motorists, storming out of their cars! How many actor/directors have had their producers do that for them? They were wonderful people and I think they were both thrilled to be asked. Richard and Michael, along with all the production crew, were a major part of not only the success of the programme itself, but also the harmony around the office. When I left *The Bill,* I asked if I could be considered to direct an episode or three... I still await an answer!'

Tim Vaughan (Script Editor)

'We had several writers on *The Bill* who had experience of policing at the sharp end — such as Barry Appleton and the late John Milne. When I joined the show, Barry was already well established with the programme and a very good writer, probably Ken Ware's most esteemed contributor. I'll never forget Barry's episode *Hold Fire*, where, after turning up late for his firearms refresher course and deliberately failing it, Ted Roach walks into a pub and asks the barmaid, "have you ever pointed a gun at anyone? You squeeze the trigger, almost to the point of no return, then just that little fraction more... and you blow someone away... for good." Writers like Barry, with all their experience of front line policing, gave the show enormously valuable credibility, and that was a typical example of how much we owe him.'

'In 1988, two of the new writers we introduced to the show had similar connections to law and order, though from rather different sides of it. The first was the late Brendan J. Cassin, who wrote eight stories for us, starting with *Chasing The Dragon*. Brendan had grown on the streets of Peckham, where he'd had a very dangerous upbringing, running drugs around the estates. The "J" in Brendan's name didn't actually stand for anything at all. I once asked him what the "J' stood for and he said, "Well, I noticed you used this bloke called Peter J. Hammond, and he gets loads of work here, so I thought, if I call myself Brendan J Cassin, I might do as well as him". Sadly, Brendan never got to eclipse Peter J Hammond, but he was still a highly talented young man and a good writer. He later had a terrible time with the Hollywood machine, which offered the world, before finally and heartlessly spitting him out, a calamity that, tragically, he never really recovered from.'

'Arthur McKenzie, who went on to write for *Wycliffe* and penned the film *Harrigan* for Stephen Tomkinson, was a real one-off. While John Milne, Brendan Cassin and Barry Appleton were dyed-in-the-wool Londoners, Arthur was a seasoned C.I.D. officer from Newcastle and a giant of a man, who'd worked happily in the roughest parts of the city through the Sixties and Seventies. He came to us with his own Northern idioms and sometimes it was hard to keep up with him — At first, we editors were faced with the baffling job of trying somehow to translate what he had to say into London English, but we quickly gave up, because Arthur's stuff was visceral, and went at its own fast pace: to have tinkered with it would have been to adulterate it.'

'*Snout* was Arthur's first episode of *The Bill* and I would become his script editor for the next three years on another 16 stories. When we later worked together on *Wycliffe*, he used to travel down from Newcastle for meetings, and stayed at my house. Arthur was then, and doubtless still is now, an enthusiastic man with scores of stories to tell and, while I knew him well enough to feel perfectly comfortable in his company, my wife used to wilt whenever I told her I'd invited Arthur to stay. On one of his visits I was ordered to prepare the way by going to the local video store to hire the longest film there was in there. I returned with Oliver Stone's *Nixon*, which we all watched with rapt attention – so my wife was happy, as well as Arthur and me!'

Paul Harrison (Director)

'I was completely rubbish at school and I left when I was fifteen. Dad said he'd get me into Elstree, printing floor plans for the studio as a holiday relief job. Then it would be up to me to get more work. I did that job for two weeks, where I made lots of cups of tea and the designers told me off a lot because I was always in the studio watching what was going on. When that finished, I was asked if I would like to assist a stage manager. I was sent to a rehearsal room, where I met a wonderful stage manager called Sheila Atha, who took it upon herself to teach me everything about stage management in both theatre and television.'

'When I finished that contract, I went to the office to be told I was taking over a show where the stage manager's husband had just died, three days before they were going into studio. I started on the Wednesday and on the Saturday I stage managed my first television show, on my 17th birthday! I did loads for ATV as a freelancer and by the time I was 19, I went into the HR department and said I wanted to be a director! The guy laughed, so I said if I wasn't one by the time I was 21 that I would leave! He took me seriously and told me to get as much experience as I could, so I went off and learned how to be a location manager and a first assistant director. They then said I needed to have had a staff job before I could apply to be a director, so they sent me down for an interview to be a floor manager, which I really didn't want to do. I actually took my shoes off and sat cross-legged on the desk in a lotus pose, because I wasn't comfortable... and they still gave me the job! I was a floor manager for a year and then I got a trainee director's job. They were great days at ATV, the like of which we shall never see again.'

'The main driving force in *Snout* was Burnside and I really liked working with Chris Ellison, we had a lot of fun on that episode, which was written by Arthur Mackenzie - a lovely man and the real deal. I later directed a 90-minute *Wycliffe* that he wrote. Though when I played my first cut of *Snout* to Peter Cregeen and Richard Bramall, who were brilliant to work with, they said, "Paul, that first half is too dark to be shown at 8:00pm. We'd like you to do it again, but can you make it funny?" They let us do the whole of the first act again and I remember thinking "I'm going to do it differently this time..." There was one ambitious shot from the original version that didn't make it into the comedy reshoot. Our production offices were right above the set and I'd said to Rolie, "I want to find a new way of moving the camera..." I tied a rope around Rolie's waist and I tied the other end to a dodgy old radiator in my office and we got a shot of the yard with him swinging backwards and forwards on a rope out of the window. You'd get sued now, but Rolie was brilliant like that and we had competitions with the other units about how long a shot could be, or could we get to lunch in one take. It was just the most liberating experience for a director, it was fabulous.'

'What I loved most about it was there was such a great team of people and it's the only show I've ever been on where all the directors were literally one door down from each other, so you could actually talk to each other. You very rarely meet other directors in television, because we're not in a department like camera or sound or makeup, you are basically working on your own most of the time. But on *The Bill* because you literally opened the office door, walked down the corridor and were on the set, you could just walk in and watch another director working and you could talk to them about their episodes. Everybody was really generous. Once I tasted single camera work on *The Bill*, my agent and I decided that I only wanted to move onto single camera film, which I really wanted to do because I love the look that you get with film. But I was also very lucky in that period of my career, because I loved directing situation comedies as well and I was blessed for the next five years, when I did a studio sitcom on five cameras in front of an audience in the winter and then I would shoot a series on film in the summer. It was so good to mix and match between those two disciplines and I've always been very grateful to *The Bill* for giving me the opportunity to show that I could direct single camera drama.'

OLD HABITS
Written by Nicholas McInerny
Directed by Barry Davis

Series 4: Episode 39
Broadcast: Tuesday 29 November 1988

Case Narrative
Following a burglary at her home, an old lady has a fatal heart attack. It is
the first death that W.P.C. Brind has to deal with – and the case is far
from simple.

Regular Cast
W.P.C. Brind (Kelly Lawrence), Sgt. Penny (Roger Leach), D.S. Roach
(Tony Scannell), D.C. Dashwood (Jon Iles), Insp. Frazer (Barbara Thorn),
Ch. Insp. Conway (Ben Roberts), P.C. Hollis (Jeff Stewart), P.C. Edwards
(Colin Blumenau), P.C. Melvin (Mark Powley).

Guest Cast
S.O.C.O. (John Yeates), Maurice Harvey (Ralph Nossek), Whickham
(Geoffrey Beevers), Mrs. Lomax (Hilary Mason), Neighbour (Veda Warwick),
Ambulance Man (David Finch), Nurse (Josephine Clarke), Mrs. Leigh
(Nina Baden-Semper), Mrs. Tucker (Nancy Gabrielle), Day Centre Members
(Dennis Edwards, Julie May), Mrs. West (Aimée Delamain), Terry Newton
(Lee Macdonald).

Production Team
Casting Director (Brian Wheeler), Title Music (Andy Pask, Charlie Morgan),
Costume (Maggie Chappelhow), Make Up Designer (Gilly Wakeford),
Graphics (Ethan Ames), Videotape Editor (Colin Bocking), Lighting
(Graham Jaggers), Camera (Peter Edwards), Sound (Alan Norman, Paul
Langwade), Production Buyer (Sarah Prebble), Location Manager
(Sheila Loughrey), First Assistant Director (Kit Williams), Stage Manager
(Nigel J. Wilson), Production Manager (Brian Heard), Production Assistant
(Julie Church), Technical Adviser (Wilf Knight), Script Editor
(Barbara Cox), Series Script Editor (Kenneth Ware), Design
(Stuart McCarthy, Jill Reedman), Executive Producer (Peter Cregeen),
Producer (Michael Ferguson).

Observation Notes

Old Habits (Production No: D4055, VTR No: THS/45290) was shot between Monday 3rd and Friday 7th October 1988.

The opening shot of *Old Habits* was filmed on the South Kilburn estate, with Brind seen outside Blake Court, which has since been redeveloped.

The scenes where Frazer talks to residents about home security at the Salisbury Day Centre were filmed inside Boxmoor House, Queensdale Crescent, W11. The exterior scene with Dashwood talking to Frazer and Brind outside the centre was also filmed outside Boxmoor House.

The scene where Dashwood follows Terry Newton was shot on Silchester Road, W10. Actor Lee McDonald was filmed entering Kingsnorth House, while Jon Iles shot his scenes from Dashwood's car on Kingsdown Close.

Kelly Lawrence and Lee McDonald then filmed their scene where Newton tells Brind about Harvey in St Mark's Park, W10. The building in the background is the former Princess Louise Hospital. This area has been redeveloped and is now the site of Kensington Memorial Park.

Old Habits was the first episode overseen by veteran director Barry Davis, who would direct a further seven stories. Davis' many television credits included *Coronation Street, Tales of the Unexpected, Play for Today* and the BAFTA-winning *Telford's Change*, starring Peter Barkworth, Hannah Gordon, Tessa Peake-Jones and Nula Conwell. Barry Davis passed away after a fall at home in 1990, aged 54.

Old Habits saw Kelly Lawrence become the first actress in *The Bill* to receive top billing on the closing credits. In the character notes distributed to writers, W.P.C. Brind is described as a 20 year old "South-of-the-River Londoner. The daughter of a former DI (retired on medical grounds following injuries sustained in an off-duty road accident) and a still-serving District Nurse, Brind is a forthright, comparatively uncomplicated lady, who really does love "the job" – especially the elements which threaten to stretch her to the limit."

Witness Statements

Nicholas McInerny (Writer)

'When I look back at my writing career, I've had my customary amount of scripts rejected and I've been kicked off a show; every writer will have a story like that. In the beginning, I was quite naïve and because it was relatively straightforward to get these two episodes made, I thought it was going to be easy. I had gone from writing radio plays and a few episodes of *Gems*, to suddenly having 12 million people watching my work on *The Bill*, which was mind-blowing. These early half-hour episodes also used to be repeated on a Friday afternoon, which meant I got a lovely full-fee royalty cheque, which was very welcome as a young writer. I then thought I'd have my own series by the time I was 30, have a play put on at the National and then move to Hollywood. I was still very, very young and I remember after *Old Habits* I kept submitting ideas to *The Bill* and not getting anywhere and my writing went off the boil for a while.'

'*The Bill* was like a finishing school, where I learned how to tell a story. Everybody I've ever met who wrote well for *The Bill* approached it without cynicism and always tried to write the very best episodes they could. Michael Ferguson, who produced *Old Habits*, gave me a really good piece of advice. He said that every police story had already been done, but not every angle on every story. With a story on *The Bill*, you were trying to find a small crime that the people watching at home could relate to, like the old lady who has been burgled. Then, what started as a small chink of light would open up into a larger world, as you revealed more throughout the story. That was the secret of writing for the show.'

'As a writer, exposition is always the most difficult thing to get across on screen. Nowadays we all know from Aaron Sorkin's great show *The West Wing* that the best thing to do is put exposition on the move, where you'd have those signature scenes of highly intelligent people walking down corridors, giving you the exposition on the go. Whilst *The Bill* didn't have advanced Steadicams in these early days, there was always an attempt to add a dynamism to those station scenes, where the handheld cameras would capture the officers walking down corridors, picking up bits of information from one person, then moving onto another. As a writer I got better along the way at knowing how to pull off those little tricks and those moments of fluidity always helped when you had to give out plot details.'

'One of the rules of series television that has always frustrated me is when a tragedy happens and your characters have a reaction to that event, but they are expected by the next episode to have already moved on and left it in the past. Whereas in real life, when people have a bereavement, a break up or a piece of bad news, it can haunt you for weeks. So I thought it would be interesting in *Old Habits* to explore W.P.C. Brind experiencing her first death and how it is still affecting her the next day, because in a professional situation like that you would not just get over it by the end of the shift. *The Bill* at this time was a series about people at work, and it is undoubtedly true that we lost something when we had to move the show more into exploring the private lives of the police officers, rather than focusing on them dealing with crimes.'

'It was great when the show just focused on the work environment in the station and any character that had a slightly outsider status, either because of their race or gender or sexuality, gave an opportunity for me to explore a slightly different take on policing. To write for those characters was always fantastic, as indeed of course was writing for the bad boys like Ramsey or Roach, who were so popular, particularly amongst the female viewers, because they broke the rules, were charming and slightly arrogant and did things on the sly and the audience adored them. We could always come up for more stories for those characters, especially later on when we started to introduce some corrupt coppers. Writers always want to write for the villains!'

'I find the continual appeal of *The Bill* fascinating and I'm very proud to have been part of it. The series had its fluctuations and we all have our favourite eras, but *The Bill* was always pretty consistent in its quality and its intention to faithfully explore and address crime and criminality in a big city and how you policed that city. I think London has a million stories and through *The Bill* we tried to tell some of those stories. Weirdly, when you watch it now, there's a slightly nostalgic element to it. In fact, I was at a hospital appointment recently and when I told the nurse that I used to write for *The Bill* she said, "Oh that was my Mum's favourite programme!" That's what I get now whenever I mention the series, it harkens back a little bit to the reassuring platitudes of *Dixon of Dock Green*, whilst also looking at things in an unsentimental way, which was a really difficult combination to pull off.'

'I think there should always be a police series on television reflecting society, especially now when we are living through very strange times in a more fractious and volatile world. The police have an even more impossible job than ever to do and the fact that *The Bill* is not still being made to show those challenges is a great shame. I think it's really missed, not just by the audience, but also within the industry, where it offered huge opportunities to people both in front of and behind the camera. It was a training ground for everybody. I'm very flattered that people still watch the series and it's wonderful that new audiences are still coming to it from all over the world. I was actually in Australia years ago and I was caught speeding. When the police officer came up to the car, my then wife said, "Go on, say it..." I explained that I wrote for *The Bill* and he made a very funny comment, "You're not trying to bribe me are you Sir?" It was a really nice little interaction... I hasten to add that he still fined me!'

Sheila Loughrey (Location Manager)

'The community centre scenes in *Old Habits*, where Barbara Thorn and Kelly Lawrence attend that residents meeting, were filmed in a block of flats on the Silchester estate. That area is quite well known, because nearby is where 10 Rillington Place was located, the home of John Christie the serial killer. The house doesn't exist anymore, as that street was all pulled down. That area around the Westway was still pretty rough, so I had to be careful as I used to take photos of the different options on my recces using quite an expensive camera. I would then get the photos developed for the design department. I remember once looking around for a particular kind of street in North London...'

'I parked the car and got out to take a photo looking up the street. I then turned around to take a photo in the other direction, when a young guy jumped out of a council bus and accused me of taking pictures of him. He stood right in front of my car so that I couldn't drive it away and it got really quite hairy. It made me realise that if someone stands right in front of your parked vehicle, there's nothing you can really do. All I could do was wind up the window and lock the door until he went away. I don't know what this guy had to hide, but he was paranoid that I was taking his picture. I went straight home after that, because it did shake me up a bit.'

Barbara Thorn (Insp. Christine Frazer)

'I never felt threatened by the whole fame thing really, people used to say hello to me in the supermarket, though maybe not always realising why they were saying hello to you. I used to get "Did you go to the same school as me?" quite a lot, when it turned out they had seen me on the television. There is a way that if you want to remain anonymous, you can avert your glance and not really look at people, though I was always happy to say hello and I ended up having lovely conversations with people. What I did find was that my neighbours would knock on my door and say, "Barbara, can you help us, this car is parked across my drive - get them to move it!" I used to explain, "I'm not really a policewoman, I am just an actress!" Though getting recognised from *The Bill* was nothing compared to when I did a major storyline in *EastEnders*, which was another level entirely and one I did find a bit scary.'

'I was brought up in Chelsea, where my mum and dad rented a lovely place and I went to a school in The Boltons. Every year, they used to put on a pantomime and I always wanted to be in it, but every year I got ill and couldn't be in it! Even as a grown up, I've never been in a pantomime. But that was when the acting seed was planted and when I went to secondary school, I used to volunteer to do the scenery for the school plays. One day, I noticed on a notice board that they were going to do a production of Shakespeare's *Twelfth Night*, and you were encouraged to put your name down if you would like to play a big part, a middle-sized part, or a small part...'

'Next thing I know, the Deputy Headmistress is congratulating me for being cast as Viola! But I hadn't put my name down, one of my friends had because she thought it would be a jolly good laugh! Then I discovered that the Deputy Headmistress had herself trained as an actress at LAMDA. She and all my teachers came to see me in the play and really encouraged me and supported me. I was terrified about doing it, but felt elated by the end of it, which is how I've felt about every job I've ever done.'

'I was told by a lot of people that I needed to get another skill, so I went off and did a secretarial course, which I hated. I then got a job at the Theatre Royal in Lincoln, where I worked in the office and then as an assistant stage manager, which is how I got my Equity card. I then came back to London and got a job as an ASM at the Watford Palace Theatre, followed by a job as an understudy on a musical called *Happy as a Sandbag* at the Ambassadors Theatre. I then went to Webber Douglas drama school, who used to let me have Tuesday and Thursday afternoons off so that I could work on the show. My theatre career really went from there.'

THE SILENT GUN

Written by Christopher Russell
Directed by Terry Marcel

Series 4: Episode 40
Broadcast: Thursday 1 December 1988

Viewing Figures: 13.05m
ITV Chart Position: 7

Case Narrative

A gunman locks himself in an upper-storey room and provokes a full-scale alert for Sun Hill officers. It's a waiting game, and no-one can take any chances...

Regular Cast

Sgt. Cryer (Eric Richard), Ch. Supt. Brownlow (Peter Ellis), Ch. Insp. Conway (Ben Roberts), D.S. Roach (Tony Scannell), D.C. Carver (Mark Wingett), Sgt. Peters (Larry Dann), P.C. Haynes (Eamonn Walker), P.C. Smith (Robert Hudson), W.P.C. Brind (Kelly Lawrence), P.C. Edwards (Colin Blumenau), W.P.C. Martella (Nula Conwell), P.C. Melvin (Mark Powley), P.C. Frank (Ashley Gunstock).

Guest Cast

Insp. Hallett (Peter Caffrey), Sgt. Towers (James Gaddas), Roger (Ron Webster), Miss Foulkes (Damaris Hayman), Bailiff (Keith Taylor), Polish Interpreter (Ania Marson), 1st Resident (Richard Bonehill), 2nd Resident (Dennis Banks), Elderly Woman (Lois Penson), Spanish Girl (Maria Isabel Hernandez), Asian Landlord (Kursheed Ullah Khan), Asian Shopkeeper (Raj Patel), Lublin (Milo Sperber).

Production Team

Casting Director (Julia Lisney), Title Music (Andy Pask, Charlie Morgan), Costume Designer (Maggie Chappelhow, Peter Roberts), Make Up Designer (Gilly Wakeford), Graphics (Ethan Ames), Videotape Editor (John Sharland), Lighting (Christopher Davies), Camera (Chas Watts), Sound (Robert Newton, Paul Gartrell), Production Buyer (Derek Rhys), Location Manager (Quenton Annis), First Assistant Director (Barry Beckett), Floor Assistant (Richard Marson), Stage Manager (Marilyn Edwards), Production Manager (Brian Heard), Production Assistant (Sylvia Rumney), Technical Adviser

(Wilf Knight), Script Editor (Tim Vaughan), Series Script Editor (Kenneth Ware), Designers (Robin Parker, Peter Joyce), Executive Producer (Peter Cregeen), Producer (Richard Bramall).

Observation Notes

The Silent Gun (Production No: D4057, VTR No: THS/45292) was shot between Monday 10th and Friday 14th October 1988. The recce of the locations took place on Monday 3rd October. Filming took place on York Road, Acton, W3. The main location was No. 6, two doors down from No. 2, which had been used as the women's refuge in the episode *Domestics*.

On Friday 2nd December, the day after *The Silent Gun* was broadcast, writer J.C. Wilsher received his first script commission for *The Bill*, after submitting storylines for the past six months. *In The Cold* would not be shot until May 1989, eventually broadcast in October 1989.

In overall charge of the siege in *The Silent Gun* is Chief Superintendent Charles Brownlow. The Character Notes issued to writers on the series detailed Mr. Brownlow as being 50 years old and described him as "a cool, remote administrator, dedicated to the pursuit of Scotland Yard's new horizons. He is a limited, conventional, unimaginative man, unquestioningly sympathetic to whatever directive the Commissioner's office issues. Keeping within budget, producing tidy files and impressive records are his principal concerns. He does not like making waves – and tells bad jokes, badly. He cultivates acquaintances, not friends, among the local councillors and dignitaries. At Sun Hill, he feels more comfortable with Sgt Cryer and the uniformed staff than he does with the CID officers. CID men tend to go their own way too much. To Charles Brownlow, that smacks of indiscipline. Good general behaviour, tidiness, and a "proper demeanour" are what he looks for in his ideal policeman; qualities frequently lacking in the CID. Brownlow is married with two children. He lives in the Home Counties and plays golf, as much for the contacts he can exploit as for the fun he gets out of the game. It is unlikely, in fact, that he gets any "fun" out of it (or anything else) at all."

Witness Statements

Christopher Russell (Writer)

'*The Silent Gun* was based on a similar siege incident that a friend of mine in the police was involved in. They didn't know who the person in the flat was, or whether or not he was dangerous. It was assumed that he was dangerous and then you had the pile up of resources on the scene, who weren't able to get anything sensible done, because they didn't know what they were dealing with. What I wanted to show in this episode was how a large number of police officers could end up sitting around, not quite sure what was happening. Whilst a potential gunman is not a funny subject, there were a number of funny things about the situation. As human beings will always find a way to entertain themselves, it was enjoyable to show this group of police officers watching football and almost acting as if it is a holiday, then occasionally remembering that there might be a lethal gunman upstairs.'

'It was Wilf Knight, the police advisor, who told me that it would be the Chief Inspector who would act as the negotiator and *The Silent Gun* was the first episode that saw Conway fulfil this role. This was an advantage for the story, because we hadn't seen him do anything like this before in *The Bill* and it was always good to be able to use Ben Roberts more actively in a story. I can't take any credit for Inspector Hallett being a pipe smoker, which wasn't written in the script and I was quite surprised when I first saw it. I assume this was a bit of business worked out between actor Peter Caffrey and director Terry Marcel. Terry handled the action and the tension well, because he didn't like scenes to be still and he kept things on the move. He also cast Damaris Hayman, who I thought was super in this episode, as Miss Foulkes.'

'*The Silent Gun* was also a good vehicle for studying human nature, because you had all the local residents behind the cordon, who were trying to live their normal lives. This siege scenario was a way of showing a cross-section of society, all of whom are normally totally unconnected to each other, until they become connected by this 1000/1 incident, which is now getting in the way of them living their lives. How most people initially see a situation like this, is that the police aren't trying to protect them, they are just getting in their way. It doesn't matter that there might be a dangerous man with a weapon behind that door; these people just want to get home and have their tea!'

Peter Ellis (Chief Supt. Charles Brownlow)
'I was very fond of Ben Roberts, who had been an engineer before he started acting. At one stage he was building himself an aeroplane, which he was going to fly! He was a wonderful actor and lovely to work with. Because *The Bill* was shot so fast, we very rarely

had a chance to talk to each other about the scripts before we turned up and did them. Very often, when we arrived in the morning, we'd find out we would be doing several bits from different episodes. After *The Bill*, we shot a pilot together up in Suffolk, called *The Mortician's Tea Party*, which was written by my son, Hugh. It was about two Northern morticians and we had lot of fun making it. We intended to develop it into a TV series and it attracted some interest. We did have a great deal of fun making it! Hugh later wrote for *The Bill*, including my final episode, as well as a feature film starring Robert Carlyle called *Summer*.'

'I think a huge part of the success of *The Bill* early on was that the producers valued the writers. Chris Russell wrote me some very good episodes. It was only on episodes like *The Silent Gun* that I ever got recognised by members of the public, because I was there with everyone else from the cast. Other than that, nobody ever really took much notice of me, though that's mainly because I looked very scruffy out of the uniform in real life. Oddly, I got recognised more in Australia when I did a couple of tours out there, though I was still surprised. The strangest one was after I had played a villain in *Z Cars* and I got pushed up against a wall by a guy in Shepherd's Bush, who said, "I bloody know you..." It doesn't occur to you at the time to ask, "Did you watch television last night?" instead you just think, "Oh God what have I done?"'

Tim Vaughan (Script Editor)

'I have a lot of favourite *Bill* episodes and it would be difficult to pick one I'd call the best of the lot — but *The Silent Gun* has always been around the top of my list. I love the fact that it isn't until well into the second half of the programme that Yorkie finds out that the man upstairs believed to have a firearm — and who, for the past six or so hours, they've all been trying to coax into coming out and putting his hands up — is actually deaf. That was a very funny moment in the sort of "slow farce" that Chris created for us. Peter Ellis was also really good in this episode: he was so understated and had that great line "This situation is in danger of drifting..." which was a perfect line for the Chief Super to say and sounded so good coming from him. It was hilariously funny that whilst he was saying this, his officers were in the next room watching the football... and when suddenly a shout went up, and you thought something dramatic had just happened, it was actually someone failing to score a goal! It all added to Brownlow's frustrations in *The Silent Gun*, who had been seconds away from spending the weekend on a getaway trip with his wife! I also thought Terry Marcel did a very good job on *The Silent Gun*. One of the really good ingredients of his direction was that he liked to have unusual things going on in the background. The further he went, the more hilarious it became. It wouldn't have surprised me if he'd added a dancing bear in the background!'

Terry Marcel (Director)

'I think *The Silent Gun* stands up quite well. Christopher Russell is a good writer and I was fortunate to direct two more of his scripts. All directors are tested, and this episode was a test for me in terms of how was I going to make it different? I just had to keep looking at it and thinking about how I could make it stand out from everybody else's episodes. I think I pushed it as far as I could, though I could not have done anything without that team. As a director you need support and I got tremendous support from Peter Cregeen, who backed me up and encouraged me if I came up with a great idea that could work and wasn't too expensive. That's how I later worked with my directors when I produced *The Enid Blyton Adventure Series* and both seasons of *Dark Knight*. I gave them as much support as I could, because Peter Cregeen had shown me that's what being a good producer is all about.'

'Preparation is so important, it's no good walking onto a set umming and ahhing and still making your mind up. I used to work it all out on the script, so that when I walked on set, I could say, "This is what I want and this is how I want it. Let's do it." It was whilst working with some directors earlier in my career, who were very poor and really didn't understand the business, that really made me start to think, "I could do this..." I can remember distinctly working on one particular picture and saying to the second assistant, "I'm not going to do this anymore." I wanted to do my own stuff and when the film industry went really dead, I put together a very small horror film called *Prey*, which I produced on a budget of £30,000. I learned a very big lesson about how not to do certain things, but the bug really bit me and I thought I knew enough about the business to become a director myself. I had an old friend called Martin Schute, who was a great producer and was then working for Ray Cooney, the big theatre impresario. Ray had written a play called *Why Not Stay For Breakfast?*, which I felt we could turn into a little movie... I said I could shoot a full-length feature in two weeks, including a New York shoot... which is exactly what I did, including a one-day location shoot in New York!'

Marilyn Edwards (Stage Manager)

'One of the stage manager's responsibilities in the early days was to actually research the storyline and make sure that it was feasible and would happen in real life. That didn't apply to our more experienced writers like Geoff McQueen and Christopher Russell, who did their own research, but when new writers were pitching prospective storylines for the half-hours, we were constantly being assured by our various contacts in the police that their ideas would never happen in a million years. We became quite unpopular when we'd have to explain to the producers that the storyline was wrong and would have to be re-written. Research was very important on *The Silent Gun*. I had a very good firearms officer, who got us the correct guns and we knew we were safe with him. My abiding memory of this episode is that Terry Marcel thought it would be fun during this tense siege to have Damaris Hayman's character handing out cups of tea. We were in an empty house, which Peter Joyce had dressed, but we didn't have cups and saucers or anything like that because this wasn't in the script. I managed to rustle up some tea and china, but then Tony Scannell decided that he wanted to be spooning sugar into his tea... Our caterers weren't nearby, because we had blocked the street off and filled it with police vehicles and supporting artists... so this huge production was held up for a good ten minutes while I ran around looking for a teaspoon!'

Richard Marson (Floor Assistant)

'I would get to Barlby Road for 5am and I do remember the days were very long and relentless. When you're a floor assistant, you get people in and out of makeup, fetch people sandwiches and cups of tea and generally help out. On location, I was once sent to ask someone to turn their car engine off, because the sound of it running was being picked up by the microphone. Because we had these radios, we looked like plain clothes police officers, so when I walked over to ask the driver to turn the engine off, the car screeched off because they thought I was going to nick them! We used to shoot in not very salubrious parts of London, before they became gentrified. I loved that *The Bill* shot in parts of London that other shows wouldn't and these episodes are now a real time capsule into those areas.'

'After each day's filming, a really dreary job for a floor assistant was to make sure that those crew radios had been brought back in and were loaded up to recharge overnight, because if you got that wrong and someone's battery was flat the next day, you were really screwed. This was before mobile phones and so the radios were our only way of communicating, which meant recharging them was a really important job. Sometimes I would still be chasing stragglers who hadn't handed their radios back in until maybe eight or nine at night, and I didn't dare leave until I knew they were all charged, which might take until midnight. So one night, I didn't go home and just slept in the kit room!'

'*The Silent Gun* had a lot of extras, who I got saddled with looking after. Jack Rosenthal once wrote a brilliant play, *Ready When You Are, Mr. McGill*, about an extra getting his big break, which of course Ricky Gervais' character was always chasing in *Extras*. Back then, you had these serial extras, who had been doing it for donkey's years and had worked on every show going. The truth of it was that some of them weren't very nice people; they'd just turn up and want the free bacon rolls and coffee. I was warned beforehand, "Be careful with the ones who bring shooting sticks..." We'd hired them to be a rowdy crowd, but suddenly you'd see all these heads sinking down out of shot, because they were sitting down! I had to go and confiscate them, because they weren't allowed them and had been told not to bring them. It was like being a schoolteacher, only to 70-year-old extras, which isn't exactly why I wanted to work in television.'

'The extras would be given set parts to play, so the ones who weren't needed for a scene would be stored on the bus, in reserve for when we did the next set-up. I remember the first assistant director barking, "Go and get me two ugly old bags!" so off I went to the bus. I was very eager to please and quite RP in those days, saying, "Madam, would you and your friend like to come with me please?" Then this really impatient first AD yelled down the radio "HAVE YOU GOT THOSE UGLY OLD BAGS YET?" It came out as clear as day and there was no getting away from it... I replied, "I've got the middle-aged shoppers..." One of the old ladies replied, "Nice try dear, but we know we're ugly old bags." That was quite embarrassing, it was a long walk with them back to the set.'

'It was also part of the floor assistant's job to do the calls for the next morning, where I had to ring around and give everyone their call times for the following day. I had been told to make sure that I actually spoke to them and not just leave a message. I phoned everybody on the list, but the only person I couldn't get hold of was one of the guest actors, James Gaddas. At that point, he was very much talked about as being the next big thing, everybody was saying that this guy was a possible James Bond and that he'd definitely be a film star in the future. I kept calling, but he didn't pick up, so I had to leave message after message. I kept going until the point where I thought it was too late, I couldn't call someone at midnight when they're meant to be in at 6am for makeup. "He must have got the message" I thought... Well the next day, he was late and I got in so much trouble. It was made worse when he said that he hadn't had a call and that there was no message on his answer phone... He then took me to one side and said "Really sorry mate, but it was you or me. You'll get over it..." There was a definite drop in temperature when he confided that he'd stayed at his girlfriend's all night. That's a really good example of shit rolling downwards in TV.'

'One of my more positive memories of *The Bill* was seeing the group of young actors playing the regular coppers, just pissing themselves laughing, despite what was a rigorous and demanding set-up for them. They didn't have the same comforts that the regulars in *EastEnders* or *Coronation Street* had, where they would rarely be leaving their cosy studio environment and all had their own dressing rooms. *The Bill* was physically the most demanding of the serials running on television at the time and the cast were turning up every day in freezing cold London, often when it was pissing with rain. They were also wearing really uncomfortable uniforms and helmets that were bloody heavy. But these young actors were at the beginning of their careers and all had that really joyous "anything's possible" camaraderie. They were having their best life, to use that cliché.'

'Eamonn Walker was one of the actors who clearly had a lot of talent and was ahead of the game even then, a really commanding actor. Another of my favourites was Mark Powley, though I remember him being really upset when I said that he reminded me of someone... Mark hoped I was about to say Steve McQueen or Robert Redford, but I said he reminded me of Simon Mayo from Radio 1! He was really insulted, "I'm way better looking than Simon Mayo!" I tried to dig myself out of the hole, saying he was the blonde boy next door and that mums would be really happy if their daughter brought him home in the future... He said "You're not making it better, I want to be edgy!" We laughed and I told him he was really dark and complex. He was a sweetheart.'

AN OLD-FASHIONED TERM
Written by Geoff McQueen
Directed by Philip Casson

Series 4: Episode 41
Broadcast: Tuesday 6 December 1988

Case Narrative
Alfred 'Tosh' Lines hasn't progressed beyond the role of Detective Constable for twelve years – but Carver discovers there's more to Tosh than meets the eye.

Regular Cast
Sgt. Cryer (Eric Richard), D.C. Lines (Kevin Lloyd), D.C. Carver (Mark Wingett), W.P.C. Martella (Nula Conwell), P.C. Edwards (Colin Blumenau), D.I. Burnside (Christopher Ellison), D.S. Roach (Tony Scannell), Insp. Frazer (Barbara Thorn), D.C Dashwood (Jon Iles), Ch. Supt. Brownlow (Peter Ellis), Sgt. Peters (Larry Dann), Sgt. Penny (Roger Leach), P.C. Melvin (Mark Powley), P.C. Smith (Robert Hudson), P.C. Haynes (Eamonn Walker).

Guest Cast
Kelly (Trevor Peacock), Doctor (Josephine Welcome), Mrs. Sansom (Anne Priestley).

Uncredited Personnel
P.C. (Oscar Peck), Press Officer (Rosane Chapman), Librarian (Bridget Moore), Secretaries (Diane Boland, Tracy Sinclair).

Production Team
Casting Director (Brian Wheeler), Title Music (Andy Pask, Charlie Morgan), Costume (Maggie Chappelhow, Carolyn Maddocks), Make Up Designer (Gilly Wakeford), Graphics (Ethan Ames), Videotape Editor (Colin Bocking), Lighting (Bill Minto), Camera (Adrian J. Fearnley), Sound (Dave Evans, Paul Gartrell), Production Buyer (Sarah Prebble), Location Manager (Brian Bilgorri), First Assistant Director (David Downing), Stage Manager (Gregory Kinchin), Production Manager (Brian Heard), Production Assistant (Susan Lewis), Technical Adviser (Wilf Knight), Script Editor (Tim Vaughan), Series Script Editor (Kenneth Ware), Designers (Stuart McCarthy,

Kyz Kistell), Executive Producer (Peter Cregeen), Producer (Michael Ferguson).

Observation Notes

An Old-Fashioned Term (Production No: D4059, VTR No: THS/45294) was shot between Monday 17th and Friday 21st October 1988. Filming for the opening scene took place at St Helens Gardens and the adjoining St Quintin Avenue, W10. The scenes where Edwards and Martella investigate the flat were shot in the top floor of No. 6 St Quintin Avenue.

The driving scenes with Carver and Lines were filmed on Southern Row, W10 and the adjoining Appleford Road, W10.

The location used for the exterior of the Magistrates Court is Ladbroke Hall, 79 Barlby Road, W10. The Grade II listed building is now Sunbeam Studios. Tony Scannell then crosses the road and joins Jon Iles at the end of St Mark's Road, W10, for the following shot where Roach and Dashwood observe Lenny leaving the court.

The later scene where they are on night-time observation was filmed opposite the Prince Of Wales pub, 48 Southern Row, W10. This building is now home to a restaurant called The Chilled Eskimo.

Witness Statements

Mark Wingett (D.C. Jim Carver)

'At the time I was living in Forest Gate, in the East End. I used to get up every day at 5.15am to go into Barlby Road, which I'm not complaining about, because that's what I signed up for and what I was being paid for. I always looked forward to going to work, because there would always be a laugh to have somewhere along the line, every day. I sometimes found myself getting up early on my days off, ready for the commute, before realising I wasn't filming that day. That was quite common for a lot of the actors, once we'd got into the quite intense routine of making *The Bill* all year round.'

'One of the great things about working in television is you are fortunate to earn some money, and I was lucky enough to start scuba diving when a friend of mine called Kenny was training to be a stuntman. Myself and two fellow actors, David John and Paul McGann, started going scuba diving with Kenny and I thought it was brilliant from the first moment I put the tank on my bank, it's an extraordinary sport. Within a year of starting training in the pool in Ladbroke Grove, I was going around the world and diving in places like the Red Sea in Egypt, which was extraordinary! I then developed an interest in marine photography and there are a mind-boggling number of shipwrecks around the coast of Britain. Many are buried under the seabed and inaccessible, though within Dover alone there are 300 exposed shipwrecks to explore, all of which are a time capsule and have a story. Getting out to sea and going underwater with a group of likeminded people is sheer escapism and became the perfect counterbalance to making *The Bill* full-time.'

'As the series became more popular, I started to have some funny encounters with the public, who knew my face, but couldn't quite place where I was from... A bloke at a set of traffic lights once asked me if I used to drive a GPO van? Or a guy in the street came up to me and said, "Excuse me mate, didn't you used to be my housing officer?" And a woman in a nightclub asked me if we'd met at the Karachi Literature Festival... So around this time, the production team needed to provide somewhere for us to sit when we were out on location. In Hollywood, actors get their famous Winnebagos... what we got was a converted library, with a translucent roof, no windows and a couple of sofas in it! We used to spend a lot of time in there, chewing the fat and having a laugh. I spent a lot of time with Kevin Lloyd, bless him. He was a joy to work with and a naughty man! When he delivered a line, he would look at you with a little twinkle in his eyes, which would make you laugh while he remained completely deadpan. He was a bugger for that and such fun!'

Gregory Kinchin (Stage Manager)

'The stage manager's job on *The Bill* was different to working on most other programmes. The script editors and the writers often did a lot of their own research and were always able to talk to our in-house police advisors, who were ex-policemen. But when it came to actually working out what needed to happen on set, some of the finer details might have got lost. Our job was to make sure that the director had everything they needed from their point of view, to be able to tell the story and to make it as accurate as possible on the floor. The designer would dress the sets and get all the major stuff in there, but it was the stage manager's responsibility to look after all the small props in the station, like the paperwork, and make sure the station was properly presented and believable.'

'The set-up in our office was that the stage manager would be on one side of the desk, with the designer on the other, because our responsibilities overlapped a little bit, so we could talk to each other and make sure we had everything covered. All the designers were very different characters; as time went on some had only ever worked for Thames, some had come from the BBC, and some were freelancers. They all had a real mix of backgrounds, which changed the way you worked with each of them, because obviously not only do you have to get on, but you also had to find the best way of communicating with each person. The designer I worked with initially was Colin Andrews, who was a very nice man, but also a quiet fellow, he didn't make a big song and dance about anything. Other designers liked to collaborate more and work more closely, whereas Colin just quietly got on with his job, so you had to ask him questions, to be sure everything was covered. He was easy going.'

'The budget for props came from the design budget. Our production buyer, Sarah Prebble, worked closely with the designer and dressed whatever sets were created on location. The buyer would spend a couple of days going out to the hire houses and ordering in all the props that they needed for the shoot, including all the vehicles that we needed as well. Then as stage managers, we were allocated a small amount from within that budget, although I never really worked to a set amount of money, because most of the stuff we used on set was minimal cost and a lot of it was either made up or acquired by ourselves. Television is all an illusion and as stage managers, we were always watching the monitor when things were being shot in the station, seeing if we could add just a little detail to the set. It might be something that the director or the actors might not even notice, but might help a viewer at home believe they were watching a real police station on their screens. There were ways of doing things in the custody area for example, which if we got wrong would make the series look shoddy. It was important to get those simple things right, to help give the series credibility.'

'When you look on the white boards in the custody area, detailing which prisoners are in each cells, there'd likely be a few recognisable names on there from the production team. Similarly when you see faces of criminals on posters in the C.I.D. office, they would often be members of the crew. We'd usually have our photos taken on the Friday coffee morning, ahead of the shoot on the Monday, which was when I would book the photographer to take photos we needed for the episode, such as surveillance photos or for set dressing. Then a whole load of us from the crew would come along and have our photos taken, which would then be used as mugshots placed around the station. Most would be quite happy to do it, it was a bit of fun and a bonus if our face was seen on screen as well.'

'We started off by mocking up a lot of the paperwork, like the custody forms and the warrants. There was also the medical side to consider as well and it was my responsibility to make sure that the forensic scenes in *An Old-Fashioned Term* were done correctly. If we didn't get those details right, it would make a mockery of the whole series really. We used to go into police stations all the time and talk to people in the force. We got to know how things worked for real and we learned more and more as we went along. Then eventually, we used to order the paperwork from the same suppliers as the police, which was an evolution of how our relationship with the police developed. Though if you ever met a policeman, they would never say, "That was really good, you got all that right!" They might give the programme a little praise, but they always liked to pick out bits that they felt weren't quite right.'

Tim Vaughan (Script Editor)

'The log line that heads this episode refers to Carver's astonishment at learning Tosh Lines has been a detective constable for twelve years, but never thought of promotion — and discovers as events unfold that there's much more to Tosh than meets the eye. That's all true, and this episode is a gripping murder story from Geoff McQueen in which Tosh demonstrates his expert deduction skills in nailing the murderer — but the real star of the episode has to be the murderer himself, Kelly, played by Trevor Peacock, the remarkable stage and screen actor, who died in 2021 at the age of 89. Geoff's script is brilliant of course: his handling of the story of the apparent suicide of a young woman is chilling and sensitive, but the character Geoff created for Trevor Peacock, playing a shabby hospital porter, makes one's blood run cold: a lecherous, depraved old man, self-pitying and tearful - but defiantly mute when the detectives ask him why he committed the crime.'

'Philip Casson's last shots in the cells, when they close the door on him and walk away, was a memorable moment. To have picked Trevor Peacock for the role was an inspired stroke by casting director Brian Wheeler and director Philip Casson. The title, *An Old Fashioned Term* is a nice touch by Geoff, distilling the ugliness of predatory characters like Trevor Peacock's Kelly. When Burnside wonders what Kelly's motive might be, Tosh replies, "Motive? That's an old fashioned term now, Guv." Some time later, long after *The Bill*, I had an idea for another TV police show. I'd done *Between The Lines, A Touch of Frost* and *Wycliffe*, but I'd lived in Leeds during the Yorkshire Ripper investigations and got to know a couple of detectives (I say "got to know" — they tried to nick me for it, and I had a job explaining to them that I was completely innocent!) But the plight of those detectives up in Leeds had always stayed with me. I must have had those words from Tosh Lines echoing in my ears when I created *Without Motive*, a story about policemen failing, which I made with my friend Russell Lewis, starring Ken Cranham, Jamie Foreman and Ross Kemp.'

'From the start of the show in 1984, there were some general rules that Geoff McQueen and Peter Cregeen set in stone for *The Bill* - probably with the advice of Lloyd Shirley, Controller of Drama at Thames TV. Every show was a one-off; everything was seen from the police point of view; and the audience never went home with the officers, or saw villains plotting, etc. Subsequent producers dismantled those rules, swapped the episode titles for numbers, and turned the show into a serial, rather than a series. I'd gone to work on other shows by then, but was saddened by the changes that were made, which I felt were to the detriment of the show. Producer Paul Marquess wanted to do things like having the first gay kiss between two police officers, and had Ackland falling in love with her own son. I'd have preferred it if he'd set up his own vehicle for for those stories, frankly, but Paul's done well with shows like *London Kills*, so, good for him. I remember having a long conversation with Mark Wingett recently about how great it would be to do *The Bill* again, but it couldn't really work now. The famous coppers' feet walking down the road that ended every episode wouldn't be possible. There aren't coppers on the beat any more: the idea of ordinary policing of the kind *The Bill* dramatised seems almost as far back as *Dixon of Dock Green*.

'I grew up with the arts in my family. My uncle, David Vaughan, was a dancer and choreographer, who after serving in India during the Second World War, moved to New York and worked with Merce Cunningham back in the 50s, later becoming his archivist. He stayed out there until he was 94 and died in 2017. He was a wonderful guy and the person in our family who we all loved more than anyone else; the avuncular uncle personified. He grew up in Brixton with my father, Paul Vaughan, who after a career as a journalist did a lot of voiceovers for *Horizon* and was the presenter of the BBC Radio 4 programme *Kaleidoscope* for about a decade.'

'When I came out of university with a degree in English, there was a researcher job going at Radio 4. I got the job, which was a strict six-month contract, covering the maternity leave for another editor/abridger called Libby Spurrier. When the contract was running out, I thought, "now what?" I rang a friend in another office, who yelled out, "I've got a mate here who needs a job, anyone got anything?" Someone shouted back that a man called Colin Schindler was looking for a script editor in TV... I thought, "That will do me!" I rang Colin, a very interesting man, who later made the film *Buster.* He invited me for an interview and I got the job on *The Masterspy.* But the moment I got started, the series was decimated by the ITV strike in 1979. We only completed six of the fourteen episodes and the series didn't come back. Colin apologised and said, "Sorry mate, I've got nothing else for you."

'Luckily, I met a guy on the set called Ben Steed, who asked me if I had an agent. When I said I didn't, he kindly said he would have a word with his... Soon after, I was sitting in my little rented flat in Mitcham and the phone rang. It was Ben, who said, "There's a job going, but don't shoot me, it's in Leeds." I said, "That's all right, what is it?" Then he said, "Again, don't shoot me, it's *Emmerdale Farm.* You'd have to live up there..." That was fine by me, so off I went to Yorkshire. When I turned up there, I was so naïve, I thought they shot everything in story order, because the only television I'd worked on were those six episodes of a little game show! The first thing they did was put a pile of scripts on my desk and told me to go over everything I thought needed changing, and do the re-writes.... I said, "You want me to do all that? By close of play today?" The producer said, "Of course, that's why you're here!" I didn't stay naïve for long!'

GETTING STRESSED
Written by Christopher Russell
Directed by Philip Casson

Series 4: Episode 42
Broadcast: Thursday 8 December 1988

Viewing Figures: 12.85m
ITV Chart Position: 5

Case Narrative
Reg Hollis is anxious to talk to everyone about possible stress problems – but with an assault, a rape and a drunk in charge of a baby, Christine Frazer has enough on her plate...

Regular Cast
Sgt. Cryer (Eric Richard), Insp. Frazer (Barbara Thorn), D.S. Roach (Tony Scannell), W.P.C. Ackland (Trudie Goodwin), D.I. Burnside (Christopher Ellison), D.C. Lines (Kevin Lloyd), D.C Dashwood (Jon Iles), Ch. Insp. Conway (Ben Roberts), Ch. Supt. Brownlow (Peter Ellis), D.C. Carver (Mark Wingett), Sgt. Penny (Roger Leach), P.C. Hollis (Jeff Stewart), P.C. Ramsey (Nick Reding), P.C. Stamp (Graham Cole), P.C. Frank (Ashley Gunstock), Sgt. Peters (Larry Dann).

Guest Cast
Maria Quinn (Emma Currie), Shirley Jervis (Victoria Burton), Mrs. Paynter (Elizabeth Kelly), Peter Gascoigne (Tim Preece), Mr. Stocks (Paul Rainbow), Car Driver (Aaron Harris).

Production Team
Stunt Arranger (Lex Milloy), Casting Director (Brian Wheeler), Title Music (Andy Pask, Charlie Morgan), Costume (Maggie Chappelhow, Carolyn Maddocks), Make Up Designer (Gilly Wakeford), Graphics (Ethan Ames), Videotape Editors (Colin Bocking, Bob Ede), Lighting (Bill Minto), Camera (Adrian J. Fearnley), Sound (John York, Paul Gartrell), Production Buyer (Sarah Prebble), Location Manager (Brian Bilgorri), First Assistant Director (David Downing), Stage Manager (Gregory Kinchin), Production Manager (Brian Heard), Production Assistant (Susan Lewis), Technical Adviser (Wilf Knight), Script Editor (Tim Vaughan), Series Script Editor (Kenneth Ware), Designers (Stuart McCarthy,

Kyz Kistell), Executive Producer (Peter Cregeen), Producer (Michael Ferguson).

Observation Notes

Getting Stressed (Production No: D4044, VTR No: THS/45279) was shot between Monday 29th August and Friday 2nd September 1988.

The opening scene where Frazer helps the driver out of his car before it explodes was filmed on Mitre Way, W10.

The later scene where Ackland apprehends the drunken mother outside an off-licence was filmed outside 5-7 Dalgarno Gardens, W10.

The bag snatch sequence was filmed in Harlesden, NW10. Ackland is attacked outside 5 Leopold Road, Harlesden, NW10. The shops on this road have since been converted into ground floor flats. The bikers escape down the Church Path back lane. When the oncoming police motorbike blocks their path, the thieves then turn off onto the appropriately named Brownlow Road, NW10. The action then jumps to Fortunegate Road, NW10, where Dashwood drives in from the adjoining Fawcett Road, NW10, forcing the motorbike back onto Church Path. The thieves then drive into Roundwood Park, using the entrance on Longstone Avenue, N10. They escape out of the park onto Harlesden Road, NW10.

Guessing Game sees June Ackland once again working in a dangerous situation, this time assaulted by the motorbike riding bag snatchers. The Character Notes described Ackland as being 33 years old and "involved in her work to a degree that is not always good for her. She finds it all too easy to identify with victims and to wish to halve their problems by sharing them. On the other hand, she is far from being "wet"; nor does she see herself as a uniformed social worker. She is a member of the police force and glad to be. She does not think of herself as a woman police officer; simply as an officer. But she has had quite a struggle to demonstrate this equality to her male colleagues – and to show herself capable of more than being expected to sit at a CAD desk all day, or do the office typing. Ackland is aware of the danger, in having to prove herself, of becoming as hard and cynical as most of the men. She is determined that this shall not happen. Ackland is single, but though she rarely talks about her private life, it is quite on the cards that she'll be seen one day being picked up outside the nick by a young man in a car. Her father recently died after a prolonged illness."

Getting Stressed also features P.C. Reg Hollis in full Police Federation Rep mode. The Background Information document issued to writers describes the role as: "becoming increasingly important, though the extent to which he is allowed to do it depends to a large degree on his senior officers. His concerns lie mainly in the areas of health and safety, recreation rooms, and the like. He is usually a man of at least 10 years experience. He is not given the time to do the job, but often wangles it – for example, by getting the post of Collator."

Getting Stressed was adapted for an episode of the Netherlands police series *Bureau Kruislaan* in 1993. The episode *Stress* was the 22nd episode of the first season and features the same storylines, though Inspecteur Christine Verwey has no assault or explosion to deal with.

Witness Statements

Christopher Russell (Writer)
'I wanted something shocking to happen to Frazer and the opening scene in *Getting Stressed* was just about the most extreme thing that could happen to her. It was important to show the audience what she was made of and how she would react in a situation like that. It was also realistic, because police have to deal with shocking situations all the time and they are certainly assaulted far more in real life than we ever showed on *The Bill*. Police officers are getting beaten up all the time, and we wanted to show that Frazer is doing the same job as a man and so she gets the same treatment as a man. We also wanted to show how she dealt with her colleagues after a situation like this, and of course Hollis was a gift in a scenario like that. Hollis was like chocolate, in that you had to be careful not to use him too much, because it would have been easy to just write more and more scenes with that character. Philip Casson was a very good director and I thought he made the motorbike chase look like a scene from a heist movie, it was an amazing sequence! I'd never seen anything like it in *The Bill* before; it was brilliantly shot and incredibly well done.'

Barbara Thorn (Insp. Christine Frazer)
'*Getting Stressed* was fantastically written by Christopher Russell and showed what a busy life Frazer had! He gave me some great throwaway lines, which reflected the humour that officers on the frontline develop in real life. The episode opened with that

extraordinary stunt, which I really enjoyed being involved with. I watched the guys do their stunts on *Hold Fire* and thought "Wow, that's amazing..." never really thinking about the fact that I might have to do some myself later on, but I did! I felt comfortable and safe, because the crew were always rock solid and alert to what was going on and we were well looked after by the lovely director Philip Casson, who I later worked with on *EastEnders*.'

'*Getting Stressed* also saw the end of Frazer and Roach's affair, which again was all very understated. Tony Scannell was always very real as Ted, much like how he was always true to himself in real life. Quite often when the rest of us were leaving make-up to go on set, Tony would be arriving, still wearing his dickie bow tie from a great night out, having not been to bed! At the time, I was quite horrified that he'd be able to work, but he always carried it off. He was a very unexpected man, always curious about everything and very funny. He was also a polite man and whenever we all used to gather at weekends, he would quite often stand with me and he was always the gentleman. You couldn't put Tony Scannell in one box, there were so many parts to him and he didn't shield anything. How he interacted with me will have been different to how he interacted with Mark Wingett or Jon Iles. He was always very open, as a person and an actor, he was his own man.'

'In recent years I taught at the Guildhall School of Music and Drama, where the basis of their training reminded me exactly of what it was like on *The Bill*, as they only take on 23 students each year and build a small ensemble. They also have a great way of working with the students, where they buddy each one up with a professional actor in their final year. I have worked with some who have gone on to become very successful. Of course students are always broke, so I used to take them out for coffee and a bite to eat. Then once a few of them became famous, I got them to take me out to the Ivy, where I'd say, "Let's have a cocktail to start with and then you can order the champagne!"'

'Two of my students got parts in *Harry Potter and the Cursed Child* at the Palace Theatre and invited me to see the final dress rehearsal before the opening night! I was glued to the show; there is something so amazing about seeing people disappear in front of your very eyes on stage. Another of my students was in *Much Ado About Nothing* at the Globe and got me a ticket. So I've got to see all these shows, which is wonderful and I am very proud of all my student buddies, who were all certainly much more confident, assured and mature than I remember being when I was training at drama school!'

Gregory Kinchin (Stage Manager)

'Building a good relationship with your director was all about communication. If you could go into the production office and ask the questions you needed answers for and get an understanding about what they were planning to do, then that made everybody's lives easier. Philip Casson had done a lot of television and was a very nice man. He was very much an actor's director and working with the cast was his focus, whilst in parallel to that he just trusted us to know what we were doing and let us get on with it.'

'If the actors brought lots of substance to their characters, the writers would obviously want to use that, because they also wanted to produce the best stuff. Nick Reding was an example of that. Ramsey was a very dodgy character, but Nick brought something to the role that made him really popular with the public. Jeff Stewart was also very clever at doing that, he really made Hollis his own and he put some very precise and unusual character traits in, which again proved very popular. Every actor on *The Bill* had their way of putting their stamp on their character.'

'*The Bill* was great to work on at this time, there was a positive vibe really flowing though the building and we were producing good stuff. You can't help but appreciate what a well-oiled machine the production was and we had such a variety of different characters working in each department. Similarly there were so many different elements that went into each episode, to make it more exciting or dramatic for the audience. And from my perspective, there was always something new to find out about the forensics or legal side, medical or police, which meant that it was always an interesting process and kept it alive.'

Tim Vaughan (Script Editor)

'Chris had established that Ramsey was capable of caring about things, like when he wanted to save the baby in *Trespasses*. Then in *Getting Stressed*, he wrote that great scene that highlighted how terrible Ramsey was, when he is on the front desk and the rape victim walks in. He'd been hoping to chat her up, but is then disappointed and doesn't even believe her! It's quite an outrageous scene, but that was the sort of thing we could do on *The Bill*, there weren't the constraints there are when making programmes these days; under the delicate supervision of Peter Cregeen, it was perfectly okay to experiment and test the boundaries. *The Bill* was a crucible for all kinds of different ideas and experiments for the writers and there was a real camaraderie between us all, everyone was singing the same tune.'

'I worked on *The Bill* for three years and for me, it was probably about as important as the three years I spent at university. It certainly gave me a completely different outlook on life. I came out of *The Bill* not only understanding a bit more about drama and how to do it, but also understanding how the police work. We spend most of our lives trying to avoid the company of police officers, but when you got to meet them working on a show like this, you unearthed the most extraordinary things. But the best thing about *The Bill*, from my perspective, was working with several brilliant writers like Chris Russell, J.C. Wilsher, and Peter J. Hammond. The doors were also wide open for new writers to come in and have a go, and I worked with some fantastic writers like Kevin Clarke, Julian Jones, Arthur McKenzie, Elizabeth Anne Wheal, and Garry Lyons, who all had much to offer the programme. I also went on to write nine episodes myself, including under the pseudonym Victoria Taylor.'

'I've enjoyed working on *Queens of Mystery* lately and I loved making shows like *A Touch of Frost*, *Between the Lines* and *The Last Detective*, but for me *The Bill* was probably the pinnacle: the place where I learned enough, ultimately, to equip me to go to work on all those other shows. *The Bill* was special for everyone who worked on it: no one who worked at Barlby Road doesn't hold the show in the highest regard. We all had a ball and I learned so much from the way Peter Cregeen, and after him, Michael Chapman, ran the series. It was a happy ship: everyone mucked in together and there was camaraderie between the writers. People would walk into the office and say, "I saw your episode last night, great job!" We all cared enormously about what we were doing, which used to motivate us all to work harder, and do better, with every production we made. Now, all those years on, I find it a complete pleasure to look back on *The Bill* and the many people I worked with, who share similar feelings about a show we all loved.'

TIGERS
Written by Edwin Pearce
Directed by Terry Marcel

Series 4: Episode 43
Broadcast: Tuesday 13 December 1988

Case Narrative
Gang violence results in a tragedy, and an unexpected and very unwelcome gift is waiting for Jimmy Carver when he turns up at Sun Hill nick.

Regular Cast
D.I. Burnside (Christopher Ellison), D.C. Lines (Kevin Lloyd), D.C. Carver (Mark Wingett), Sgt. Peters (Larry Dann), W.P.C. Brind (Kelly Lawrence), P.C. Stamp (Graham Cole), P.C. Hollis (Jeff Stewart), P.C. Haynes (Eamonn Walker), Insp. Frazer (Barbara Thorn), D.S. Roach (Tony Scannell), D.C Dashwood (Jon Iles), Sgt. Penny (Roger Leach), W.P.C. Martella (Nula Conwell), P.C. Melvin (Mark Powley), P.C. Edwards (Colin Blumenau), P.C. Ramsey (Nick Reding).

Guest Cast
Lorraine (Lisa Climie), Naseeruddin (Bhasker Patel), Mr. Faridh (Gurdial Sira), Rashid (Ayub Khan-Din), 2nd Bangladeshi (Kash Parmar), Lil (Pamela Lyne), Man (Michael Goldie), Teenage Girl (Patsy Palmer), Baby (Hannah Macadam).

Production Team
Stunt Co-ordinator (Rocky Taylor), Casting Director (Julia Lisney), Title Music (Andy Pask, Charlie Morgan), Costume Designer (Maggie Chappelhow, Peter Roberts), Make Up Designer (Gilly Wakeford), Graphics (Ethan Ames), Videotape Editor (John Sharland), Lighting (Christopher Davies), Camera (Chas Watts), Sound (Stephen Codling, Paul Gartrell), Production Buyer (Derek Rhys), Location Manager (Quenton Annis), First Assistant Director (Barry Beckett), Stage Manager (Marilyn Edwards), Production Manager (Brian Heard), Production Assistant (Sylvia Rumney), Technical Adviser (Wilf Knight), Assistant Script Editor (Elizabeth Bradley), Series Script Editor (Kenneth Ware), Designers (Robin Parker, Peter Joyce), Executive Producer (Peter Cregeen), Producer (Richard Bramall).

Observation Notes

Tigers (Production No: D4058, VTR No: THS/45293) was shot between Monday 17th and Friday 21st October 1988. The scenes set in the Indian restaurant were filmed in 357 King Street, Hammersmith W6. In 1989, the Haweli Indian restaurant opened at this location and is still in business today.

Mark Wingett and Kevin Lloyd performed the famous scene where Lines and Carver are overturned in their car on the adjoining Black Lion Lane, W6. Writer Edwin Pearce watched the filming of this scene, nicknaming Wingett and Lloyd "the upside-downers". Pearce also recalled that a member of the public tried setting fire to Mark Wingett's hair while he was on his way to the location earlier that morning...

The scene where Brind tries to resuscitate Naseeruddin was filmed at the end of Wedlake Street, next to the old footbridge over the Grand Union Canal, leading to Harrow Road, NW10. The footbridge was restored in the 1990s with both ends updated to allow step-free access.

The scene in *Tigers* where Carver searches Lorraine's flat was filmed at 39 Hormead Road, W9. Prior to the start of the half-hour episodes in 1988, script editor Tim Vaughan updated Carver's Character Notes, which detailed that "even after three years in the force, he still believes in his job and in the possibility of doing good, of helping, and even of converting bad to good. He has a slightly wry, hesitant manner and lacks confidence to an extent. The right-wing arrogance of some of his colleagues still shocks him. Hendon gave him theories about society and policing and these he still values. He finds it difficult to accept people for what they are, when what they are is not acceptable. It must be possible, he seems to think, to help them see the light! He was on probation with the CID and the attachment is now permanent. Carver is quite tough when he has to be, and in spite of his caring, concerned attitude, he is ready to join in a physical struggle, if there's no other way. His stubborn, tenacious nature also makes him unwilling to give up the chase. Like most of his colleagues at Sun Hill, Carver is unmarried."

Witness Statements

Marilyn Edwards (Stage Manager)

'Terry Marcel, the director, always wanted plenty going on in the background when we were shooting inside Sun Hill. If it wasn't decorators or builders up ladders, it was drag queens in custody. In *Tigers*, it was posters and collection boxes for the Great Ormond Street Appeal, and enough trees in the corridor to plant a forest. I think the actors may have ad-libbed around all of that, and most effectively. Although this was a very dramatic episode – where Mark Wingett and Kevin Lloyd were both very brave doing their own stunt – my favourite memory is the baby, played by my beautiful goddaughter Hannah, who was only a few months old then. We were lucky to get a couple of close-ups of her in the episode when she wasn't crying, because she was not a willing performer that day. She is now a beautiful 33-year-old, working as a veterinary surgeon in Australia, where she has dined out on this story because the series is still so popular there.'

Peter Joyce (Designer)

'The location manager was very important in terms of finding locations to fit the script. Then all the departments; camera, sound, lighting etc. would go on a tech recce to that location during the prep week. The director would talk through the shots they required and we would all have our say. I've been on shoots where we've found out early in the morning that the sunrise came bouncing through the window at the wrong angle. Then it's panic stations because we've had to redress an entire location in less than an hour, because they couldn't shoot against sunlight. That's why people the production team would schedule weather cover scenes that could be filmed with the regular cast at the last minute back at Barlby Road, so if for some reason we couldn't shoot a scene on location we always had a fail-safe.'

'The art department had a recurring problem with the police cars, which had to be kept absolutely clean, because having different degrees of dirt on the cars would have been a continuity nightmare. It was always a bone of contention that the cars were always spotless when of course in real life they would get very dirty. We also had to remove the hubcaps, so they wouldn't fly off when they were traveling at speed. For the scene in *Tigers* where the gang shove the car over onto its roof, we had to take the engine out to make it lighter to throw over. Stunts like that always had to be very well planned and take a lot of time to do.'

Chas Watts (Camera)

'There wasn't a rota for the cameramen on *The Bill*, because not everybody wanted to do it. You were put on it by request, either from a producer or a returning director. I did an awful lot of Terry Marcel's episodes, who is a great bloke. Terry liked the camera to be *in* the scene, not viewing the scene, which is an important definition and I feel what we did best on *The Bill*. For example, during the sequence in *Tigers* where the hooligans turned the car over, Terry wanted a two-shot from the back of the car, behind Mark Wingett and Kevin Lloyd. But instead of the camera going over with the car, Terry wanted the viewer's point of view to remain the right way up during the shot. Over the weekend, I invented a camera mount, with a rotating bearing, that would prevent the camera from turning over with the car... The mount was designed to rotate cameras, but I engineered it to work in reverse, so that the mount would rotate, but the camera wouldn't. Our brilliant vehicle co-ordinators took the back window out for us and I rigged the mount to a modified broom handle, which I held while the car went over. It was a very short shot, because the scene was quite rightly cut quickly to keep the pace up, but it sums up how inventive we all felt whilst working at Barlby Road.'

'I loved working on *The Bill* and I even used to have the theme tune as my ringtone. If I was walking down the street and my phone went off, people would smile as they walked towards me, because they recognised the music. It has been very interesting watching these episodes again, which I haven't seen in 100 years! It makes you look back on your life in a nice way and I'm pleased by how well they stand up. It makes you appreciate what we all did on *The Bill* as a team and it was a pleasure to be part of that gang. I am chuffed to bits that these episodes are still being watched over 34 years after we made them.'

Mark Wingett (D.C. Jim Carver)

'*Tigers* was a great episode, beautifully written by Edwin Pearce. Not only was it an unusual story from the gangland perspective, but it was also the first time we see Carver with a girlfriend - as well as the possibility that he is the father of her baby. One of the things that impresses me most when I look back on these old episodes, is the consistent quality of our guest actors. It was always very high and seldom was there a "bad performance". The lovely Lisa Climie came in for a couple of scenes as Lorraine and she made an impact. I am still in touch with Lisa, who has worked for many years as an addiction counsellor and is currently writing a PhD. I love the moment where I go to stop her from leaving and she just clinches hold of me, with all that unrequited love between us. It was a lovely little moment.'

'Though everyone was great in *Tigers*; Chris Ellison was at his absolute best as Burnside, as was Larry Dann in those improvised scenes down the station corridor. All that business with the plants was thrown in by the inimitable Terry Marcel, who was a little bit of a maverick director and a very inventive man. The drag queen wasn't in the script either, Terry just had a mischievous eye for adding these interesting moments in. He knew what he was doing and he had utter respect from us actors, we were right behind him.'

'As for the famous stunt scene in *Tigers*, that was par of the course of being in *The Bill*. The team came up with this idea and then asked me, "Mark, we want to turn a car upside down with you still inside it... are you happy with that?" I agreed, as did Kevin Lloyd, who was not the smallest man on the planet, but he was game for anything and enthusiastically said, "That'll be great, we'll have fun with that!" When we came to film the stunt, Chas Watts put a Bolex film camera in the footwell of the car, which was the first time I had ever seen a wind up camera. They wound up the camera, set it off and then tipped us over! It was great fun, until you realise that when you are upside down in a car, your seat belt tightens with the tension and you can't actually move to get out of the car. But it was a great stunt, what a blast!'

Terry Marcel (Director)

'You only really get one chance to shoot a stunt like the car being overturned in *Tigers*, so you've got to really prepare. From my point of view, doing a set-up like that wasn't a problem for me, because I'd been very lucky to spend many years working as an assistant director and a production manager. I knew how special effects worked and which camera rigs we'd have to use to best show the stunt off. I'd done the lot. That's why I think a lot of first ADs would make great directors, because they have more or less prepared everything that is going to happen and then they are standing behind that camera watching everything as it happens. I can't remember having to persuade Mark Wingett or Kevin Lloyd to be in the car as it overturned, but they'd have only done it if they had confidence in me as the director. They're the ones in front of the camera and they want to know that sitting behind that camera is a competent person, who knows what they are doing.'

'I always say that you've got to stand up and be counted as a director; you've got to be able to walk onto your set and everyone has to know who you are, what you can do and that you're in charge, it's as simple as that. I always worked on the principle that the first take was always the best take, which I think some producers hated me for because I wouldn't do a second take if it wasn't necessary. "Print and go" was my motto and I think the actors liked that, because I always found there was a certain energy in performance during a first take. Other directors have other ways of working, but I always preferred to be confident in my abilities and to show confidence in my actors. If I ever felt something wasn't quite right, I would never tell an actor in front of everyone, I would take them to one side or quietly whisper a note in their ear. In my opinion, a director should never give feedback to an actor that everyone else in the team can hear. You want your actors to have complete confidence in you, because who else have they got to rely on?'

'For me, it was the speed of *The Bill* that I enjoyed the most, we were doing between 25 and 30 setups a day. Though obviously with the speed we were working at, we were sure to make some mistakes. I can remember looking at some footage that had been cut together one day and unfortunately, there was a camera cable running right the way through the shot. The editor said, "Don't worry about that, watch this..." and he showed me what must have been one of the very first efforts at CGI. He just got a pencil on this pad and took out the cable! That was the very first time I'd seen software like that and was one of the advantages of moving away from film. Shooting on video was perfect for *The Bill*, because working on film is a totally different ball game, where you have to reload and you get scratches and can have a lot of technical problems that we wouldn't have had time for.'

'It was a sheer pleasure to work on *The Bill*; it was so well organised and made by a very professional team. As a director, you want nothing more than to work with good people on good scripts and have good support from your producers. For me, Peter Cregeen was the king - a very, very clever man who made it all possible. I still see him in Richmond and he always asks how I am. I like him a lot and would have loved to work with him again. On *The Bill,* I was allowed to express myself as a director and try new things. The show holds up in a way that a lot of others from that period don't and in terms of the television I've directed, it's number one on the list.'

GUESSING GAME
Written by Peter J. Hammond
Directed by Jan Sargent

Series 4: Episode 44
Broadcast: Thursday 15 December 1988

Viewing Figures: 12.25m
ITV Chart Position: 5

Case Narrative
A man called Kessel is found dead in his maisonette – but what might be the sinister secret that he has taken to his grave?

Regular Cast
P.C. Ramsey (Nick Reding), W.P.C. Ackland (Trudie Goodwin), Sgt. Peters (Larry Dann), D.S. Roach (Tony Scannell), D.C Dashwood (Jon Iles), D.C. Carver (Mark Wingett), Ch. Insp. Conway (Ben Roberts), W.P.C. Martella (Nula Conwell).

Guest Cast
Audrey (Jean Warren), Neighbour (Lizzie Queen).

Production Team
Casting Director (Julia Lisney), Title Music (Andy Pask, Charlie Morgan), Costume Designer (Maggie Chappelhow, Dennis Hogan), Make Up Designer (Gilly Wakeford), Graphics (Ethan Ames), Videotape Editor (John Sharland), Lighting (Graham Jaggers), Camera (Peter Edwards), Sound (Alan Norman, Mike Fairbairn), Production Buyer (Derek Rhys), Location Manager (Eddie Mares), First Assistant Director (Dickie Beighton), Stage Manager (Susan Shattock), Production Manager (Brian Heard), Production Assistant (Ruth Parkhill), Technical Adviser (Wilf Knight), Series Script Editor (Kenneth Ware), Designers (Stuart McCarthy, Neil Thomson), Executive Producer (Peter Cregeen), Producer (Richard Bramall).

Observation Notes
Guessing Game was shot in October 1988, with the scenes set in and around Mr. Kessel's home filmed on the notorious Stonebridge estate, Harlesden, NW10. Later when C.I.D. arrive to investigate Kessel's home, Carver parks the car on Knatchbull Road, NW10. The estate has since

been significantly redeveloped, though despite regeneration, remains one of the most dangerous places in the UK, with a high violent crime rate.

The scene where Carver visits the Rosa Hairdressing Salon was shot on Golborne Road, W10. The following driving scene was shot further down Golborne Road, with Mark Wingett driving by the Prince Arthur and Earl of Warwick pubs, both of which have since closed down. Wingett then turns left into Elkstone Road, W10 and parks under Trellick Tower, where the subsequent garage and tower scenes were shot.

Guessing Game was adapted for the Netherlands police series *Bureau Kruislaan* in 1993. *Giswerk* was the 24th episode of the first season.

Guessing Game was the first of 15 episodes over the next decade directed by Jan Sargent, a prolific director of theatre and television. Her many credits include *Big Deal*, *Desmonds*, *Juliet Bravo*, *Soldier Soldier*, *Perfect Scoundrels*, *Dangerfield* and *Where the Heart Is*.

Witness Statements

Peter J. Hammond (Writer)

'Out of all *The Bill* episodes I've written, *Guessing Game* is probably my favourite. It's about strange Mister Kessel and rope. And I was blessed with a fine production team. Part of the fun was to have our main player already dead and to keep the audience guessing, which was a trick I used lots of times later in *Midsomer Murders*. You've got to grab the audience early, so originally I wanted to start *Guessing Game* with the body in the hallway, but then they explained a policeman had to be in every scene, so I couldn't do that unless it was through the eyes of a policeman. So I had to have Ramsey arrive and looking through the letterbox first. But they were good rules to stick by and you never went home with the coppers in the early days, which was good.'

'Larry Dann was always good as Peters; a simple, honest bloke who liked his gardening and was a bit of a nerd. It was lovely in *Guessing Game* when Ackland was showing him the pictures suggesting the bondage and it was all beyond him, he just couldn't see it. Then he takes the information to Ted Roach, who unravels the story from something simple like a picture on a wall, to there potentially being another victim. I was very pleased with the pace of *Guessing Game*, which was thanks to our very good director, Jan Sargent, who also captured all those mean streets in the area around Barlby Road, which were ideal for filming.'

'I liked to keep things on the move, like the scene in *Guessing Game* where Carver updates Roach and Dashwood as he drives them to Trellick Tower. I think walking and talking scenes have been taken on a lot since *The Bill*, but I think we were the first to get away from people sitting down talking at desks. I was a big fan of writing scenes on staircases or through doors, anything to keep it moving. I also preferred writing for the lower ranks like Dashwood, who was a good character. I also liked writing for Roach and I was very sad when I heard Tony Scannell had passed away. He was a loveable rogue as a copper, but he was an honest one and he pulled no punches. I thought he was great and many years later when it had become a soap, I was invited back to *The Bill* and was asked to write about old coppers finding out what had happened to Roach, who had been killed off-screen. I welcomed that, because it meant reintroducing Peters and Bob Cryer. But sadly when I started to write it, they told me that a third of the script had to adopt an ongoing soap situation, which kind of spoiled it for me. I found it difficult to write something that I knew nothing about and wasn't interested in; I just wanted to write a short story about the old coppers.'

'*The Bill* meant a lot to me and came at the right time in my career, because I'd been away from crime drama for a while and had only been doing odd bits and pieces. I was eventually put on blocks, where I'd be commissioned to write three scripts at a time, which was a good discipline. I became one of their regular writers for the next ten years and wrote 39 episodes in total, so it was a big part of my career. It's nice to know that the good old days of half-hour episodes are still remembered and being enjoyed, it's quite a compliment.'

Sue Shattock (Stage Manager)

'Stage management had to liaise with our police advisers, as well as the real police, to make sure that the way information came up on the computer screen in the CAD room was accurate. In *Guessing Game*, there is a sequence where Nula Conwell is bringing up Mr. Kessel's aliases. I knew there was going to be a close-up of the screen, which was really nervewracking because, as far as I was aware, this hadn't been done before in the history of *The Bill*. It was tricky because I had no reference material to use and it took time to find out how the information should be presented. Then I had the technicians build a template from scratch.

The screens in the CAD room weren't actually connected to a real computer, so to make this information appear, I sat in an adjacent room using a computer, feeding in the information to appear on the screen in the CAD room on cue. I had to press of the buttons on my computer in sync with when Nula was pressing her CAD keyboard, so that the information came up live on the screen at exactly the right moment.'

'We also had to dress the desks in C.I.D. and make sure that everyone had working pens and the right paperwork. Each character would also have their own personal props for their desk; for example Jon Iles smoked cheroot cigarettes as Dashwood, so I would make sure he always had a supply of those and a lighter. The actors all knew their characters so well that, if stage management got something wrong, they would notice and be able to tell you pretty quickly. I liked all the actors, none of them were difficult or challenging, they were all lovely. Our job was to make sure that things were in the right place at the right time, so that the cast and the director had everything they needed.'

Jan Sargent (Director)

'I've loved drama since I was a child and grew up with it in the family. When I was six, my father made me a puppet theatre and I started doing plays with friends. Then I was in a skiffle group and later joined a jazz group. I was supposed to go to Oxford, but I didn't go in the end because my father died, so after doing a short teaching course I came back to live with my mother and help with my brother and sister. It was then that I started doing amateur dramatics, first as an actor and then as a director, which is when I decided that's what I wanted to do. I went to Rose Bruford College, followed by Drama Centre, which is where I learned how to be a director properly. I then worked for ten years in the theatre, before I learned how to do film at the National Film School. And the rest, as they say, is history.'

'My TV career began when I got to direct a *Play for Today*, before the BBC stopped making them. I then thought I had better start directing series, because that seemed to be the way television was moving. I directed series like *Juliet Bravo, Casualty, Big Deal* and *Truckers*. Then I got started on *The Bill*, which was magical because when you joined the series, you had this powerful team waiting for you. You had the script editor working with the writer; you had somebody finding your locations; you had Nigel Wilson helping you fit your schedule around the actors – who were often making several episodes at the same time. You had the station set with all the costumes and the details; everything was just there ready for you. My job was made easy because of the work already done by the team around me; all I had to do was say "Action" and everything happened, which was wonderful. It was a real ensemble piece, which is what I like best. You just had to avoid bumping into the crew making a different episode, who you could often hear through the wall!'

'I had a wonderful time making *Guessing Game* with a great crew. I remember early on asking Peter Edwards, one of our fantastic cameramen, "How do you do this?" He said, "Come on, let's do a shot now..." He got two of the actors to walk down the corridor and we just followed them. It was easy – 'Action-Follow-Cut'. Peter's camera work was excellent, especially when you consider he was lugging around a really heavy camera in those days. The actors were also very good at these shots, because by this time they were all trained in the art of *The Bill* - they knew how to walk with the camera and that we wouldn't be going in for any close-ups, so they would look to the side when we followed them. The joy of the series was that we rarely had to do any retakes, whereas on other series you had to do loads of takes because you needed other shots to tell the story, which was more difficult. *The Bill* was never difficult, because everybody knew what they were up for.'

'We didn't have rehearsals beforehand, which I found mind-blowing at the time, but I can't remember having trouble with any of the cast. What I had learned about working with actors in the theatre was the Stanislavski method, where everything is based around action. The action for the actor is "what does their character want"? That was the basis for me working with the actors in each scene and because *The Bill* was action-based, it was very simple. An example of this in *Guessing Game* is the scene where Roach goes to the canteen to see Peters, having initially tossed the case aside as nothing important. When I asked Tony Scannell, "What do you want in this scene?" he said, "I want to get to the canteen quickly". He initiated the action in this scene, as it was his choice to go steaming fast down the corridor and we just followed him. I thought Tony was brilliant; he somehow transitioned the character from not giving a fuck in the beginning, to gradually becoming more furious once he'd read this man's record. That's why I loved the series; it was police-driven and the characters were instrumental to every shot.'

'My only sadness on *The Bill* was that I never met the writers, therefore the script editor was very important when you were breaking down the script and I enjoyed working with Tim Vaughan. Peter's script was clever because he kept you guessing, even from the beginning outside the front door where there are two unopened milk bottles, hinting that he's been dead for a couple of days. Then in each scene he wrote in a new clue, like the pictures on the wall, which the design team created for Ackland to find. Then we just had to block the scene with Trudie, who is a very good actor with an inquisitive and intelligent manner. She had very nice chemistry with Larry Dann, another lovely actor. I enjoyed working with them both again on later episodes.'

'Those pictures gave us a very clear picture of what this man's victim was going to go through. Then when the audience sees the empty chair in the tower later on, they understand because they've already got that image in their mind. It was my suggestion to use Trellick Tower, because I had always wanted to film up there. Peter's camera work was really good here, going up in the lift, along the gantry and then out onto the balcony with lovely Jon Iles and looking out over the edge. That was my favourite part of the episode, though I felt embarrassed by the line that Roach had where he asks if anybody could ever "live happily in this hellhole..." because at the time, I had a friend who lived there in a very nice flat and was actually very happy, thank you very much Roach!'

'Gradually all the clues added up to the scene where Jean Warren talks about the treats. Jean was wonderful and I later cast her in another episode I directed called *On the Cards*. *The Bill* was the best experience I ever had as a director, I just adored it. I got to direct a couple of episodes every Christmas for ten years. I think it's terrible that the series hasn't got more recognition, because it was such a long-running and superb series. The subject matter was always relevant and interesting and the clever discipline of every scene being told from the police person's point of view made it straightforward storytelling and I loved it. I'm really surprised and knocked out that anyone is interested in our memories of making the programme and I'm very grateful to have been asked to take a look back at *Guessing Game*, it's been a real joy.'

THE ASSASSINS

Written by Douglas Watkinson
Directed by Terence Daw

Series 4: Episode 45
Broadcast: Tuesday 20 December 1988

Viewing Figures: 11.00m
ITV Chart Position: 9

Case Narrative

The Assassins, a gang of upper-class thugs, indulge in their favourite pastime: trashing restaurants. Mr. Cooper, meanwhile, worries about damage of another kind.

Regular Cast

Sgt. Cryer (Eric Richard), D.I. Burnside (Christopher Ellison), D.C. Lines (Kevin Lloyd), P.C. Smith (Robert Hudson), P.C. Haynes (Eamonn Walker), Sgt. Penny (Roger Leach), W.P.C. Martella (Nula Conwell), P.C. Melvin (Mark Powley), P.C. Stamp (Graham Cole).

Guest Cast

Kuzalo (Hakeem Kae-Kazim), Strathvane (Daniel Flynn), Caroline Day (Mary Cornford), Charlesworth (Andrew Alston), Balderstone (Nick Dunning), Skinner (John Judd), Kuzalo Senior (Errol Shaker), Magistrate (Seymour Green), Solicitor (Owen Brenman), Mr. Cooper (Frank Mills), Mrs. Cooper (Jeanne Watts), Hopkins (Martyn Whitby), Sue Hopkins (Lynne Verrall), Mrs. Lines (Lesley Duff), Breakdown Man (Richard Ratcliffe).

Production Team

Fight Arranger (Stuart St. Paul), Casting Director (Brian Wheeler), Title Music (Andy Pask, Charlie Morgan), Costume (Maggie Chappelhow, Peter Roberts), Make Up Designer (Gilly Wakeford), Graphics (Ethan Ames), Videotape Editor (Dave Lewinton), Lighting (Christopher Davies), Camera (Roy Easton), Sound (Bill Rawcliffe, Mike Fairbairn), Production Buyer (Sarah Prebble), Location Manager (Ian Elsey), First Assistant Director (David Cherrill), Stage Manager (Nigel J. Wilson) Production Manager (Brian Heard), Production Assistant (Valerie Muncey Sanders), Technical Adviser (Wilf Knight), Script Editor (Barbara Cox), Series Script Editor

(Kenneth Ware), Designers (Stuart McCarthy, Jill Reedman), Executive Producer (Peter Cregeen), Producer (Michael Ferguson).

Observation Notes

The Assassins was shot between Monday 31st October and Friday 4th November 1988. On Tuesday 1st November, a film crew captured behind the scenes footage of the café scenes from *The Assassins*, as well as interviews with Chris Ellison and Robert Hudson, for the documentary *One Day in the Life of Television,* broadcast exactly one year later in 1989. The location used for the café scene was 20 Station Terrace, NW10, which had previously been used as the army surplus store in *They Say We're Rough.* The scene where P.C. Haynes and P.C. Smith investigate the broken down removal van was shot outside Austen House, Cambridge Road, NW6. This 18-storey high-rise building was constructed as part of the South Kilburn RDA project in 1971.

The Assassins was the first of two episodes directed by Terence Daw, whose 40-year career as a director includes episodes of *Brookside, Heartbeat, Thief Takers, Emmerdale* and the feature film *Surviving Evil.*

Witness Statements

Douglas Watkinson (Writer)

'I think television should be a bit rough around the edges for it to be believable and Terence Daw achieved this with his direction of *The Assassins*, which I mean as a total compliment. It worked beautifully, because nobody polished it until it was so shiny that it just slid off your memory into oblivion. It had an identity of its own, because it was done properly. Terence also assembled such a talented guest cast, from the young actors playing the "Assassins", who were all so good that you just wanted to smack them, to Frank Mills playing the character moving to Grasmere Avenue, which looking back was slightly corny, but I loved his performance. I also thought Chris Ellison filled the screen as Burnside; the moment he came on, you went straight to him and you couldn't take your eyes off him. Eric Richard was also excellent as Cryer. I divide actors between those who you believe and those you can't, and with Eric you believed every single word that came out of his mouth.'

'I still get residuals every so often from the most extraordinary places where *The Bill* and other programmes I've written have been shown, on channels that I didn't even know existed. I often wonder what on earth do they make of *Heartbeat* in Latvia and Estonia? I realise now how lucky I've been as a writer. I've never been out of work, except from choice, and in those days to be constantly working was a treat, but I didn't realise then how lucky one was to be asked again and again to do something else. Though after 40 years, which is an awful long time, I found myself being asked to write the same thing over and over again for television. In fact, a producer did once actually ask me to do "the same, only different..." those were his very words. I felt that I'd done enough, so I began writing novels and am currently working on my seventh in my Nathan Hawk series of crime and mystery books. In my later years, I have no idea what else I might do, so I just can't resist carrying on writing. I expect I shall drop dead over this computer.'

Terence Daw (Director)

'I grew up in television, right from playing small parts as a child actor. I just loved the whole idea of working in television and when I left school, I managed to get a job as a post boy at Rediffusion Television, who were making shows like *Ready, Steady, Go!* The 1960s was a wonderful period to be working in TV and that company was an astonishing place to work. From there I moved into post-production at what became Thames TV and worked as a trainee, then first assistant, film editor in the cutting rooms for a number of years. Later, I moved into Promotions at London Weekend TV, where I was writing and producing all their trailers, for shows like *Upstairs Downstairs* and *Within These Walls.*'

'I wanted to move into directing, but it was a chicken and egg situation then, because you couldn't officially become a director if you didn't have a union card, but you couldn't get the card unless you had directed something! So you had to find a way around it and I managed to direct a couple of documentary films for the Central Office of Information, which got me my ticket. From there I was able to move into directing TV and I started by doing lots of live shows like *Good Afternoon* and *Magpie*. Live TV is about the most challenging thing I think you can do, but it was a wonderful training ground. What I really wanted to do all along was drama and I was lucky because I got to direct an arts and culture show in Birmingham that had a drama section. I started directing these short plays and from there I was able to move onto dramas like *Brookside*, working with the great Jimmy McGovern.'

'I was thrilled when in 1988 I was offered two episodes of *The Bill*, which felt like a big step up for me and I loved the idea that every episode was a self-contained little story. There were obviously certain character threads, but in general as a director I could just concentrate on the specific story and the characters that take part in each episode, whereas on other shows like *Emmerdale* you constantly had to keep up with what the characters had been up to last week. I think *The Bill* broke a lot of ground at the beginning, there wasn't really anything else like it around at the time and the way it was produced was quite innovative.'

'The turnaround was very fast and by the time I was working on it, there were three units filming different episodes at once, to keep up with the demands of the twice-weekly schedule. The machine moved very quickly, so as a director you really had to jump on that moving carousel and be prepared to deliver your episodes. Because of that fast turnaround, the directors hardly ever got to meet the writer, though I will have talked to Douglas Watkinson on the phone. Whereas on *Brookside* for instance, even though that was a very tight schedule, I always had meetings with the writers, where we would sit down with the producer and go through each episode. That was pretty amazing, considering the amount of episodes that *Brookside* turned out, because that was a very writer-led show. I thought Douglas delivered a lovely piece of writing with *The Assassins* and I loved the diplomatic immunity angle, which was very good and still relevant today.'

'I remember directing *The Assassins* very well, it doesn't seem that long ago, even though I've done a lot of other things since then. *The Bill* had a nice ensemble of actors, though they obviously weren't all in every episode. I think a lot of the directors loved having Chris Ellison's character Burnside in their story, since he was a bit on the dodgy side, which was great because it immediately made him and the stories more interesting. I also enjoyed working with Kevin Lloyd, who was a very nice man, and Eric Richard, who made it look easy. I cast Frank Mills, a lovely character actor and very familiar face, who did a lovely job of playing this gentleman who the police initially dismiss as being a silly old fool, but in the end was right about some dodgy removal people. I suggested to Frank that it would be fun if every time he goes to the station, he would always push the front door the wrong way, which was a nice bit of business. *The Bill* also gave opportunities to younger actors who have gone on to do interesting work, including Daniel Flynn, who returned to *The Bill* to play Supt. Heaton... so perhaps crime does pay?'

'You had five days to film an episode, and so any days where you were filming outside of the Barlby Road set would eat into your time, because the whole unit had to travel to location. For *The Assassins* we only had one day to complete all the scenes in the café for example, which was an empty lot that the location department had rented for the day. The design team went in early in the morning and created this set for us, which we then needed to trash in the story. Because the schedule was so tight, we didn't have much time to rehearse. I would go in with a plan in my head about how I was going to shoot it and how people were going to move around, but then it was a case of collaborating with the crew and the cast to work out exactly how it was going to go.'

'During our filming of the fight in the café, there was a moment where someone throws a stool at a large mirror on the wall. I must have shot that eight times, because the mirror would not break! I remember thinking to myself that we didn't have much time and we hadn't even broken the bloody mirror yet. Nowadays as a director I always use two cameras, but *The Bill* was a single camera show, because the brief from Peter Cregeen was that they wanted a slightly documentary feel, not too much wobbly camera, but at the same time not getting into the nitty gritty of stylised shots and lighting. So that fight sequence took a long time, because there were lots of individual shots within the action, which in other cases you might pick up with a couple of cameras. Because I come from an editing background, I tend to think very much in terms of how the shots are going to cut together, which in a situation like that where we didn't have a lot of time was very helpful, because I could edit the sequence in my head as we were going to a certain extent.'

'I have grown up in the film and television business, it's all I know and I still love it. I continue to work as a writer and director, currently developing a slate of scripted TV drama series' and feature films through my company Audience Films Ltd. You do so many things in your career that you tend to forget about some of them, but *The Bill* has always stayed in my memory and it's nice to revisit that period of my life again and remember the people that I worked with. It was lovely to be part of *The Bill,* it helped me move up the drama ladder, for which I am grateful. It's great that there's still an enthusiastic audience out there for the series and it's very nice that our work is still being seen and appreciated.'

OUTMODED
Written by Barry Appleton
Directed by Terry Green

Series 4: Episode 46
Broadcast: Thursday 22 December 1988

Viewing Figures: 12.55m
ITV Chart Position: 4

Case Narrative
Sun Hill is plagued by bogus emergency calls, W.P.C. Ackland helps a victim of repeated muggings venture out of her flat, and a car is hauled out of the river.

Regular Cast
Sgt. Cryer (Eric Richard), D.S. Roach (Tony Scannell), D.C Dashwood (Jon Iles), W.P.C. Ackland (Trudie Goodwin), D.C. Carver (Mark Wingett), Sgt. Penny (Roger Leach), W.P.C. Martella (Nula Conwell), P.C. Ramsey (Nick Reding), P.C. Haynes (Eamonn Walker), P.C. Smith (Robert Hudson), P.C. Edwards (Colin Blumenau), Sgt. Peters (Larry Dann), P.C. Frank (Ashley Gunstock), P.C. Stamp (Graham Cole).

Guest Cast
Mrs. Jenkins (Mel Churcher), Parker (Wayne Goddard), Jason Scott (Dominic Arnold), Prof. Wallis (Michael Fenton Stevens), Mr. Finch (Brian Miller), Mrs. Scott (Wendy Allnutt), Mrs. Joseph (Ruth Goring).

Production Team
Casting Director (Julia Lisney), Title Music (Andy Pask, Charlie Morgan), Costume (Allard Tobin, Dennis Hogan), Make Up Designer (Gilly Wakeford), Graphics (Ethan Ames), Videotape Editor (John Sharland), Lighting (Graham Jaggers), Camera (Peter Edwards), Sound (Alan Norman, Alan Lester), Production Buyer (Trevor Young), Location Manager (Douglas Macdonald), Floor Manager (Aidan Boulter), Stage Manager (Marilyn Edwards), Production Manager (Brian Heard), Production Assistant (Caroline O'Reilly), Technical Adviser (Wilf Knight), Series Script Editor (Kenneth Ware), Design (Robin Parker, Peter Joyce), Executive Producer (Peter Cregeen), Producer (Richard Bramall).

Observation Notes

Outmoded (Production No: D4050, VTR No: THS/45285) was shot between Monday 19th and Friday 23rd September 1988.

Responding to the opening bogus shout in *Outmoded,* Nick Reding drives the panda car under the railway bridge on Colborn Road, Mile End E3. Rather than follow the area car onto the adjoining Tredegar Road, Ramsey's local knowledge means Reding continues driving down Colborn Road and then onto Antill Road.

The conclusion of this scene was filmed at Clare House on the Monteith Estate, Hawthorn Avenue, E3. This 22-storey building opened in 1968, containing 129 flats. In 2021, following the Grenfell disaster, an inspection determined that the 207ft building would be vulnerable to collapse. All residents were moved into temporary accommodation while Clare House has been scheduled for demolition.

The scene where Patrick's car is pulled out of the river was filmed in the Royal Docks, E16. For the scene where Roach and Carver go to find Parker, the camera pans down Christ Church Spitalfields, an Anglican church designed by Nicholas Hawksmoor and built between 1714 and 1729. Tony Scannell and Mark Wingett leave their car parked on Brushfield Street and enter Old Spitalfields Market. The scenes with Ackland visiting Mrs Jenkins at her flat were filmed at Antrim House, Old Ford Road, E3. This 22-storey high-rise building was demolished in 2002. Actor Michael Fenton Stevens was erroneously credited on screen, with Graham Cole listed as playing Prof. Wallis.

Outmoded was adapted for an episode of the Netherlands police series *Bureau Kruislaan* in 1993. The title of the episode *Dood door Schuld* translates as "Death by Fault" and was the 14th episode of the season. The episode features a car being hauled out of the river, containing the body of a girl. The driver is revealed to be the son of Adjutant Bob Voskuil.

Originally, of course, this storyline was written for Sgt. Bob Cryer, who is described in the Character Notes as a "father-figure to his lads on the beat. Having done the job for sixteen or seventeen years, he has the weight of experience behind him which enables him to go to the senior-management, if the need arises, and shout the odds in defence or his men, particularly in their working relationship with CID who, he believes, will always try to take advantage of woodentops. Bob Cryer does not appear to have ambition beyond his sergeant's rank. He is a natural leader, at that level; and is happy to stay there. He is married to Shirley, with a teenage son (Patrick) who is mad about football – both as a spectator and a young player."

Witness Statements

Barry Appleton (Writer)

'I wanted to show that there was more to June Ackland than being a police officer. She was caring and taking Mrs Jenkins, who was scared to leave her flat, to the shops and offering to put her up was all above the call of duty. I also thought it would be interesting to do something about hacking. My daughter Sacha and my son Simon gave me all of the information about computers for *Outmoded*, which I would never have been able to write without their help. I also wanted to continue giving more of the actors something extra to play with and I thought Eric Richard played that scene where he found out about Patrick really, really well. It pulled at the heartstrings seeing Cryer like that and I continued that storyline in *Digging up the Past*.'

Caroline O'Reilly (Production Assistant)

'It was my job to help the production and make sure everything worked and flowed between each department. During shooting for example, the production assistant became the eyes and ears of the editor. I logged every shot recorded for *Outmoded* and then gave all my notes over to John Sharland, detailing which shots he had to cut together. Every shot had a number, which related to the slate number, which in turn related to the script, so he knew where the shots were and which ones to use for particular coverage. I was beside the director all the time, so I would also log which takes featured the performances they liked best. I would also keep an eye on the continuity and it was my job to make sure that each take matched the previous one, especially where props were concerned. I would also detail what went wrong with a take, because by the time the director got to the edit, they might have forgotten details from the shoot. If they ask the editor why they hadn't used their favourite take, my notes would say "plane noise" or "missed dialogue" or any number of things that can go wrong during shooting.'

'*The Bill* was a fast-paced production and it could be quite stressful for the directors, especially because we were sharing actors with other units. If they fell behind, it wasn't just their own production that they had to consider. On *Outmoded*, Eric Richard was also shooting other episodes with the Red unit at the same time, so if we held onto him longer than we were supposed to, we'd be holding up the Red unit, which just could not be allowed to happen. Normally on other shows, a director could compromise on what they shot in the afternoon, if they had fallen behind in the morning. They couldn't do that on *The Bill* if it affected another unit, so that added pressure for them. Terry Green was one of the directors who found the scheduling a little bit tricky at first and needed some time to get into the style of how to shoot *The Bill*.'

'When someone came looking for Terry after work one night, I said they would find him in the pub, looking like an endearing version of Roland Rat. He was a very talented director and a real East End boy who had directed a lot of *Minder* and *The Sweeney*. East London was his manor. There was a shot in *Outmoded* where Cryer goes to the computer hacker's house and the camera looks up in a bedroom where there was a circular hole in the ceiling, with the hacker looking over the balcony. Well that was Terry's bedroom; we shot those scenes in his home near Roman Road in East London! I thought it was quite strange that he had his son's bedroom above his own, with a minstrels' gallery in the ceiling! Terry didn't have a mobile phone or a landline either, so if I wanted to speak to him I had to ring the local pub and they would go to the end of the garden and shout over the fence. He would then come over the fence and answer the phone! He was a funny guy, but lovely and easy to get on with. I think his son played one of the skateboarders in *Outmoded*.'

Michael Fenton Stevens (Prof. Wallis)

'Around this time, I had started making choices about where I was going as an actor. When I was young, I'd imagined turning up at a theatre every evening to perform. But I'm afraid to say that I followed the money and took the work that was paying me the most, which was television and advertising. I turned down some really fantastic theatre jobs, including a two-and-a-half-year contract with the English Shakespeare Company, where I would have toured the world with Michael Pennington playing some brilliant parts. But I also had young children, which influenced my choice enormously. I came through comedy and had brilliant fun making the sketch show *KYTV*. Then all of a sudden, I started being seen for dramatic roles and *The Bill* was my first TV drama. I think they wanted me to play the Professor because I didn't sound like all the other East End blokes in the show, though it's very strange now listening to my voice in anything from that far back, because I realise that my voice has dropped about an octave!'

'Considering the speed of the production and the enormous pressure the team were under, I thought *The Bill* was a programme of good quality. I remember meeting Eric Richard in the canteen in the morning and then going through our lines together on the bus going to location. After filming with me, Eric was then going to have to dash off and film another batch of scenes. He was a very nice man and a very good actor. Also in *The Bill* at this time was Roger Leach, who I worked with when we did *Around the World in 80 Days* together at Buxton Opera House, an absolutely gorgeous theatre. I played Passepartout and Roger played loads of parts in this beautiful musical, which had some really lovely songs in it. I later stayed with Roger when we played the Salisbury Playhouse a couple of times. He was a really sweet man and is sadly missed. I loved it when he really relaxed, because his Australian accent came through.'

'My first scene in *Outmoded* opens with a very strange shot, where we go up a staircase and it doesn't cut into us at all, we're kept in the distance. Terry Green had been a designer before becoming a director, so perhaps he was more interested in the angles of the building than us? I also had to sound like a computer expert and talk about modems, though I knew nothing about computers at that point and didn't know what I was talking about. When you look at those rows of square boxes in the episode, you remember just how ugly computers were back then. We also did a walking scene where we went through door after door after door. I remember thinking "Why can't we just be in the room?" When you can just stand and talk to somebody, you can concentrate on saying the lines right. It's so much harder to act when you've also got to walk and lead the way opening doors, especially when you're trying to make it look very relaxed and natural, like your character has walked down those corridors hundreds of times before. I've had a number of scenes like that in my career, where you think "Really? Why did you write it like this?"'

'Another job that springs to mind is an episode of *As Time Goes By* with Judi Dench and Geoffrey Palmer, who were both consummate comic actors. I was playing the part of their daughter's boyfriend, but they didn't know she had a boyfriend. They come back early from their holiday to discover me, wearing their daughter's dressing gown, tidying up their home. It was a very funny scene, because my character knew where everything was in the house and had clearly been there loads of times, but they'd never met me. We then go into the kitchen and whilst asking them about their holiday, I then proceed to cook breakfast for them! I had to do the entire scene in one take, in front of a live audience, and time my dialogue with the toaster, which was being controlled by a props guy hidden behind the counter. The whole point was my character was supposed to be extremely relaxed, while in reality I was absolutely terrified. I thought if I can pull that off, I must be a bloody genius!'

'I remember feeling like a bit of a fraud when I made *The Bill*, because I hadn't come through the same route as Eric, Roger and the other actors. I hadn't done any training, I'd just drifted into it and I was learning on the job. As an actor, I am still learning and over the course of the last two years, I have learned another skill - podcasting! When everybody got locked down in 2020, I started a podcast with my son called *My Time Capsule*. The premise is that the guests choose five things from their life to put into a time capsule; four things that they love and one thing they'd like to get rid of. I thought it would just be me talking to people, who would tell me interesting anecdotes and funny stories about their careers and their lives. But it's become much more than that and some of the things that people have spoken to me about have been astonishing and really moving really. I've cried with laughter listening to the funny stories and then I've cried with emotion over the sadness of some of the stories I've heard.'

Aidan Boulter (Floor Manager)

'We shot the scene in *Outmoded* where the car got pulled out of the river in the Royal Docks, which is unrecognisable now from what it was then. As a young lad I went to London Nautical School and we used to do our seamanship training in that very dock, which is now where the Excel Arena is! *Outmoded* was directed by Terry Green, a former BBC production designer and a real character. Terry was a proper East End lad, who lived in Bethnal Green and hated the idea of coming into the production office in Barlby Road for our script meetings. Instead, he insisted on me going to meet him at his home, which was a bit of a nightmare, but he was the director and that was what he wanted and so that's what we did.'

'Sadly, *Outmoded* was my last episode of *The Bill* at Barlby Road and I only returned once more for an episode made at Merton. I wish I had known then what I know now about human nature and how to treat people properly, as I suspect my time on the series might have been a bit longer than it actually was. But one of the problems with being an AD is that you become the Sergeant Major; you're the one badgering people and making sure they stick to your schedule, because there's nothing worse when you've spent a week putting a schedule together and by the second day it's all gone out the window. If that happened, you'd be going back to the office after the shoot and rewriting your schedule until 11:00 at night. My personal life at the time was also absolute madness: I'd recently got married and had a baby, and we'd just bought a house in Buckinghamshire, which meant I had to leave at 5:00 in the morning to get into work ready for each 10-hour day. So getting people to stick to my schedule as much as I could was always in the forefront of my mind. Knowing what I know now, maybe I should have just let that go and given people a bit more freedom to be artistic. But I'm hugely proud and so grateful to have worked on *The Bill*, which was a fantastic foundation for everything that came afterwards in my career.'

Eric Richard (Sgt. Bob Cryer)

'People have asked me over the years why I stayed with the show for so long. I was still a jobbing actor then, as I am now. As well as being paid a reasonable amount of money, I knew that I was guaranteed at least a dozen high calibre scripts every year, where Sgt. Cryer would be an active participant. It was a gift for a professional actor and an example of that was the sequence of episodes written by Barry Appleton, beginning with *Outmoded* and continuing with *Digging up the Past*, where Sgt. Cryer is struggling to come to terms with his son Patrick's being involved with a young woman tragically losing her life. I also knew that in between those scripts, I would be supporting the other members of the cast with their storylines. What was not to like about that? I was having a fabulous time working with the cast as a whole, we were a very close company and there was no one who felt that they needed to be "the star" or to have their own Winnebago or dressing room, we didn't have any of that crap at all. This might sound slightly emotional, but my old mantra as an actor is "I want a good part, in a good production, with good people, in a good place..." I was lucky on *The Bill* to have all four of those.'

DIGGING UP THE PAST

Written by Barry Appleton
Directed by Barry Davis

Series 4: Episode 47
Broadcast: Tuesday 27 December 1988

Case Narrative

Building workers unearth a skeleton, Ramsey and Edwards investigate a ticket forger, and Sgt. Cryer faces the fact that his son has been charged with a serious offence.

Regular Cast

Sgt. Cryer (Eric Richard), D.I. Burnside (Chris Ellison), Ch. Insp. Conway (Ben Roberts), D.S. Roach (Tony Scannell), D.C Dashwood (Jon Iles), W.P.C. Martella (Nula Conwell), Insp. Frazer (Barbara Thorn), P.C. Ramsey (Nick Reding), P.C. Edwards (Colin Blumenau), P.C. Melvin (Mark Powley), W.P.C. Ackland (Trudie Goodwin), P.C. Frank (Ashley Gunstock), P.C. Smith (Robert Hudson), Sgt. Penny (Roger Leach), D.C. Carver (Mark Wingett).

Guest Cast

S.O.C.O. (Tessa Peake-Jones), Ch. Insp. Waltham (Glynn Sweet), Barnes (Gawn Grainger), Burgess (Dicken Ashworth), Albert (Mike Savage), Shirley Cryer (Jackie Abbey-Taylor), Peter Schwartz (Ron Berglas).

Production Team

Stunt Arranger (Stuart St. Paul), Casting Director (Brian Wheeler), Title Music (Andy Pask, Charlie Morgan), Costume (Maggie Chappelhow, Dennis Hogan), Make Up Designer (Gilly Wakeford), Graphics (Ethan Ames), Videotape Editor (Dan Carter), Lighting (Graham Jaggers), Camera (Peter Edwards), Sound (Alan Norman, Paul Gartrell), Production Buyer (Sarah Prebble), Location Manager (Sheila Loughrey), First Assistant Director (Kit Williams), Stage Manager (Nigel J. Wilson), Production Manager (Brian Heard), Production Assistant (Julie Church), Technical Adviser (Wilf Knight), Series Script Editor (Kenneth Ware), Design (Stuart McCarthy, Jill Reedman), Executive Producer (Peter Cregeen), Producer (Michael Ferguson).

Observation Notes

Digging up the Past (Production No: D4056, VTR No: THS/45291) was shot between Monday 10th and Friday 14th October 1988. All the building site scenes were filmed on St. Mark's Road, W10, with the skeleton buried where No. 70 and 70B St. Mark's Road now stand today.

The scene where Ramsey and Edwards visit Albert's flat was filmed at 70 Neville Close, Queens Park, NW6. The following driving scene with Ramsey and Edwards was filmed on Lonsdale Road, NW6, with Nick Reding driving the Porsche in from the adjoining Salusbury Road. Later, Reding turns back into Lonsdale Road from Donaldson Road at the opposite end. The later scenes where Ramsey and Edwards break into the warehouse and discover the counterfeit money were filmed in 2 Lonsdale Road, NW6, which is now used as a beauty supply store.

Digging Up The Past was adapted for an episode of the Netherlands police series *Bureau Kruislaan* in 1993. The title of the episode *Een ijzige Reputatie* translates as "An Icy Reputation" and was the 15th episode of the season. As with *Outmoded* and *Digging up the Past*, *Een ijzige Reputatie* continues with the story of Bob Voskuil avoiding his son, though has a slightly different conclusion, with the officer visiting his son in his cell and then personally releasing him.

Witness Statements

Barry Appleton (Writer)

'Watching *Digging up the Past* again after all these years, I couldn't believe that I'd written it! I got the idea from something I read in the newspaper and then I adapted it to make it work for the story. I loved the idea of getting them all fighting in the mud and water! For the subplot, I'd already established Ramsey and Taffy as having a bit of conflict in *Save the Last Dance for Me*, when Ramsey had challenged Taffy to a game of three-card brag and Cryer had confiscated Taffy's winnings for the poor box. It was good to explore this further with the dodgy theatre tickets and I loved that last scene with Ramsey and Taffy, when the doors open and they're stood with all that money in their hands, that was great. Though at this time the production was getting so big on *The Bill* that I was starting to feel a little out of it. At Artichoke Hill I really felt like part of the family, everybody knew me and I could walk into anybody's office for a chat.'

'Thames were impressed with my work on the series and started to commission me to write pilot scripts. I wrote so many during this period and because they kept renewing the option on them, presumably to stop me taking them to other channels, I kept getting the same money back again and again for several years. I wrote some good series that never came to light, because Thames lost the franchise. My favourite pilot was one called *Two Drummers Drumming*, about a young lad and his girlfriend who were nicked for housebreaking. They got community service and had to go to a school and entertain some kids dressed as clowns, which they didn't want to do at all. They ended up out on the street having a big argument, pushing each other around, still dressed as these clowns. People walking past them and thought it was part of an act, so started throwing money down for them and they suddenly got interested. They were trying to save up enough money to restore an old American car, which was always on blocks on their council estate. And the copper who nicked them was always coming over to their flat, because he fell in love with the lad's mother. I loved that script, though it would be a bit dated now. It's a pity none of the pilots went to series, I could have been a millionaire by now!'

Nula Conwell (W.P.C. Viv Martella)

'We had so many writers working on the half-hours, who all had their favourite characters to write for. I was lucky that Barry Appleton wrote very well for me and understood how to represent the equality of women working in the police force. I feel we were successful on *The Bill* at representing both genders and showing how they could resolve situations by working together. I also didn't want Martella taking a back seat when it came to the action scenes, I wanted her to be out with the guys, getting stuck in. Barry used to take the time to come in and talk to us and he got to know how I wanted to portray Viv and so he wrote scenes like the building site fight in *Digging up the Past* for me, where I had a lot of fun.'

'I distinctly remember filming in that muddy ditch, where a photo taken of me waving my fist in the air and yelling "I'll have you!" was later entered into a competition. This episode was directed by the late Barry Davis, who I first worked with as a teenager when he cast me in a *Play for Today*, and later again as a regular in the series *Telford's Change*. It was also lovely to work with Tessa Peake Jones on *Digging up the Past*. She was a contemporary of mine and we have seen each other again more recently at an *Only Fools & Horses* convention. Like *The Bill*, *Only Fools* continues to enjoy a new life and has a huge appreciation society. I'm quite lucky to have been a part of them both.'

Nigel J. Wilson (Stage Manager)

'It wasn't always easy for new actors to slot into an established cast, though this episode featured a good performance from Nick Reding and a classic contribution from Chris Ellison, both of whom found their feet very quickly. The addition of new characters in the half-hour episodes often had a subtle effect on other longstanding relationships, which also gave the writers new opportunities to explore even established relationships further. What I remember most about *Digging up the Past* was the splendid punch-up in the rain, which ended with Nula taking a mud bath! Viewers will also have spotted Tessa Peake-Jones as the forensics officer, who went on to later fame, and I hope fortune, as Del Boy's wife Raquel in *Only Fools and Horses*. Directing this episode was the late Barry Davis, who was a very experienced drama director. He was a rather shy man, who enjoyed his work and the odd pint to go with it. I recall that he rarely missed an opportunity to tell anyone who would listen how wonderful an actress Hannah Gordon was, who he had directed in *Telford's Change*.'

Sheila Loughrey (Location Manager)

'*Digging up the Past* was directed by the late Barry Davis, who was one of my favourites, Barry was only a small guy, with unkempt hair and an unkempt beard. When I walked into a pub with Barry, people used to think I had brought him in off the street, because he used to keep his trousers up with a piece of string, I kid you not! He was a fantastic director though and very experienced. We made a good team with Kit Williams as Barry's first assistant director and the late Julie Church as his P.A; we had such good fun. I remember Barry telling me he was going to try to cast Tessa Peake-Jones, who he had worked with before on *Telford's Change*. Barry was also very fond of Nula Conwell, who he had also directed on *Telford's Change* and so it made him happy to have them both in this episode, they were two of his favourite actresses.'

'At that time around Ladbroke Grove, there hadn't been much development and there were still big gaps in between buildings, which had been bomb sites. It wasn't until later that London suddenly started shooting up. The building site in *Digging up the Past* was not far from Barlby Road, which gave us all the maximum amount of time to set up, as I think we had to film all those scenes in one day. The first thing I had to do was find out who owned that land and then see if the building firm would be agreeable to us filming there, bearing in mind they had their own schedule. Then I just had to negotiate the least amount of money I possibly could, because we never had much money on *The Bill*, we used to pay in the low hundreds for locations, rather than thousands. But because people liked *The Bill* so much, they wouldn't mind giving us permission to film.'

'As a staff location manager, after I had finished my allotted six week block on *The Bill*, I would go back to Teddington and then be assigned to another programme. I worked a lot on *The Sooty Show*, and we used to film the location scenes in and around a little farm in Chessington. I'll never forget the floor manager, Fizz Waters, saying something very funny when we were shooting a scene on a little high street. The puppeteers were walking Sooty's legs along the road and there were some pedestrians stood in the back of shot. Fizz walked up to these people and politely said, "Excuse me, would you mind not standing there please, because if we get your legs in the background, this is going to look silly..." We all just fell about, we used to have so much fun.'

Mark Wingett (D.C. Jim Carver)

'Towards the end of 1988, the late Geraint Morris joined *The Bill* as our third producer. The Green unit was introduced, meaning we now had three units working in tandem at Barlby Road to fulfil the schedule. Ben Roberts once beautifully described the set-up: "Green unit shouted "Action!" Blue went for a take, and the Red unit told everyone to fucking shut up!" That sums up just how close we all were to each other in that building, we were a bit cramped for space. But it was so exciting to do and for me these were the halcyon days *of The Bill*; there was a real buzz about the show back then and it was getting more and more popular. There was a great social life at this time as well. The studio was based just off the Westway, an elevated section of the A40. To join this road meant passing the Pavilion Public House in Shepherd's Bush. Everyone used to pop in there for a drink on their way home, the excuse being that we were all waiting for the traffic to die down... The Pavilion was a friendly place with a beer garden and we spent many a good night in there.'

TAKEN INTO CONSIDERATION
Written by Lawrence Gray
Directed by Christopher Hodson

Series 4: Episode 48
Broadcast: Thursday 29 December 1988

Case Narrative
Kevin Boswell enjoys his frequent visits to Sun Hill, and charges against him can rarely be made to stick – but are Carver and Dashwood finally about to succeed?

Regular Cast
D.C Dashwood (Jon Iles), D.C. Carver (Mark Wingett), W.P.C. Ackland (Trudie Goodwin), D.I. Burnside (Christopher Ellison), Sgt. Penny (Roger Leach), W.P.C. Martella (Nula Conwell), Sgt. Peters (Larry Dann), P.C. Melvin (Mark Powley), P.C. Stamp (Graham Cole), P.C. Hollis (Jeff Stewart).

Guest Cast
Kevin Boswell (Matthew Sim), Daphne Johnson (Yvonne Marshall), Landlord (Andre Thornton Grimes).

Uncredited Personnel
Press Officer (Rosane Chapman), Secretaries (Diane Boland, Tracy Sinclair), Accountant (John Kellard), Rigger (Dave Peacock), Props Chargehand (John Ayling), Make Up Assistants (Carolyn Wills, Kate Rudlin), Floor Assistant (Richard Marson), Assistant Stage Manager (Annie Scott).

Production Team
Casting Director (Maggi Sangwin), Title Music (Andy Pask, Charlie Morgan), Costume (Maggie Chappelhow, Carolyn Maddocks), Make Up Designer (Gilly Wakeford), Graphics (Ethan Ames), Videotape Editor (John Sharland), Lighting (Nino La Femina), Camera (Jamie Acton-Bond), Sound (Brian Moray, Mike Fairbairn), Production Buyer (Derek Rhys), Location Manager (Joe McDonald), First Assistant Director (Glynn Purcell), Stage Manager (Joan Walker-Smith), Production Manager (Brian Heard), Production Assistant (Janice Brackenridge), Technical Adviser (Wilf Knight), Script Editor (Barbara Cox), Series Script Editor (Kenneth Ware),

Design (Stuart McCarthy, Peter Joyce), Executive Producer (Peter Cregeen), Producer (Richard Bramall).

Observation Notes
Taken Into Consideration (Production No: D4067, VTR No: THS/45302) was shot between Monday 7th and Friday 11th November 1988.

The scene where Carver and Dashwood apprehend Kevin Boswell was filmed outside 2 St. Charles Place, W10. Ackland and Martella talk to the landlord on the doorstep of 1 St. Charles Square; the rear of that property was used for the scene where Kevin climbs down a drainpipe.

The episode marked the return to the series for director Christopher Hodson, who had helmed seven of the original hour-long episodes in the first and second series – including *A Dangerous Breed*, the first episode of *The Bill* to be recorded. Hodson directed 40 episodes in total within a career that spanned six decades. His other television credits included *The Gentle Touch*, *Raffles*, *Within These Walls*, *Campion*, *Mr. Palfrey of Westminster* and *Upstairs, Downstairs*, for which he received an Emmy nomination. Christopher Hodson passed away in 2015, aged 86.

Witness Statements

Lawrence Gray (Writer)
'I was born in Bridlington, but grew up in London. I got the writing bug after university when I was unemployed and couldn't get a job. I was living in a little room in Muswell Hill, wondering what to do with myself. I started writing so I could tell girls that I was a writer, rather than "I'm an unemployed dickhead." I started on an old typewriter, which was missing the letter T and so any time I got to that letter, I had to write it by hand. That's basically how I started and after a ten-year hard slog to try and get out of the slough of despondent frustration and into television, I finally got this episode of *The Bill*. Though when I got into the industry, I found that people were even more miserable than I was and that frustration never, ever leaves you... there's always bitterness.'

'I come from a family of policemen, my father was a policeman and I was brought up with them all around me. My brother-in-law was also a policeman and my nephew is still a serving officer. I knew that policemen were always up all night, my father never came home. Sometimes he would go to the Turkish baths and sleep it off there or he would meet local geezers for information to get ahead of the game, knowing who's who and what's what on the manor. They would therefore still be half cut sometimes when they turned up to a day's work the next morning. I didn't feel like CID were doing this much on *The Bill*, but the producers didn't want corrupt policemen on the programme at this time. So instead of them being corrupt, I wrote that they were overworked and under pressure.'

'That led to the idea for *Taken Into Consideration*, where to ease that workload, Dashwood was putting pressure on poor old Kevin to admit to a load of other burglaries, so he could then tick them off his list to help clear up his books. And this was also based on reality, where my father was dealing with these idiots who would confess to anything, just for the love of the attention. In those days people were nicking VCRs, whereas nowadays its mobile phones. It always struck me that whenever you shacked up with someone; you would end up with two copies of the same videos. That's why they assume Kevin is their guy, because he's got two of everything and it's all in packing cases. Well I've spent my entire life surrounded by packing cases, always ready for yet another move.'

'I put Burnside's gag about Kevin being well known like Bob Monkhouse because he used to do stand-up at police dos, where my dad said he told very blue jokes. I believe my original script was 40 minutes long, which was then edited down to 25 minutes. At the time, my friends thought *Taken Into Consideration* rattled through rather too quickly and they were rather confused as to what was going on. But now time dilation has taken place, it seems to be the normal speed that things are made nowadays. I was disappointed when they stuck the credits in immediately after Dashwood picked up Kevin's famous whiskey bottle, full of coins. My father had one like that on our doorstep, so I put that in for him, but you didn't see it long enough for the pay off.'

'I actually wrote a couple of scripts for *The Bill*. My other story was about sexism in the police. Back then, the female police constables were known as WPCs, until this changed in 1999 when they removed the sexual differentiation. The big thing for me with *The Bill* was that they always seemed to be relegated to dealing with finding dogs or domestics. They were presented as social workers, but half the women I knew growing up were no different to the policemen. I wrote this hard-hitting storyline where poor old June Ackland was raped and she was told to keep it quiet because it would ruin her career. That was an edgy script based on a real life story that my brother-in-law told me, where a policewoman he knew had been involved in "an unfortunate incident" and hadn't reported it because it would be just too much trouble for her future career. Even though it was never made by *The Bill*, that script went around in the industry and got me work on shows like *Medics* and *Yellowthread Street*, which was a really exciting show to get on. *Yellowthread Street* took us to Hong Kong at an incredibly exciting period. After I came home, I didn't want to go back to just signing on the dole and scratching around looking for writing work, I wanted to go on more adventures. Then my wife was offered a job in Hong Kong at the Chinese University and we settled down there and stayed for 30 years! I learned Cantonese and worked on lots of Chinese scripts and then I got sucked into directing. I ended up directing my first feature film at the grand old age of 59 and more recently we've been making documentaries about the history of Malaysia... a long way from Sun Hill.'

Jamie Acton-Bond (Camera)

'*The Bill* wasn't like filmed drama where you would do a lot of separate shots that would be edited together later; the whole idea was to mainly do continuous shots. There's a driving shot in *Taken Into Consideration* for example, where Jon Iles parks the car and Mark Wingett gets out and we follow him down the alley, all in one shot. The camera rig was on the outside of the car, with me waiting on the pavement, ready to derig the camera as soon as Jon hit his mark. Nowadays, of course, that shot would be so much easier to do with smaller cameras. Those continuous shots in *The Bill* were something that Chris Hodson had established. He was a really good director and his shoots always flowed and worked without aggravation, I don't recall any arguments.'

'*The Bill* really was a team effort and Barlby Road was a great place to work. We would all meet in the canteen in the morning. Everybody helped each other, from the professional actors right through to our producers, we all learned about this new way of shooting television drama together. It was a new way of shooting drama and a great learning curve for all of us and a great springboard for our careers. Everybody who came onto *The Bill* enjoyed working on the series. My manager at Teddington once said, "We are privileged to be paid to do a hobby." That's what we all felt about the industry in those days, we were very lucky.'

Matthew Sim (Kevin Boswell)

'I'd hardly done any telly since leaving drama school in 1982 and *The Bill* was so good at giving opportunities to young actors. You didn't have to be well known to get a bite at the cake and every week you would see a raft of new faces. *Taken Into Consideration* was cast by Maggi Sangwin, though by weird coincidence I already knew the director, because Chris Hodson was a friend of my parents. My dad was a theatre photographer and my mum was an actress, who I think might have worked with Chris years ago. I remember auditioning for Kevin, who was a similar character to the two other roles I later played on *The Bill*; just normal guys. I would never get cast in those kind of parts now; I've since been pigeonholed into playing psychos and weirdos or I've played women and crossdressers, all kinds of stuff. Parts like Kevin don't really come my way now, a normal geezer who was a bit of a div.'

'It was such a good script that I didn't have to worry about acting, it came naturally and I was just enjoying having good dialogue. Obviously, being a young actor I was probably a bit scared, because I knew it was such a high turnover and wanted to do a good job and not affect the schedule by fluffing my lines. I just wanted to be as good as the show and to do the cast justice. If I'd tried to be funny, then I wouldn't have been, because comedy scares me shitless. I loved the line when Dashwood goes to record the interview and Kevin asks, "Are we having some sounds, then?" I enjoyed working with Jon Iles, he was great and I already knew Mark Wingett because I was at the National Youth Theatre with him. I was with Mark when he got plucked from there to be in *Quadrophenia*. I still see Trudie Goodwin a lot too, because she lives around the corner from me.'

'*The Bill* was a fantastic job to get and I'm amazed when I look back on some of the opportunities I got when I was young. I remember one day lying in bed and I heard the letterbox go. I thought "Wouldn't that be nice if that was a script for a job..." And sure enough, there was a script for an amazing play at Northampton. I obviously had to audition, but it was one of the best jobs I ever did. That doesn't happen anymore, I might still occasionally get a great job, but they seemed better early in your career, rather than when you've been doing it for 30 years.'

'*Taken Into Consideration* came out just after Christmas and I'd been invited to spend New Year with a couple of friends from drama school. They lived in Wales and so we watched the episode there. I'd driven up from London and on the way my car was playing up, so they booked me into a garage the next day. I went to this industrial estate in the middle of nowhere, and I walked into this Portacabin. I said I was looking for the garage and this woman looked at me and shrieked, "Weren't you on TV last night?!" She nearly had a complete spasm; she couldn't believe that somebody she had seen on TV the night before had walked into her Portacabin. I was similarly gobsmacked to be asked to talk about the episode all these years later! I couldn't believe it, but I'm very grateful to have been asked and I'm thrilled that the episode is still being enjoyed. It's a loss to the schedules that *The Bill* isn't still filling that 8pm slot for the whole family to watch. And it's a huge loss to the profession, there's not been anything since that's given the same opportunities to young actors.'

Jon Iles (D.C. Mike Dashwood)

'Watching *Taken into Consideration* back after 85 years or however long it's been, the thing that came flooding back was Matthew Sim's guest performance, because he literally stole every scene he was in. He was so funny and matter of fact. I laughed out loud when we bring him into the station and he says, "Oh, hello Mr. Penny." It was so superbly underplayed, like being back in custody was the most natural thing in the world. Kevin was a great foil for Dashwood, who was getting more and more infuriated with him. The more Dashwood threw his toys out of the pram, the more Matthew responded by underplaying Kevin's reactions, which I think created a fabulous conflict in those interview scenes. I just loved his performance and can't praise him enough.'

'Within the week that *Taken into Consideration* was broadcast, I was also a special guest on the *Wheel of Fortune* Christmas special, as well as playing a footballer in a sketch with Bruce Forsyth and Ronnie Corbett for their BBC comedy extravaganza on Boxing Day, which was just extraordinary. The *Wheel of Fortune* was filmed in Scotland and I won a set of pine table and chairs for a mental health charity. I was then invited to the after show party, but I couldn't go because I was doing *The Bill* the next morning. I was taken straight from the studio on a motorbike, still wearing my dinner jacket and in full slap, to get on a commuter plane back down to London at 11:00 at night, so I would be back and ready for filming first thing in the morning. I never rose above that dizzying week, where I was in three different programmes and got top billing on *The Bill*'

Peter Cregeen (Executive Producer)

'I have always maintained a connection with *The Bill*. I attended leaving parties for both Trudie and Eric when they retired from the programme. I also attended a big party when the series finished, which was extraordinary. Some people I didn't know of course, but Graham Cole was the compere for evening and was up on stage making announcements. It was a great experience, as well as being a sad experience as well. I have to confess that I wasn't really watching it by the time it was drawing to a close, even though I'm sure Jonathan Young was doing a very good job on it. I don't know what the rationale was for taking it off the air, because at the time it was pulling in four million, which now of course would be perfectly respectable.'

'I suspect it was primarily for commercial reasons, because people tend to forget that commercial television is exactly what that's about, the programmes sell the advertising, which was as true of *The Bill* as any other ITV programme. Which reminds me of an experience I shall never forget from earlier in my career, when I attended a Christmas party at Yorkshire Television. The sales people were all based in one building, while the YTV production teams all worked in a much smaller building around the corner. The party was held in the sales building, where the chairman got up and made a speech about what a great year it had been and the sales were all up! He then passed on his congratulations to the sales team, who had raised the revenue of the company... He never said a word about programmes in his speech at all!'

'The following year, at the next Christmas party, the Chairman's speech included, "I've been told I've got to say something about programmes..." Then he told us the "great news" that we were all going to be moving around the corner, to work in the same building. I first went to that building for a meeting with Michael Ferguson, who was producing a series called *Airline*, which in the end I never worked on. When Michael and I both arrived at the front of this building, the commissionaire said "Morning gentlemen, can I see your passes?" which we produced. He replied "Oh... you're production. No, I'm afraid you have to go around the corner and use the entrance at the back of the building. Only sales people are allowed to come through the front." It was extraordinary; he might have been suggesting it was a quicker route to our office, but we both took grave exception and that perhaps illustrates how commercial television operates.'

WHO GOT THE DRUMS: 1988

The half-hour episodes of *The Bill* saw the introduction of a drum-beat over the final shot, prior to the closing credits. Here are the members of the regular cast who got "the drums" in 1988 – and the number of times they got them, either on their own or shared as a group of legends:

Tony Scannell	11
Eric Richard	10
Jon Iles	8
Chris Ellison	6
Robert Hudson	5
Larry Dann	4
Roger Leach	3
Mark Wingett	3
Colin Blumenau	3
Mark Powley	3
Trudie Goodwin	2
Eamonn Walker	2
Graham Cole	2
Ashley Gunstock	1
Nick Reding	1

TOP OF THE BILL: 1988

Here are the legends who "topped the bill" on the closing credits:

Eric Richard	34
Chris Ellison	3
Nick Reding	3
Colin Blumenau	2
Eamonn Walker	2
Larry Dann	1
Jon Iles	1
Kelly Lawrence	1
Tony Scannell	1

TOP OF THE COPS: 1988

From the 48 episodes broadcast that year, here are the number of appearances that the regular cast each made in 1988:

Jon Iles	34
Eric Richard	34
Mark Wingett	32
Larry Dann	31
Colin Blumenau	30
Nula Conwell	30
Tony Scannell	28
Robert Hudson	28
Eamonn Walker	28
Roger Leach	27
Trudie Goodwin	26
Mark Powley	24
Barbara Thorn	24
Nick Reding	23
Ben Roberts	23
Chris Ellison	20
Jeff Stewart	20
Graham Cole	19
Ashley Gunstock	19
Peter Ellis	13
Kelly Lawrence	13
Kevin Lloyd	11

SERIES 4?

For those wondering why this book was not called *Witness Statements: Making The Bill (Series 4)...* The impression that each year was a standalone "Series" has been created for the marketing of DVD releases. The half-hour episodes produced over the next ten years were all part of a continuous production, and the term "Series 4" was in fact used on all scripts and paperwork to label every half-hour episode made until 1998, prior to the return of the hour-long episode format. For example, the late great Kevin Lloyd's final episode as D.C. Tosh Lines, *A People Person* (Prod No: B4290, VTR/THS/94957), was Series 4 Episode No: 1261, filmed between Tuesday 9th and Saturday 13th December 1997.

MISSING EVIDENCE

Three Story Outlines - Written by Garry Lyons in 1988

In 1988, writer Garry Lyons was invited by script editor Tim Vaughan to submit four *The Bill* story outlines, without featuring specific Sun Hill characters. *The Coop* was commissioned, while the other three episodes; *Beastie Boys*, *Community Arts* and *Contact Sports*, were discussed but ultimately not commissioned. These outlines have been reproduced below with kind permission from Garry, who later wrote three more *The Bill* episodes that were produced between 1989-90. Read on for a fascinating glimpse into the pitching process and imagine some "lost" 1988 cases.

BEASTIE BOYS

Written by Garry Lyons

Case Narrative

The Bill are doing a trawl around Sun Hill, rounding up kids involved in nicking Volkswagen car badges. The trawl has been ordered by a senior officer, who has just had his own car badge nicked. Some of the officers regard the job as a drag. Others, especially the WPCs, are unhappy about the way the kids are being rounded up and expected to grass on their friends. They think the methods are unnecessarily draconian.

Meanwhile a group of junior detectives bust a con man for a wedge of phoney traveller's cheques. A search of the villain's house turns up a large parcel of evidence. The Bill bring him back to the nick. He has form for this kind of crime. The con man is casual and confident. He answers some of the questions, but insists on seeing a senior officer (whom he mentions by name). "Why do you want to see him?" the cops ask. "I want to make a statement," says the con. "You can make a statement to us," say the cops. "I want **him**," says the con.

By now the station is packed with kids and their parents. Officers are delivering lectures about the life of crime, and are threatening convictions. News comes in that someone has sprayed a VW insignia on a parked police car. The questioning is intensified. The senior officer (the same one mentioned?) is furious. Some of his juniors see the funny side.

The detectives wait while the con man talks to the senior officer. There are mumbles about a 'deal' being struck. The senior officer returns. He says the con will duck his nut to £400 of phoney cheques. The detectives protest, they caught the villain red-handed. The senior officer says the con is a well-known and useful informer. The detectives are still unhappy. The senior officer says the Yard is hunting for a big travellers' cheque con gang. The man in the cells has told him the name of a big fish who gave him the cheques. The detectives find this difficult to believe. One of them accuses the senior officer of accepting a bribe. The senior officer dresses him down and says that is a very serious allegation. He orders the station sergeant to bail the villain immediately.

At the magistrates' court, a stream of juveniles are being conditionally discharged for car badge theft. It's wall-to-wall stuff. The con man's case comes up. The prosecuting solicitor says how helpful the villain has been. When the magistrate asks for details of 'previous', he leaves out the prison sentences. The con man gets six months suspended and walks free. The junior detectives are furious and are deeply suspicious of the senior officer, but can prove nothing. The senior officer arrives at the nick in his VW. The garage has just given him new car badges. When he goes back out to the car park, the badges are now gone.

COMMUNITY ARTS
Written by Garry Lyons

Case Narrative
There has been a spate of breaking and entering in a Sun Hill neighbourhood. One of the beat bobbies is on the job. The usual suspects are rounded up. But they swear innocence and give alibis. Witnesses talk about two suspicious youths – one with a tattoo around his neck. Attention turns to a local community arts centre. Run by the local authority, it is a place where a lot of the unemployed youths hang out. The Bill get doubly suspicious when – on a routine visit – they stumble upon an anti-police drama workshop and discover they are being videoed.

Meanwhile, colleagues are having trouble with the local vagrants. They have been pestering pedestrians, swearing at them and begging. They are well-known to Sun Hill officers, and usually there's some give-and-take. But they've been overstepping the mark recently and getting into fights. The Bill have been forced to come the heavy. There's been a succession of winos in the cells and the courts. During one confrontation, one of the winos tells a bobby "Lay off! You'll need us one day!" The Bill laugh.

Things develop at the arts centre when the director – a bit of a graduate lefty – reports thefts from the box office and bar. This increases The Bill's suspicions. It must be an inside job. They start to question the arts centre users, a bit too aggressively for the director's taste. "Do you want to find the culprits or not?" he is told. The Bill cannot believe that security is so slack. Anyone, apparently, can get a key to the centre. Strangers can just stroll around at will. The director tries to explain this is a policy of open access. He likes the building to be used 24 hours a day. All this only adds to the prejudices of some of the cops. One or two on the other hand – those involved in amateur dramatics – get quite excited about the work the centre is doing. This causes some on-the-job tension and mirth.

A body is found in a canal. A vagrant. No foul play. Looks like suicide or accident. No identification. Not someone known to the Sun Hill nick. One of the PCs is ordered to get a name. He does a profitless search through the missing person files. Then he has to eat humble pie, and go and talk to the well-known winos. They laugh. "Now the boots on the other foot, now you want sunnink." Down among the winos, the PC is finding out very little. Eventually, for the price of a cup of tea, he is told that a number of new winos have been moving in on the regulars' patch. This is what has been causing some of the aggro. His informer gives him a name and a sketchy story about the dead man. Enough to do some checking.

A crime prevention officer has been sent to the arts centre. He advises on alarm systems and extra locks. The director says this would destroy access. The view that the centre couldn't organise a piss-up in a brewery is further confirmed when one of its Transit vans – parked outside on a hill with the handbrake off – rolls across the road into an oncoming car. The Bill debate whether to press a traffic charge. Then at night, villains smash through the front doors of the centre, load the centre's old cast iron safe onto some wheels and into the back of a truck. The Bill find the safe, drilled through, on a waste tip the next morning.

The arts centre director protests vehemently to The Bill that they are not doing anything to clear up the recent thefts. The Bill tell him to watch it, or he'll be in trouble for the Transit incident. Besides which, the fire department are unhappy about his emergency precautions and there are irregularities with the performance licence. The centre could be closed down. Then Sun Hill gets a phone call from the centre. The director has just been talking to two suspicious men in the foyer. They were shifty looking, as if they were casing the joint. When questioned, they asked for leaflets. "We wanna know what's on at the featre tonight." The director gives a description. One of the men has a tattoo round his neck. The Bill drive over and apprehend them.

After much footslogging and computer checking, the PC is none the wiser about the dead vagrant's identity. He is forced to conclude that his wino informer's story was a fiction.

CONTACT SPORTS
Written by Garry Lyons

Case Narrative

One of the junior PCs is having a hard time. His record on nicks is not impressive recently. He gets a bad assessment. One night he and another PC swoop in on a street brawl. Several youths are carted off to the station. But when he gets them there, the PC is told to let them all off with a caution. There is an emergency to attend (a big fire). Frustrated, the PC rows with his superior. The PC is severely reprimanded.

The following Saturday, the PC is playing rugby for the Metropolitan Police at Imber Court, Thames Ditton. It is a rough match. The other side goad the Met for being 'the filth'. One particularly nasty ruck turns into a brawl. The PC takes out his frustrations by thumping an opponent, who is carried off injured. The PC is sent off. There are mutterings in the bar afterwards. The team captain tells him that a suspension is likely.

The PC is in a sulk when he arrives at work on Monday morning. But things are even worse than he realises. Everybody's avoiding him, or feeling sorry for him. He finds this odd. Then he finds out his on-the-pitch punch-up has made the press. The Rugby Union are investigating. The victim – who sustained a suspected broken jaw – is threatening to press charges of G.B.H. or A.B.H.

The PC is called in to see a senior officer. He is told the force take a dim view of his behaviour. Two officers from Surrey Constabulary are turning up later in the day to interview him as a result of the victim's and the referee's complaints. He may be suspended on full pay while inquiries proceed. If charges are not pressed, then the PC will at least face internal disciplinary measures.

The Surrey police arrive and question the PC. They are embarrassed. It is not the grilling the PC feared. It seems as if they are looking for a way not to have to charge him, rather than throwing the book. The PC protests that he was provoked. The Surrey police apologise, but say that if the victim is determined it may be hard for them to stop the case coming to court. They then go in to see the senior officer at Sun Hill. The PC assumes this is the end of the line for him.

The senior officer explains to the Surrey men the mitigating circumstances surrounding the PC's actions. He tells them what an outstanding young officer the PC is. Plainly he blames himself to a certain extent. But he tells the Surrey men that if his PC did wrong, then he should be punished. He wants no cover-ups.

The matter proceeds. The RFU suspend the PC for a few matches. The victim's injuries are not nearly as serious as first imagined. The Police Federation get involved. Meanwhile, the youth the PC arrested at the beginning of the story is apprehended again. It turns out that their fighting was by no means a spontaneous gang scrap. It was an organised affair associated with organised street crime – drugs. The senior officer is made to feel very awkward. If he hadn't been so hard on the PC the first time round, the young men might not have got in so much trouble.

After a few days leave, the PC is called in to see the senior officer. When he arrives he is shocked to discover his victim sitting there. The senior officer says that the victim has kindly agreed to withdraw his charges. The victim says that on consideration, after chatting to the senior officer, he would not wish to blight the young man's career. The PC is relieved, if puzzled. He shakes hands with the victim. They call it quits. The victim turns to leave. But the senior officer stops him. He asks if the pair of them would be prepared to repeat that handshake outside. He has arranged for a press photographer to capture the moment.

The pair of adversaries reluctantly agree. The victim leaves. The PC turns to the senior officer, "How did you manage to persuade him?" "I appealed to his sense of decency" says the senior officer. "And when that didn't work, I threatened to disclose to the press what he got up to at his club's last annual dinner." "What did he get up to?" "Oh the Surrey lads were very helpful there. Nothing extremely criminal, you understand. But things his wife wouldn't want to read about in the press." End.

AUTHOR ACKNOWLEDGEMENTS

I am hugely grateful to the cast and crew who shared their memories:

Jamie Acton-Bond, Barry Appleton, Aidan Boulter, Colin Blumenau, Diana Bramall, John Challis, Kevin Clarke, Graham Cole OBE, Nula Conwell, Derek Cotty, Peter Cregeen, Larry Dann, Gareth Davies, Terence Daw, Marilyn Edwards, Peter Ellis, Chris Ellison, Karen England, Michael Fenton Stevens, Trudie Goodwin, Ashley Gunstock, Lawrence Gray, Peter J. Hammond, Paul Harrison, Robert Hudson, Jon Iles, Julian Jones, Peter Joyce, Greg Kinchin, Stan Lee, Niall Leonard, Russell Lewis, Derek Lister, Sheila Loughrey, Garry Lyons, Terry Marcel, Richard Marson, Nicholas McInerny, Julian Meers, Caroline O'Reilly, John Osborne, Oscar Peck, Mark Powley, Robert Putt, Nick Reding, Jonathan Rich, Eric Richard, Christopher Russell, Jan Sargent, Sue Shattock, Matthew Sim, Barbara Thorn, Tim Vaughan, Eamonn Walker, Fizz Waters, Douglas Watkinson, Chas Watts, Nigel J. Wilson and Mark Wingett.

I also grateful to the following for their kind help and support:

Sacha Appleton, Anne Barfield, Kim Bowers, Maureen Brock, David Brunt, Carol Challis, Jerry & Julie Crocker, Helena Crocker, Mervyn Cumming, Andrew Diack, George Fairbrother, Lynne & Ray Francis, David French, Vic Gallucci, Ronnie Grainge, Ian Greaves, Toby Hadoke, David J. Howe, Bryony Kelly, Kyz Kistell, Paul Langwade, Benjamin Leach, Becky Lee, Vicki Lee, Chris Leviston, Kat Lister, Brenda Longman, Rolie Luker, Derek Lyons, Andrew Mackintosh, Suzanne Maddock, Simon McGoldrick, Vaughan Millard, Paul Morris, Stuart & Jen Morris, John O'Brien, Edwin Pearce, Ben Peyton, Yvonne Quenet, Garance Rawinsky, David Richens, Natalie Roles, Andrew Ruff, Christine Russell, Michael Seely, Andrew T. Smith, Derrick Smith, Frank W. Smith, Jennie Tate, Tom Theakston, Tony Virgo, Natalie Wayland, Sarah Went & Jane Wyatt.

Special thanks to John Hancock, Dean Francis Goodfellow, David & Amanda Knights (authors of *Acton Through Time*) and Kurt Roberts for sharing their local knowledge and identifying multiple filming locations.

Special thanks to Barry Appleton, Diana Bramall, Ellie Gleave, Jon Iles, Garry Lyons, Richard Marson, Chas Watts and Nigel J. Wilson for sharing their invaluable paperwork and diary entries from 1988.

Special thanks to the genius Robert Hammond for his glorious artwork.

Special thanks to Benjamin Adams for researching vehicles, Rob Cook for novelisation details and Jason Singerling for identifying music changes.

Special thanks to Barry Appleton, Diana Bramall, Terence Daw, Paul Harrison, Stan Lee, Niall Leonard, Richard Marson, Chas Watts and Nigel J. Wilson for kindly sharing photographs for this book.

Special thanks to the co-producers of *The Bill Podcast*: Benjamin Adams, Rob Cook, Sarah Keiper, Alex Mockler, Laura Pini-Fay and Simon Wolf.

Special thanks to the executive producers of *The Bill Podcast*: Isobel Allen, Ben Ashmore, Alana Dewar, Andrew Diack, Paul Dunn, Dan Evans, George Fairbrother, Luke Heagerty, Daniel Johnson, Edward Kellett, James Ledain, Simon McGoldrick, Lucy McNeill, Gary Moncur, Steph Morris, Stuart & Jen Morris, Claire Norbury, Tom Sherrington, Angel Stannard, Patrick Stratford, Michael While and Sarah Went of *The Billaton*.

The Bill Podcast is made in association with georgefairbrother.com mcgoldrickwatchrepairs.com and mistymoonfilmsociety.com

The Bill Podcast presents in-depth interviews with the legends of *The Bill*. Played over 300,000 times in more than 50 countries worldwide, the Podcast is available on iTunes and soundcloud.com/thebillpodcast

Over 65 hours of bonus *The Bill Podcast* content is available on Patreon, including 60 cast and crew episode commentaries, *Billgrimage* location videos, exclusive *Off the Beat* podcasts, reaction and analysis videos and much more. Join the investigation - patreon.com/thebillpodcast

After recording his interview for this book, the mighty John Challis passed away. He was very kind and supportive. Rest in peace John.

I also lost four treasured friends during the writing of this book, who all gave me such support and encouragement over the years: Ian Cullen (actor/writer), Mervyn Cumming (director), Bernard Holley (actor/VO artist) and Frank Williams (actor/playwright). I miss them every day.

Special thanks to my darling wife and proofreader: Tessa Crocker. You are my best friend and I am so grateful for your support, encouragement, love and belief. During the making of this book, we lost our beloved cat, Rocco. He was a darling boy and we had ten wonderful years with him. We have since adopted a cat from the RSPCA, called Fawkes, who is bringing us some new joy. Both boys sat with me as I wrote this book x

WITNESS STATEMENTS: MAKING THE BILL (SERIES 1-3)
Featuring interviews with 40 cast and crew
(ISBN 978-1838281908)

ALSO AVAILABLE FROM DEVONFIRE BOOKS

ALL MEMORIES GREAT & SMALL
Featuring interviews with 75 cast and crew about the making of
the classic BBC series. (ISBN 978-1838281915)